JOHN GOETSCH

NATHAN BIRT

REVIVAL TODAY

365 CHALLENGING DEVOTIONS FROM REVIVAL HISTORY

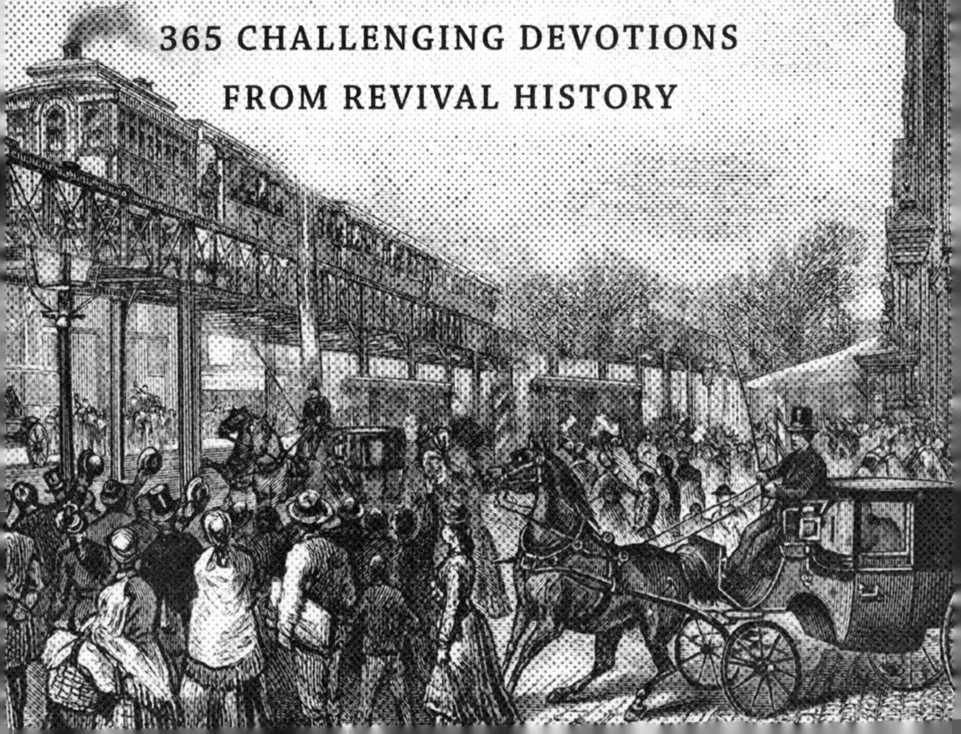

First published in 2018 by Striving Together Publications, a ministry of Lancaster Baptist Church, Lancaster, CA 93535. Striving Together Publications is committed to providing tried, trusted, and proven books that will further equip local churches to carry out the Great Commission. Your comments and suggestions are valued.

Striving Together Publications
4020 E. Lancaster Blvd.
Lancaster, CA 93535
800.201.7748

Cover design by Andrew Jones
Layout by Craig Parker
Edited by Monica Bass

The contents of this book are the result of decades of spiritual growth in life and ministry. It is not our intent to claim originality with any quote or thought that could not readily be tied to an original source.

ISBN 978-1-59894-370-2

Printed in the United States of America

Table of Contents

A Word from the Authors

Revival *today*—do you believe it could happen?

Or do you believe that revival was only for *yesterday*. Have times changed and society worsened so that a reviving of God's people is no longer probable...or even possible? When we hear of the great revivals of yesteryear, we tend to forget that they were all preceded by great spiritual darkness. After all, God doesn't send revival to those who don't need it!

This is why we have compiled these devotions. Each devotion describes an event or individual from the past that God has used to bring revival. It is an on-this-day book, with most readings featuring a historic event that took place on the same day you will read it, some years prior. Don't read these miraculous events of history and assume they were only for history. Read them and be reminded that the same God who worked in the past continues to work today. As Hebrews 13:8 assures us, "Jesus Christ the same yesterday, and to day, and for ever."

In the back of the book, you'll find a bibliography of sources we used, including the direct quotes you'll read throughout the daily readings. We've included a wide range of people and events in this volume. Although we may not endorse every aspect of each person's beliefs or ministry practices, these are people whom God used, and we have been encouraged and challenged by the ways in which He used them.

We have endeavored to make each devotion not only historically beneficial, but also practical and applicable from Scripture. We trust you'll read with an open heart to God's Word and the Holy Spirit. Please don't let these devotionals be a substitute for reading the greatest book ever written on revival—the Bible! At the end of each day's reading, you'll find a suggested passage to read, which will take you through the entire Bible in a year. Bible reading schedules are also included in the front.

We pray that the Lord uses this book to encourage you that His work of reival is not just for yesterday—it is for *today!* We pray with the psalmist, "Wilt thou not revive us *again:* that thy people may rejoice in thee?" (Psalm 85:6).

Sincerely in Christ,
John Goetsch and Nathan Birt

PRACTICES OF EFFECTIVE CHRISTIANS

The Effective Christian Memorizes Scripture

The following principles for effective Scripture memory are taken from *Homiletics from the Heart,* written by Dr. John Goetsch.

1. **Choose a specific time and a quiet place.**
   What gets scheduled gets accomplished. When memorizing the Word of God, you want to free yourself from all distractions.

2. **Organize by topic.**
   Many people attempt to learn the "Golden Chapters" or whole books of the Bible. While this is a noble attempt, it is not the way the Word of God will be used while teaching or preaching. Choose a topic you would like to study and then memorize every verse that deals with it. The next time you are speaking on that particular subject, your mind will be able to tie these verses together to truly allow you to "preach the Word…"

3. **Work out loud.**
   Even though it may sound odd, your mind memorizes better and faster that which it audibly hears. This is why you should choose a specific time and a quiet place!

4. **Walk while you memorize.**
   Your body has a natural sense of rhythm. This is why we memorize the words of songs so quickly. We will memorize much more quickly (and retain it longer) if we are walking around.

5. **Review, review, review.**
   Repetition is the key to learning. The one who is serious about memorizing Scripture cannot simply keep learning new passages weekly. Rather, he must also make the time to review the previous passages already committed to memory. It becomes readily apparent that memorization will take work, but the rewards are worth it!

6. **Set goals of time.**
   If you are not careful, you may ask for disappointment by setting goals of verses per week. The reason why is that some verses are more difficult to learn than others. If you set goals of time spent in memorization, God will honor that.

On the following pages you will find many major Bible doctrines and key verses to memorize. It is time to put into practice these six principles.

The Bible

Psalm 119:160—*Thy word is true from the beginning: and every one of thy righteous judgments endureth for ever.*

Isaiah 40:8—*The grass withereth, the flower fadeth: but the word of our God shall stand for ever.*

2 Timothy 3:16–17—*All scripture is given by inspiration of God, and is profitable for doctrine, for reproof, for correction, for instruction in righteousness: That the man of God may be perfect, throughly furnished unto all good works.*

Hebrews 4:12—*For the word of God is quick, and powerful, and sharper than any twoedged sword, piercing even to the dividing asunder of soul and spirit, and of the joints and marrow, and is a discerner of the thoughts and intents of the heart.*

John 17:17—*Sanctify them through thy truth: thy word is truth.*

Matthew 24:35—*Heaven and earth shall pass away, but my words shall not pass away.*

1 Thessalonians 2:13—*For this cause also thank we God without ceasing, because, when ye received the word of God which ye heard of us, ye received it not as the word of men, but as it is in truth, the word of God, which effectually worketh also in you that believe.*

God

Psalm 111:9—*He sent redemption unto his people: he hath commanded his covenant for ever: holy and reverend is his name.*

Isaiah 57:15—*For thus saith the high and lofty One that inhabiteth eternity, whose name is Holy; I dwell in the high and holy place, with him also that is of a contrite and humble spirit, to revive the spirit of the humble, and to revive the heart of the contrite ones.*

Lamentations 3:22–23—*It is of the LORD's mercies that we are not consumed, because his compassions fail not. They are new every morning: great is thy faithfulness.*

Deuteronomy 32:4—*He is the Rock, his work is perfect: for all his ways are judgment: a God of truth and without iniquity, just and right is he.*

Psalm 138:2—*I will worship toward thy holy temple, and praise thy name for thy lovingkindness and for thy truth: for thou hast magnified thy word above all thy name.*

John 4:24—*God is a Spirit: and they that worship him must worship him in spirit and in truth.*

Psalm 90:2—*Before the mountains were brought forth, or ever thou hadst formed the earth and the world, even from everlasting to everlasting, thou art God.*

Jesus Christ

John 1:1, 14—*In the beginning was the Word, and the Word was with God, and the Word was God. And the Word was made flesh, and dwelt among us, (and we beheld his glory, the glory as of the only begotten of the Father,) full of grace and truth.*

Philippians 2:6–8—*Who, being in the form of God, thought it not robbery to be equal with God: But made himself of no reputation, and took upon him the form of a servant, and was made in the likeness of men: And being found in fashion as a man, he humbled himself, and became obedient unto death, even the death of the cross.*

Colossians 1:16–17—*For by him were all things created, that are in heaven, and that are in earth, visible and invisible, whether they be thrones, or dominions, or principalities, or powers: all things were created by him, and for him: And he is before all things, and by him all things consist.*

1 Timothy 2:5–6—*For there is one God, and one mediator between God and men, the man Christ Jesus; Who gave himself a ransom for all, to be testified in due time.*

Hebrews 1:8—*But unto the Son he saith, Thy throne, O God, is for ever and ever: a sceptre of righteousness is the sceptre of thy kingdom.*

Luke 19:10—*For the Son of man is come to seek and to save that which was lost.*

Holy Spirit

John 14:16—*And I will pray the Father, and he shall give you another Comforter, that he may abide with you for ever;*

John 14:26—*But the Comforter, which is the Holy Ghost, whom the Father will send in my name, he shall teach you all things, and bring all things to your remembrance, whatsoever I have said unto you.*

John 15:26—*But when the Comforter is come, whom I will send unto you from the Father, even the Spirit of truth, which proceedeth from the Father, he shall testify of me:*

John 16:13–14—*Howbeit when he, the Spirit of truth, is come, he will guide you into all truth: for he shall not speak of himself; but whatsoever he shall hear, that shall he speak: and he will shew you things to come. He shall glorify me: for he shall receive of mine, and shall shew it unto you.*

1 Corinthians 3:16—*Know ye not that ye are the temple of God, and that the Spirit of God dwelleth in you?*

Ephesians 4:30—*And grieve not the holy Spirit of God, whereby ye are sealed unto the day of redemption.*

Ephesians 5:18—*And be not drunk with wine, wherein is excess; but be filled with the Spirit;*

Mankind

Genesis 1:26–27—*And God said, Let us make man in our image, after our likeness: and let them have dominion over the fish of the sea, and over the fowl of the air, and over the cattle, and over all the earth, and over every creeping thing that creepeth upon the earth. So God created man in his own image, in the image of God created he him; male and female created he them.*

Job 14:1, 14—*Man that is born of a woman is of few days, and full of trouble. If a man die, shall he live again? all the days of my appointed time will I wait, till my change come.*

Psalm 8:4–5—*What is man, that thou art mindful of him? and the son of man, that thou visitest him? For thou hast made him a little lower than the angels, and hast crowned him with glory and honour.*

Isaiah 64:6—*But we are all as an unclean thing, and all our righteousnesses are as filthy rags; and we all do fade as a leaf; and our iniquities, like the wind, have taken us away.*

Romans 3:10–11—*As it is written, There is none righteous, no, not one: There is none that understandeth, there is none that seeketh after God.*

Romans 3:23—*For all have sinned, and come short of the glory of God.*

Sin

Numbers 32:23—*But if ye will not do so, behold, ye have sinned against the* LORD*: and be sure your sin will find you out.*

Ezekiel 18:20—*The soul that sinneth, it shall die. The son shall not bear the iniquity of the father, neither shall the father bear the iniquity of the son: the righteousness of the righteous shall be upon him, and the wickedness of the wicked shall be upon him.*

Romans 6:23—*For the wages of sin is death; but the gift of God is eternal life through Jesus Christ our Lord.*

James 1:15—*Then when lust hath conceived, it bringeth forth sin: and sin, when it is finished, bringeth forth death.*

1 John 1:8–10—*If we say that we have no sin, we deceive ourselves, and the truth is not in us. If we confess our sins, he is faithful and just to forgive us our sins, and to cleanse us from all unrighteousness. If we say that we have not sinned, we make him a liar, and his word is not in us.*

1 John 3:4—*Whosoever committeth sin transgresseth also the law: for sin is the transgression of the law.*

Jeremiah 17:9—*The heart is deceitful above all things, and desperately wicked: who can know it?*

Salvation

Isaiah 45:22—*Look unto me, and be ye saved, all the ends of the earth: for I am God, and there is none else.*

Isaiah 43:11–12—*I, even I, am the Lord; and beside me there is no saviour. I have declared, and have saved, and I have shewed, when there was no strange god among you: therefore ye are my witnesses, saith the Lord, that I am God.*

John 14:6—*Jesus saith unto him, I am the way, the truth, and the life: no man cometh unto the Father, but by me.*

Acts 4:12—*Neither is there salvation in any other: for there is none other name under heaven given among men, whereby we must be saved.*

Romans 10:9–10—*That if thou shalt confess with thy mouth the Lord Jesus, and shalt believe in thine heart that God hath raised him from the dead, thou shalt be saved. For with the heart man believeth unto righteousness; and with the mouth confession is made unto salvation.*

Ephesians 2:8–9—*For by grace are ye saved through faith; and that not of yourselves: it is the gift of God: Not of works, lest any man should boast.*

Titus 3:5—*Not by works of righteousness which we have done, but according to his mercy he saved us, by the washing of regeneration, and renewing of the Holy Ghost;*

Church

Matthew 16:18—*And I say also unto thee, That thou art Peter, and upon this rock I will build my church; and the gates of hell shall not prevail against it.*

Colossians 1:18—*And he is the head of the body, the church: who is the beginning, the firstborn from the dead; that in all things he might have the preeminence.*

Ephesians 5:25–27—*Husbands, love your wives, even as Christ also loved the church, and gave himself for it; That he might sanctify and cleanse it with the washing of water by the word, That he might present it to himself a glorious church, not having spot, or wrinkle, or any such thing; but that it should be holy and without blemish.*

Acts 2:46–47—*And they, continuing daily with one accord in the temple, and breaking bread from house to house, did eat their meat with gladness and singleness of heart, Praising God, and having favour with all the people. And the Lord added to the church daily such as should be saved.*

1 Corinthians 12:13—*For by one Spirit are we all baptized into one body, whether we be Jews or Gentiles, whether we be bond or free; and have been all made to drink into one Spirit.*

1 Timothy 3:15—*But if I tarry long, that thou mayest know how thou oughtest to behave thyself in the house of God, which is the church of the living God, the pillar and ground of the truth.*

Angels

Genesis 3:24—*So he drove out the man; and he placed at the east of the garden of Eden Cherubims, and a flaming sword which turned every way, to keep the way of the tree of life.*

Psalm 148:2, 5—*Praise ye him, all his angels: praise ye him, all his hosts. Let them praise the name of the* LORD*: for he commanded, and they were created.*

Isaiah 6:1–3—*In the year that king Uzziah died I saw also the* LORD *sitting upon a throne, high and lifted up, and his train filled the temple. Above it stood the seraphims: each one had six wings; with twain he covered his face, and with twain he covered his feet, and with twain he did fly. And one cried unto another, and said, Holy, holy, holy, is the* LORD *of hosts: the whole earth is full of his glory.*

Mark 13:32—*But of that day and that hour knoweth no man, no, not the angels which are in heaven, neither the Son, but the Father.*

Hebrews 1:5–6—*For unto which of the angels said he at any time, Thou art my Son, this day have I begotten thee? And again, I will be to him a Father, and he shall be to me a Son? And again, when he bringeth in the firstbegotten into the world, he saith, And let all the angels of God worship him.*

1 Thessalonians 4:16—*For the Lord himself shall descend from heaven with a shout, with the voice of the archangel, and with the trump of God: and the dead in Christ shall rise first:*

End Times

1 Thessalonians 4:13–18—*But I would not have you to be ignorant, brethren, concerning them which are asleep, that ye sorrow not, even as others which have no hope. For if we believe that Jesus died and rose again, even so them also which sleep in Jesus will God bring with him. For this we say unto you by the word of the Lord, that we which are alive and remain unto the coming of the Lord shall not prevent them which are asleep. For the Lord himself shall descend from heaven with a shout, with the voice of the archangel, and with the trump of God: and the dead in Christ shall rise first: Then we which are alive and remain shall be caught up together with them in the clouds, to meet the Lord in the air: and so shall we ever be with the Lord. Wherefore comfort one another with these words.*

John 14:1–3—*Let not your heart be troubled: ye believe in God, believe also in me. In my Father's house are many mansions: if it were not so, I would have told you. I go to prepare a place for you. And if I go and prepare a place for you, I will come again, and receive you unto myself; that where I am, there ye may be also.*

Acts 1:10–11—*And while they looked stedfastly toward heaven as he went up, behold, two men stood by them in white apparel; Which also said, Ye men of Galilee, why stand ye gazing up into heaven? this same Jesus, which is taken up from you into heaven, shall so come in like manner as ye have seen him go into heaven.*

Revelation 22:20—*He which testifieth these things saith, Surely I come quickly. Amen. Even so, come, Lord Jesus.*

How to Lead a Person to Christ

Someone once said, "The fruit of a Christian is another Christian." There is a lot of truth in that statement. The Christian leader will influence people to be more soul-conscious. Yet, sometimes a person will be very active in sharing the gospel, but will not see much fruit. It is the responsibility of the Christian leader to train others to not only be available, but effective in their witness. Here are some truths that every soulwinner must remember as he prepares to help another soul spend an eternity with Christ.

1. **A soulwinner should start with the truth of God's love for every individual.**
   John 3:16 is perhaps the most familiar verse in all the New Testament. *"For God so loved the world...."* There are sinners living today who actually believe that God hates them and wants them to go to Hell because of their sin. A sinner will never accept a Saviour who he believes will never love him.

2. **A soulwinner must emphasize the fact that we are all sinners—there are no exceptions.**
   There have been some who understand the "love" of God and feel that He would never send anyone to Hell. These sinners must also understand that the God of "love" is also first, and foremost, holy. All men fall short of the holy standard He has set. As a result of this "falling short," we are condemned to an eternity in Hell. Romans 3:23 includes all men everywhere.

3. **A soulwinner must teach the sinner that his sin carries with it an expensive price tag.**
   According to Romans 6:23, *"the wages of sin is death...."* In Ezekiel 18:20, the Israelites learned that the soul that sinned would die. As a soulwinner, the person you are dealing with has the wrath of God already abiding on him (John 3:36).

4. **A soulwinner should demonstrate the good news that Jesus has already paid this price.**
   Not only does Romans 6:23 deal with the penalty of sin, it also deals with the promise of salvation. Romans 5:8 continues with this theme by showing the sinner that Christ died for us while we were yet sinners.

5. **A soulwinner must remember that a sinner must personally accept Christ as Saviour.**
   This promise is given in Romans 10:13—"*For whosoever shall call upon the name of the Lord shall be saved.*" A sinner may believe that God loves him, may understand the fact that he is a sinner, and may further understand that Jesus died to pay his sin debt and still be lost. The soulwinner is not after a simple mental assent to a list of subscribed facts. He is looking for a sinner to repent, to confess, and to know the joy of being a Christian.

6. **Ask the sinner, "Is there anything that would hinder you from trusting Christ right now, today, as your Saviour?"**
   This question will show the soulwinner if there are still any "obstacles" that must be removed before a sinner trusts Christ. It will also serve as a good transition into drawing the gospel net. After a sinner is saved, the Great Commission is still unfulfilled. We are commanded to go, to win, to baptize, and to teach (disciple). An effective soulwinner will determine to see each aspect of the Great Commission come to fruition with those he leads to Christ.

Verses Remembered by Effective Christians

When you lose sight of His greatness:

Jeremiah 32:17; Jeremiah 33:3; Psalm 147:5; Romans 11:33–36; and 1 Chronicles 29:11–14

When you have needs:

Matthew 6:33; Philippians 4:19; Psalm 37:3; Psalm 37:25; and Deuteronomy 2:7

When you are overwhelmed:

Psalm 55:5; Psalm 55:18; Psalm 107:6–8; and 2 Corinthians 4:16

When problems seem insurmountable:

2 Corinthians 4:15–18; Romans 8:18; Psalm 32:7; Psalm 60:12; Psalm 61:2; and Psalm 62:6–8

When you need purpose:

1 Corinthians 10:31; Ephesians 3:16–21; John 10:10; and Psalm 139:14

When you have stress:

Philippians 4:4–7; Deuteronomy 20:1–4; and Jeremiah 32:27

When you are under pressure:

Psalm 27:1–2; Psalm 27:13–14; Psalm 46:1–2; and 2 Corinthians 12:9–10

When you worry:

Philippians 4:6–7; 1 Peter 5:7; Psalm 55:22; and Psalm 46:10

When you are afraid:

Psalm 56:3; Genesis 15:1; Psalm 27:1; 2 Timothy 1:7; and John 14:27

When you have a big decision to make:

Psalm 32:8; Psalm 143:10; Psalm 40:8; Proverbs 3:5–6; and Psalm 37:3–6

When you are discouraged:

1 Samuel 30:6; Joshua 1:9; Isaiah 41:10; Isaiah 40:26–28; and 2 Corinthians 4:15–16

When you are disheartened:

Joshua 1:5–9; Psalm 73:2; Psalm 73:17; and Psalm 73:24–26

When you are facing opposition:

2 Timothy 3:12; 2 Timothy 2:3; 1 Peter 4:12–13; 1 John 4:4; and Romans 8:31–32

When friends seem to let you down:

2 Timothy 4:16–17; Hebrews 12:2–3; Matthew 28:20; and Deuteronomy 32:27

When you are lonely:

Isaiah 41:10; Hebrews 13:5–6; Acts 18:9–10; and Isaiah 43:2

When you ask if it is worth it:

Matthew 25:21; 1 Corinthians 15:58; Galatians 6:9; and 2 Corinthians 4:17

The Effective Christian's Daily Bible Reading

Christians used by God have one thing in common: a daily walk with God. A Christian's daily walk is based upon the foundation of Bible reading and prayer. It has often been said, "The Book will keep you from sin, or sin will keep you from the Book."

Printed at the bottom of the page for each day is a segmented reading calendar that will allow you to read through the Old and New Testaments during the course of a year.

When considering whether or not to spend time in the Word of God, it is advisable to listen to the words of David, a man after God's own heart, who under the inspiration of the Holy Spirit wrote:

Psalm 119:105
"*Thy word is a lamp unto my feet, and a light unto my path.*"

Psalm 119:9
"*Wherewithal shall a young man cleanse his way? by taking heed thereto according to thy word.*"

May God's Word draw you closer to Him, and help you be the Christian He saved you to be.

One-Year Bible Reading Schedule

January

❑	**1**	Gen. 1–3	Matt. 1
❑	**2**	Gen. 4–6	Matt. 2
❑	**3**	Gen. 7–9	Matt. 3
❑	**4**	Gen. 10–12	Matt. 4
❑	**5**	Gen. 13–15	Matt. 5:1–26
❑	**6**	Gen. 16–17	Matt. 5:27–48
❑	**7**	Gen. 18–19	Matt. 6:1–18
❑	**8**	Gen. 20–22	Matt. 6:19–34
❑	**9**	Gen. 23–24	Matt. 7
❑	**10**	Gen. 25–26	Matt. 8:1–17
❑	**11**	Gen. 27–28	Matt. 8:18–34
❑	**12**	Gen. 29–30	Matt. 9:1–17
❑	**13**	Gen. 31–32	Matt. 9:18–38
❑	**14**	Gen. 33–35	Matt. 10:1–20
❑	**15**	Gen. 36–38	Matt. 10:21–42
❑	**16**	Gen. 39–40	Matt. 11
❑	**17**	Gen. 41–42	Matt. 12:1–23
❑	**18**	Gen. 43–45	Matt. 12:24–50
❑	**19**	Gen. 46–48	Matt. 13:1–30
❑	**20**	Gen. 49–50	Matt. 13:31–58
❑	**21**	Ex. 1–3	Matt. 14:1–21
❑	**22**	Ex. 4–6	Matt. 14:22–36
❑	**23**	Ex. 7–8	Matt. 15:1–20
❑	**24**	Ex. 9–11	Matt. 15:21–39
❑	**25**	Ex. 12–13	Matt. 16
❑	**26**	Ex. 14–15	Matt. 17
❑	**27**	Ex. 16–18	Matt. 18:1–20
❑	**28**	Ex. 19–20	Matt. 18:21–35
❑	**29**	Ex. 21–22	Matt. 19
❑	**30**	Ex. 23–24	Matt. 20:1–16
❑	**31**	Ex. 25–26	Matt. 20:17–34

February

❑	**1**	Ex. 27–28	Matt. 21:1–22
❑	**2**	Ex. 29–30	Matt. 21:23–46
❑	**3**	Ex. 31–33	Matt. 22:1–22
❑	**4**	Ex. 34–35	Matt. 22:23–46
❑	**5**	Ex. 36–38	Matt. 23:1–22
❑	**6**	Ex. 39–40	Matt. 23:23–39
❑	**7**	Lev. 1–3	Matt. 24:1–28
❑	**8**	Lev. 4–5	Matt. 24:29–51
❑	**9**	Lev. 6–7	Matt. 25:1–30
❑	**10**	Lev. 8–10	Matt. 25:31–46
❑	**11**	Lev. 11–12	Matt. 26:1–25
❑	**12**	Lev. 13	Matt. 26:26–50
❑	**13**	Lev. 14	Matt. 26:51–75
❑	**14**	Lev. 15–16	Matt. 27:1–26
❑	**15**	Lev. 17–18	Matt. 27:27–50
❑	**16**	Lev. 19–20	Matt. 27:51–66
❑	**17**	Lev. 21–22	Matt. 28
❑	**18**	Lev. 23–24	Mark 1:1–22
❑	**19**	Lev. 25	Mark 1:23–45
❑	**20**	Lev. 26–27	Mark 2
❑	**21**	Num. 1–2	Mark 3:1–19
❑	**22**	Num. 3–4	Mark 3:20–35
❑	**23**	Num. 5–6	Mark 4:1–20
❑	**24**	Num. 7–8	Mark 4:21–41
❑	**25**	Num. 9–11	Mark 5:1–20
❑	**26**	Num. 12–14	Mark 5:21–43
❑	**27**	Num. 15–16	Mark 6:1–29
❑	**28**	Num. 17–19	Mark 6:30–56

March

❑	**1**	Num. 20–22	Mark 7:1–13
❑	**2**	Num. 23–25	Mark 7:14–37
❑	**3**	Num. 26–28	Mark 8
❑	**4**	Num. 29–31	Mark 9:1–29
❑	**5**	Num. 32–34	Mark 9:30–50
❑	**6**	Num. 35–36	Mark 10:1–31
❑	**7**	Deut. 1–3	Mark 10:32–52
❑	**8**	Deut. 4–6	Mark 11:1–18
❑	**9**	Deut. 7–9	Mark 11:19–33
❑	**10**	Deut. 10–12	Mark 12:1–27
❑	**11**	Deut. 13–15	Mark 12:28–44
❑	**12**	Deut. 16–18	Mark 13:1–20
❑	**13**	Deut. 19–21	Mark 13:21–37
❑	**14**	Deut. 22–24	Mark 14:1–26
❑	**15**	Deut. 25–27	Mark 14:27–53
❑	**16**	Deut. 28–29	Mark 14:54–72
❑	**17**	Deut. 30–31	Mark 15:1–25
❑	**18**	Deut. 32–34	Mark 15:26–47
❑	**19**	Josh. 1–3	Mark 16
❑	**20**	Josh. 4–6	Luke 1:1–20
❑	**21**	Josh. 7–9	Luke 1:21–38
❑	**22**	Josh. 10–12	Luke 1:39–56
❑	**23**	Josh. 13–15	Luke 1:57–80
❑	**24**	Josh. 16–18	Luke 2:1–24
❑	**25**	Josh. 19–21	Luke 2:25–52
❑	**26**	Josh. 22–24	Luke 3
❑	**27**	Judges 1–3	Luke 4:1–30
❑	**28**	Judges 4–6	Luke 4:31–44
❑	**29**	Judges 7–8	Luke 5:1–16
❑	**30**	Judges 9–10	Luke 5:17–39
❑	**31**	Judges 11–12	Luke 6:1–26

April

❑	**1**	Judges 13–15	Luke 6:27–49
❑	**2**	Judges 16–18	Luke 7:1–30
❑	**3**	Judges 19–21	Luke 7:31–50
❑	**4**	Ruth 1–4	Luke 8:1–25
❑	**5**	1 Sam. 1–3	Luke 8:26–56
❑	**6**	1 Sam. 4–6	Luke 9:1–17
❑	**7**	1 Sam. 7–9	Luke 9:18–36
❑	**8**	1 Sam. 10–12	Luke 9:37–62
❑	**9**	1 Sam. 13–14	Luke 10:1–24
❑	**10**	1 Sam. 15–16	Luke 10:25–42
❑	**11**	1 Sam. 17–18	Luke 11:1–28
❑	**12**	1 Sam. 19–21	Luke 11:29–54
❑	**13**	1 Sam. 22–24	Luke 12:1–31
❑	**14**	1 Sam. 25–26	Luke 12:32–59
❑	**15**	1 Sam. 27–29	Luke 13:1–22
❑	**16**	1 Sam. 30–31	Luke 13:23–35
❑	**17**	2 Sam. 1–2	Luke 14:1–24
❑	**18**	2 Sam. 3–5	Luke 14:25–35
❑	**19**	2 Sam. 6–8	Luke 15:1–10
❑	**20**	2 Sam. 9–11	Luke 15:11–32
❑	**21**	2 Sam. 12–13	Luke 16
❑	**22**	2 Sam. 14–15	Luke 17:1–19
❑	**23**	2 Sam. 16–18	Luke 17:20–37
❑	**24**	2 Sam. 19–20	Luke 18:1–23
❑	**25**	2 Sam. 21–22	Luke 18:24–43
❑	**26**	2 Sam. 23–24	Luke 19:1–27
❑	**27**	1 Kings 1–2	Luke 19:28–48
❑	**28**	1 Kings 3–5	Luke 20:1–26
❑	**29**	1 Kings 6–7	Luke 20:27–47
❑	**30**	1 Kings 8–9	Luke 21:1–19

May

❑	**1**	1 Kings 10–11	Luke 21:20–38
❑	**2**	1 Kings 12–13	Luke 22:1–30
❑	**3**	1 Kings 14–15	Luke 22:31–46
❑	**4**	1 Kings 16–18	Luke 22:47–71
❑	**5**	1 Kings 19–20	Luke 23:1–25
❑	**6**	1 Kings 21–22	Luke 23:26–56
❑	**7**	2 Kings 1–3	Luke 24:1–35
❑	**8**	2 Kings 4–6	Luke 24:36–53
❑	**9**	2 Kings 7–9	John 1:1–28
❑	**10**	2 Kings 10–12	John 1:29–51
❑	**11**	2 Kings 13–14	John 2
❑	**12**	2 Kings 15–16	John 3:1–18
❑	**13**	2 Kings 17–18	John 3:19–36
❑	**14**	2 Kings 19–21	John 4:1–30
❑	**15**	2 Kings 22–23	John 4:31–54
❑	**16**	2 Kings 24–25	John 5:1–24
❑	**17**	1 Chr. 1–3	John 5:25–47
❑	**18**	1 Chr. 4–6	John 6:1–21
❑	**19**	1 Chr. 7–9	John 6:22–44
❑	**20**	1 Chr. 10–12	John 6:45–71
❑	**21**	1 Chr. 13–15	John 7:1–27
❑	**22**	1 Chr. 16–18	John 7:28–53
❑	**23**	1 Chr. 19–21	John 8:1–27
❑	**24**	1 Chr. 22–24	John 8:28–59
❑	**25**	1 Chr. 25–27	John 9:1–23
❑	**26**	1 Chr. 28–29	John 9:24–41
❑	**27**	2 Chr. 1–3	John 10:1–23
❑	**28**	2 Chr. 4–6	John 10:24–42
❑	**29**	2 Chr. 7–9	John 11:1–29
❑	**30**	2 Chr. 10–12	John 11:30–57
❑	**31**	2 Chr. 13–14	John 12:1–26

June

❑	**1**	2 Chr. 15–16	John 12:27–50
❑	**2**	2 Chr. 17–18	John 13:1–20
❑	**3**	2 Chr. 19–20	John 13:21–38
❑	**4**	2 Chr. 21–22	John 14
❑	**5**	2 Chr. 23–24	John 15
❑	**6**	2 Chr. 25–27	John 16
❑	**7**	2 Chr. 28–29	John 17
❑	**8**	2 Chr. 30–31	John 18:1–18
❑	**9**	2 Chr. 32–33	John 18:19–40
❑	**10**	2 Chr. 34–36	John 19:1–22
❑	**11**	Ezra 1–2	John 19:23–42
❑	**12**	Ezra 3–5	John 20
❑	**13**	Ezra 6–8	John 21
❑	**14**	Ezra 9–10	Acts 1
❑	**15**	Neh. 1–3	Acts 2:1–21
❑	**16**	Neh. 4–6	Acts 2:22–47
❑	**17**	Neh. 7–9	Acts 3
❑	**18**	Neh. 10–11	Acts 4:1–22
❑	**19**	Neh. 12–13	Acts 4:23–37
❑	**20**	Esther 1–2	Acts 5:1–21
❑	**21**	Esther 3–5	Acts 5:22–42
❑	**22**	Esther 6–8	Acts 6
❑	**23**	Esther 9–10	Acts 7:1–21
❑	**24**	Job 1–2	Acts 7:22–43
❑	**25**	Job 3–4	Acts 7:44–60
❑	**26**	Job 5–7	Acts 8:1–25
❑	**27**	Job 8–10	Acts 8:26–40
❑	**28**	Job 11–13	Acts 9:1–21
❑	**29**	Job 14–16	Acts 9:22–43
❑	**30**	Job 17–19	Acts 10:1–23

July

❑	1	Job 20–21	Acts 10:24–48
❑	2	Job 22–24	Acts 11
❑	3	Job 25–27	Acts 12
❑	4	Job 28–29	Acts 13:1–25
❑	5	Job 30–31	Acts 13:26–52
❑	6	Job 32–33	Acts 14
❑	7	Job 34–35	Acts 15:1–21
❑	8	Job 36–37	Acts 15:22–41
❑	9	Job 38–40	Acts 16:1–21
❑	10	Job 41–42	Acts 16:22–40
❑	11	Ps. 1–3	Acts 17:1–15
❑	12	Ps. 4–6	Acts 17:16–34
❑	13	Ps. 7–9	Acts 18
❑	14	Ps. 10–12	Acts 19:1–20
❑	15	Ps. 13–15	Acts 19:21–41
❑	16	Ps. 16–17	Acts 20:1–16
❑	17	Ps. 18–19	Acts 20:17–38
❑	18	Ps. 20–22	Acts 21:1–17
❑	19	Ps. 23–25	Acts 21:18–40
❑	20	Ps. 26–28	Acts 22
❑	21	Ps. 29–30	Acts 23:1–15
❑	22	Ps. 31–32	Acts 23:16–35
❑	23	Ps. 33–34	Acts 24
❑	24	Ps. 35–36	Acts 25
❑	25	Ps. 37–39	Acts 26
❑	26	Ps. 40–42	Acts 27:1–26
❑	27	Ps. 43–45	Acts 27:27–44
❑	28	Ps. 46–48	Acts 28
❑	29	Ps. 49–50	Rom. 1
❑	30	Ps. 51–53	Rom. 2
❑	31	Ps. 54–56	Rom. 3

August

❑	1	Ps. 57–59	Rom. 4
❑	2	Ps. 60–62	Rom. 5
❑	3	Ps. 63–65	Rom. 6
❑	4	Ps. 66–67	Rom. 7
❑	5	Ps. 68–69	Rom. 8:1–21
❑	6	Ps. 70–71	Rom. 8:22–39
❑	7	Ps. 72–73	Rom. 9:1–15
❑	8	Ps. 74–76	Rom. 9:16–33
❑	9	Ps. 77–78	Rom. 10
❑	10	Ps. 79–80	Rom. 11:1–18
❑	11	Ps. 81–83	Rom. 11:19–36
❑	12	Ps. 84–86	Rom. 12
❑	13	Ps. 87–88	Rom. 13
❑	14	Ps. 89–90	Rom. 14
❑	15	Ps. 91–93	Rom. 15:1–13
❑	16	Ps. 94–96	Rom. 15:14–33
❑	17	Ps. 97–99	Rom. 16
❑	18	Ps. 100–102	1 Cor. 1
❑	19	Ps. 103–104	1 Cor. 2
❑	20	Ps. 105–106	1 Cor. 3
❑	21	Ps. 107–109	1 Cor. 4
❑	22	Ps. 110–112	1 Cor. 5
❑	23	Ps. 113–115	1 Cor. 6
❑	24	Ps. 116–118	1 Cor. 7:1–19
❑	25	Ps. 119:1–88	1 Cor. 7:20–40
❑	26	Ps. 119:89–176	1 Cor. 8
❑	27	Ps. 120–122	1 Cor. 9
❑	28	Ps.123–125	1 Cor. 10:1–18
❑	29	Ps. 126–128	1 Cor. 10:19–33
❑	30	Ps. 129–131	1 Cor. 11:1–16
❑	31	Ps. 132–134	1 Cor. 11:17–34

September

❑	1	Ps. 135–136	1 Cor. 12
❑	2	Ps. 137–139	1 Cor. 13
❑	3	Ps. 140–142	1 Cor. 14:1–20
❑	4	Ps. 143–145	1 Cor. 14:21–40
❑	5	Ps. 146–147	1 Cor. 15:1–28
❑	6	Ps. 148–150	1 Cor. 15:29–58
❑	7	Prov. 1–2	1 Cor. 16
❑	8	Prov. 3–5	2 Cor. 1
❑	9	Prov. 6–7	2 Cor. 2
❑	10	Prov. 8–9	2 Cor. 3
❑	11	Prov. 10–12	2 Cor. 4
❑	12	Prov. 13–15	2 Cor. 5
❑	13	Prov. 16–18	2 Cor. 6
❑	14	Prov. 19–21	2 Cor. 7
❑	15	Prov. 22–24	2 Cor. 8
❑	16	Prov. 25–26	2 Cor. 9
❑	17	Prov. 27–29	2 Cor. 10
❑	18	Prov. 30–31	2 Cor. 11:1–15
❑	19	Eccl. 1–3	2 Cor. 11:16–33
❑	20	Eccl. 4–6	2 Cor. 12
❑	21	Eccl. 7–9	2 Cor. 13
❑	22	Eccl. 10–12	Gal. 1
❑	23	Song 1–3	Gal. 2
❑	24	Song 4–5	Gal. 3
❑	25	Song 6–8	Gal. 4
❑	26	Isa. 1–2	Gal. 5
❑	27	Isa. 3–4	Gal. 6
❑	28	Isa. 5–6	Eph. 1
❑	29	Isa. 7–8	Eph. 2
❑	30	Isa. 9–10	Eph. 3

October

❑	1	Isa. 11–13	Eph. 4
❑	2	Isa. 14–16	Eph. 5:1–16
❑	3	Isa. 17–19	Eph. 5:17–33
❑	4	Isa. 20–22	Eph. 6
❑	5	Isa. 23–25	Phil. 1
❑	6	Isa. 26–27	Phil. 2
❑	7	Isa. 28–29	Phil. 3
❑	8	Isa. 30–31	Phil. 4
❑	9	Isa. 32–33	Col. 1
❑	10	Isa. 34–36	Col. 2
❑	11	Isa. 37–38	Col. 3
❑	12	Isa. 39–40	Col. 4
❑	13	Isa. 41–42	1 Thess. 1
❑	14	Isa. 43–44	1 Thess. 2
❑	15	Isa. 45–46	1 Thess. 3
❑	16	Isa. 47–49	1 Thess. 4
❑	17	Isa. 50–52	1 Thess. 5
❑	18	Isa. 53–55	2 Thess. 1
❑	19	Isa. 56–58	2 Thess. 2
❑	20	Isa. 59–61	2 Thess. 3
❑	21	Isa. 62–64	1 Tim. 1
❑	22	Isa. 65–66	1 Tim. 2
❑	23	Jer. 1–2	1 Tim. 3
❑	24	Jer. 3–5	1 Tim. 4
❑	25	Jer. 6–8	1 Tim. 5
❑	26	Jer. 9–11	1 Tim. 6
❑	27	Jer. 12–14	2 Tim. 1
❑	28	Jer. 15–17	2 Tim. 2
❑	29	Jer. 18–19	2 Tim. 3
❑	30	Jer. 20–21	2 Tim. 4
❑	31	Jer. 22–23	Titus 1

November

❑	1	Jer. 24–26	Titus 2
❑	2	Jer. 27–29	Titus 3
❑	3	Jer. 30–31	Philemon
❑	4	Jer. 32–33	Heb. 1
❑	5	Jer. 34–36	Heb. 2
❑	6	Jer. 37–39	Heb. 3
❑	7	Jer. 40–42	Heb. 4
❑	8	Jer. 43–45	Heb. 5
❑	9	Jer. 46–47	Heb. 6
❑	10	Jer. 48–49	Heb. 7
❑	11	Jer. 50	Heb. 8
❑	12	Jer. 51–52	Heb. 9
❑	13	Lam. 1–2	Heb. 10:1–18
❑	14	Lam. 3–5	Heb. 10:19–39
❑	15	Ezek. 1–2	Heb. 11:1–19
❑	16	Ezek. 3–4	Heb. 11:20–40
❑	17	Ezek. 5–7	Heb. 12
❑	18	Ezek. 8–10	Heb. 13
❑	19	Ezek. 11–13	James 1
❑	20	Ezek. 14–15	James 2
❑	21	Ezek. 16–17	James 3
❑	22	Ezek. 18–19	James 4
❑	23	Ezek. 20–21	James 5
❑	24	Ezek. 22–23	1 Peter 1
❑	25	Ezek. 24–26	1 Peter 2
❑	26	Ezek. 27–29	1 Peter 3
❑	27	Ezek. 30–32	1 Peter 4
❑	28	Ezek. 33–34	1 Peter 5
❑	29	Ezek. 35–36	2 Peter 1
❑	30	Ezek. 37–39	2 Peter 2

December

❑	1	Ezek. 40–41	2 Peter 3
❑	2	Ezek. 42–44	1 John 1
❑	3	Ezek. 45–46	1 John 2
❑	4	Ezek. 47–48	1 John 3
❑	5	Dan. 1–2	1 John 4
❑	6	Dan. 3–4	1 John 5
❑	7	Dan. 5–7	2 John
❑	8	Dan. 8–10	3 John
❑	9	Dan. 11–12	Jude
❑	10	Hos. 1–4	Rev. 1
❑	11	Hos. 5–8	Rev. 2
❑	12	Hos. 9–11	Rev. 3
❑	13	Hos. 12–14	Rev. 4
❑	14	Joel	Rev. 5
❑	15	Amos 1–3	Rev. 6
❑	16	Amos 4–6	Rev. 7
❑	17	Amos 7–9	Rev. 8
❑	18	Obad.	Rev. 9
❑	19	Jonah	Rev. 10
❑	20	Micah 1–3	Rev. 11
❑	21	Micah 4–5	Rev. 12
❑	22	Micah 6–7	Rev. 13
❑	23	Nahum	Rev. 14
❑	24	Hab.	Rev. 15
❑	25	Zeph.	Rev. 16
❑	26	Hag.	Rev. 17
❑	27	Zech. 1–4	Rev. 18
❑	28	Zech. 5–8	Rev. 19
❑	29	Zech. 9–12	Rev. 20
❑	30	Zech. 13–14	Rev. 21
❑	31	Mal.	Rev. 22

90-Day Bible Reading Schedule

Day	Start	End	✔
1	Genesis 1:1	Genesis 16:16	❑
2	Genesis 17:1	Genesis 28:19	❑
3	Genesis 28:20	Genesis 40:11	❑
4	Genesis 40:12	Genesis 50:26	❑
5	Exodus 1:1	Exodus 15:18	❑
6	Exodus 15:19	Exodus 28:43	❑
7	Exodus 29:1	Exodus 40:38	❑
8	Leviticus 1:1	Leviticus 14:32	❑
9	Leviticus 14:33	Leviticus 26:26	❑
10	Leviticus 26:27	Numbers 8:14	❑
11	Numbers 8:15	Numbers 21:7	❑
12	Numbers 21:8	Numbers 32:19	❑
13	Numbers 32:20	Deuteronomy 7:26	❑
14	Deuteronomy 8:1	Deuteronomy 23:11	❑
15	Deuteronomy 23:12	Deuteronomy 34:12	❑
16	Joshua 1:1	Joshua 14:15	❑
17	Joshua 15:1	Judges 3:27	❑
18	Judges 3:28	Judges 15:12	❑
19	Judges 15:13	1 Samuel 2:29	❑
20	1 Samuel 2:30	1 Samuel 15:35	❑
21	1 Samuel 16:1	1 Samuel 28:19	❑
22	1 Samuel 28:20	2 Samuel 12:10	❑
23	2 Samuel 12:11	2 Samuel 22:18	❑
24	2 Samuel 22:19	1 Kings 7:37	❑
25	1 Kings 7:38	1 Kings 16:20	❑
26	1 Kings 16:21	2 Kings 4:37	❑
27	2 Kings 4:38	2 Kings 15:26	❑
28	2 Kings 15:27	2 Kings 25:30	❑
29	1 Chronicles 1:1	1 Chronicles 9:44	❑
30	1 Chronicles 10:1	1 Chronicles 23:32	❑
31	1 Chronicles 24:1	2 Chronicles 7:10	❑
32	2 Chronicles 7:11	2 Chronicles 23:15	❑
33	2 Chronicles 23:16	2 Chronicles 35:15	❑
34	2 Chronicles 35:16	Ezra 10:44	❑
35	Nehemiah 1:1	Nehemiah 13:14	❑
36	Nehemiah 13:15	Job 7:21	❑
37	Job 8:1	Job 24:25	❑
38	Job 25:1	Job 41:34	❑
39	Job 42:1	Psalm 24:10	❑
40	Psalm 25:1	Psalm 45:14	❑
41	Psalm 45:15	Psalm 69:21	❑
42	Psalm 69:22	Psalm 89:13	❑
43	Psalm 89:14	Psalm 108:13	❑
44	Psalm 109:1	Psalm 134:3	❑
45	Psalm 135:1	Proverbs 6:35	❑

Day	Start	End	✔
46	Proverbs 7:1	Proverbs 20:21	❑
47	Proverbs 20:22	Ecclesiastes 2:26	❑
48	Ecclesiastes 3:1	Song 8:14	❑
49	Isaiah 1:1	Isaiah 13:22	❑
50	Isaiah 14:1	Isaiah 28:29	❑
51	Isaiah 29:1	Isaiah 41:18	❑
52	Isaiah 41:19	Isaiah 52:12	❑
53	Isaiah 52:13	Isaiah 66:18	❑
54	Isaiah 66:19	Jeremiah 10:13	❑
55	Jeremiah 10:14	Jeremiah 23:8	❑
56	Jeremiah 23:9	Jeremiah 33:22	❑
57	Jeremiah 33:23	Jeremiah 47:7	❑
58	Jeremiah 48:1	Lamentations 1:22	❑
59	Lamentations 2:1	Ezekiel 12:20	❑
60	Ezekiel 12:21	Ezekiel 23:39	❑
61	Ezekiel 23:40	Ezekiel 35:15	❑
62	Ezekiel 36:1	Ezekiel 47:12	❑
63	Ezekiel 47:13	Daniel 8:27	❑
64	Daniel 9:1	Hosea 13:6	❑
65	Hosea 13:7	Amos 9:10	❑
66	Amos 9:11	Nahum 3:19	❑
67	Habakkuk 1:1	Zechariah 10:12	❑
68	Zechariah 11:1	Matthew 4:25	❑
69	Matthew 5:1	Matthew 15:39	❑
70	Matthew 16:1	Matthew 26:56	❑
71	Matthew 26:57	Mark 9:13	❑
72	Mark 9:14	Luke 1:80	❑
73	Luke 2:1	Luke 9:62	❑
74	Luke 10:1	Luke 20:19	❑
75	Luke 20:20	John 5:47	❑
76	John 6:1	John 15:17	❑
77	John 15:18	Acts 6:7	❑
78	Acts 6:8	Acts 16:37	❑
79	Acts 16:38	Acts 28:16	❑
80	Acts 28:17	Romans 14:23	❑
81	Romans 15:1	1 Corinthians 14:40	❑
82	1 Corinthians 15:1	Galatians 3:25	❑
83	Galatians 3:26	Colossians 4:18	❑
84	1 Thessalonians 1:1	Philemon 25	❑
85	Hebrews 1:1	James 3:12	❑
86	James 3:13	3 John 14	❑
87	Jude 1	Revelation 17:18	❑
88	Revelation 18:1	Revelation 22:21	❑
89	Grace Day	Grace Day	❑
90	Grace Day	Grace Day	❑

JANUARY

January 1, 1896

Pride Is Always a Hindrance to Revival

"If my people, which are called by my name, shall humble themselves..."
—2 Chronicles 7:14

Gypsy Smith returned to America to hold his fifth revival crusade in the United States. As he walked through the city where his first meeting would begin, he meditated on the sermon he was about to preach and prayed for souls to be saved. Near the rented auditorium, a large sign caught his eye. "Gypsy Smith: The Greatest Evangelist in the World." The Holy Spirit pricked his heart, and upon entering the meeting hall, he demanded that the sign be taken down immediately.

We tend to think of pride as an insignificant issue—at least in our own lives. But God sees it as an abomination. "Every one that is proud in heart is an abomination to the LORD" (Proverbs 16:5a). It is ludicrous to think that we can have revival without God, yet we drive Him away through our pride and self-sufficiency. "Though the LORD be high, yet hath he respect unto the lowly: but the proud he knoweth afar off" (Psalm 138:6). God is not attracted to our boasting but to our brokenness. "The LORD is nigh unto them that are of a broken heart; and saveth such as be of a contrite spirit" (Psalm 34:18).

Humility is the common thread that ties all of God's usable servants together. The letter "I" is the middle letter in the word *pride,* and it is the middle letter in the word *sin*. As we begin a new year, let's be sure to have a funeral for self. The "I" of our lives must die and be buried if revival will ever come to our lives, our churches, and our communities.

When we ponder what Christ has done for us, we will pray and live the words of the Apostle Paul in Galatians 2:20, "I am crucified with Christ: nevertheless I live; yet not I, but Christ liveth in me: and the life which I now live in the flesh I live by the faith of the Son of God, who loved me, and gave himself for me." Begin this new year by dying to self. Revival is born on the grave of pride.

January 2, 1863

God Calls His People to Be Bold

"And now, Lord, behold their threatenings: and grant unto thy servants, that with all boldness they may speak thy word."—**Acts 4:29**

No other battle in the Civil War would result in the casualties and losses as the Battle of Stones River near Murfreesboro, Tennessee. Death would come to 1,677 on the Union side and 1,294 on the Confederate side. As the Union forces seized control on this January day in 1863, one voice could be heard through dark and smoke-filled air. The man's name may be familiar to many Christians, for he would become one of the greatest evangelists the world has ever seen—Dwight Lyman Moody. During the heat of battle, Moody would run in and out of the explosions and seek out a wounded soul desperate for help. Over the gruesome noise of nineteenth-century warfare, each soldier would hear the same battle cry from the lips of Moody, "Are you a Christian?"

"The thief cometh not, but for to steal, and to kill, and to destroy" (John 10:10a). Satan has waged war against mankind ever since his fall from Heaven. The death toll from sin mounts as Satan's war against Christ and the Gospel intensifies. Every day we meet the wounded who are perishing without hope. "Wherein in time past ye walked according to the course of this world, according to the prince of the power of the air, the spirit that now worketh in the children of disobedience...That at that time ye were without Christ...having no hope, and without God in the world" (Ephesians 2:2, 12).

Will we, like the apostles in Acts 4 and D. L. Moody in the Civil War, ask God for boldness to proclaim God's message of hope to the lost and dying around us? When the cannons of life are stilled and the weapons laid to eternal rest, may it not be said of our generation, "I looked on my right hand, and beheld, but there was no man that would know me: refuge failed me; no man cared for my soul" (Psalm 142:4). May we boldly seek out the perishing and proclaim the message of the Gospel.

January 3, 1897

Little Is Much When God Is in It

"...And thy Father, which seeth in secret, shall reward thee openly."
—Matthew 6:18

In Zechariah 4:10, God asks, "For who hath despised the day of small things?" Most of the world's population have never made their way to the small town of Garner, Iowa. This little spot on the map, however, is well-known to God. It was here that J. Wilbur Chapman had been scheduled to preach a revival but canceled because God led him to step out of revival work and take a pastorate. He wrote the pastor of the little church in Garner letting him know that he would not be able to come for the meeting. The pastor was greatly disappointed and wrote to tell Chapman that he and the church family had already invested much prayer and preparation. Chapman replied, "I will send my assistant; he will do a fine job."

When Chapman informed his assistant of this decision, the young intern was shocked and protested, "But, I don't have any sermons!" Chapman took out the notes to eight of his well-known sermons and handed them to Billy Sunday and said, "Here, preach these. They are tried and tested." Thus, the first revival that Billy Sunday preached was in a little town in Iowa with the sermons of his mentor, J. Wilbur Chapman, on January 3, 1897. God blessed that meeting with a miraculous, supernatural power, and from that humble beginning, a great work of revival began.

You may be virtually unknown in the world, and your ministry in the church may seem small and insignificant to those around you. But do not underestimate what God wants to do through you. "But God hath chosen the foolish things of the world to confound the wise; and God hath chosen the weak things of the world to confound the things which are mighty. And base things of the world, and things which are despised, hath God chosen, yea, and things which are not, to bring to nought things that are: That no flesh should glory in his presence" (1 Corinthians 1:27–29). Be faithful in whatever you do and wherever you are. God will take care of the results.

January, 1897

God Is Greater than the Power of Any Sin

"For the weapons of our warfare are not carnal, but mighty through God to the pulling down of strong holds;"—**2 Corinthians 10:4**

In the same month and year as God would use Billy Sunday in his first revival crusade in Iowa, God was at work in the heart of a broken and battered life a couple hundred miles east in the city of Chicago. The life of Mel Trotter was soiled and spoiled by drunkenness and depravity, and when his two-year-old little girl died, he vowed he would never touch liquor again. But two hours later, he sold his daughter's shoes to buy another drink. Later, as he walked to a bridge near Lake Michigan where he intended to end his life, God stood in the way, much as He had done in the life of Saul of Tarsus in Acts 9. Entering the Pacific Garden Mission that night, Mel Trotter found Christ as His Saviour, and his life was radically transformed.

No bondage of sin can match the miracle working power of the Gospel. God has turned murderers into missionaries, sailors into saints, and pirates into preachers. Moses, David, and Paul were all men who committed murder at one point in their lives. Yet, God transformed them and made them some of His finest servants. "Therefore if any man be in Christ, he is a new creature: old things are passed away; behold, all things are become new" (2 Corinthians 5:17). The devil loves to convince people they are too far into sin to ever be saved. But no one has stooped so low that God's grace cannot reach him. "But where sin abounded, grace did much more abound" (Romans 5:20b). God's saving grace can reach you today.

Christian, God has power over the habits that have enslaved you. The strongholds of your sinful past are no greater than the walls of Jericho, the giant named Goliath, or the raging tempest on the Sea of Galilee. As a child of God, the Holy Spirit now dwells within you, and "...greater is he that is in you, than he that is in the world" (1 John 4:4b). Mel Trotter's past was no match for God's power. A few steps from suicide, God turned his life around and used him to preach the Gospel. Let the same God pull down a stronghold of sin in your life today.

January, 1901

The Eternal Is Far More Important than the Earthly

"Set your affection on things above, not on things on the earth."
—Colossians 3:2

Do you ever find yourself in a battle between what you want and what God wants? The truth is, every decision in life is a war between self and God. There are only two choices on the shelf: pleasing God or pleasing self. Our lives will be characterized by either Philippians 1:21 or Philippians 2:21. The first says, "For to me to live is Christ" while the latter states, "For all seek their own, not the things which are Jesus Christ's." Where are your eyes today? Are they on the temporal things that can satisfy for a moment or on the eternal which has unending reward?

Mordecai Ham wrote of this battle in his soul: "My call to the ministry was a continuous and irresistible urge. I fought it when I started out as a salesman, because God had not completely whipped me, and I did not want to be a preacher until I had first made a fortune." After studying twenty-seven books, praying earnestly for God's will, and writing essays of meditation, this Christian businessman finally laid aside his personal plans and accepted God's call of ministry upon his life. Though it was a hard decision for the moment, Ham would soon see the eternal rewards of a life lived in God's service.

In the temporal, the temporary seems important. But in eternity, nothing temporal will be important at all. That is why we must not focus on things here but rather on the hereafter. Solomon was successful in gathering to himself everything that life could offer. Whatever his heart desired, he had the resources or power to obtain. But at the end of his life, he declared that it was all vanity and vexation of spirit (see Ecclesiastes 2). His storehouses were full, but his soul was empty. Make sure you have an "upward look" today. The hymn writer put it this way: "Turn your eyes upon Jesus; Look full in His wonderful face. And the things of earth will grow strangely dim, in the light of His glory and grace."

January 6, 1850

It Is Never Foolish to Serve the Lord

"A faithful man shall abound with blessings;"—**Proverbs 28:20a**

"Look unto me, and be ye saved, all the ends of the earth: for I am God, and there is none else" (Isaiah 45:22). The unpolished and unskilled layman preacher would preach: "Young man, you look very miserable. Young man, look to Jesus Christ. Look. Look. Look!" That humble but faithful preacher did not know the young man sitting in the service who had come in only to get out of the snowstorm. But God sure did! And He would use that little meeting of fifteen people and the poor sermon of a faithful man of God to bring about the salvation of one who would later be called "The Prince of Preachers." That man was Charles Haddon Spurgeon.

Spurgeon would later say: "Between half-past ten o'clock, when I entered that chapel, and half-past twelve o'clock, when I was back again at home, what a change had taken place in me! Simply by looking to Jesus, I had been delivered from despair, and I was brought into such a joyous state of mind that, when they saw me at home, they said to me, 'Something wonderful has happened to you,' and I was eager to tell them all about it. Oh! There was joy in the household that day, when all heard that the eldest son had found the Saviour and knew himself to be forgiven."

The world would look at a small gathering of fifteen people as foolishness. Skeptics would ask, "How could anything meaningful or influential come out of such a pointless meeting?" But God delights in using those who are faithful. That preacher and congregation would never know of the tens of thousands who would come to Christ through the ministry of that young teenager. They could not have imagined that his sermons would still be read and quoted today. "Now unto him that is able to do exceeding abundantly above all that we ask or think, according to the power that worketh in us" (Ephesians 3:20). Will you be faithful today and let God show Himself strong on your behalf?

January 7, 1832

Investing in a Child Can Change the Future

"But Jesus said, Suffer little children, and forbid them not, to come unto me: for of such is the kingdom of heaven."—**Matthew 19:14**

Working with children, whether they are your own or someone else's, can be challenging and tedious. Yet, the time we invest and the seeds of truth we sow can spring forth into a mighty harvest.

When T. DeWitt Talmage was born in Bound Brook, New Jersey, his parents had no idea the effect that their baby boy would have on the world. Charles Spurgeon said of Talmage's preaching: "His sermons take hold of my inmost soul. The Lord is with this mighty man. I am astonished when God blesses me but not surprised when He blesses him." Talmage preached to over 8,000 people every week, his sermons reaching over 25,000,000 readers. Queen Victoria would keep his sermons as one of her favorite books, and the Czar of Russia would call him his personal friend. God had great plans for this little baby boy, and thankfully his parents brought him up in the nurture and admonition of the Lord.

The most important work you do today may well be with your children or grandchildren. Your greatest opportunity in your church may be on a bus route, a Sunday school class, junior church, or the nursery. Timothy was thankful he had a mother and grandmother who invested in him. "When I call to remembrance the unfeigned faith that is in thee, which dwelt first in thy grandmother Lois, and thy mother Eunice; and I am persuaded that in thee also...And that from a child thou hast known the holy scriptures, which are able to make thee wise unto salvation through faith which is in Christ Jesus" (2 Timothy 1:5; 2 Timothy 3:15).

As you minister to infants and children, you may never know the impact you will have on their lives and the impact that they will have on the world. Don't ignore them and look over them. Love them and teach them the Word of God. Your influence on their lives may be the reason that thousands more souls are saved. Will you help a young person today to learn the Word of God?

January 7, 1902

The Applause of Men or the Approval of God?

"He hath remembered his mercy and his truth toward the house of Israel: all the ends of the earth have seen the salvation of our God."—**Psalm 98:3**

Few Christians today would be familiar with the name Hyman Appelman. If you asked preachers to list ten great evangelists of the past, Appelman's name would not be mentioned by most. Appelman was born into a Jewish family on January 7, 1902 and called by God to evangelism shortly after his conversion. God used him in a powerful way throughout the world. During a six-month campaign in Australia in 1949, 8,600 people were saved. During a twelve-month meeting in Britain in 1951, 1,400 people came to Christ. During a three-month revival in India, 5,893 people were born again. At the end of his ministry, over 445,000 people had trusted Christ in his meetings, and over 270,000 of those joined a local church.

Dr. Lee Roberson said of Appelman's ministry: "The first time that I listened to him preach my heart was stirred by his fervor, zeal, and passion for souls...for thirty-five years there has been no abatement of his zeal and his concern for the souls of men." God used him to reach his own people, the Jews and countless Gentiles as well. Over four hundred preachers would later say they were called to preach under Appelman's preaching. This choice servant of God has faded into obscurity in the minds of most modern-day Christians. But God never forgets.

Whether or not anyone remembers our ministry is unimportant. We can always be sure that God will. "For God is not unrighteous to forget your work and labour of love, which ye have shewed toward his name, in that ye have ministered to the saints, and do minister" (Hebrews 6:10). We must not live and labor for the applause, accolades, or awe of men, but rather for the approval of God. When we stand before Him, He will be all that matters anyway.

January 9, 1839

God's Word Always Works

"So shall my word be that goeth forth out of my mouth: it shall not return unto me void, but it shall accomplish that which I please, and it shall prosper in the thing whereto I sent it."—**Isaiah 55:11**

A revival meeting was scheduled to take place at a small country general store in Abingdon, Virginia. As word got around of the meeting, a boy named Robert Sheffey would attend, but with the sole purpose of causing trouble. Yet, when God's Word is faithfully preached, it is the Sword of the Spirit that causes the trouble. Sheffey was convicted of his sin that night and trusted Christ as Saviour. God would take this young trouble-maker and use him as one of the most influential circuit-riding preachers of the 1800s.

We must never underestimate the power of God's Word. Whether we are preaching it, teaching it, quoting it, singing it, or testifying of it, the Scripture will always do its work in the hearer. "The prophet that hath a dream, let him tell a dream; and he that hath my word, let him speak my word faithfully. What is the chaff to the wheat? saith the Lord. Is not my word like as a fire? saith the Lord; and like a hammer that breaketh the rock in pieces?" (Jeremiah 23:28–29).

Your words may or may not be remembered. You may say something so succinctly that your children will quote it to their children. Perhaps it may be quoted for generations or written in a book. But as powerful as our words are today, God's Words are even more so, for they are eternal. What you share with someone today from God's Word will never return void. "Heaven and earth shall pass away: but my words shall not pass away" (Mark 13:31).

Do not underestimate the importance of taking time to let God's Word minister to you today. Then, as it influences you, ask God to help you weave into your conversations that same Word so that it can change the lives of those around you. God's Word through you could be a seed that God uses to raise up the next Robert Sheffey.

January, 1904

Music Is a Universal Language

"Let the word of Christ dwell in you richly in all wisdom; teaching and admonishing one another in psalms and hymns and spiritual songs, singing with grace in your hearts to the Lord."—**Colossians 3:16**

The combination of Spirit-filled singing and Spirit-filled preaching has never been evidenced more than in the evangelistic team of R.A. Torrey and Charles Alexander. Torrey was a brilliant Bible scholar with a powerful delivery, and Alexander was an outstanding musician who could get anyone to sing. Many called Alexander "Mr. Happy" as he would lift the hearts and voices of revival congregations all over the world. The music would soften and ready hearts for the preaching of God's truth.

When R.A. Torrey and Charles Alexander reached Birmingham in their tour of England, they did not realize the power of God that they would witness there. They had worked and prayed, but nothing could have prepared them for the marvelous work that lay ahead. Every seat in the eight-thousand-seat Bingley Hall was filled with two thousand left standing in the wings. The singing, led by Alexander, echoed throughout the large concert hall, and the voice of Torrey preaching the Bible arrested the hearts of all. After thirty days of meetings, seven thousand conversions were recorded in Birmingham, and God was glorified.

Are you participating in the services of your church or do you just attend as a spectator? Do you sing during the song service? Do you enter into prayer when someone prays from the pulpit? Do you give in the offering or intercede for the lost at the invitation? Are you ready to greet a visitor or answer the questions of an inquirer?

You will get out of church exactly what you put in to it! The next time the doors are open at church, go with an anticipation of participation. Maybe someone will call you "Mr. Happy" and listen to the message to find out how to become like you.

January, 1930

Stewarding Every Means for the Gospel

"Redeeming the time, because the days are evil."—**Ephesians 5:16**

In 1901, Guglielmo Marconi completed the first successful transatlantic radio communication, and the radio quickly became the best means of communication in the world. Almost thirty years later, on a cold day in January of 1930, a quick thought ran across Charles Fuller's mind as he meditated on this rather new invention of the radio. Why not use this new technology to further the Gospel of Jesus Christ? From that thought, the Old Fashioned Revival Hour was born. Fuller started the radio program broadcasting his Sunday services only, but the program would become much more in the coming years. The Old Fashioned Revival Hour became a staple of Christianity and evangelism throughout its years on the air.

Technology is rarely created for the sole purpose of spreading the Gospel. Instead, most modern conveniences are invented to make life easier, allow us to work faster, make more money, or in some cases make sin more convenient. As Christians, it is for these reasons that we are often skeptical of bringing this technology into the church or ministry. It is tainted in our minds or labeled as "worldly."

In Acts 8:4, the Bible says, "Therefore they that were scattered abroad went every where preaching the word." The command that Jesus had given them was to take the Gospel to every creature. Thus, they saw no place or people group as off limits. Even when they were arrested and imprisoned, they used those opportunities to preach God's Word. If the apostles were alive today, would they use technology to carry out the Great Commission? Would they use social media? Would they livestream their preaching or create websites to present the Gospel? The answer seems rather obvious.

How then will you use the technology in your hand today? Sinful purposes? Selfish purposes? Just because the days are evil doesn't mean we have to be. Let's look at our technology as a way to be a greater steward of the opportunity we have to get the Gospel to the whole world.

January 12, 1723

Will God Be Glorified through You Today?

"That we should be to the praise of his glory, who first trusted in Christ."
—Ephesians 1:12

Have you ever asked yourself, "What am I living for?" "Why am I here?" "What is my purpose?"

In 1723, on today's date, a young Jonathan Edwards discovered the purpose of his life and wrote about his newfound realization in his journal. With great conviction and determination he penned these words: "Never to do any manner of things, whether in soul or body, less, but what tends to the glory of God...." Edwards could not imagine how God would soon bless this purpose statement. God would use him to spark the First Great Awakening in America.

Is life about you today? Your happiness? Your dreams? Your comfort? Your success? In John 8:29, Jesus gave His purpose statement in relation to His Father, "...for I do always those things that please him." That meant leaving Heaven and all of its glory and coming to a sin-cursed world to die for sinners like you and me. Yes, He "...made himself of no reputation, and took upon him the form of a servant, and was made in the likeness of men: And being found in fashion as a man, he humbled himself, and became obedient unto death, even the death of the cross" (Philippians 2:7–8). Had Jesus Christ lived for Himself, we would never know the forgiveness of sin or have the hope of eternal life.

Will you glorify Christ with your life today? Will He be praised through your actions and reactions? Will He be pleased with your thoughts and attitudes? Will He be glorified through your walk, your work, and your worship? "Whether therefore ye eat, or drink, or whatsoever ye do, do all to the glory of God" (1 Corinthians 10:31). Resolve today to glorify God with your life. We owe it to Him! "And that he died for all, that they which live should not henceforth live unto themselves, but unto him which died for them, and rose again" (2 Corinthians 5:15).

January 13, 1916

I Surrender All

"I beseech you therefore, brethren, by the mercies of God, that ye present your bodies a living sacrifice, holy, acceptable unto God, which is your reasonable service."—**Romans 12:1**

A young man walked over to a chaparral bush, his eyes filled with tears and his spirit sober. He would finally decide to give God his entire life—his hopes, his dreams, his future—everything. He had been battling God's will for his life, but now it was time to surrender. This would not be mere lip service either. The young man truly meant it. In the same month he would pack his bags and begin a trip to Decatur Bible College, some 125 miles away, with $9.25 in his pocket. This kid meant business. This kid was John R. Rice. God would take this life offered to Him and turn him into a wonderful soulwinner, evangelist, and author.

Have you presented your life as a living sacrifice to God? Christ gave His life for you. He bought your life with a price. How arrogant to think that we can live our lives for ourselves after accepting God's precious gift of salvation! "What? know ye not that your body is the temple of the Holy Ghost which is in you, which ye have of God, and ye are not your own? For ye are bought with a price: therefore glorify God in your body, and in your spirit, which are God's" (1 Corinthians 6:19–20). It is not unreasonable for God to ask us to give something to Him that already belongs to Him.

No doubt a few weeks ago, you received some gifts at Christmas time. Have the givers of those gifts come back to you since and asked to have them back? If they did, you would question their love or sincerity in the first place. Yet so often, we take our lives back from the one who purchased it with His own blood.

Surrender all today. Present your life to God. He will do far more with it than you could ever do on your own. Give Him your life and don't ever ask to have it back.

January, 1898

The Great Commission or the Great Omission?

"And he said unto them, Go ye into all the world, and preach the gospel to every creature."—**Mark 16:15**

While not a household name in most circles, a preacher by the name of Shubal Stearns was responsible for changing the very heart of the South during the Great Awakening. It took over one hundred years for someone to finally realize his importance and write a biography of his life. The "Bible belt" of the nation was, by and large, the result of Shubal Stearns' ministry. In his biography of Shubal Stearns, Charles Taylor wrote in 1898, "He was undoubtedly one of the greatest ministers that ever presented Jesus to perishing multitudes. Had he been a Roman priest, he would have long since been canonized and declared the patron saint of Carolina. Fervent supplications would have ascended and stately churches would have been dedicated to the holy and blessed saint Shubal Stearns, the apostle of North Carolina and the adjacent states."

God may or may not call you to be a church planter, but He has called each of us to be a Gospel planter. Approximately sixty percent of the world's population has never heard a clear presentation of the plan of salvation. Not all of those people live across an ocean on foreign soil. Have your neighbors heard the Gospel? You may assume they have, but how can you be sure? Have you ever shared it with them? What about your loved ones or co-workers? Every person is either a missionary or a mission field.

The Great Commission is not a suggestion; it is a command! How long would you keep your job if you disobeyed the orders of your employer? How long would someone be allowed to serve in the military but disregard the base commander? Can we expect the blessings of God in our lives or pray for revival in our nation when we are living in disobedience to our Lord's command? As you enter *your* world today, tell someone about Jesus Christ. Shubal Stearns was just one man, but his impact is still felt today. Who will you impact this week?

January, 1930

We Walk by Faith—Not by Sight

"For I am not ashamed of the gospel of Christ: for it is the power of God unto salvation to every one that believeth; to the Jew first, and also to the Greek." —**Romans 1:16**

When God saved Paul Levin in 1930 at an early age, He got his whole life. Dr. Paul, as he was affectionately known, preached daily on his radio program called "Bible Echoes," printed millions of tracts, preached hundreds of youth weeks at the Bill Rice Ranch beginning in 1953, and conducted revival meetings throughout the country until God called him home. His energy for God's work was contagious, and his humility won the hearts of many a friend and foe.

Dr. Levin did not impress the average onlooker. He was as common as the farms he grew up around in rural Iowa. *Dignified* or *intellectual* were not words used to describe this evangelist. But as a small boy, he knelt one day to pray a simple prayer of surrender. God heard that prayer and placed His power upon him to do a great work for God. Dr. Paul had his share of heartaches and battles, but through them all he saw an opportunity for God to do something great. He preached, "I believe this is a great hour of opportunity, and all evangelists, pastors, and Christians of sound, separated churches ought to go all out in soulwinning, knocking on doors, extensive bus ministries, gear up for evangelism, and forget all about why you can't have successful evangelistic meetings and why you can't see many people saved these days."

What excuses are keeping you from serving the Lord with your all today? Satan would have us believe that we are not talented enough or our resources are insufficient or the world is too far gone. These are lies that have birthed a fatalism in our churches that prevents revival. We may not see how we can make a difference or what good our witness would do or how we could have revival in such wicked days. But remember, "we walk by faith, not by sight" (2 Corinthians 5:7). Faith is not based in what we can see, but in the One who is unseen! Ask the Lord to increase your faith today.

January 16, 1968

Be Strong in the Lord

"Even the youths shall faint and be weary, and the young men shall utterly fall: But they that wait upon the LORD shall renew their strength; they shall mount up with wings as eagles; they shall run, and not be weary; and they shall walk, and not faint."—**Isaiah 40:30–31**

A powerful preacher crossed the finish line after a faithful life on this day in 1968. While many today only know Bob Jones, Sr. as the founder of Bob Jones University in Greenville, South Carolina, this fiery evangelist was one of the most courageous preachers to ever take a stand for the Word of God and biblical fundamentalism. Dr. Bob's last words before God took him home were, "Get my shoes; I must go preach." Even on his last day on this earth, he still had a fire in his bones to preach the literal, infallible, inerrant, inspired Word of God. He truly heeded his own advice: "Do right till the stars fall."

No matter what age you are, God can still use you. Don't let your youth or your lack of it keep you from serving the Lord. God's power can flow through you and can change lives all around you. There is no age limit to God's promise in Isaiah 40:31. People of every age will get tired in the race that God has called us to run, but God promises to renew our strength as we rely on Him. "Not that we are sufficient of ourselves to think any thing as of ourselves; but our sufficiency is of God" (2 Corinthians 3:5). The Apostle Paul realized that he could accomplish all things only one way: "...through Christ which strengtheneth me" (Philippians 4:13).

Are you relying on God's strength today for the tasks ahead or are you trusting your own? "Thus saith the LORD; Cursed be man that trusteth in man, and maketh flesh his arm, and whose heart departeth from the LORD" (Jeremiah 17:5). You will flounder and fail today in your own strength. This is why it is important that you heed the admonition of Ephesians 6:10: "...be strong in the Lord, and in the power of his might." With his strength, you too can "do right till the stars fall."

January 17, 1920

Let Your Light Shine

"Ye are the light of the world. A city that is set on a hill cannot be hid."
—Matthew 5:14

Because of the labors of the great evangelists Billy Sunday and Sam Jones, Congress passed a prohibition of alcoholic beverages and its sale in the United States, and on this day in 1920, the eighteenth amendment would take effect. Despite the criticism and mocking of others, Christians did in fact influence the government and set in order a ban of the wicked drink that now plagues our society once again. To pass an amendment in the Constitution of the United States took great influence and courage for those early twentieth-century Christians. Billy Sunday wrote in a magazine article: "I am the sworn, eternal, and uncompromising enemy of the liquor traffic and have been for thirty-five years. I saw that nine-tenths of the misery, poverty, wrecked homes, and blighted lives were caused by booze. I put twelve states dry before we voted on the Eighteenth Amendment. The real reason for the Federal Prohibition Amendment is that the wet minority has never respected the law and has never allowed the dry majority to be dry. The liquor traffic always has been criminal and lawless, caring nothing for human well-being, fighting for its own privilege to exploit the people."

We realize that government cannot bring revival. But that does not mean that we should abandon all influence in our government. Elijah in 1 Kings 17–18 influenced the government of Ahab and Jezebel, the most wicked duo to ever sit on a throne of power. Daniel took his stand in Daniel 6 and prayed even though the government had made it illegal to do so. When God protected Daniel in the den of lions, the king later declared that the God of Daniel was indeed the true God.

Have you prayed for your government leaders this week? Have you written them? When is the last time you voted in an election? All of the darkness in this world cannot put out one light. So, "Let your light so shine before men, that they may see your good works, and glorify your Father which is in heaven" (Matthew 5:16).

January 18, 1889

God's Plan Is Always Greater than Our Own

"For I know the thoughts that I think toward you, saith the LORD, thoughts of peace, and not of evil, to give you an expected end."—**Jeremiah 29:11**

A handful of preachers had invited Gypsy Smith to come to America for the purpose of holding revival meetings. But when he reached this "new world," he soon found that most of the preachers who had invited him to preach had either died or had become indifferent to his ministry. A discouraged Gypsy Smith walked the streets of New York City, wondering if this was truly what the Lord wanted for his life. Through this trying time, God would show Himself strong. One day, Dr. Prince of the Nostrand Avenue Methodist Episcopal Church of Brooklyn opened up his pulpit to Smith for a three-week crusade. The 1,500-seat auditorium was packed, and over 300 souls were added to Heaven as a direct result of Smith's determination and faithfulness to follow God's leading. Gypsy Smith's legendary ministry in America had begun.

Something that we know in our minds and should comfort our hearts is the fact that God knows more than we do. God has a plan for our lives. We may not understand it fully; in fact, most often we do not. But God continues to work and lead in our lives with His ultimate care and wisdom. Don't be discouraged when things don't go your way. God has never made a mistake, and He won't make His first one on you. Sometimes He will bring hard times into our lives to test us and to grow us. You must choose whether you will allow those times to make you bitter or better. It will be one of the two.

In the rough patches of life, stay in love with the Lord and true to His will for your life. You can be confident even in those dark days that God is in control and will turn the trial into triumph. "And we know that all things work together for good to them that love God, to them who are the called according to his purpose" (Romans 8:28).

January 19, 1897

God's Grace Is Available to All

"That if thou shalt confess with thy mouth the Lord Jesus, and shalt believe in thine heart that God hath raised him from the dead, thou shalt be saved."
—**Romans 10:9**

As he contemplated suicide, a twenty-seven-year-old Mel Trotter walked past the Pacific Garden Mission in Chicago. Something tugged at his heart to go in, and God took over from there. He was so drunk that the usher at the door had to prop him up against the wall for him to stand. In the back of that auditorium, he listened to the salvation testimony of Harry Monroe. Little did Mel know that Monroe was praying as he watched him come in: "Oh God, save that poor, poor boy!" The Holy Spirit cut through the alcohol, depression, and suicidal thinking in Mel's heart that night, and when Monroe gave an invitation, Mel walked the aisle and trusted Christ to save him. When asked later how he knew that he was on his way to Heaven, he replied, "I was there when it happened, January 19, 1897, ten minutes past nine, Central time, Pacific Garden Mission, Chicago, Illinois, USA."

We should be thankful for the simple yet powerful Gospel that can break through any heart and save those who believe. We are all sinners—maybe we haven't sunk to the depths of sin as a Mel Trotter, but our sin nature separates us from a Holy God and bars us from Heaven. The only solution to the sin problem is Jesus Christ who declared, "…I am the way, the truth, and the life: no man cometh unto the Father, but by me" (John 14:6). Being a good person will not save you, nor will religion. "Neither is there salvation in any other: for there is none other name under heaven given among men, whereby we must be saved" (Acts 4:12).

God made the way of salvation simple so that all could understand. To be saved, we simply need to agree (confess) that sin has separated us from God; believe that Jesus Christ is the Son of God, died for us, and rose from the dead; and call upon God to save us. "For whosoever shall call upon the name of the Lord shall be saved" (Romans 10:13). Have you made that decision? If not, will you decide today?

January 20, 1874

A New Song

"He brought me up also out of an horrible pit, out of the miry clay, and set my feet upon a rock, and established my goings. And he hath put a new song in my mouth, even praise unto our God: many shall see it, and fear, and shall trust in the LORD."—**Psalm 40:2–3**

Moody's meetings in Edinburgh, Scotland, ended on this date after more than two months of Christ-honoring singing and Christ-exalting preaching. The people in the town had sung only Psalms for hundreds of years in their churches. Ira Sankey, Moody's music man, introduced Gospel hymns to the people for the first time. As a result, crowds packed out their two thousand-seat auditorium, and many were saved. Moody's and Sankey's methods, however, did not go without criticism, so Dr. Horatius Bonar wrote a letter describing the character of the two evangelists: "These American brethren bring us no new Gospel, nor do they pretend to novelty of any kind in their plans, save perhaps that of giving greater prominence to the singing of hymns.... We may trust them. They fully deserve our confidence; the more we know of them in private the more do we appreciate them.... These men are self-denying, hard-working men, who are spending and being spent in a service which they believe to be not human but divine. These men have the most definite of all definite aims—winning souls to everlasting joy, and they look for no fame and no reward save the Master's approval."

God's special gift of music should be stewarded wisely. Music can control our emotions and influence us in ways like little else can. Satan knows the power of music and uses it consistently to advance his agenda. But God's music will teach us truth from His Word, lift our spirits, encourage our hearts in service to Him, and ultimately glorify God in our lives. Does the music you listen to draw you closer to God or drive you away from His plan for your life? "I will sing unto the LORD as long as I live: I will sing praise to my God while I have my being" (Psalm 104:33). Sing to the Lord and for the Lord today.

January 21, 1894

God Will Never Forsake You

"Verily thou art a God that hidest thyself, O God of Israel, the Saviour."
—Isaiah 45:15

The people in the front rows could sense that something was wrong with their beloved pastor. Pastor Talmage ascended the platform and stood behind the pulpit. He then preached a sermon entitled "God shall wipe away all tears from their eyes." After he had completed his sermon, Talmage announced to his church that he had some difficult news to share. Everyone in the church was shocked as he read to them his resignation. His voice quivered as he declared, "My plans after resignation have not been developed, but I shall preach both by voice and newspaper press so long as my life and health are continued." With a heart full of defeat and discouragement, Talmage descended the platform.

"We are troubled on every side, yet not distressed; we are perplexed, but not in despair; Persecuted, but not forsaken; cast down, but not destroyed; Always bearing about in the body the dying of the Lord Jesus, that the life also of Jesus might be made manifest in our body. For we which live are alway delivered unto death for Jesus' sake, that the life also of Jesus might be made manifest in our mortal flesh" (2 Corinthians 4:8–11). Throughout this very difficult time in Talmage's life, he did not give up on God or stop trusting the promises of His Word. As a result, God would use this preacher to lead a great revival that would take the nation's capital by storm.

Sometimes God will hide Himself from us to test or correct us. When these times come, we should ask ourselves: Has sin crept into my life? Am I living a pleasing life for the Lord? If we sincerely and honestly know that sin has not caused this trial, then we must trust God and call upon Him for strength. God will help us in the time of trouble, and oftentimes that trouble is what brings us so much closer to Him. Diamonds are made and polished by friction. So are the children of God. The Lord has not forsaken you, nor has He given up on you. He is near, and your faith in His promises honors Him.

Exodus 1–3 // Matthew 14:1–21

January 19, 1876

God Blesses the Faithful

"Then Agrippa said unto Paul, Almost thou persuadest me to be a Christian."
—Acts 26:28

All heads turned as the most powerful man in the world entered Moody's auditorium. While holding meetings in Washington D. C., Dwight Moody received an honored guest, the current President of the United States—Ulysses S. Grant. Surely the air was tense as the president, known for his bad temper and excessive drinking, listened to this preacher and what he had to say. Grant, as a victorious Civil War general, had heard Peter Cartwright preach the Gospel as well. Only eternity will tell if Grant's curiosity of these two preachers resulted in his salvation. We don't know where that seed of the Gospel fell in President Grant's heart that night, but we know that Moody preached with the same grace and the same truth as he always had.

In Acts 26, we read of another Christian leader fearlessly preaching the Gospel to a government official. King Agrippa listened to Paul that day and responded with, "Almost thou persuadest me to be a Christian" (Acts 26:28). Don't be intimidated by the leaders God has put in your life. He has given you opportunities to spread the Gospel and uplift Christ in a sphere of influence that only you possess. Some leaders may be interested while others like Grant and Agrippa may be only curious. Either way, we must "Preach the word; be instant in season, out of season; reprove, rebuke, exhort with all longsuffering and doctrine" (2 Timothy 4:2).

We may not always be fruitful, but we can and must always be faithful. How people respond to God's message is not our decision. Our decision is to be faithful in delivering that message. Will you take the opportunities God gives you today to share His message of salvation? Don't worry about the response. We must accept our responsibility and let God take care of the response.

January 19, 1940

Full Surrender

"And he gave some, apostles; and some, prophets; and some, evangelists; and some, pastors and teachers; For the perfecting of the saints, for the work of the ministry, for the edifying of the body of Christ:"—**Ephesians 4:11–12**

Burdened for the souls of men and filled with the burning desire for evangelism, John R. Rice gave up the pastorate in exchange for the office of the evangelist. In his book *The Evangelist*, written in 1968, Rice describes the high calling and duty of those who serve in this office: "Christ gave evangelists! He gave them to the whole body of Christ, the church. Evangelists are exactly as much in the plan of God as are apostles, prophets, pastors, and teachers. The church can never do without evangelists. Evangelists are intended to edify and build up the body of Christ, to prepare the saints for service. This is to the end that souls will be saved as Christ's spiritual body—the church—is taught and edified and developed to increase itself by soulwinning." Rice truly believed in the office of evangelist and sought to see others successfully follow in his footsteps. He described his purpose for writing such a book: "We plead for compassion and forbearance on the part of those who read and, oh, we pray that God may stir many a heart to win souls, that He will give people a hunger for old-fashioned revival preaching and revival results where cities will feel a great moral revolution and the impact on society will be what revivals have been in the past and can be today."

Whatever God has planned for your life, obey. If God wants you to be a pastor, serve your church with all your heart. If God wants you to be an evangelist, preach the Gospel everywhere you go. If God wants you to be a teacher, faithfully explain the truths of the Word of God. If God wants you to be a layman, be faithful to the Lord in your work and support the church and pastor God has given you. We are laboring together. "I have planted, Apollos watered; but God gave the increase. So then neither is he that planteth any thing, neither he that watereth…For we are labourers together with God…" (1 Corinthians 3:6–9).

January 24, 1738

God Abhors Hypocrisy

"Not by works of righteousness which we have done, but according to his mercy he saved us, by the washing of regeneration, and renewing of the Holy Ghost;"
—Titus 3:5

On this day in 1738, in his much published journal, an unconverted John Wesley wrote of his longing for peace and forgiveness. He had arrived in Savannah, Georgia, to reach the Indians, but his efforts had been a disaster. This frustrated and hopeless missionary wrote, "I went to the Americas to convert the Indians, but, oh, who shall convert me? Who, what is he that shall deliver me from this evil heart?" Spiritual death cannot bring forth spiritual life.

There was a man in the first century whose name started with the letter "J" and ended in the letter "S." He was a great preacher and teacher. He did miracles of all sorts. He was conservative, revered, liked, and trusted. But you might be surprised at the name of the one to whom I'm referring—Judas! Just because a person serves God does not mean they are one of His children. There are many who consistently try to work themselves into favor with God, but God is clear in His Word that good works do not work! "Where is boasting then? It is excluded. By what law? of works? Nay: but by the law of faith. Therefore we conclude that a man is justified by faith without the deeds of the law" (Romans 3:27–28).

If we could be saved by our works, we could not call eternal life a gift, which God clearly does: "For the wages of sin is death; but the gift of God is eternal life through Jesus Christ our Lord" (Romans 6:23). If something is a gift, you cannot work for it; if something is obtained by work; it dare not be called a gift. "And if by grace, then is it no more of works: otherwise grace is no more grace. But if it be of works, then is it no more grace: otherwise work is no more work" (Romans 11:6). So which is it? "For by grace are ye saved through faith; and that not of yourselves: it is the gift of God: Not of works, lest any man should boast" (Ephesians 2:8–9). If your salvation is not through faith in Jesus Christ, you have no salvation.

January, 1936

Christians Are Saved to Bear Fruit

"Ye have not chosen me, but I have chosen you, and ordained you, that ye should go and bring forth fruit, and that your fruit should remain: that whatsoever ye shall ask of the Father in my name, he may give it you."—**John 15:16**

If you enjoyed various kinds of fruit, you could plant some fruit trees in your yard. On our farm as a boy, we had apple trees, pear trees, and cherry trees. We also had hickory and walnut trees. These trees provided a good bit of our annual food supply and were valuable to us. We heated the old farmhouse with a wood-burning furnace; therefore, if any of those trees quit yielding fruit, they were quickly cut down and used for firewood. We didn't grow those trees for firewood however. We planted them and nurtured them so that they would bear fruit.

During a campaign in Binghampton, New York, John R. Rice formed the Billy Sunday Club. This group of men would serve as ushers for the revival meetings. Each of these ushers had been saved in a Billy Sunday crusade held in that city ten years before! What a thrill it must have been for Dr. Rice to see this fruit from the life of an evangelist who had gone before him. That fruit from Billy Sunday's efforts soon brought forth "more fruit" when 378 were saved in the revival conducted by John R. Rice!

Are you a fruit-bearing Christian? You may look nice on Sundays and use your talents in many ways. But God didn't save you to look good or take up a spot in the church house. He desires that you bear fruit. Ask the Lord today to help you win someone to Christ. It may start with simply inviting a neighbor or friend to a church service. God could use a Gospel tract in someone's life if you would carry one with you and give it out. Get involved in your church's soulwinning efforts. "Herein is my Father glorified, that ye bear much fruit; so shall ye be my disciples" (John 15:8).

January 26, 1896

The World Needs Godly Mothers

"She hath done what she could: she is come aforehand to anoint my body to the burying."—**Mark 14:8**

A godly mother is a precious commodity. Dwight Moody's heart was mourning and grieving over losing his dear mother. Her epitaph on her tombstone would quote Mark 14:8, "She hath done what she could." And she certainly did. Her son would honor her in the eulogy at her funeral: "It is not the custom, perhaps, for a son to take part in such an occasion, but, if I can control myself, I should like to say a few words. It is a great honor to be the son of such a mother. I do not know where to begin; I could not praise her enough.... Friends, it is not a time of mourning. I want you to understand we do not mourn. We are proud that we had such a mother. We have a wonderful legacy left us. What more can I say? You have lived with her, and you know about her. I want to give you one verse, her creed. It was very short. Do you know what it was? I will tell you. When everything went against her, this was her stay: 'My trust is in God.'"

Even when we are unaware, our children are watching us and learning from us. Just as many watched Mary pour the ointment on Jesus' feet, your children are watching your attitude toward God and your service to Him. They hear and understand more than you think. Those little eyes and ears are observing your walk with the Lord every single day. What kind of an example are you giving them to follow? "That the aged men be sober, grave, temperate, sound in faith, in charity, in patience. The aged women likewise, that they be in behavior as becometh holiness, not false accusers, not given to much wine, teachers of good things; In all things shewing thyself a pattern of good works...." (Titus 2:2–3, 7).

Would you want your children to be just like you? If not, what needs to change in you today? Our Saviour has given us an example that we might follow in His steps. Are we doing the same for our children? The next D. L. Moody may be watching you!

January, 1940

God Uses Those Who Let Him

"And the lord said unto the servant, Go out into the highways and hedges, and compel them to come in, that my house may be filled."—**Luke 14:23**

Mel Trotter would preach his last sermon in January of 1940 in the place where it more or less began. After his conversion from a life of drunkenness and shame at the Pacific Garden Mission in Chicago, Trotter returned to his home town of Grand Rapids, Michigan. It was there that he opened a rescue mission to reach the homeless and needy with the Gospel. That mission became a template for sixty-six others that Trotter helped to organize all across the United States. After preaching for forty years with men like R.A. Torrey and Billy Sunday, Trotter returned to Grand Rapids for the fortieth anniversary of the mission and preached his final time.

Mel Trotter did not possess a brilliant mind like Torrey or have a storied baseball career like Billy Sunday. He was simply a sinner saved by grace who knew that everybody, no matter what their lot in life, needed a Saviour. God is not looking for certain "kinds" of people to be saved. "For this is good and acceptable in the sight of God our Saviour; Who will have all men to be saved, and to come unto the knowledge of the truth" (1 Timothy 2:3–4). And God is not limited to using certain "kinds" of people to reach others with the Gospel. The abilities that God needs are pliability, reliability, and dependability. If you will let God mold your life and place yourself at His disposal, you will have more opportunities than you can imagine.

Don't excuse yourself from God's service because of your past or present inadequacies and failures. The Apostle Paul had some stains on his past but gave us good advice: "…forgetting those things which are behind, and reaching forth unto those things which are before, I press toward the mark for the prize of the high calling of God in Christ Jesus" (Philippians 3:13–14). Rather than thinking yourself unuseable because of your past, reach forward in the present for Christ, and reach out to those He would allow you to serve.

January 28, 1856

Invest in the Next Generation

"And the things that thou hast heard of me among many witnesses, the same commit thou to faithful men, who shall be able to teach others also."
—2 Timothy 2:2

Today the great evangelist R.A. Torrey was born in 1856. D. L. Moody would take Torrey under his wing and train him to take the baton of the Gospel to the next generation. As the official successor of Moody, Torrey would be greatly and mightily used of God to see thousands saved and many churches revived. Torrey travelled the world preaching the Gospel to every person he would meet. He is known for his convicting books on prayer and his sermon in booklet form, "Why God Used D. L. Moody," a classic in Christian literature. It was said of him, "Possessed with a brilliant, well-trained mind, he was logical, penetrating, positive, thorough and convincing, whether preaching, teaching or doing personal work." He would later preach in the London Tabernacle, "I would rather win souls than be the greatest king or emperor on earth; I would rather win souls than be the greatest poet, or novelist, or literary man who ever walked the earth. My one ambition in life is to win as many souls as possible. Oh, it is the only thing worth doing, to save souls; and men, and women, we can all do it!"

The Gospel light must be passed from generation to generation. Training the next generation is vital to the health of a church. Do you see the children and teenagers in your church as someone you could influence and mentor for ministry? If we don't train them for Christ, we can be sure that Satan will bring someone along to mentor them in the ways of the world and sin. Vladimir Lenin, the Communist leader, once stated, "Give me a child for the first five years of his life, and he will be mine forever." If we do not take seriously our responsibility of passing on truth to the next generation, we can be sure that someone will pass on error. Start writing the history of the future by investing your life in a child today. Generations to come will thank you.

January 28, 1706

The Perfect Will of God

"And be not conformed to this world: but be ye transformed by the renewing of your mind, that ye may prove what is that good, and acceptable, and perfect, will of God."—**Romans 12:2**

Many give credit to preacher and church planter Shubal Stearns, who was born on this day in 1706, for the spread of sound Baptist churches in the South. After hearing Jonathan Edwards and George Whitefield preach in the northern colonies, Stearns preached the Gospel in the South. He and his church would plant hundreds of churches, and the evidence is still present today. God raised up this man in a specific time period for a specific purpose. History shows that he fulfilled that God-given mission.

The young Queen Esther was reluctant to approach the king. Her people were in trouble as Haman was plotting to kill the Jews—God's chosen people. Mordecai sent an urgent message to Esther in chapter four and verse fourteen, "For if thou altogether holdest thy peace at this time, then shall there enlargement and deliverance arise to the Jews from another place; but thou and thy father's house shall be destroyed: and who knoweth whether thou art come to the kingdom for such a time as this?" An entire nation of people hung in the balance. Would Esther obey God or follow her fears and doubts? How different would history read if God's people in these critical moments had disobeyed the will of God?

You and I are not alive today by happenstance or accident. We are a part of God's eternal plan. God has a perfect will for us to fulfill with our lives, and we can't improve on perfect! If we settle for anything less that God's will, we are settling for mediocre at best. Follow the steps that the Apostle Paul gives us in Romans 12:1–2. Stay pure from sin; stay presented to God as a living sacrifice; and you will then prove that good and acceptable and perfect will of God.

January 28, 1906

God Gives the Increase

"Every branch in me that beareth not fruit he taketh away: and every branch that beareth fruit, he purgeth it, that it may bring forth more fruit."—**John 15:2**

Some would say that revival meetings do not have much lasting value. An evangelist comes in and preaches for a week and then is gone. All of the time, expense, and effort seems to be of little value for such a short-term effort. For that reason, many churches no longer schedule weeks of revival services. The results just don't justify the cost.

But can we truly tabulate all that God does in a service or meeting? During a revival campaign with R.A. Torrey and Charles Alexander, a man named Oswald Smith listened intently. During the invitation, he came forward and was saved. Oswald J. Smith would become one of the greatest Bible preachers of Canada. He would travel the world preaching the Gospel and recruiting missionaries to go to the utmost parts of the earth. It was just one decision in January of 1906, but the fruit from that one revival convert has been multiplied over and over again.

We must never get weary in well-doing, especially when we are using biblical methods to communicate God's truth. Not all fruit can be calculated on a decision card at the end of the week. Never underestimate the potential of one soul reached for Christ. Philip was preaching in the city of Samaria, and Acts 8 indicates that the whole city was affected by his preaching. Yet, the Holy Spirit commanded Philip to leave the great work God was doing there and go out into the desert and reach one man. No doubt that seemed odd to the preacher. Most of us would have protested or complained. But Philip obeyed, and as a result of that obedience, the Ethiopian eunuch was saved and took the Gospel to his own country that had been previously unreached.

The conversion of Oswald Smith or the Ethiopian eunuch may have seemed humanly insignificant. But with God, those single decisions impacted the world. We must keep doing as God has commanded and let Him multiply the results.

Exodus 23–24 // Matthew 20:1–16

January, 1877

Nothing Is Small to a Big God

"I say unto you, that likewise joy shall be in heaven over one sinner that repenteth, more than over ninety and nine just persons, which need no repentance."
—Luke 15:7

Moody's Boston Crusade ended with all six thousand seats filled in the rented auditorium. After this crusade, Moody decided to turn to the smaller towns of New England for the rest of the year and throughout 1878 as well. Moody was a humble man who sought not only the large crowds of the bustling city, but also the individual soul in the small country town. This was no doubt due to the fact that Moody himself had been saved because his Sunday school teacher visited him to confront him about his salvation. Had Edward Kimball not been faithful in reaching one, God would never have had the opportunity to reach the thousands through D. L. Moody.

You may not have an opportunity to preach to an auditorium of six thousand people, but you do have an opportunity where God has placed you to tell someone about Jesus. All of Heaven rejoices over one sinner who is saved rather than over the ninety and nine who are already safely in the fold. Do we rejoice when there is an opportunity to tell one? Perhaps God used men like Moody in a big way because there was no opportunity that was too small. The biblical principle is clear in Luke 16:10, "He that is faithful in that which is least is faithful also in much: and he that is unjust in the least is unjust also in much."

We cannot expect God to give us big opportunities if we are not faithful in the small ones. Determine today to be sensitive to the Holy Spirit as He brings people across your path and opens the door for you to share Christ with them. If we were to "preach" to just one today; and every day, we too could preach to over six thousand in less than ten years. Little is indeed much, when God is in it!

FEBRUARY

February 1, 1905

God's Enabling Always Accompanies God's Calling

"And it shall come to pass, as soon as the soles of the feet of the priests that bear the ark of the Lord, the Lord of all the earth, shall rest in the waters of Jordan, that the waters of Jordan shall be cut off from the waters that come down from above; and they shall stand upon an heap."—**Joshua 3:13**

J. Wilbur Chapman had a burden. God had placed on his heart to hold mass evangelistic meetings, but he had no way of financing them. As he stepped out by faith, God allowed his path to cross with John W. Converse, a Christian businessman on this day in 1905. Upon hearing of Chapman's vision, Converse knew that God wanted him to have a part in this work for God financially. Because of his support, Chapman was able to bring Charles Alexander on board as his music man, and for decades God used this team to reach thousands with the Gospel in their evangelistic crusades.

"But without faith it is impossible to please him: for he that cometh to God must believe that he is, and that he is a rewarder of them that diligently seek him" (Hebrews 11:6). God doesn't say it is merely *improbable* or *unlikely* to please Him without faith. He says it is *impossible!* What step in your Christian life would God have you take today by faith? Jesus pondered something in Luke 18:8: "...Nevertheless when the Son of man cometh, shall he find faith on the earth?" If the Lord came back today, would He find you living by faith?

How sad to think that we are limiting the power of God by our lack of faith. Listen to this telling statement in Matthew 13:58, "And he did not many mighty works there because of their unbelief." The problem is not a lack of revival—the problem is a lack of faith. The problem is not that sinners no longer get saved—the problem is that Christians do not believe that they will. The waters of the Jordan River did not roll back until the priests stepped into the water. Take that step of faith today, and watch what God will do.

February 2, 1900

The Power of Personal Testimony

"Long time therefore abode they speaking boldly in the Lord, which gave testimony unto the word of his grace."—**Acts 14:3a**

God commands us to let others know about what He has done in our lives. "Let the redeemed of the Lord say so, whom he hath redeemed from the hand of the enemy" (Psalm 107:2). Have you shared your testimony of God's grace recently with anyone? Your life can be like an open letter, declaring God's salvation to others. "Ye are our epistle written in our hearts, known and read of all men: Forasmuch as ye are manifestly declared to be the epistle of Christ ministered by us, written not with ink, but with the Spirit of the living God; not in tables of stone, but in the fleshly tables of the heart" (2 Corinthians 3:2–3).

A preacher by the name of Harry Monroe of the Pacific Garden Mission in Chicago decided to take four men who had been saved from lives of wicked sin to an evangelistic crusade in Grand Rapids, Michigan on this day in 1900. The men shared their testimonies of God's grace to the crowds of people. The four men were Charles Palmer, Tom Sullivan, Frank Williams, and the soon-to-be great evangelist Mel Trotter. Trotter's biography tells us, "From the beginning God's hand was upon this young convert from Chicago. God prospered him and raised him up to be one of the greatest evangelists of his day and one of the best-known and most-loved-mission men of the world." It all started with him merely sharing from his heart what God had done for Him.

A testimony can be a powerful tool to share the Gospel. The Bible gives us many instances when the apostles shared their testimonies with those around them. From kings and politicians, to the people on the street and in the marketplace, the apostles seized every opportunity to share what God had done in their lives. Simply letting those around us know what God has done in our lives, combined with a clear Gospel presentation, can make the difference in someone's eternal destiny. Ask God to let you share your testimony with someone today.

February 3, 1908

Faith Is Required to Please God

"But without faith it is impossible to please him: for he that cometh to God must believe that he is, and that he is a rewarder of them that diligently seek him."
—Hebrews 11:6

One of the great keys to the success of Billy Sunday's evangelistic crusades was the simple fact that Sunday believed that God could and God would work. It is called "walking by faith rather than sight." We cannot always "see" what God is doing or wants to do, but we must trust by faith that He is bigger than what we can see.

Early in Billy Sunday's ministry in Bloomington, Illinois, God gave Sunday his largest crowd yet to which to proclaim the Gospel. By faith, the wooden tabernacle meeting place was built to seat five thousand, the largest to be built to date for his crusades. On February 3, 1908, God not only filled that tabernacle but overflowed it with people. On the last night of the campaign, Sunday could do nothing but thank God for what He had wrought in that place. Dr. Elijah Brown would describe this meeting in his biography of the evangelist: "This meeting resulted in forty-seven hundred people taking their stand for God and righteousness."

God requires faith for salvation, but that decision is only the beginning of the journey of faith throughout the Christian life. Jesus wondered in Luke 18:8, if when He returned to this earth He would find anyone living by faith. Hebrews chapter eleven is filled with amazing accounts of what God did through men and women of Bible times. But each amazing story is preceded by the words, "By faith" or "Through faith." What amazing miracle in your life is right around the corner as you live today by faith? In Matthew 13:58 we read some sad words, "And he did not many mighty works there because of their unbelief." May that never be true in our lives, our church, or our generation!

February 1876

Equipping for Battle

"Wherefore take unto you the whole armour of God, that ye may be able to withstand in the evil day, and having done all, to stand."—**Ephesians 6:13**

The *Cameron Herald* reported in February 1914 that Mordecai Ham was praying for his brother's life. His brother had just been diagnosed with a "whiskey heart," and Ham was determined to intercede for his life. After eighteen hours of prayer, Ham's brother eventually recovered and later trusted Christ. Mordecai was later quoted: "I would never cease to fight the evil drink as long as I should live. My precious brother was spared and is today a happy Christian with the bright hope of Heaven, and I am trying to make good my covenant with God who spared him."

As Christians, we must actively engage the world, the flesh, and the devil. We must not sit by and let the armies of Hell capture souls again and again. We must daily put on the armor of God and ask for God's strength to stand. The helmet of salvation brings assurance of our eternal destination. The breastplate of righteousness guards our hearts from the temptation of the devil. The belt of truth holds all of the armor together with honesty and sincerity. The feet shod with the preparation of the Gospel of peace ensures that we will be ready to share the good news of salvation with anyone around us. The shield of faith protects us from the fiery darts. And the sword of the Spirit, the only offensive weapon in our arsenal, the Word of God, guarantees victory if we know it and use it.

Don't start your day without putting on the armor of God. The devil watches and waits for that moment when we are careless or complacent: "Lest Satan should get an advantage of us: for we are not ignorant of his devices" (2 Corinthians 2:11). One unprotected area of our lives leaves a target for Satan, and just one fiery dart could prove to be fatal. "Be sober, be vigilant; because your adversary the devil, as a roaring lion, walketh about, seeking whom he may devour: Whom resist stedfast in the faith, knowing the same afflictions are accomplished in your brethren that are in the world" (1 Peter 5:8–9).

February 5, 1837

Turning the World Upside Down

"And when they found them not, they drew Jason and certain brethren unto the rulers of the city, crying, These that have turned the world upside down are come hither also."—**Acts 17:6**

No one could have anticipated what God was going to do with this little baby boy born on February 5, 1837. Dwight Lyman Moody would turn the world upside down for Christ. Dr. Fred Barlow would later describe this implausible candidate for evangelism: "For if anyone ever appeared to be less qualified for the evangelist's office, it was D. L. Moody. He was unschooled (he quit after six years); he was unconventional (he refused ordination and rejected being called by any title other than 'Mr. Moody'); he was unseemly in appearance (he was a short, heavy-looking—nearly three hundred pounds—commonplace man without grace of look or gesture); he was unpolished and ungrammatical in his preaching (his words rushed from his bearded face like a torrent; often two hundred and thirty per minute...short staccato sentences; imperfect pronunciation. Spurgeon said, 'the only man I ever knew who said 'Mesopotamia' in one syllable....Many 'aint's' and 'have got's'). Yet Moody was a success in evangelism; aye, he was a superlative, even supernatural success."

There was a group in the Book of Acts who were used in a similar way to do the unexpected. They were called the house of Jason in the town of Thessalonica. The Jews had stirred up the town so much that the people took Jason and his family to the rulers and accused them of turning the world upside down. What an accusation! Unknowingly, the enemies of God paid them a great compliment. In a day when so many Christians are trying to blend into the culture without the world knowing it, we need people who will abandon all self-interest and aspirations and live to please Jesus Christ and Him alone. The reason God used D. L. Moody was not because of his abilities but because of his complete surrender to God. Will you surrender your all to the Lord today and be part of a generation that turns the world upside down for Christ?

February 6, 1738

Addicted to the Ministry

"I beseech you, brethren, (ye know the house of Stephanas, that it is the firstfruits of Achaia, and that they have addicted themselves to the ministry of the saints,)"—**1 Corinthians 16:15**

While sailing to America, the powerful evangelist George Whitefield describes in his journal a typical day on the ocean vessel: "Read prayers and preached to the soldiers as usual. Interceded warmly for absent friends and for all mankind, and went to bed full of peace and joy. Thanks be to God for his unspeakable gift!" Whitefield's typical daily life still preaches a convicting sermon to modern-day Christians. Our days are often filled with thoughts of this world and how we can be more comfortable and secure. The Bible reminds us that we are soldiers in a battle and must live to please the One who chose us: "Thou therefore endure hardness, as a good soldier of Jesus Christ. No man that warreth entangleth himself with the affairs of this life; that he may please him who hath chosen him to be a soldier" (2 Timothy 2:3–4).

What is your passion? What consumes your time and energy? What drives you to get out of bed in the morning? Jim Elliot, the martyred missionary once said, "He is no fool who gives up what he cannot keep to gain what he cannot lose." Jesus states it this way in Mark 8:35, "For whosoever shall save his life shall lose it; but whosoever shall lose his life for my sake and the gospel's, the same shall save it." It was said of the house of Stephanus, "...that they have addicted themselves to the ministry of the saints" (1 Corinthians 16:15).

Are we addicted to Bible reading and prayer? Are we addicted to attending church, soulwinning, tithing, and serving in ministry? We become addicted to work, hobbies, recreation, and sports teams. There may be nothing specifically sinful about any of these, but do we have that same passion for the things of God? Or do we get excited about the earthly and make excuses about the eternal? Make sure something you do today has something to do with eternity.

February 7, 1876

Mission Possible

"And Jesus looking upon them saith, With men it is impossible, but not with God: for with God all things are possible."—**Mark 10:27**

D. L. Moody had just turned thirty-nine years of age and was ready to begin his revival crusade in New York City. His meeting was held on Madison Avenue, where the Madison Square Garden stands today. Moody's heart was undoubtedly thrilled by the thousands of souls saved already in England and America, but he was not ready to rest. Because of his continued determination, six thousand souls would be saved during this ten-week crusade. Every day sixty thousand people would attend the three to five services that were held. Such numbers stagger the modern-day Christian's imagination, but it still is possible.

Jesus described to His disciples how rare the occurrence was for a rich man to be saved. "It is easier for a camel to go through the eye of a needle, than for a rich man to enter into the kingdom of God," Jesus explained. The disciples were confused, and asked, "Who then can be saved?" Looking them straight in the eyes, Jesus proclaimed, "With men it is impossible, but not with God: for with God all things are possible." In the context of the salvation of lost souls in the passage, we can truly believe that a spiritual awakening is possible today. The world would scoff at such a claim. "The world is too far gone!" they would shout. But we can look them in the eye and say with confidence, "With men it is impossible, but not with God: for with God all things are possible" (Mark 10:25–_27).

We are not called to a "Mission Impossible." No soul is beyond the reach of God's grace. No church is beyond hope and no city or nation is beyond revival. If Nineveh could have revival, so can your city. If King Ahab would admit that the Lord was God, wicked leaders today can be brought to say the same by the power of the Gospel. If God could save a man with a legion of devils living inside of him, God can save anyone today! Let's not surrender to the lies of impossibilities, but rather serve the Lord who makes all things possible.

February 8, 1736

The Power of God

"It is the spirit that quickeneth; the flesh profiteth nothing: the words that I speak unto you, they are spirit, and they are life."—**John 6:63**

Excited about the prospects of their new missionary work, John and Charles Wesley finally reached Savannah, Georgia, on February 8, 1736. Weary in body, their hearts were ready to see amazing things. But the excitement would be short-lived. All the Wesley's would find in Georgia was failure after failure after failure. The reason? John Wesley was not yet saved. He was living for himself and had not trusted Christ for his salvation. His ongoing efforts would prove vain and useless without the power of God.

The twelve disciples had trained under the greatest teacher and preacher of all. They had watched and listened to Jesus for three years. Now the Lord's mission was accomplished. As eye-witnesses of the death, burial, and resurrection, the disciples were more than ready to take that message to the world. Christ had commanded them to do so, but not without the power of the Holy Spirit. "And that repentance and remission of sins should be preached in his name among all nations, beginning at Jerusalem. And ye are witnesses of these things. And, behold, I send the promise of my Father upon you: but tarry ye in the city of Jerusalem, until ye be endued with power from on high" (Luke 24:47–49).

The disciples did tarry and trusted exactly what God had said. "But ye shall receive power, after that the Holy Ghost is come upon you: and ye shall be witnesses unto me both in Jerusalem, and in all Judaea, and in Samaria, and unto the uttermost part of the earth" (Acts 1:8). God's work simply cannot be done without God. Do you know Christ as your Saviour? Do you have the Holy Spirit's power upon your life?

Once John Wesley was saved and yielded his life to the Lord, the results were amazing.

February 9, 1709

The Furnace of Affliction

"Behold, I have refined thee, but not with silver; I have chosen thee in the furnace of affliction."—**Isaiah 48:10**

On a cold February night in 1709, the parsonage was quickly burning to the ground with young John Wesley trapped inside. After what would seem an eternity for his family, John was finally snatched from the flames and rescued from certain death. God had a purpose for Wesley's life that would start with his salvation some years later. Once saved, this childhood experience gave him a sense of urgency to live each day for Christ.

When trials come into our lives, our first desire is that God will remove them quickly. Like the Apostle Paul who on three occasions asked God to remove his thorn in the flesh, we want to put trouble behind us. It is through these trials, however, that God fashions and makes us to be like Him and to do His work more effectively. "And he said unto me, My grace is sufficient for thee: for my strength is made perfect in weakness" (2 Corinthians 12:9a).

Job was a man in the Old Testament who suddenly lost everything he had—his possessions, his children, his health, and his friends. Even his own wife told him to "curse God and die." Job's response is amazing, "Though he slay me, yet will I trust in him: but I will maintain mine own ways before him" (Job 13:15). God brought Job through these difficulties in his life as a shining example to all who come after him.

With God in control of our lives, the trouble that comes can turn into triumph. We may not understand God's plan in the middle of a trial, but we can trust Him as much in a loss as we can in a victory. Had the Wesleys become bitter or angry at God as they stood homeless and at the brink of death, we may never have heard of John and Charles Wesley. Are you missing a blessing because of bitterness? Ask God to forgive you and go forward in His sufficient grace.

February 8, 1874

Always Be Ready

"But sanctify the Lord God in your hearts: and be ready always to give an answer to every man that asketh you a reason of the hope that is in you with meekness and fear:"—**1 Peter 3:15**

D. L. Moody preached his evangelistic crusade in Glasgow, Scotland, in February of 1874. The meetings were held in the 4,000-seat Crystal Palace. After three months of preaching there, Moody could not even enter the building because of the crowds. Upwards of 30,000 people would flock to the meetings and try to enter the building. Searching for a solution, Moody decided to speak from a carriage outside, with the choir singing from the roof of a shed nearby. What an amazing spirit of revival must have been there in Glasgow for the outdoor service that night! A witness described the event: "We thought of the days of Whitefield, of such a scene as that mentioned in his life, when, in 1753 at Glasgow, twenty thousand souls hung on his lips as he bade them farewell. Here there were thirty thousand eager hearers, for by this time the thousands within the Crystal Palace had come out, though their numbers quietly melting into the main body did not make a very perceptible addition to the crowd; and many onlookers who knew something of such gatherings were inclined to estimate the number much higher."

We must not wait for everything to be "just right" to share the Gospel. Too often we over-analyze the situation and decide that something can't be done for God because it doesn't fit into our thinking or plan.

In the Book of Acts, the apostles did not wait for the ideal circumstance. They preached during trials to people who wanted to kill them. They preached to philosophers who would undoubtedly mock them. And they preached to anyone and everyone who would listen. Don't let circumstances stop you from fulfilling the mission God has given to you. Step out by faith and watch what God will do. Whether it's one or 30,000, let's be ready today to share the good news of the Gospel!

February 3, 1826

Biblical Revival Produces Changed Lives

"Therefore if any man be in Christ, he is a new creature: old things are passed away; behold, all things are become new."—**2 Corinthians 5:17**

True and lasting revival is not simply a week of special services or a scheduled event on the church calendar. It may begin there as Christians set aside a time to seek the Lord, gather for prayer and preaching, and make decisions that God desires. When God works in revival, He doesn't leave things status quo in the lives of Christians or the church. Sin is confessed and forsaken. The fleshly patterns are replaced with Spirit-filled living. Apathy is replaced by fervency. The world takes notice when a people and a church are experiencing revival.

Such was the case following the revival preaching of Charles Finney in Rome, New York, in 1826. One newspaper reporter wrote: "[It] exceeds anything of the kind of which I have ever heard, except the day of Pentecost...Every store has been converted into a house of prayer." What a testimony to the power of God!

Can you point to changes in your life that God has made in the past six months? What about over the last five years? Or ten? Spiritual growth and maturity does not happen because we are disciplined or motivated enough to make those changes on our own. All of our righteousness is as "filthy rags" (Isaiah 64:6). Without Christ, we can do nothing, but with Christ working in us, "I can do all things through Christ which strengtheneth me" (Philippians 4:13).

What does God want to change in your life today? What is it that displeases Him? Are you willing to allow God to make that change today? Ask God through His power to remove the old and make all things new in your life.

Instead of wondering if God will do His part, our focus should be on the responsibility we have as individuals to do our part. What step does God want you to take today to put yourself in a condition for God to send a powerful revival to our generation?

February 13, 1913

God Blesses Those Who Serve

"Knowing that of the Lord ye shall receive the reward of the inheritance: for ye serve the Lord Christ."—**Colossians 3:24**

The revival meetings led by Billy Sunday in Columbus, Ohio, were about to conclude. February 13, 1913, would be the final day of the crusade. The numbers on record from this revival are staggering. Every night at least 12,000 people attended. It is estimated that close to 1,000,000 people attended the meetings throughout the two-month crusade. The number of salvations was totaled at 18,333, of which 2,189 came forward the very last night. Interestingly, it is recorded that 1,884 babies were kept in nurseries across the street in a separate building! That would have been the night for the nursery workers to pray for a short sermon!

The work of God is not possible without a team of devoted volunteers. Ushers, choir members, nursery workers, Sunday school teachers, bus workers, mechanics, janitors, counselors, and other ministries of service are needed for God's work to be accomplished. Are you a part of that work force? Have you found a place to put your hand to the plow in your local church? If not, you are missing out on the great joy of the Christian life. There is no greater joy than the joy of serving Jesus Christ. Someone has said, "Those jobs don't pay much, but the benefits are out of this world! "Colossians 3:23–24 admonishes, "And whatsoever ye do, do it heartily, as to the Lord, and not unto men; Knowing that of the Lord ye shall receive the reward of the inheritance: for ye serve the Lord Christ."

Christianity is not a spectator sport. God didn't save us to sit, soak, and sour; He saved us to stand, strive, and serve. Let's not be content to merely watch God work but rather determine to be a part of that work. Remember, "...God is not unrighteous to forget your work and labour of love, which ye have shewed toward his name, in that ye have ministered to the saints, and do minister" (Hebrews 6:10).

February 13, 1918

Opposition Is to Be Expected

"Remember the word that I said unto you, The servant is not greater than his lord. If they have persecuted me, they will also persecute you; if they have kept my saying, they will keep yours also."—**John 15:20**

J. Wilbur Chapman and Charles Alexander completed their final evangelistic crusade in Elisabeth, New Jersey in 1918. It was not their intent for this to be the last, but the evangelical world was losing interest in mass revival crusades. Many had become critical of these kinds of meetings and most no longer celebrated the saving of souls as had once been the case. The passion for revival in America had waned as the desires for other things had choked away the truths preached and sung by Chapman and Alexander. With their work now despised, they were forced to end the large revival campaigns that had once been a staple in American religious history.

Jesus told His followers that they would face criticism and opposition. "If the world hate you, ye know it hated me before it hated you. If ye were of the world, the world would love his own: but because ye are not of the world, but I have chosen you out of the world, therefore the world hateth you" (John 15:18–19). When persecution comes, our first thought should not be, "What are we doing wrong?" The world did not crucify Jesus because He was wrong—they crucified Him because He was right!

What is perhaps more difficult to understand is when so-called Christians oppose us. Their words can often be harsh and hurtful and their actions demeaning and damaging to our reputation and character. We must learn to turn these critics and their criticism over to the Lord. Paul said in 2 Timothy 4:16–17, "At my first answer no man stood with me, but all men forsook me: I pray God that it may not be laid to their charge. Notwithstanding the Lord stood with me, and strengthened me; that by me the preaching might be fully known…." A good practice is to die both to criticism and compliments. Live to please Jesus only!

February 4, 1905

Can Revival Take Place in Our Generation?

"Come, and let us return unto the LORD: for he hath torn, and he will heal us; he hath smitten, and he will bind us up."—**Hosea 6:1**

The average Christian today has become a fatalist when it comes to revival. We have become convinced that great movements or revival awakenings are part of the historical record of Christianity but are impossible in any part of the foreseeable future. We have believed that what God has performed in the past is no longer available to us today.

One of the greatest revival crusades in history began with an average attendance of 5,500 people per service. Between the singing of Charles Alexander and the preaching of R.A. Torrey, London had not seen anything like them since Moody and Sankey or Wesley or Whitefield. The power of this revival team can only be described by the amazing results of this crusade. It is estimated that around 1,114,650 Englishmen attended the 202 meetings. Over 17,000 professions of faith resulted from Torrey and Alexander's efforts. One writer proclaimed: "It seemed as if all of London was singing revival hymns!"

Our hearts should be stirred by stories such as these. They remind us that God is not dead, and He can do much more than we can ask or think. Can God repeat these outpourings of His blessing and power? Will He? The answer depends in large part upon us. Will we return unto the Lord in our generation? Will we seek him? Will we humble ourselves? Will we pray? Will we turn from sin and make things right with God and one another?

Instead of wondering if God will do His part, our focus should be on the responsibility we have as individuals to do our part. What step does God want you to take today to put yourself in a condition for God to send a powerful revival to our generation?

February 15, 1727

Preach the Word

"Preach the word; be instant in season, out of season; reprove, rebuke, exhort with all longsuffering and doctrine."—**2 Timothy 4:2**

Fourteen years before his monumental sermon "Sinners in the Hands of an Angry God," Jonathan Edwards was ordained to preach. This twenty-four year old young man could not imagine how God would use his life to impact his entire (future) nation with revival. He did not even know what the United States of America would be, let alone how he would be so used of God in the nation's beginnings. But his young heart undoubtedly dreamed of being used by God in an amazing way.

In 1734, Edwards would preach a lesser known sermon of his, "That Every Mouth May Be Stopped," that characterized his bold preaching: "Look over your past life....How little regard you have had for the Scriptures, to the Word preached, to the Sabbaths and sacraments! What low thoughts you have had of God and what high thoughts of yourselves. Many of you by the bad examples you have set, by corrupting the minds of others, by your sinful conversation, by leading them in sin and by the mischief you have done in human society other ways, have been guilty of these things that have tended to other's damnation. If God should forever cast you off and destroy you, it would be agreeable to your treatment of Himself, of Christ, of your neighbors and yourself."

The First Great Awakening in America depended on a young preacher being true to the faithful preaching of God's Word. While the results did not come immediately, God used Edwards to launch a revival that impacted the founding of our nation and beyond. We must never get weary of proclaiming the truth. God promises to use His Word as we faithfully proclaim it, whether from a pulpit or in our daily conversations. When God opens a door today to speak for Him—use His Word. It will never return void!

February 16, 1758

God's Way Is Perfect

"As for God, his way is perfect; the word of the Lord is tried: he is a buckler to all them that trust in him."—**2 Samuel 22:31**

Jonathan Edwards saw God's hand of power move across Colonial America during the years of the First Great Awakening. He desired more than anything else that this spirit of revival would continue. He knew that for God's work to continue in God's way, young men would need to be trained for ministry. It was thus with great joy that he accepted the position of president of the Princeton Theological Seminary on February 16, 1758. He longed for God to use him in training future laborers in the revival harvest.

Yet in just one month, Edwards would die and be buried in Princeton Cemetery.

God often works in mysterious ways. We might wonder if God has made a mistake or has miscalculated.

We have assurance from the Bible, however, that God's way is always perfect. In life's blessings, He is perfect. In life's struggles, He is perfect. In life's service, His way is perfect. In everything, God's way is always and will forever be perfect. God has never made a mistake, and He isn't going to start making them with your life or future.

Are you pushing against God's plan for your life today because you don't understand it or because it isn't what you think is best or right? Be careful. Let God be God. "Nay but, O man, who art thou that repliest against God? Shall the thing formed say to him that formed it, Why hast thou made me thus? Hath not the potter power over the clay?" (Romans 9:20–21a). There is always safety in submission. Trust God—we see life from the playing field, but God sees life from the blimp! He has a better view of the big picture than we do, and He promises to go with us every step of the way. Ask God to forgive your resistance along with the anger, bitterness, or frustration that has accompanied it. Remember, you can't improve on perfect—and His way is always perfect!

February 17, 1889

The Power of Preaching

"For the preaching of the cross is to them that perish foolishness; but unto us which are saved it is the power of God."—**1 Corinthians 1:18**

The twenty-six year old Billy Sunday preached his first message in Chicago as a baseball player. As he stood behind the pulpit and began to preach the Word of God for the first time, the city of Chicago roared on by, not realizing the significance of this event. The preaching of this young evangelist would turn the nation upside down and bring about the Eighteenth Amendment to the U. S. Constitution. In his lifetime, Sunday would preach to over one hundred million people in person and see nearly one million of them saved.

Billy Sunday would travel with evangelist J. Wilbur Chapman, who wrote a letter describing Sunday's early preaching: "One day in Urbana, Ohio, I had a request from someone out of town for a speaker, and I asked Mr. Sunday to accept the invitation. He seemed greatly frightened and assured me that he could not do such a task. Finally it was determined that he should go and simply tell the story of his conversion. Following that day's services the most interesting reports were made to me of the impression which he had made upon his audience, and I then had the conviction that he ought to do more of this sort of work. I suggested to him that he ought to go to a number of places and stay for a week's meetings. When he told me that he did not have sermons, I asked him to make use of anything that he had heard me say and told him that I should feel highly honored at his doing so. It was thus that he started so far as I can remember." Thus the great evangelist's ministry had begun.

Titus 1:3 declares that God "…hath in due times manifested his word through preaching." There is no higher calling on earth than to preach God's Word! There is no greater activity that we engage in than hearing the Word of God preached. It may seem like a foolish exercise to the unbeliever, but not to the child of God. God uses preaching to change lives!

February 18, 1678

A Life-Long Journey

"Dearly beloved, I beseech you as strangers and pilgrims, abstain from fleshly lusts, which war against the soul."—**1 Peter 2:11**

While in jail for preaching the Gospel, John Bunyan had a burden on his heart. He wrote his thoughts down on the milk bottle stoppers that he was given in the prison. On February 18, 1678, *Pilgrim's Progress* was published and began its miraculous journey around the world to millions of readers. Only the Bible has outsold this classic in Christian literature over the years. Christians throughout the centuries from all different backgrounds and nationalities have been encouraged to press on for higher ground in the Christian life through this masterpiece.

The Christian life is a journey that at times is difficult and filled with trials, troubles, and tests. What "Pilgrim" experienced is picturesque of what each Christian faces as they make their way to the Celestial City. The battles with "Apollyon" will weary us at times, and quitting will seem like the logical and easy thing to do. The struggles, however, will be worth it all when we reach our final Home.

An old song puts it this way, "Sometimes the day seems long, Our trials hard to bear. We're tempted to complain, to murmur and despair. But Christ will soon appear to catch his bride away! All tears forever over in God's eternal day! It will be worth it all when we see Jesus! Life's trials will seem so small when we see Christ. One glimpse of his dear face, all sorrow will erase. So bravely run the race till we see Christ." The third verse puts it into a finish line perspective: "Life's day will soon be o'er, all storms forever past; We'll cross the great divide to Glory, safe at last! We'll share the joys of heaven: a harp, a home, a crown; The tempter will be banished, We'll lay our burdens down."

Stay in the battle dear friend no matter what the test—it will be worth it when we see Christ.

February 18, 1917

Fervent in Spirit

"This man was instructed in the way of the Lord; and being fervent in the spirit, he spake and taught diligently the things of the Lord..."—**Acts 18:25**

Apollos was a young preacher in the Book of Acts who demonstrated a fervency and passion that is so needed in God's work today. We get passionate about the stock market, our favorite sports team, or a new app on our smart phone; but when it comes to the things of God, we are apathetic, indifferent, and non-committal.

The fire of the Bob Jones Crusade was indescribable on the opening night in Zanesville, Ohio, in February of 1917. Seventeen churches participated in this area wide revival, and over 5,000 people listened to Dr. Bob Jones, Sr. preach that opening night. By the last night of the crusade, the nightly attendance would be 18,000 people, and the total attendance for the meeting was just over 266,000. As Jones preached the Word of God, he became so passionate about the Gospel message that he broke the pulpit as he pounded on it. By the end of the crusade, a total of 3,284 decision cards were signed for salvation.

Amazingly, we lose our voices screaming at ball games and may even throw things in frustration when our team loses, but how passionate are we about sharing the Gospel? We're not advocating a riot or simply doing something to call attention to ourselves, but that we live with a holy, fervent passion. The Apostle Paul wrote, "Knowing therefore the terror of the Lord, we persuade men" (2 Corinthians 5:11a).

Will you share the Gospel today? Will those you witness to know that you truly believe what you are saying? Will they hear the fervency in your voice? See it on your face? Sense it from your heart? Let's be "...zealous of good works" (Titus 2:14).

February 20, 1957

A Woman's Influence

"Who can find a virtuous woman? for her price is far above rubies."
—Proverbs 31:10

"No account of the career and achievements of Rev. W. A. Sunday would be complete or accurate unless it made full recognition of the part Mrs. Sunday had in both." Such was the priceless importance of the wife of Billy Sunday. As one reads through the biographies of many great men of God, sometimes the only mention of their wives is the date of their wedding. Then it seems as if their wives fade into the background, never to be seen again. But this was not true of Billy Sunday's wife, affectionately called "Ma" Sunday. In many ways, she was the lifeblood of her husband's campaigns as she encouraged and lifted him up countless times. Even after her husband's death, she would frequently stop by the homes of friends in Winona Lake, Indiana, and speak of her beloved husband and encourage God's people to be faithful. On February 20, 1957, she would meet her husband again in Heaven.

A virtuous woman is a precious and priceless encouragement in serving the Lord. Women have a powerful influence on those around them. The strength and stability of our homes, local churches, and nation is dependent upon godly women. Many miraculous conversions and powerful revivals can be traced to the prayers of a godly woman.

Ladies, you may never receive the recognition you deserve here on Earth, but Heaven will be filled with stories of your influence. We need your prayers, your encouragement, and your example. Men, be sure to thank your wife or mother for the impact they have daily on your life and ministry. Their influence is beyond price! Don't take it for granted. Find an older lady in your church this week and thank her for being faithful to the Lord and His work. May the Lord find in our generation multitudes of virtuous women.

February 17, 1886

God's Definition of Success

"This book of the law shall not depart out of thy mouth; but thou shalt meditate therein day and night, that thou mayest observe to do according to all that is written therein: for then thou shalt make thy way prosperous, and then thou shalt have good success."—**Joshua 1:8**

As evangelist Sam Jones hopped off the train in Chicago on this day in 1886, he could sense the hardness and apathy of the people whom he had come to reach. His goal was to hold a six-week revival crusade. As he looked across the bustling, godless city, a vivid illustration came to mind. "It is like biting pumpkin; your teeth won't take hold of it," he muttered to himself. But he soon would "bite the pumpkin" as it were, and God's teeth would take hold of the city of Chicago.

God does not define success as becoming wealthy, powerful, or famous. As Joshua prepared to cross the Jordan River to conquer the Promised Land, God encouraged him with the secret to success. Meditating on God's Word day and night and then doing what the Bible says is God's formula for a successful life. As Joshua looked over the Jordan at an almost impenetrable fortress, he was encouraged to know that the key to victory was not in himself or some brilliant military strategy, but in a simple but powerful motto: Know God's Word—meditate on it—and obey it!

God does not expect us to pull strings and fight our way up the ladder to success. He says if we know His Word and obey Him, He will take care of the rest.

Do you feel sometimes that you are "biting the pumpkin?" Does some task seem impossible? Go to the Word of God. Claim one of God's eternal promises. Think on it throughout the day and obey it in every way that God instructs you. That may seem like a foolish strategy to the average person, but it brought down the walls of Jericho for Joshua!

February 22, 1913

Be Careful of Jealous Comparisons

"For we dare not make ourselves of the number, or compare ourselves with some that commend themselves: but they measuring themselves by themselves, and comparing themselves among themselves, are not wise."
—2 Corinthians 10:12

Today in 1913, Pastor W.M. Randies commented on the number of conversions during the Billy Sunday campaign of Wilkes-Barre, Pennsylvania: "With regard to the number of converts, this needs to be said, quite a number were members going forward to take others forward, some were members that by this expressed a desire to reach "higher ground" or to leave out of their lives things that they had been led to see were wrong. Some pastors report a number of duplications, some of the duplicate cards bearing different dates (I think this came through new converts taking others forward a little later and thus being counted twice.) On the other hand this does not count the large number converted in the weeks following the meeting. As an example my church received 184 cards, yet to date we have added 240 to full communion, almost all of which can be said to have been the result of the meeting. I think that a very conservative estimate would be that 15,000 were added to the churches of the Wyoming Valley." Despite the ongoing criticism of "evangelistically speaking" numbers, this pastor defended the Billy Sunday campaign and rejoiced in even greater results than those recorded!

In this life, human error is a certainty. Western culture is obsessed with statistics and numbers that can often be made to say whatever we like. The Bible teaches us that God rejoices over one sinner who comes to repentance. Oftentimes, we become competitive when we hear of other churches seeing certain results or other Christians having more success than ourselves, but we must remember that we are all on the same team. Paul warns the Corinthian believers of comparing themselves with each other. This wasn't a wise practice in the first century or in 1913 and is still unwise today. Be faithful to plant and water—God will give the increase!

February 23, 1791

A Great Cloud of Witnesses

"Wherefore seeing we also are compassed about with so great a cloud of witnesses, let us lay aside every weight, and the sin which doth so easily beset us, and let us run with patience the race that is set before us."—**Hebrews 12:1**

The eighty-eight year old John Wesley made his way to the pulpit for the last time in Leatherhead, England. Surely the ears of the people were especially attentive to the wise old preacher who had seen and accomplished so much for Christ. One can almost see the thin bony finger of this dear old servant of God pointing in emphasis one last time as he preaches the Book he had come to know and love so well. Wesley would soon pass the baton to the next generation as He would join his Saviour in Heaven and watch from the skyline the advances of Christ's kingdom.

We have a great heritage in the Lord. Thousands of past generation Christians are now in the grandstands watching us serve the Lord. Does the Lord allow them to see our apathy and neglect? Are they aware of our casual and comfortable Christianity today? Many of them were thrown to wild animals or burnt at the stake for Christ. Others were tortured cruelly and even martyred for their faithfulness to the Gospel. Hebrews 11:38 refers to these as those "of whom the world was not worthy." We must remember men like John Wesley who would stop at nothing to preach the Gospel to every creature.

As God's people we have a "...goodly heritage" (Psalm 16:6), and we must run our race faithfully as so many have done before us. The grandstands of Heaven are filled with those cheering us from the other side. They would tell us to fight a good fight, finish the course, and keep the faith (2 Timothy 4:7). What a challenging and convicting testimony these previous generations have left us. Will you follow in their footsteps today?

February 24, 1791

Make a Difference through Encouragement

"Let us therefore follow after the things which make for peace, and things wherewith one may edify another."—**Romans 14:19**

To whom would the elderly John Wesley write his last letter? This was his very last chance to influence someone, to help and encourage a dear friend. Would it be to a fellow preacher or to an old friend? Was it sent to his brother Charles, whom he loved dearly? John Wesley's last correspondence was to his close friend William Wilberforce. Wilberforce was almost single-handedly responsible for the eradication of slavery in Great Britain and endured many battles in his fight to free the slaves. John Wesley had much influence on this British statesman, and he would write his last letter to encourage his dear friend.

We may not know when our "last" opportunity will be to encourage someone else. Let's not wait for that "last" opportunity. Determine today to edify someone in the work of the Lord. Hurting people are all around us. We often sit right next to them at church or live right across the street from them or pass them in a store or work right beside them in an office. Are we so focused on our to-do lists or absorbed with our own problems that we pass by needy people like the priest and Levite did in Luke 10?

Who would benefit from a word of encouragement from you today? A friend? An enemy? A family member? Your pastor? A co-worker? A stranger? "Let no corrupt communication proceed out of your mouth, but that which is good to the use of edifying, that it may minister grace unto the hearers" (Ephesians 4:29). Be ready today to encourage someone in the Lord and for the Lord! It may not be your last chance, but if it is, you'll be mighty glad you did.

February 17, 1909

This Is Our Generation

"The night is far spent, the day is at hand: let us therefore cast off the works of darkness, and let us put on the armour of light."—**Romans 13:12**

Every generation presents new challenges to the spreading of the Gospel and revival. The God we serve, however, does not change. "For I am the LORD, I change not..." (Malachi 3:6). What God did one hundred years ago, He is able to do once again.

When J. Wilbur Chapman and Charles Alexander got off the train in Boston, little did they know what God would do. As the Boston campaign concluded, it would go down in history as their most successful crusade. With 990 services in Boston, a total of 764,000 people attended, and over 7,000 trusted Christ as Saviour. On February 22, the pastors involved in the Boston campaigns, wrote: "The Chapman-Alexander Evangelistic Campaign having concluded, we who have cooperated in the movement desire to place on record our sincere convictions regarding its results. We rejoice and thank God for the manifest presence and power of the Divine Spirit guiding and ruling in all of our preparations and deliberations, and especially for His evident direction of the messages from the lips of the evangelists, and the convicting and converting grace so marvelously exhibited. Boston has been thoroughly awakened. Thousands have been brought to God. The whole Christian church has been reinvigorated. What has been wrought in the hearts and homes cannot be tabulated or registered and will never be known until the Books of Heaven are opened...."

Yes, our day is different than it was in the early 1900s, but God's power is not limited to past generations. "Of old hast thou laid the foundation of the earth: and the heavens are the work of thy hands. They shall perish, but thou shalt endure: yea, all of them shall wax old like a garment; as a vesture shalt thou change them, and they shall be changed. But thou art the same, and thy years shall have no end" (Psalm 102:25–27). The only thing limiting God is our unbelief that He can work in our generation.

February 5, 1893

There Is Power in God's Word

"For the word of God is quick, and powerful, and sharper than any twoedged sword, piercing even to the dividing asunder of soul and spirit, and of the joints and marrow, and is a discerner of the thoughts and intents of the heart."
—Hebrews 4:12

Dr. Ford Porter was born on February 5, 1893. Undoubtedly, Dr. Porter was best known for a grey and pink tract he wrote entitled, "God's Simple Plan of Salvation." Thousands of testimonies could be given of ordinary people receiving this tract from a friend or finding one on their door or in a public place, and as a result of reading it trusting Christ as their Saviour.

In that tract, they would read: "My Friend: I am asking you the most important question of life. Your joy or your sorrow for all eternity depends upon your answer. The question is: Are you saved? It is not a question of how good you are, nor if you are a church member, but are you saved? Are you sure you will go to Heaven when you die?" Only God knows the number of people who will be in Heaven one day because of this little tract that was filled with the truth of salvation.

Our power does not lie in ourselves, nor does it lie in our efforts or words. Our power is from the Word of God, the spiritual Sword that pierces the soul. Only God's Word will make a difference in someone's life for eternity. "It is the spirit that quickeneth; the flesh profiteth nothing: the words that I speak unto you, they are spirit, and they are life" (John 6:63).

Do not underestimate the power of God's Word today. You may never preach an entire sermon from a pulpit, but you could share a Scripture verse today that could change someone's life. Your destination may never be to a foreign field as a missionary, but you could hand someone a Gospel tract today to change their destination from Hell to Heaven! Give someone God's truth today—watch God do the rest!

Winter 1872

Thus Saith the Lord

"If we receive the witness of men, the witness of God is greater: for this is the witness of God which he hath testified of his Son."—**1 John 5:9**

D. L. Moody invited one of his close friends, Henry Moorehouse, to preach once again at his church in Chicago. The first time Moorehouse preached at Moody's church, Moody was reluctant as he would be out of town the first and second nights of the meeting. When Moody returned to Chicago, he asked his wife how the meetings were going. Emma Moody told her husband, "He tells the worst of sinners that God loves them." Moody responded, "Then he is wrong." "I think you will agree with him, when you hear him," his wife replied, "because he backs up everything he says with the Bible." And Emma was right. As Moody listened to the preaching of Henry Moorehouse, his perspective on ministry changed forever, not from Henry Moorehouse's words, but because he backed everything up with the Bible..

Our words cannot change lives. They are no different than the thousands of other words people hear every day. God's words, however, are eternal and life-changing. "And ye shall know the truth, and the truth shall make you free" (John 8:32). The Holy Spirit accompanies His Word as it is spoken or preached. That is the power behind it! "It is the spirit that quickeneth; the flesh profiteth nothing: the words that I speak unto you, they are spirit, and they are life" (John 6:63). God commands us to "Preach the Word" and "Speak the truth." When we do, the Holy Spirit guides it to the very heart of the hearer, and it always accomplishes what God sends it to do (Isaiah 55:11).

This is why it is vital that we read, meditate on, and study God's Word. We cannot give someone else something that we do not possess. How much of God's Word are you hiding in your heart? When is the last time you memorized a portion that could be used to help someone else? Don't hoard God's truth today—share it with anyone you can. It can change their life!

February 28, 1899

Don't Run from God

"They that observe lying vanities forsake their own mercy."—**Jonah 2:8**

Unfortunately, revival doesn't come to many until there is some tragedy in their life to arrest their attention. The funeral parlor or the hospital waiting room has often been that place where someone stops running from God and gets serious about spiritual things. Sadly, many opportunities are wasted while we run from God's will in our lives.

Mordecai Ham had been resisting God for his entire life, but the Lord got his attention in 1899 as Mordecai's much loved grandfather passed away. This was an extremely traumatic moment for Mordecai, and he knew deep inside God wanted his life. God wanted his all—his goals, his dreams, his future, his money, his desires, and his love. Sadly, it took the death of a loved one to get his attention. Mordecai Ham would soon forsake his rebellion against God and become one of America's powerful evangelists.

Don't wait for the storm to turn to God. Our obstinate will does not change God's omniscient will! God will get your attention the easy way or the hard way. We cannot run from an all-powerful, all-present God. "Whither shall I go from thy spirit? or whither shall I flee from thy presence? If I ascend up into heaven, thou art there: if I make my bed in hell, behold, thou art there. If I take the wings of the morning, and dwell in the uttermost parts of the sea; Even there shall thy hand lead me, and thy right hand shall hold me. If I say, Surely the darkness shall cover me; even the night shall be light about me. Yea, the darkness hideth not from thee; but the night shineth as the day: the darkness and the light are both alike to thee" (Psalm 139:7–12). Inside the belly of the whale, Jonah learned a valuable lesson: those that run away from God forsake God's mercy. Don't repeat Jonah's mistake!

February 28, 1864

God Uses and Blesses the Local Church

"That he might present it to himself a glorious church, not having spot, or wrinkle, or any such thing; but that it should be holy and without blemish."
—Ephesians 5:27

The Illinois Street Church opened its doors in 1864 with D. L. Moody as its pastor. Moody had become a mature influential Christian in Chicago, and after building a massive Sunday school and constantly winning souls, he planted a church in downtown Chicago. Through this church, he would see thousands saved and added to the membership. It would become a symbol of Christ's love for Chicago throughout the years. After Moody's death, this church would be renamed "Moody Church" or sometimes referred to as "Moody Memorial Church" in honor of his sacrifice and love for the church that was closest to his heart.

God promises to bless the local church. Christ is the founder of the church and gave Himself for it. Revival takes place through God's vehicle for the Great Commission—the local New Testament church. It is through this visible local body of believers that He works and accomplishes His plan. No church is perfect, because we as members are imperfect. A local church may have some flaws and always has its critics, but it is still God's plan in this age.

Are you a member of a thriving local church? Are you attending faithfully and serving in ministry in that church? Don't let a bad experience in the past or a hypocrite keep you from God's plan for your life. "Not forsaking the assembling of ourselves together, as the manner of some is; but exhorting one another: and so much the more, as ye see the day approaching" (Hebrews 10:25). In the Book of Acts, we find the believers gathering together every day for worship, prayer, and service. Yet today, as we get closer to the Lord's return, we think that if we give God an hour a week on Sunday morning, we are doing Him a favor!

The blessing of God on your life will be in direct proportion to your commitment to His church.

MARCH

March 1, 1907

Satan Hates Revival

"But foolish and unlearned questions avoid, knowing that they do gender strifes."—**2 Timothy 2:23**

How sad the evangelist's heart must have been when his crusade was forced to cease. Over four thousand people were attending every night, but Satan had gotten the victory. Arguments about petty issues amongst the churches were destroying the work of God. With the unity of believers disrupted, a new teaching—that of speaking in tongues—had also crept in. Between the petty arguments and the confusion of tongues breaking out in the services, Mordecai Ham was forced to close his revival crusade in Houston, Texas. How many more might have been saved? How many backsliders might have been reclaimed? How many broken homes might have been healed? How many churches might have been revived? But in 1907, Satan had won this battle in Houston.

When God is at work, we can be sure that Satan will counter punch and try to destroy all that God is doing. First Peter 5:8 warns, "Be sober, be vigilant; because your adversary the devil, as a roaring lion, walketh about, seeking whom he may devour." The devil will always step up his game when God's people desire revival. The battle between God and the devil is never greater than when God's people humble themselves, pray, seek God's face, and turn from sin. The wicked one never sits idly by or gives up in his attempt to block the work of God.

Satan doesn't care how he destroys revival. Whether disunity or outright false teaching, his goal is to keep the sinner from being saved and the Christian from being revived. We must not be ignorant of his devices, and we must guard our hearts and minds through the Word of God and prayer. Are you being sober and vigilant? Are you guarding your heart against the division that can so easily come between you and another Christian? Are you carefully protecting your heart from error by saturating yourself daily in truth? We can win this battle "...because greater is he that is in you, than he that is in the world" (1 John 4:4)!

March 2, 1875

There Is Power and Blessing in Christian Unity

"Only let your conversation be as it becometh the gospel of Christ: that whether I come and see you, or else be absent, I may hear of your affairs, that ye stand fast in one spirit, with one mind striving together for the faith of the gospel."
—**Philippians 1:27**

In Liverpool, England, D. L. Moody stood in front of the brand new YMCA building in Liverpool, England, for which he had raised funds during his campaigns in England. He placed the memorial plaque on the building which read: "This memorial stone was laid by D. L. Moody, of Chicago, March 2, 1875." Someone present at the dedication service described the spirit of revival in the city: "Men who wrote and spoke against the movement, men who laughed at it, went to hear and came away with changed thoughts—six thousand people at the midday prayer meeting, six thousand at the afternoon Bible lecture, and ten thousand at the evening meeting, with the inquiry rooms full, is something that even 'The Exchange' has to admit. But beyond this is the mighty power of God's spirit, working and acting, which no tables can register, no numbers record."

God works in mighty ways through His people when they strive, not against one another, but together for the cause of the Gospel. We have a real enemy who tries to bring disunity and conflict in our churches. We must stand together in one accord and one faith against the enemy and for the Gospel. One of the keys to the power of the first-century church at Jerusalem was the unity of God's people. Phrases like "with one accord," "all things common," and "singleness of heart" are found often throughout the first two chapters of the Book of Acts. No wonder God could rain down His power on the Day of Pentecost where three thousand were saved, baptized, and added to the church.

We cannot produce revival, but we can make sure that we are right one with another. Are you at odds with a brother or sister in Christ? Make it right today! It may be the very key to the next great revival.

March 2, 1995

How Will You Finish?

"Look to yourselves, that we lose not those things which we have wrought, but that we receive a full reward."—**2 John 8**

Many people start out in their Christian lives with energy, zeal, and vision. They desire to grow in God's grace and knowledge of the Word of God. They want to win as many of their family members and friends to Christ as they can. They can't wait to get to church and find a place to serve and be a blessing. Over time, however, the Christian life can become routine and our love for Christ can wane. William Booth, the founder of the Salvation Army, often said, "Look well to the fire of your soul, for it is always the tendency of fire to go out."

As his aging body was being eaten up by cancer, Curtis Hutson knew that his life was almost over. He decided to record some of the lessons that he had learned in life and ministry. He began at 1:00 PM on Wednesday and finished at 3:00 PM on Thursday; twenty-six hours of wisdom and praise. Before going to Heaven a short time later, this evangelist and soulwinner would even win the nurse who attended to him to Christ.

How will you finish your course? God has designed life as a marathon rather than a sprint. Our desire should be to say with the Apostle Paul, "I have fought a good fight, I have finished my course, I have kept the faith: Henceforth there is laid up for me a crown of righteousness, which the Lord, the righteous judge, shall give me at that day: and not to me only, but unto all them also that love his appearing" (2 Timothy 4:7–8). Regardless of our age or station in life, we should fix our eyes upon the finish line and determine to run with patience the race that is set before us. There will be obstacles, head winds, injuries, and detours to tempt us to leave the course designed for us. Ask the Lord today to keep you faithfully running until the finish.

March 5, 1738

Harden Not Your Heart

"He, that being often reproved hardeneth his neck, shall suddenly be destroyed, and that without remedy."—**Proverbs 29:1**

John Wesley was in the ministry but was not yet converted. By his own account, he was convicted of his sin and knew that he needed a personal faith in Christ, but was putting it off. He wrote in his journal about his unbelief and hypocrisy in March of 1738. "I found my brother at Oxford, recovering from his pleurisy; and with him Peter Bonier; by whom, in the hand of the great God, I was, on Sunday, the fifth, clearly convinced of unbelief, of the want of that faith whereby alone we are saved. Immediately it struck into my mind, 'Leave oft preaching. How can you preach to others, who have not faith yourself?'"

John Wesley was "clearly convinced of unbelief" in his heart, but he did nothing about it. His heart was convicted by the Holy Spirit's working, but he did not respond until much later. We should be grateful that God is a God of multiple chances. "It is of the Lord's mercies that we are not consumed, because his compassions fail not. They are new every morning: great is thy faithfulness" (Lamentations 3:22–23).

What a terrible risk it is to put off what we know God wants us to do today. In Acts 24:25, we read of a man named Felix who heard Paul preach. "And as he reasoned of righteousness, temperance, and judgment to come, Felix trembled, and answered, Go thy way for this time; when I have a convenient season, I will call for thee." There is no record in Scripture that Felix ever asked for another meeting with Paul or ever trusted Christ as Saviour. The "convenient season" never came.

If something is the right thing to do, it ought to be done today. The decision to delay is often a deadly decision. Say *yes* to all that God speaks to you about today through His Word and His Holy Spirit. You will never regret immediate obedience to the still small voice of God.

March 5, 1995

Honesty Is Always the Best Policy

"Having your conversation honest among the Gentiles: that, whereas they speak against you as evildoers, they may by your good works, which they shall behold, glorify God in the day of visitation."—**1 Peter 2:12**

After a long battle with cancer, it was on this day in 1995 that Dr. Curtis Hutson went to be with the Lord. Dr. Tom Malone said this about his friend: "After hundreds of hours together, I can say that Dr. Curtis Hutson was the most pure gold man I have ever met. He was honest in every area of his life. He was a great preacher and a great leader. He was fully surrendered to Christ. I miss him so much."

Would those close to you say that you are honest in every area of your life? Dr. Hutson would not have seen the power of God working through his life and ministry had he not been honest with himself, honest with God, and honest with others. The writer of Hebrews put it this way, "Pray for us: for we trust we have a good conscience, in all things willing to live honestly" (Hebrews 13:18). Proverbs 23:23a admonishes us to "Buy the truth, and sell it not."

The world will not listen very long to our message if they sense that we are dishonest in the way that we live. In a culture of deception, trickery, cheating, and lies, the honest Christian will stand out as a great testimony to the grace of God.

Our God is a God of truth! In fact, it is impossible for God to lie (Titus 1:2). Do we as His children resemble our Father? We ought to. Make sure that in your family, your church, your neighborhood, and your place of employment that you have a reputation of honesty. It's always the best policy and Peter in our verse above reminds us that honesty always impacts the lost world around us for God's glory and honor.

March 6, 1830

God Works Best in Softened Hearts

"Sow to yourselves in righteousness, reap in mercy; break up your fallow ground: for it is time to seek the Lord, till he come and rain righteousness upon you."
—**Hosea 10:12**

With a growing burden for revival, Charles Finney published the first edition of his periodical "The New York Evangelist" on this day in 1830. In this magazine, Finney relayed stories and testimonies about God's work in revival meetings. He desired that these accounts would stir up the hardened hearts of many of God's people and set the stage for an even greater awakening.

A farmer would not expect much of a crop if he were to simply throw some seeds on hardened soil. In reality, a good farmer would spend hours during the early spring to break up the hardened soil in order to prepare it for the seed that is to be planted. Even after this preparation, throughout the growing season of the crop, the farmer cultivates the soil so that the rain will reach the roots and the weeds can be eliminated.

We are often guilty of thinking that God will just miraculously produce revival. While He is capable of doing so, we should cultivate a spirit of revival in our own hearts. Are we spending any time preparing our hearts *before* we read God's Word or attend a preaching service? Have we removed the stones from the ground of our hearts and pulled up the thorns that choke the Word? Have we broken up the fallow ground so that God's Word can penetrate deeply into our minds and hearts and produce fruit for His glory?

To reap the harvest of revival, we must prepare by breaking up the hardened soil of our own hearts. That may not be attractive, but it is an absolute in the soil and in the soul.

March 7, 1929

Serve God While You Are Young

"Let no man despise thy youth; but be thou an example of the believers, in word, conversation, in charity, in spirit, in faith, in purity."—**1 Timothy 4:12**

After practicing his sermon in a Florida swamp, Monroe Parker, a young man who had just been called to preach, stood in front of a human audience for the first time to preach God's Word. After expounding to the frogs and the crickets of the swamp, he boldly preached the Gospel to the congregation. God would move in a special way as ten people came forward for salvation at the invitation time.

Monroe Parker was eighteen years old when he preached his first sermon. God had placed an anointing on his life, and his age was not going to hold him back. The young Dr. Parker could have given God excuse after excuse as to why he was not able to preach. But because of his boldness, ten more souls were added to the kingdom of God. If you are young, don't let anyone despise you for your youth. God can use anyone who is willing to be used regardless of their age. Have humility and respect for the older generation, but don't wait until you are older to serve God. Do it now! If you are older, looking back at the generation coming behind you, be kind and supportive of them. Don't put them down just because they are young. They will make mistakes, just like you did, and they will be in need of correction, but don't despise them because of their youth.

There is never a wrong time to serve the Lord. Whether young, old, or in between, our hearts should be to give our all for the One who gave His life for us. "And that he died for all, that they which live should not henceforth live unto themselves, but unto him which died for them and rose again" (2 Corinthians 5:15). God used an eight-year-old king named Josiah to lead a mighty revival in the nation of Israel. He also used a ninety-year-old man named John to be the human author of the Book of Revelation. He can use you today if you are willing!

March 8, 1736

Are You Saved?

"Many will say to me in that day, Lord, Lord, have we not prophesied in thy name? and in thy name cast out devils? and in thy name done many wonderful works? And then will I profess unto them, I never knew you: depart from me, ye that work iniquity."—**Matthew 7:22–23**

What a contradictory thing it is to preach the grace of God without experiencing it yourself. And yet, every time John Wesley stood to preach the Word of God in those early years of his ministry, he was convicted in his heart of his hypocrisy and deceitfulness in his religion. In his journal, he wrote of his failing ministry in Georgia and his guilt when he preached as an unconverted minister: "I do here bear witness against myself, that when I saw the number of people crowding into the church, the deep attention with which they received the word, and the seriousness that afterwards sat on all their faces; I could scarce refrain from giving the lie to experience and reason and Scripture all together." John Wesley could not preach the Word of God with a clear conscience because of his hypocrisy. He would speak about the things of God, and those around him would listen with sincerity and seriousness, but he had never actually experienced the Christian life himself.

One of Jesus' own disciples was a man who looked and acted the part but was lost. Judas Iscariot preached, cast out demons, and did some wonderful things in ministry, but lacked a personal relationship with the Saviour, Jesus Christ. How sad to think that our churches may have those who serve in various ways and participate weekly in worship and yet do not know the Lord.

Do you have a personal relationship with Jesus Christ? You may call yourself a Christian, but what does God say? Romans 8:16 reminds us, "The Spirit itself beareth witness with our spirit, that we are the children of God." Would God call you one of His children? If you are not sure, you can be sure today! "But as many as received him, to them gave he power to become the sons of God, even to them that believe on his name" (John 1:12).

March 9, 1875

Revival Always Follows Genuine Prayer

"Continue in prayer, and watch in the same with thanksgiving; Withal praying also for us, that God would open unto us a door of utterance, to speak the mystery of Christ, for which I am also in bonds."—**Colossians 4:2–3**

When Moody arrived in London, he was handed a list of spiritual needs from the city's pastors: "117,000 habitual criminals are on its police register…more than one-third of all the crime in the country is committed in London; 23,000 persons live in its common lodging-houses; its many beer shops and gin palaces would, if placed side by side, stretch…a distance of 73 miles; 38,000 drunkards appear annually before its magistrates; It has as many paupers as would occupy every house in Brighton; It has upward of a million habitual neglecters of public worship; It has 60 miles of shops open every Lord's day…."

Only the power of an Almighty God can awaken a city in those desperate conditions. But with a thousand people praying for this meeting, Moody knew that it was time to open the doors of the rented Agricultural Hall and begin preaching God's Word. They had knocked on the doors of homes throughout all of London and had passed out flyers advertising the event. They had met with pastors and churches all across the city. Now it was time to see what God would do. On March 9, 1875, the meetings commenced. In the words of William Moody: "The hall was quickly filled, seats and standing room, and thousands went away disappointed, though 17,000 people were crowded into the great building. Mr. Moody won all hearts in the very beginning by asking the vast audience to "praise God for what He was going to do in London."

Have you prayed for revival? A prayer meeting with over a thousand people staggers the imagination. But God doesn't require a thousand people to pray to see revival. All he needs is a righteous man or woman to pray fervently to Him. We cannot expect God to send revival in our hearts, in our church, and in our nation, if we do not ask Him. "The effectual fervent prayer of a righteous man availeth much" (James 5:16b).

March 9, 1899

The Word of God Is Quick and Powerful

"For the word of God is quick, and powerful, and sharper than any two-edged sword, piercing even to the dividing asunder of soul and spirit, and of the joints and marrow, and is a discerner of the thoughts and intents of the heart." **—Hebrews 4:12**

T. DeWitt Talmage retired to give his time to writing books and sermons. Talmage would become one of the most widely read Christian authors of his time. It is estimated that he wrote over three thousand journals reaching 25 million readers in his day. What talent did this servant of the Lord possess that God could use him in such a fantastic way?

When Talmage was in training at the New Brunswick Theological Seminary, the president of the institution had this to say about his preaching: "...frankly, and in all kindness, I must tell you that I solemnly think you have made a mistake in your calling. Get a position selling goods behind a dry goods counter or take a clerkship in a law office, or if necessary, follow the plough, but do not think of becoming pastor of a church. You are not fitted for it at all. It is a great mistake for you to waste your time."

No words could have been less prophetic! No doubt, the president was right in his evaluation of the personality and abilities of this young preacher. But the secret to be used is not in natural ability but in the supernatural power of God. "And I, brethren, when I came to you, came not with excellency of speech or of wisdom, declaring unto you the testimony of God. For I determined not to know any thing among you, save Jesus Christ, and him crucified. And I was with you in weakness, and in fear, and in much trembling. And my speech and my preaching was not with enticing words of man's wisdom, but in demonstration of the Spirit and of power: That your faith should not stand in the wisdom of men, but in the power of God" (1 Corinthians 2:1–5). Forget the hype, the emotion, and the flash of man—there will be no revival without the piercing, penetrating power of the Word of God!

March 12, 1856

What Are We Living For?

"For to me to live is Christ, and to die is gain."—**Philippians 1:21**

"Mr. Moody thinks he has some progress since he was here before—at least in knowledge. Has maintained his habits of prayer and reading the Bible. Believes God will hear his prayers, and reads the Bible. Is fully determined to adhere to the cause of Christ always...Will never give up his hope, or love Christ less....His prevailing intention is to give up his will to God."

In this statement from the minutes of his membership committee at Mount Vernon Church on March 12, 1856, we learn why God used the young D. L. Moody so greatly: his faith, his prayer, his devotion, his hope, and his cause. What are you living for? We hear it often but it is nonetheless true: "Only one life, twill soon be past; and only what is done for Christ will last." The world has much to offer that can easily consume our days, our years, and our lives. All of these earthly things, however, are temporary at best. It is for this reason that we are exhorted to "Set your affection on things above, not on the things of the earth" (Colossians 3:2). Focusing on the eternal while on earth is not easy but a discipline that will have the blessing of God.

Perhaps like some in the past, we should take a moment today to write down what we are living for. What is preeminent in our lives and schedules? Will anything on our "bucket list" be eternal? Is our to-do list approved by God? Epaphras prayed for the church at Colossae in Colossians 4:12 that they would "...stand perfect and complete in all the will of God." One day in heaven the only thing that will matter is if we completed the will of God for our lives. That has to start with us doing what we know to be God's will today! Remember, the devil doesn't care what you plan to do, as long as you don't start doing it until tomorrow. Defeat his devices by doing what you know is right and honoring to Christ today.

March 12, 1908

Teamwork Makes the Dream Work

"These all continued with one accord in prayer and supplication, with the women, and Mary the mother of Jesus, and with his brethren."—**Acts 1:14**

The crusade was in Philadelphia, a city founded on "brotherly love." Today, J. Wilbur Chapman's dream of reaching Philadelphia would become a reality. This was his first "simultaneous campaign," meaning that he organized more than one service per night, and with a new music man, Charles Alexander, who had travelled with R.A. Torrey years before. Chapman's heart was no doubt racing as the auditorium began to fill. He had divided the city into 42 sections, covered by 21 evangelist/musician teams to promote the services. Around 300 churches worked together for the meetings. Two main services were held on each side of the city, and Chapman preached in both each night. Charles Alexander's wife would later write of the large-scale meeting: "Noonday gatherings for business men and women were held each day in the Garrick Theatre, and meetings for men only, on Sunday afternoons. In addition to the simultaneous church services at night, other meetings through the daytime were held in factories, in public-houses, prisons, and in the open air, wherever a crowd could be gathered. There were five thousand singers in the district choirs; five thousand personal workers; two thousand ushers; one thousand volunteer "door-bell ringers" for house-to-house visitation, and two hundred and fifty district leaders." As the crusades continued, about 35,000 came every night to the two locations. God was changing Philadelphia one service at a time.

Are God's people willing to work together for a grand cause of that magnitude today? God has created different personalities and given His people a variety of gifts, but all of us should be willing to work together for revival and soulwinning. President Ronald Reagan often said, "It would be amazing what could be accomplished if no one cared who got the credit." Next time you engage in ministry, don't worry about what is in it for you or whether it is done the way that fits or pleases you best. Serve instead "with good will doing service, as to the Lord, and not to men" (Ephesians 6:7).

March 13, 1899

Bold as a Lion

"The wicked flee when no man pursueth: but the righteous are bold as a lion."
—Proverbs 28:1

Sam Jones had entered the town of Toledo, Ohio, to hold evangelistic crusades. When he began the meetings, he sensed a hindrance to the work. After much prayer, he discovered that the new mayor in the town was the problem. Fearlessly, he confronted the new mayor, whose name happened to also be Sam Jones. The mayor had adopted a "Golden Rule" philosophy that kept the doors of 700 saloons and 150 "gambling dens" open. At his preaching meeting with over 6,000 men attending, Evangelist Jones exclaimed, "If the devil were mayor, he wouldn't change a thing!" On March 13, 1899, the newspaper headlines in Toledo, Ohio, read, "Evangelist's Hot Shot."

God commands us to be bold in our fight for righteousness. Courage comes as a result of being clean. An unrighteous man or woman will never be bold or take a stand for Christ. When we stand for truth, we never stand alone. God aligns Himself with those who align with His Word. Today Christianity is in the minority. In many ways we see a discrimination against God's people because of their beliefs and behavior. Laws in government, policies in the work place, and the bias of the media all make it increasingly difficult for Christians to take their stand. We can take confidence in the words of the psalmist, "The LORD is on my side; I will not fear: what can man do unto me?" (Psalm 118:6).

As God's people we have an intangible on our side that the world knows nothing about. That intangible is God Himself! Why would we be afraid or timid when we have the Creator of the Universe standing beside us and fighting for us? We don't have to be crude or crass, but we can be confident. Be bold today as you live before others. When a door opens to speak for Christ—don't hesitate! We are on the winning side!

March 14, 1914

Never Give Up on the Lost

"Come now, let us reason together, saith the Lord: though your sins be as scarlet, they shall be as white as snow; though they be red like crimson, they shall be as wool."—**Isaiah 1:18**

Another lesser-known name in evangelism is E. Howard Cadle. After completely ruining his life with gambling, alcohol, and adultery, doctors informed him that he would have only six months to live. His mother had told him many times: "Always remember, Son, that at eight o'clock every night I'll be kneeling beside your bed, asking God to protect my precious boy." One instance, during a fight while gambling, Cadle drew his gun out and pulled the trigger to shoot a man, but the gun did not fire. He looked at the clock, and it was exactly 8:00 PM. His mother's powerful prayers had protected her son. Finally, he returned home to his godly mother. With tears in his eyes, he cried, "Mother, I'm tired of sin. I've broken your heart, betrayed my wife, broken my marriage vows—I'd like to be saved, but I've sinned too much." His mother replied, "Son, I've prayed twelve years to hear you say what you have just said." Then she shared with him Isaiah 1:18, "Come now, let us reason together, saith the Lord: though your sins be as scarlet, they shall be as white as snow; though they be red like crimson, they shall be as wool." That day, Howard accepted Christ as his Saviour and immediately found his wife. "Forgive me for all the wrongs I've done to you, Ola," he confessed. With tear-filled eyes, she kissed her husband and replied, "I have forgiven you—long ago, honey."

Never give up praying for those who need to accept Christ. No one is beyond the grace and love of God. The Lord can cleanse and redeem anyone who comes to Him in repentance. Who are you praying for today? Who *should* you be praying for? Have you given them the Gospel? Have you shared your concern for them? Don't give up! God would clean up the sin of Cadle's life and use him in the field of evangelism for the remainder of his life. God loves doing what seems impossible to men. Let's pray for and witness to some impossible cases today.

March 15, 1752

A Shelter in the Storms

"In God is my salvation and my glory: the rock of my strength, and my refuge, is in God."—**Psalm 62:7**

Storms—both physical and spiritual—are a part of life. God's protection through physical storms serve as wonderful reminders that He will keep us through the spiritual tempests as well. He is our refuge and strength and always a present help in time of trouble (Psalm 46:1).

John Wesley wrote of an experience in a storm while preaching: "While I was preaching at West Street in the afternoon, one of the most violent storms I ever remember came up. In the midst of the sermon, a great part of a house opposite to the chapel was blown down. We heard a huge noise, but knew not the cause; so much the more did God speak to our hearts: and great was the rejoicing of many in confidence of his protection. Between four and five, I took horse, with my wife and daughter. The tiles were rattling from the houses on both sides; but they hurt not us."

The song writer wrote, "Why should I feel discouraged; Why should the shadows come? Why should my heart feel lonely, and long for heaven above? When Jesus is my portion; A constant friend is He. His eye is on the sparrow, And I know He watches me. His eye is on the sparrow, And I know He watches me." Yes, if God cares for the sparrows and the lilies of the field, we can be sure He never takes His eye off of us no matter what the circumstance or situation. As Jesus told His disciples in Luke 12:6–7, "Are not five sparrows sold for two farthings, and not one of them is forgotten before God? But even the very hairs of your head are all numbered. Fear not therefore: ye are of more value than many sparrows."

Go to Him today with your trial and trouble. He is the rock of your strength, and a refuge in times like these. "Casting all your care upon him; for he careth for you" (1 Peter 5:7).

March 2, 1791

Humanly Speaking

"For thus saith the high and lofty One that inhabiteth eternity, whose name is Holy; I dwell in the high and holy place, with him also that is of a contrite and humble spirit, to revive the spirit of the humble, and to revive the heart of the contrite ones."—**Isaiah 57:15**

In 1791, the great preacher John Wesley entered eternity. Very few men have had a more powerful influence on Christianity; an influence that is still seen three centuries after his life. Wesley would forever change the world. His life and testimony would influence hundreds of thousands to enter Christ's service. His journal is an inspirational classic that continues to be read to this day. John Wesley's influence is far beyond what one man could humanly perform. Though many would have certain differences with him, no one can deny that God's hand rested mightily on this man of God.

None of us can understand the potential of one life for God. As we read through certain histories of revival, many of biblical proportions, we must remember that everything that happened was because of God's ultimate power. Humanly speaking, revival is impossible, but with God, all things are possible. Humanly speaking, one life does not matter in the grand scheme of humanity, but with God, that one life can be multiplied to influence thousands, if not millions, of people for eternity. Humanly speaking, the humility and prayer of one person means nothing, but with God, the answer to that prayer can change the course of history.

Can God use you today? You are just one—but you are one! Jonathan told his armour bearer as they faced an uncountable host of Philistines, "...there is no restraint to the Lord to save by many or by few" (1 Samuel 14:6). God is not limited by "the odds" for or against. He is God! And He wonderfully invites us to place our lives at his disposal to use for His glory. The yielding of your life to Him today could affect eternity!

March 17, 1892

No Looking Back

"And Jesus said unto him, No man, having put his hand to the plough, and looking back, is fit for the kingdom of God."—**Luke 9:62**

An up-and-coming professional baseball player known for his speed and agility surrendered his life to Christ in 1892. He had been wrestling with God about quitting baseball, and he prayed that if the National League would give him an opportunity to be released, he would take it. St. Patrick's Day, 1892, Billy Sunday received word that he could be released from his contract, if he wanted to. He wired back, "I do, send it." He would leave a major league baseball contract to work at the YMCA for $83.33 a month. Many would consider this decision a horrible mistake, leaving a well-paying career and national fame. "And for what?" the critic would ask. But God wanted Billy Sunday's life to do something unique in history. Sunday would soon join J. Wilbur Chapman as an assistant and go on to shake the nation for Christ in ways that many preachers could only dream, never looking back and never regretting his decision.

What tempts you to look back? Is money shouting your name? Is your past life calling you back? Their call is hollow and filled with deception. They will not reveal to you that they cannot offer anything of lasting value. The temporary pleasure they advertise often comes at a high price. But their voice is loud and constant. Jesus in our verse today reminds us that the devil only wants us to "look" back. Satan knows that if he can distract us from God's plan and path, it won't be long until our direction is severely altered. Later in Luke's Gospel, Jesus said, "Remember Lot's wife" (Luke 17:32). This lady never returned to Sodom and Gomorrah as the fire and brimstone fell—she merely "looked back."

Solomon gives good advice to his son in Proverbs 4:25–27 that is good for us today. "Let thine eyes look right on, and let thine eyelids look straight before thee. Ponder the path of thy feet, and let all thy ways be established. Turn not to the right hand nor to the left: remove thy foot from evil." Keep your eyes on the eternal prize!

March 18, 1968

Guided by Critics or by Christ?

"By faith Noah, being warned of God of things not seen as yet, moved with fear, prepared an ark to the saving of his house; by the which he condemned the world, and became heir of the righteousness which is by faith."—**Hebrews 11:7**

After thousands of broadcasts over the radio, Charles Fuller of "The Old-Fashioned Revival Hour" passed away on this date in 1968. "The Old-Fashioned Revival Hour" was a beacon of truth for America during the Great Depression, World War II, and up to the late 1960s. Many preachers were skeptical of using this new tool called "radio." They would preach that since the devil is "the prince of the power of the air" (Ephesians 2:2),using radio would open oneself to Satan's power. But God would silence the critics, and use Charles Fuller's ingenuity to spread the Gospel across the nation and around the world. The program, however, was cancelled the same year as Fuller's death, and a much-needed lighthouse in the land of radio dimmed its light. Thankfully, many preachers have picked up the baton of Charles Fuller, as they continue to spread the Gospel all around the world through the tool of radio and other modern forms of media today.

Never let the critics dictate your service to the Lord. As the well-known saying goes, "No one ever built a monument to a critic." God is looking for servants who will not be discouraged when those around them criticize and complain. Noah had his fair share of critics, but he continued to build the ark. Peter called him a "preacher of righteousness" because of his faithfulness in spite of the scorners around him (2 Peter 2:5). Noah saved his family because of that faithfulness to God.

Is your commitment to Christ wavering because of a critic? "The fear of man bringeth a snare: but whoso putteth his trust in the LORD shall be safe" (Proverbs 29:25). Step out by faith and obey God in all that He commands. We will not be judged one day by the onlookers but by the One who has saved us and called us to serve Him.

March 19, 1925

Not Willing That Any Should Perish

"Brethren, my heart's desire and prayer to God for Israel is, that they might be saved."—**Romans 10:1**

Born into Judaism, the evangelist Hyman Appelman later said of his salvation: "It was a culmination of a conscious lifetime search for inner peace and satisfaction...Before then, I was an orthodox Jew living up to the Judaistic religion as much as I could. I always believed in God, in the Old Testament, in a resurrection, a judgment, a Heaven, and a Hell. All Dr. Davis had to do was to show me that Jesus of Bethlehem was the promised Messiah; that He was more than a man; and that He died and rose again." Appelman's faith in Christ would spread to thousands, as he would preach "...to the Jew first, and also to the Gentile" (Romans 2:10) in the spirit of the Apostle Paul.

Appleman preached: "Revival will come today when enough of us go back—back to Pentecost, back to the book of Acts, back to the Upper Room of prayer, back to the tarrying commanded by the Lord for Holy Ghost power, back to restudy, reanalyzing, and realigning ourselves and our churches to the program of the apostolic days; when with nothing but surrendered lives filled with the Holy Spirit showing the world Jesus Christ. Twelve apostles, one hundred and twenty disciples, five hundred followers of the lowly Nazarene, rose from their knees fire-baptized, going forth to preach the Gospel that changed the world and keeps on changing it for God, for men, for time, for eternity."

How we need God's people today to follow in the footsteps of men like the Apostle Paul and Hyman Appelman and take the Gospel to the Jew and the Gentile—to every person in every place. Every tribe, every culture, every race, and every tongue needs the Saviour. Who can you tell about Jesus today?

March 20, 1751

Is It in the Bible?

"That we henceforth be no more children, tossed to and fro, and carried about with every wind of doctrine, by the sleight of men, and cunning craftiness, whereby they lie in wait to deceive; But speaking the truth in love, may grow up into him in all things, which is the head, even Christ:"—**Ephesians 4:14–15**

Shubal Stearns was greatly bothered by a doctrine that had been received in his denomination. This "doctrine" had been a tradition for centuries, but he could not find the evidence in the Bible to support it. The false doctrine of infant baptism was nowhere to be found in the Bible. Only after someone was saved in the Bible, did he see baptism performed. After seeing the flaws of infant baptism in his denomination, Shubal Stearns was ordained on March 20, 1751, as a Baptist preacher. Soon, Stearns would plant local churches all across the South. The term "Bible Belt" has its roots in the work that God accomplished through Shubal Stearns.

Everything we believe must come from the Bible. The Bible is our foundation, and without it we would be "tossed to and fro...with every wind of doctrine" (Ephesians 4:14). The "sleight of men and cunning craftiness" is around everywhere we look. Only with wisdom from the Bible can we discern truth from error. Be careful about those who do not use Scripture to support their teachings or use Scripture out of context. We should strive to be like the "noble" Bereans in Acts 17:11..."in that they received the word with all readiness of mind, and searched the scriptures daily, whether those things were so."

Don't just read the Bible today—let it read you. After you study the Bible for a spell—let it study you! We must not bend Scripture to support our beliefs, but rather bend our beliefs to Scripture. "Order my steps in thy word: and let not any iniquity have dominion over me" (Psalm 119:133).

March 1908

Stand in the Gap

"And I sought for a man among them, that should make up the hedge, and stand in the gap before me for the land, that I should not destroy it: but I found none."—**Ezekiel 22:30**

As Christians, we dare not become intimidated by the wickedness of our world. Unfortunately, the Bible tells us that the world will not become less sinful any time soon. "But evil men and seducers shall wax worse and worse, deceiving, and being deceived" (2 Timothy 3:13). But just because evil increases, God's people are not given a pass on their responsibility. In the very next verse, Paul writes: "But continue thou in the things which thou hast learned and hast been assured of, knowing of whom thou hast learned them" (2 Timothy 3:14). It is in the darkest of conditions that the light has the most effect.

With tremendous faith in God, Mordecai Ham started a revival crusade in New Orleans in the middle of the Mardi Gras festival. With great success, many Christians distributed Gospels of John throughout the city. Soon the Roman Catholics in the town saw Mordecai Ham's efforts and commanded their people to burn the Scripture portions they had received. Despite Satan's powerful opposition in New Orleans, three thousand souls were saved and added to the church.

Mordecai Ham mirrored the boldness of the Apostles in his life. Wherever Satan had dominion, he wanted to be there to "stand in the gap." Who will stand in the gap today? In Ezekiel's day, God was looking for a man to make a difference, but He found none. God needs a man or woman of God to stand in the gap of sin and call everyone to a Saviour. As you see wickedness around you, be careful not to develop a complaining spirit, but pray for our nation and those who need Christ. Remember, where sin is great—the grace of God is greater.

March 22, 1758

A Broken and Contrite Heart

"The sacrifices of God are a broken spirit: a broken and a contrite heart, O God, thou wilt not despise."—**Psalm 51:17**

The world looks for and follows after celebrities. Even in our churches, it is often the flamboyant or polished preachers who are sought after and admired. God, however, is not looking for the celebrity Christian but the surrendered Christian.

After witnessing God's power in a way that few men in history had seen, Jonathan Edwards went to be with the Lord on this day in 1758. Edwards had seen an awakening that was only explainable by the power of God. He often spoke of the First Great Awakening as "the surprising work of God." Edwards was anything but flashy in the pulpit. He read his sermons with the notes fully hiding his face from the audience. He used no expression of voice, bodily movements, or gestures. One of his biographers wrote: "Though Edwards was cut off in the fullness of power, his life does not suggest incompleteness. Rather, it rounded into a perfect whole because it had a fixed and single center—that burning core of conviction that had flashed upon him in his youth.... God as a Being who was to him at once majestic and holy, beautiful and loving, and in comparison with whom everything else in the world of nature and of man was nothing."

God does not need the most talented, entertaining men to spread His Word. Often those who have more talent than others do not accomplish what everyone thinks they will. God does not need your talent—He needs your heart. God uses ordinary people who are completely surrendered and obedient to His will.

We often discard that which is broken because we consider it useless and valueless. God, on the other hand, uses only that which is broken. The broken and contrite spirit is a requirement in God's economy. When the alabaster box was broken and the ointment poured on Jesus feet, the odor of that fragrance filled the room (Mark 14:3). May our broken lives send out a sweet-smelling savor of our Saviour today that is undeniable.

March 29, 1788

God Inhabits the Praises of His People

"Let every thing that hath breath praise the LORD. Praise ye the LORD."
—Psalm 150:6

Charles Wesley, John Wesley's brother, passed away in late March of 1788. God used this man to write over six thousand hymns and Gospel songs. Some of his most loved hymns are "And Can It Be," "Christ the Lord Is Risen Today," "Hark! the Herald Angels Sing," "Jesus, Lover of My Soul," and many more that are still used in worship to the Lord today. Meditate on the words of praise from Wesley's hymn "O For a Thousand Tongue to Sing:"

> O for a thousand tongues to sing my great Redeemer's praise;
> The glories of my God and King, the triumphs of his grace!
>
> Jesus! the name that charms our fears; That bids our sorrows cease;
> 'Tis music in the sinner's ears; 'tis life, and health, and peace.
>
> He breaks the power of canceled sin; He sets the prisoner free;
> His blood can make the foulest clean; His blood availed for me.
>
> Hear him, ye deaf; his praise, ye dumb; Your loosened tongues employ;
> Ye blind, behold your Saviour come, and leap, ye lame, for joy.

Thank God for the preachers who sing and write hymns of love and devotion for Him. Psalm 150 concludes the book of Psalms with a call to all of creation to praise the Lord. Praise Him with music and instruments! Praise Him for His "excellent greatness!" You may not be able to write or sing music like Charles Wesley, but all of us should make a joyful noise unto the Lord today. He would love to hear you sing!

March 24, 1874

Take the Next Step

"Then shall we know, if we follow on to know the LORD: his going forth is prepared as the morning; and he shall come unto us as the rain, as the latter and former rain unto the earth."—**Hosea 6:3**

Dwight Moody asked a man named Philip Bliss to join him in his evangelistic crusades. Unsure if he should join the evangelist, Bliss decided to "put out a fleece" and committed to sing for the evangelist for only a few meetings. That first service on March 24, 1874, he sang the song "Almost Persuaded." God empowered the words of the hymn as he sang and drove them into the hearts of the audience. Many were moved to a decision that night for Christ as a result. The next afternoon, Bliss surrendered his life to Christ. He gave God everything—his career, his voice, his fame, and his future. Little did P.P. Bliss know how his life would impact Christian music forever.

Sometimes the will of God is very clear while other times we are unsure of God's plan. When life is blurry, we can trust that if we obey Him in our simple actions, He will guide us in the more complex decisions. Hosea reminded the people of Israel that if they followed the Lord, "He shall come unto us as the rain." Have you ever seen the rain on the horizon and felt the wind as it was blowing the storm your way? Soon, you can feel the spray of the rain as the clouds make their way closer. If we follow God in obedience, He will come just as the rain on the horizon.

Take that next step for Christ today. It may not seem like a giant leap of faith, but obeying in the simple areas will reveal God's plan in the more complex. The more you obey, the more God will reveal. God's plans are so much greater than our own. Trust Him. You won't be disappointed.

March 1, 1914

Billy Sunday Blizzard

"For thou hast been a shelter for me, and a strong tower from the enemy."
—Psalm 61:3

We are often unaware of God's protection in our lives until the calamity or threat to our well-being is past. We are sometimes surprised by "what could have been" had we stepped out of God's will in that moment or been somewhere other than the place He put us.

During a Billy Sunday crusade in March of 1914, a huge blizzard hit the area hard during one of the preaching services. No one knew how long the snow would fall, but the two thousand people remained inside the tabernacle and gave attention to the preaching of God's Word. After the blizzard ended and people began to make their way home, news spread that four people had died in the storm. Those who stayed in the tabernacle that night were thankful they were in a place of God's protection.

Regardless of the storm, whether physical or spiritual, there is protection in the center of His will. Time after time in the Bible, we read of those who were protected by God's providential hand because of their obedience to Him. Noah, Abraham, Elijah, Elisha, Jeremiah, and Paul all experienced the supernatural protection of God in obedient service to the Lord. But we should not take God's protection for granted. Only when we live by faith in complete service and obedience to Him can we experience security and safety. We cannot expect the absence of struggles and trials, for those are how God molds us into His image (Romans 8:28–29). But when they come, we can rest in God's promises of protection.

Don't venture out of God's plan for your life today. The storms can be brutal and without God's protection, we are vulnerable and can easily fall. With His protection, however, we can rest in the confidence that we are invincible until our work for Him is complete.

March 26, 1909

God's Command to Go

"Go ye therefore, and teach all nations, baptizing them in the name of the Father, and of the Son, and of the Holy Ghost: Teaching them to observe all things whatsoever I have commanded you: and, lo, I am with you alway, even unto the end of the world. Amen."—**Matthew 28:19-20**

As the captain announced, "All ashore who's going ashore!" J. Wilbur Chapman prayed once again for God's power. Leaving Vancouver, British Columbia, on March 26, 1909, J.Wilbur Chapman and Charles Alexander began their first worldwide evangelistic crusade. On the itinerary was "Melbourne, Sydney, Ipswich, Brisbane, Adelaide, Ballarat, Bendigo, and Townsville in Australia; Manila in the Philippines; Hong Kong, Kowloon, Canton, Shanghai, Hankow, Peking and Tientsin in China; Seoul, Korea; Kobe, Kyoto, Tokyo, and Yokohama in Japan." Multitudes around the world would soon hear the clear Gospel and accept Jesus Christ as Saviour because of the faith of these two men of God who were willing to leave their comfort zones and go to all the world with the Gospel.

Where does God want you to go? Our itinerary may be different than an evangelist of yesteryear or today, but God still commands us to go. The command remains, "Go ye therefore and teach all nations." Many times we get comfortable where we are. We tend to enjoy the comforts of our living room or office. But God commands us to go! Our schedules get filled with the necessities of life along with "time off" for ourselves. But when do we take time to go with the Gospel to someone in need? Do we have a regularly scheduled time each week? Are we accountable to a partner within our local church? We dare not keep the Good News to ourselves when God commands us to take it to every creature. We must not allow ourselves to become apathetic or lazy. Until everyone has heard, we must continue to go.

March 31, 1860

You Are Not Insignificant

"For thou hast possessed my reins: thou hast covered me in my mother's womb. I will praise thee; for I am fearfully and wonderfully made: marvellous are thy works; and that my soul knoweth right well."—**Psalm 139:13–14**

In a small gypsy camp in Europe, a young woman gave birth to a precious baby boy. No one of any importance would think twice about this infant born in late March of 1860—but God did. Many despised and thought poorly of the wandering gypsy people. God, however, had sent a special messenger for them. He cared about this seemingly insignificant group of people and raised up a mighty evangelist from their midst. As the sun set on the first day of Rodney "Gypsy" Smith's life, in no way could his humble village understand the future God had planned. Gypsy Smith would shake two continents for Christ and see multitudes saved in his joyous ministry.

God didn't make a mistake when He created you. You won't understand all the twists and turns your life will take, but God is never out of control. He hasn't given up in His plan to use you. Your life didn't happen by accident. Your birth didn't surprise God. "My substance was not hid from thee, when I was made in secret, and curiously wrought in the lowest parts of the earth. Thine eyes did see my substance, yet being unperfect; and in thy book all my members were written, which in continuance were fashioned, when as yet there was none of them" (Psalm 139:15–16).

Humanism would lecture us about our purposeless existence on earth, but the Lord teaches otherwise. He crafted us in the womb with great love and purpose. How it must grieve our God when we live our lives like we are in control. God has a plan so much bigger, better, and brighter than anything we could imagine. "Now unto him that is able to do exceeding abundantly above all that we ask or think, according to the power that worketh in us.." (Ephesians 3:20).

Don't mess up God's plan by living for yourself. You'll never improve on your Creator's careful design for your life. You are fearfully and wonderfully made on purpose and for a purpose.

March 28, 1858

Sin Hinders Revival

"Your iniquities have turned away these things, and your sins have withholden good things from you."—**Jeremiah 5:25**

Charles Hadden Spurgeon mounted the pulpit to deliver a sermon on revival. All ears were attentive to this magnificent orator as he preached God's Word. With supernatural power, he described the current prayer meeting revival and declared, "Men, brethren, and fathers, the Lord God hath sent us a blessing. One blessing is the earnest of many. Drops precede the April showers. The mercies which He has bestowed upon us are but the forerunners and the preludes of something greater and better yet to come. He has given us the former, let us seek of Him the latter rain,that His grace may be multiplied among us and His glory may be increased. There are some of you to whom I address myself this morning who stand in the way of revival of religion. I would affectionately admonish you and beseech you not to impede the Lord's own work...God will never bless an unholy people; and in proportion to our unholiness, He will withhold the blessing from us."

Over 150 years later, his message still rings true in the hearts of believers seeking revival. We must examine our lives and ask God to examine us as well. We must not stand in the way of revival. We often discuss the need for humility and prayer, but God cannot bless until we turn from our wicked ways. The smallest covetous thought or prideful look can hinder God's working in our lives, in our churches, and in our nation. We can complain about the wickedness we see on the news, but if we do not turn away from sin ourselves, God will not heal our land.

"But in a great house there are not only vessels of gold and of silver, but also of wood and of earth; and some to honour, and some to dishonor. If a man therefore purge himself from these, he shall be a vessel unto honour, sanctified and meet for the master's use, and prepared unto every good work" (2 Timothy 2:20–21). Will you be a clean or a contaminated conduit? God only uses clean vessels for revival!

March 29, 1739

A Passion for Preaching

"Then I said, I will not make mention of him, nor speak any more in his name. But his word was in mine heart as a burning fire shut up in my bones, and I was weary with forbearing, and I could not stay."—**Jeremiah 20:9**

John Wesley writes: "I left London, and in the evening expounded to a small company at Basingstoke.... [In two days] In the evening I reached Bristol, and met Mr. Whitefield there. I could scarce reconcile myself at first to this strange way of preaching in the fields, of which he set me an example on Sunday; having been all my life (till very lately) so tenacious of every point relating to decency and order, that I should have thought the saving of souls almost a sin, if it had not been done in a church."

John Wesley and George Whitefield would have their differences in the coming years, but God would use them both to see England and the American colonies turn to God. Many believe that if it was not for the preaching of these men, the Declaration of Independence would never have been written and a nation founded "under God" would never have been born.

This open air preaching to the multitudes was a new phenomenon. Whitefield had been cast out of the churches of his day for his stand against their false beliefs, but that would not stop him from preaching. He said, "The churches are closed to me, but bless God the fields are open!" The Word of God burned inside of him. Jeremiah sensed the same burning in his heart in his time. He had even decided to give up preaching for good. But God's Word was as a fire in his heart and in his bones, as to make him weary for not preaching. The Apostle Paul exclaimed, "For though I preach the gospel, I have nothing to glory of: for necessity is laid upon me; yea, woe is unto me, if I preach not the gospel!" (1 Corinthians 9:16).

God give us men with a fire for this hour and time! We need men today who will stand up with a holy calling and in a fearless tone, preach the Word of God! Let's encourage pastors, missionaries, and evangelists to "preach the word" (2 Timothy 4:2)!

March 30, 1858

Stand Up for Jesus

"Wherefore take unto you the whole armour of God, that ye may be able to withstand in the evil day, and having done all, to stand."—**Ephesians 6:13**

Dudley Tyng, a prominent preacher during the Prayer Meeting Revival, preached to a crowd of five thousand people at the downtown YMCA. He preached a powerful sermon from Exodus 10:11 which says, "Not so: go now ye that are men, and serve the LORD. . . ." He fearlessly proclaimed, "I must tell my Master's errand, and I would rather that this right arm were amputated at the trunk than that I should come short of my duty to you in delivering God's message." Two weeks later, while examining a barn with a few preacher friends, his shirt sleeve was caught in a corn threshing machine, and a few days later he would die of deep laceration and blood loss. With his arm mangled and life slipping from him, he whispered to the preachers standing by, "Let us all stand up for Jesus." At his funeral, the preacher, George Duffield, Jr., led the congregation in singing the song he had just written in honor of the dying words of his friend:

Stand up, stand up for Jesus, Ye soldiers of the cross;
Lift high his royal banner, It must not suffer loss.

Stand up, stand up for Jesus, Stand in his strength alone;
The arm of flesh will fail you, Ye dare not trust your own.

Stand up, stand up for Jesus, The strife will not be long;
This day the noise of battle, The next the victor's song.

To those who vanquish evil, A crown of life shall be;
They with the King of Glory, Shall reign eternally.

Whether in prosperity or poverty, good health or bad, in life or in death—we must stand up for Jesus Christ. "According to my earnest expectation and my hope, that in nothing I shall be ashamed, but that with all boldness, as always, so now also Christ shall be magnified in my body, whether it be by life, or by death" (Philippians 1:20). Stand up for Jesus Christ today!

Judges 9–10 // Luke 5:17–39

March 31, 1826

Ye Are the Light of the World

"Righteousness exalteth a nation: but sin is a reproach to any people."
—Proverbs 14:34

America had forgotten where she came from. The First Great Awakening with the preaching of Jonathan Edwards and George Whitefield had faded and would soon be forgotten by a new generation. With a skeptical president and humanistic writers, a small group of Christians began to pray. By March 31, 1826, over two thousand people were saved and added to a church in Rome, New York, after Charles Finney preached in that northern town. The Second Great Awakening was beginning to sweep across the entire New World as preachers like Finney preached fearlessly the truths of God's Word.

America is in need of another awakening. She has once again forgotten her heritage and moved away from the God who made her great. Prayer and the Bible have been removed from public life, and to speak of Jesus Christ is considered politically incorrect. But before we are filled with righteous indignation about our society, let us be filled with righteous inspection of our own lives. We can get upset with the sin in our nation, rightly so, but God does not use the unsaved to spread His light through neighborhoods and schools. He uses His children.

"Ye are the salt of the earth: but if the salt have lost his savour, wherewith shall it be salted? it is thenceforth good for nothing, but to be cast out, and to be trodden under foot of men. Ye are the light of the world. A city that is set on an hill cannot be hid. Neither do men light a candle, and put it under a bushel, but on a candlestick; and it giveth light unto all that are in the house. Let your light so shine before men, that they may see your good works, and glorify your Father which is in heaven" (Matthew 5:13–16). All of the darkness in this world cannot put out one light! Let your light shine brightly today!

APRIL

April 726 B.C.

Tear Down the Idols

"Little children, keep yourselves from idols. Amen."—**1 John 5:21**

After years of living under a wicked ruler, the people of Judah had a leader who was willing to follow the Lord and His Word. King Ahaz had led the nation in turning their backs against God as he promoted the worship of idols in the nation. Ahaz thought that worshipping the gods of the Syrians would bring military success to the crumbling nation of Judah, but his idol worship was the very reason for the destruction that now ransacked the country. Ahaz had gone so far as to sell the treasures of the Temple of God to win over foreign governments, and he had commanded the high priest to construct a new altar in the Temple, one like he saw in Damascus. As King Hezekiah ascended the throne of his father, he no doubt remembered the sin of his father, especially the sacrifice of his own brother to Syrian idols in the valley of Hinnom. But now it was his turn to make a decision for himself and the people of his nation. Would he follow in the footsteps of his father and live for his own selfish desires, or would he live for God? Thankfully, Hezekiah made the right decision. It was time to tear down the idols and rebuild the Temple of God.

The idols of today are just as destructive to our lives and our nation as the idols of Israel were to them. The idols of selfish materialism, sensual pleasure, haughty academia, and greed-filled power are no less ruinous and a great hindrance to revival in our hearts. Every day we must tear down the idols in our own hearts of pride, selfishness, lust, bitterness, jealousy, and covetousness. God does not share His glory or worship with anyone or anything: "I am the LORD: that is my name: and my glory will I not give to another, neither my praise to graven images" (Isaiah 42:8). Do we ascribe more worth—that is, more time and attention to our jobs, retirement, possessions, friendships, entertainment, or recreation, than we do to our God? If so, we have some idols to pull down. "Thou shalt have no other gods before me" (Exodus 20:3). We stumble at the very first commandment of the Law, and because we do, our nation, our lives, and our churches fall.

April 2, 1739

Come Out from Among Them

"Wherefore come out from among them, and be ye separate, saith the Lord, and touch not the unclean thing; and I will receive you. And will be a Father unto you, and ye shall be my sons and daughters, saith the Lord Almighty."
—**2 Corinthians 6:17–18**

Breaking away from something we have put time and energy into is never easy. History reveals that many individuals have remained in a church or movement because it was easier to compromise their beliefs than to contend for the Bible. There is a human tendency to believe that we can change something from the inside if we just stay with it. But this is contrary to God's command. "Can two walk together, except they be agreed?" (Amos 3:3). Separating from those who are teaching error may not be easy, but it is always right and brings with it the wonderful blessings of God.

John Wesley and George Whitefield were no longer allowed to preach in the Anglican Church by April of 1739. Because they were rightly dividing the Word of Truth, they were banished from the pulpits in England. These two men joined together and went to the coal mining fields and preached to the common man. Thousands upon thousands would gather around them daily and hear the preaching. Crowds of twenty thousand or more were not uncommon in these open-air meetings. Hundreds of these hardened and sinful men were turning to Christ every day!

Are you compromising some area of God's Word because of your fear of family or friends? You will need God's grace and strength to take your stand and do what is right, but the blessings will be immeasurable. Your marriage, your children and grandchildren—the future of Christianity as we know it—depends on bold decisions to obey Scripture in our generation. Remember, the cost of obedience is never as great as the cost of disobedience. "If ye be willing and obedient, ye shall eat the good of the land: But if ye refuse and rebel, ye shall be devoured by the sword: for the mouth of the LORD hath spoken it" (Isaiah 1:19–20).

April 2, 1877

A Goodly Heritage

"The lines are fallen unto me in pleasant places; yea, I have a goodly heritage."
—Psalm 16:6

If you have been raised in a Christian family that placed a priority on God, His Word, and His house, you are blessed and should be very thankful. If you have or had a parent or grandparent who prayed for you daily, you are fortunate.

On a small farm near Scottsville in southern Kentucky, a mother held her newborn baby for the first time. His name was Mordecai, and he would become one of the most powerful evangelists of his time. Mordecai Ham could trace his lineage back to eight generations of Baptist preachers, back to Roger Williams. He once stated, "From the time I was eight years old, I never thought of myself as anything but a Christian. At nine, I had definite convictions that the Lord wanted me to preach." Ham would become a great spokesman for prohibition and would preach across the country in meetings and on radio against the sin of alcohol. His preaching was used by God to bring many to Christ as Saviour and churches to revival.

Perhaps you are a first generation Christian and did not have the privilege of being taught early on about Christ like Mordecai Ham. Will you dedicate yourself today to be the "first" in a long line of generations who will know and serve God in your family? The laborers needed in the harvest fields will not come simply because we have good local churches and excellent training schools and colleges. We must have homes, where early on the character of God and the contents of the Bible are carefully taught and practiced early.

Wouldn't it be wonderful if God could use your home to produce eight generations of Baptist preachers? God will bless a family with a goal like that!

April 4, 1900

A Faithful God

"The grass withereth, the flower fadeth: because the spirit of the LORD bloweth upon it: surely the people is grass. The grass withereth, the flower fadeth: but the word of our God shall stand for ever."—**Isaiah 40:7–8**

D. L. Moody had passed away four months before, and now due to a great fire in Kansas City, the location of Moody's last message went up in smoke. During his last message, he profoundly stated: "'I have no sympathy with the idea that our best days are behind us,' and he smiled as he related the impression that he had a year before when he saw in the papers that 'Old Moody is in town.' 'Why,' he said, 'I am only sixty-two; I am only a baby in comparison with the great eternity which is to come.'" Yet the memory of Dwight Moody was beginning to fade. It was the turn of a new century, with new hardships, new battles, and new ideas. But God and His Word never change. What is true is true for all centuries. Whether the date is 1900 or 2000 or 3000, nothing changes about the God of truth.

We are tempted to think that times are different and revivals of the past are a part of history but no longer possible in our day. The waves of skepticism, doubt, and unbelief overwhelm any vision or thought of an awakening in our generation. The very lack of revival, however, is our fatalistic and unbelieving hearts. "And he did not many mighty works there because of their unbelief" (Matthew 13:58). Jesus was more than willing to miraculously work in His own area of Nazareth where He had grown up, but passed them by because of their lack of faith. Will our generation miss the revival God planned for us because of our unbelief?

Great men may be gone, and buildings may crumble or burn, but our God lives and His Word has power to change lives today! We don't need something new—we need something old—or should we say *timeless?* Our God has no beginning or ending—He is eternal. His Word is true from the beginning, and when Heaven and earth pass away, it will still endure (Mark 13:31)! There is a good foundation to build our faith for another great revival.

April 5, 1886

The Primacy of Preaching

"Then Philip went down to the city of Samaria, and preached Christ unto them... And there was great joy in that city."—**Acts 8:5, 8**

Most of the great revivals of the past have been characterized by the powerful preaching of God's Word. Today it seems that preaching is de-emphasized with the canceling of what used to be regular Sunday evening and mid-week services in many churches. Even the preaching time on Sunday mornings is often reduced by our appetite for fellowship and entertainment. In the Bible we view scenes of people standing from morning until evening hearing the Word of God. Revivals in previous centuries would last for weeks rather than days.

On April 5, 1886, the Chicago Tribune described the revival crusade led by Sam Jones in Chicago. "The great five-week revival meeting...is over. The finish was reached in a veritable blaze of glory and without a solitary essential lacking to crown it a magnificent success...People [last night] stood along the aisles on the main floor, stood six and seven deep on the promenade and in the gallery, stood on the stairways, and, in fact, stood everywhere it was possible to stand. There was scarcely breathing, much less standing room. Several hundred people remaining in the building from the afternoon service, and by six o'clock nearly every seat was occupied. By half-past six people were standing, and fifteen minutes later the entrance doors were closed and no more people admitted...A careful estimate places the number of people turned away at about ten thousand, really a greater throng than was able to hear the last sermon of this series of revival meetings...The meetings...during the past five weeks have been attended by nearly two hundred and sixty thousand persons...Half an hour was spent with about a hundred penitents in the inquiry room. Thus was closed the great meeting in Chicago."

How many sermons will you hear in the next five weeks? Will you be in church each time the doors are open and give your full attention to the preaching? Revival in large part depends on it!

April 2, 1859

Will Somebody Pray?

"And he said unto them, This kind can come forth by nothing, but by prayer and fasting."—**Mark 9:29**

The economic collapse in the late 1850s was crushing businesses and leaving once-successful businessmen penniless. Two laymen decided that the only solution was prayer. They met during the noon hour at the Old Dutch Reformed Church in New York City and called upon God for a spiritual revival. The prayer meetings grew until the noon bell was calling people to prayer all across the nation. It is estimated that nearly one million people were saved during this "Prayer Meeting Revival!"

As the revival swept the nation, James Waddel Alexander, Jeremiah Lanphier's pastor in New York City, described the revival: "Though I have aimed to keep down and regulate the excitement among us, and have no additional service but an exhortation on Monday to such as seek instruction on points connected with conversion, I perceive such a degree of inquiry as has never met me in my ministry....From the start I have held myself ready to adapt measures to emerging demands; I however feel glad I have pursued the repressive method; which by the way has lost me sundry good opinions even among my own flock. Study I cannot, being run down by persons...in search of counsel. The uptown prayer meetings are very sober and edifying. I am told the general tendency in all is to increased decorum. The openness of thousands to doctrine, reproof, etc., is undeniable. Our lecture is crowded—many going away. The publisher of Spurgeon's sermons says he has sold a hundred thousand. All booksellers agree, that while general trade is down, they never sold so many religious books. You may rest assured there is a great awakening among us....and there are meetings of great size, as free from irreverence as any you ever saw."

What can you do for the cause of revival? Can you pray? Two men was all it took to birth a revival in New York City that affected the nation and the eternal destiny of one million people. Go to your knees and pray for another awakening.

April 1880

The Joy of Being Used by God

"And I thank Christ Jesus our Lord, who hath enabled me, for that he counted me faithful, putting me into the ministry."—**1 Timothy 1:12**

The ministry is not a job or vocation. It is not something we choose to do to make a living. It is a high calling of God. One that is never to be taken lightly or treated disrespectfully. There is no greater honor, and nothing gives more joy than to be a co-laborer with Christ in the ministry.

It was an exciting day for the acclaimed evangelist D. L. Moody. God had put on his heart to open a training school for preachers. In April of 1880, a ground-breaking ceremony took place for the first dormitory of this new seminary. As Moody's foot hit the shovel, he thanked God for putting him in the ministry. God was using this former shoe cobbler in ways no man could humanly explain. The anointing of God was on his life. He leaped by faith, and God had answered once again. Months later, Moody would dedicate this dormitory with the college's theme verse, Isaiah 27:3, "I the Lord do keep it; I will water it every moment: lest any hurt it, I will keep it night and day."

What a joy to know that what we do for the Lord in our service to Him will have His power, protection, presence, and provision. The ministry is God's work, not our own. Jesus declared in Matthew 16:18, "I will build my church." Paul said, "I have planted, Apollos watered; but God gave the increase" (1 Corinthians 3:6).

Is God using your life in His service? Have you ever told the Lord that He could? Are you willing to let Him use your life? What would keep you from giving more of your time, talent, and treasure to the Lord's work? There is joy in serving Jesus! His yoke is easy and His burden is light (Matthew 11:29–30). Roll up your sleeves and enter into the work of God today. You'll never be happier in your life.

April 8, 1862

Use Every Opportunity for the Lord

"I must work the works of him that sent me, while it is day: for the night cometh, when no man can work."—**John 9:4**

News of the Civil War battle of Pittsburg Landing reached the YMCA where D. L. Moody worked. Moody and several of his fellow workers quickly boarded a train the next day to supply help for the wounded soldiers. A medical doctor shared his testimony of Moody's influence on his life that night on the train: "When we were two or three hours out of Chicago and every one was getting settled down in his seat for the night (we had no sleepers then) I was aroused by a gentle tap on the shoulder and asked if I would not attend Moody's prayer meeting, which was then to be held in the front end of the car. I wasn't a Christian then and I didn't go, but nevertheless my conscience gave me a stinging rebuke and I was set thinking. In the forward end of that car was Mr. Moody, engaged in conducting a prayer meeting; in the rear end was a company of men playing cards. I couldn't help realizing the wonderful zeal of the man on his great work, and how earnest and how careful he was that no duty be neglected, no opportunity lost...I saw no more of Mr. Moody during that trip, but I have thought of this circumstance many, many times and of the intense Christian zeal by which he was always impelled."

Do we miss opportunities of service because our minds are focused on ourselves or the things of this world rather than on Christ and the eternal? We can become so consumed with our earthly needs that there just isn't time for anything else. Jesus taught, "Lay not up for yourselves treasures upon earth, where moth and rust doth corrupt, and where thieves break through and steal: But lay up for yourselves treasures in heaven, where neither moth nor rust doth corrupt, and where thieves do not break through nor steal: For where your treasure is, there will your heart be also" (Matthew 6:19–21). When an opportunity comes to serve the Lord, where is your heart? Don't miss opportunities today because your heart is misplaced.

April 9, 1911

Holy Toledo!

"Say not ye, There are yet four months, and then cometh harvest? behold, I say unto you, Lift up your eyes, and look on the fields; for they are white already to harvest."—**John 4:35**

The disciples questioned a detour that Jesus took through the city of Samaria. It seemed to be a waste of time as nothing could possibly take place there of any consequence. Little did they know that while they went to buy lunch, Jesus would win a woman stained with sin to Himself, and through her a powerful revival would take place. The fields were white unto harvest in Samaria.

Billy Sunday stepped off the train in Toledo, Ohio, on this day in 1911. He had no idea that this would be his most successful evangelistic campaign yet, but he had a desire to make a difference in the town. He merely went with the faith that God would do something great there, and God did. The town would welcome him with open arms, and by the end of the week he would see a record of 7,300 converts. Thirty thousand people would come to hear Sunday preach, and most of the businesses in the town would shut down during the services. Many believe that the phrase "Holy Toledo" came from the spark of revival that came under the preaching and leadership of Billy Sunday.

We can never witness to the wrong person. Everyone is a candidate to be saved. We may have our opinions about where revival is most likely to come, but the truth is, the fields are white everywhere. No place is an impossible place. No group of people is too hardened to be saved. No church is too far gone to experience once again the fire of revival. Let's not limit God by our preconceived notions and opinions. God is no doubt working in the heart of someone you will meet today. Jesus' disciples in Samaria learned that no lunch is worth missing a miracle for!

April 10, 1900

Live for the Glory of God

"Whether therefore ye eat, or drink, or whatsoever ye do, do all to the glory of God."—**1 Corinthians 10:31**

William R. Moody, D. L. Moody's son, set down his pen for the last time. His biography about his father's life was finally complete. He had begun this 499-page biography of his father in the spring of 1894. In his foreword, William confessed, "The preparation of my Father's biography has been undertaken as a sacred trust...Father lived solely for the glory of God and for the spread of the Gospel of Jesus Christ. It is the earnest prayer of his family that in this record of career his life's purpose may be conserved."

Are you aware that your biography is being written? Every day another page or two is recorded in the eternal records. It is an honest record of both the good and the bad. One day we will give an account for every page. Solomon urges us to think carefully about what is being recorded there. "Let us hear the conclusion of the whole matter: Fear God, and keep his commandments: for this is the whole duty of man. For God shall bring every work into judgment, with every secret thing, whether it be good, or whether it be evil" (Ecclesiastes 12:13–14).

What a challenge it is to live every moment for the glory of God! Our Saviour left us a great example of how to live. "And he that sent me is with me: the Father hath not left me alone; for I do always those things that please him" (John 8:29). Can we say that we do only and always those things that please our heavenly Father? May it be our goal! May we aspire to live more and more of our lives for God's glory rather than our own! The cry of John the Baptist would be a noble prayer today: "He must increase, but I must decrease" (John 3:30).

April 1897

When Have You Last Said, Thanks?

"In every thing give thanks: for this is the will of God in Christ Jesus concerning you."—**1 Thessalonians 5:18**

Our human nature is prone to find fault with people, complain about our circumstances, sulk when we are underappreciated, and worry about the future. We can go days and weeks with nothing but complaint on our minds and coming from our lips. We tend to count our blessings on our fingers, but pull out a calculator to tabulate our burdens.

Moody had written many letters to some of the most influential people in the world, but this letter written in April of 1897 near the end of his life would be his most important. Moody determined to give credit where credit was due in his "letter" to the Lord. He wrote a simple, retrospective letter of his thankfulness to God. He was grateful for the opportunity to be used of God for many years of ministry. He wrote, "This year it has been a great joy to be used after working forty years and not be laid aside, and then I have great reason to thank God for my health; not a cold, not a headache, but joy and strength and pleasure in the work."

You might be tempted to say, "Well, I haven't been as fortunate as Moody" or "God hasn't treated me that way. I have more problems and pains than I can number." I can assure you, D. L. Moody had his struggles. People opposed the Gospel message everywhere he preached. His weight was a constant battle and because of his lack of formal education, he struggled to speak grammatically correct English. But Moody chose to be thankful! After forty years, he could have no doubt written a book about his troubles, but instead sat down and deliberately thanked God for the blessings.

Before you close your eyes at the end of this day, why not take a moment to jot down a few of God's blessings for which you are thankful. Be careful—it may take longer than you had planned!

April 12, 1902

Our Hope Is in the Lord

"The Lord taketh pleasure in them that fear him, in those that hope in his mercy."—**Psalm 147:11**

The older we get the less hopeful we tend to be. In our youth we are idealistic at the prospects of the future, but as we age, realism sets in and our hope wanes. This should not be true, however, of the child of God. The best is yet to come! Earth may not bring all that we hope or dream of, but eternity will be far beyond what we can imagine or think!

Today in 1902, in the city of Washington D.C., T. Dewitt Talmage took his last breath. After his vacation in Mexico to recover from the flu, he became ill again. No one thought his condition was serious until a few days before he passed away. He would die of brain inflammation. Though his preaching style had waned in popularity for the past few years, God used the life of T. Dewitt Talmage to bring thousands of souls to the knowledge of Christ. In his last written sermon two months before his death, his text was Psalm 33:2. Talmage wrote: "That Gospel rocked our cradle, and it will epitaph our grave. It soothes our sorrows, brightens our hopes, inspires our courage, forgives our sins, and saves our souls. It takes a man who is all wrong and makes him all right…The grandest churches are yet to be built. The mightiest anthems are yet to be hoisted. The greatest victories are yet to be gained…The most triumphant processions are yet to march. O what a world this will be when it rotates in its orbit a redeemed planet, girdled with spontaneous harvests and enriched by orchards whose fruit are speckles and redundant, and the last pain will have been banished, and the last tear wept, and the last groan uttered, and there shall be nothing to hurt or destroy in all God's holy mountain! All that and more will come to pass, for 'the mouth of the Lord hath spoken it!'"

"The future is as bright as the promises of God," Adoniram Judson penned. Where is your hope today? Are you focused on the promises of the Lord or the problems of life? "Happy is he that hath the God of Jacob for his help, whose hope is in the Lord his God" (Psalm 146:5).

April 13, 1902

Just Say No!

"My son, if sinners entice thee, consent thou not."—**Proverbs 1:10**

We fail to understand how dangerous sin can be. We think that a little sin will not hurt us. But there is no such thing as a little sin, for there is no such thing as a little God to sin against! The problem with a little sin is that it doesn't stay little. It grows and matures until it is too big to control. How much better, as Solomon advises his son, if sin knocks at your door—don't answer it!

A New York Times journalist could not believe his eyes as he watched T. Dewitt Talmage preach one evening: He would describe his experience after Talmage's death in 1902: "One Sunday morning when the time came for him to deliver his sermon, he walked to the extreme edge on one side of his fifty-foot platform, faced about, then suddenly started as fast as he could run for the opposite side. Just as everybody in the congregation, breathless, expected to see him pitch headlong from the further side of the platform he leaped suddenly in the air and came down with a crash, shouting, 'Young man, you are rushing towards a precipice'. And then he delivered a moving sermon upon the temptations and sins of youth in a big city."

Are you running toward destruction of your life today on the path of sin? Stop! Repent! Turn around! It's not too late. It's not too hard. "There hath no temptation taken you but such as is common to man: but God is faithful, who will not suffer you to be tempted above that ye are able; but will with the temptation also make a way to escape, that ye may be able to bear it" (1 Corinthians 10:13). There is no sin that God cannot forgive and deliver you from. There is no cry of confession to God that will go unheeded. Stop denying! Stop hiding! Come clean. The only way to cover your sin is to confess it. "He that covereth his sins shall not prosper; but whoso confesseth and forsaketh them shall have mercy" (Proverbs 28:13).

April 13, 1881

Jesus Christ Is Our All in All

"*...but Christ is all, and in all.*"—**Colossians 3:11b**

How would someone describe your life? Perhaps they would mention your appearance or personality. Maybe they would talk about your career or hobbies. A business man; a reader; a family man; a sportsman; a hard worker; a friend. All of these would be good and perhaps in some way sum up your life. But would anyone speak of your resemblance to Christ?

J. Wilber Chapman's mind was flooding with the memories that brought him to this moment. He remembered when he was seventeen years old and accepted Christ as his Saviour. He remembered graduating with his bachelor of arts from Lake Forest College and enrolling in the Lane Theological Seminary in Cincinnati, Ohio. And today in 1881, he would complete his ordination. Soon, he would graduate from seminary and join the evangelistic trail with D. L. Moody. Ford Ottman would say of him in his 1920 biography: "For more than a quarter of a century Dr. J. Wilbur Chapman was a potent presence and a formative force...not as one who sought preferment or place, but as one who, for Christ's sake and the Gospel's, gave himself to the service of his fellowmen. He was great among us in that he was the servant of all....As an ambassador of Christ he was loyal to the commission and the message he received. He faithfully delivered his message, and his ministry was therefore effective and fruitful. The cardinal truths he believed and defended were the Divine Inspiration of the Scriptures, the Deity of Jesus Christ, the Personality of the Holy Spirit, the Primacy of the Atonement, and the Return of our Lord. Love for Christ was his ruling passion, the evangel of Christ was his message: in the life he lived, in the sermons he preached, in the books he wrote, in the songs he composed. He was a preacher to preachers."

God uses men and women who are most like Him to reach a world without Him. While we may try to relate to people through our interests, gifts, jobs, or families, it is Christ who people need to see in us. Make sure someone sees Jesus in you today.

April 15, 1903

God Will Use You as You Are

"But what went ye out for to see? A man clothed in soft raiment? behold, they that wear soft clothing are in king's houses. But what went ye out for to see? A prophet? yea, I say unto you, and more than a prophet."—**Matthew 11:8–9**

John the Baptist was anything but conventional. He was not your normal preacher by any stretch. Unbound by the religious systems of his day and oblivious to the opinions of others, he fearlessly prepared the way for the Messiah. People often think that we have to fit a certain mold for God to use us. We must have a dynamic personality, a gift of speech, a flamboyant approach, or a new and innovative method. Paul reminded the church at Corinth that it is God, our Creator, who fashioned us exactly as He wished and will use us just as we are: "For who maketh thee to differ from another? and what hast thou that thou didst not receive? now if thou didst receive it, why dost thou glory, as if thou hadst not received it?" (1 Corinthians 4:7).

Billy Sunday had been travelling as the advance man for J. Wilbur Chapman. He remembered with delight the moment Chapman called him in 1896 and asked him to preach in his stead. Preaching had become Billy Sunday's lifeblood, and as he wrung his sweaty hands, it was time to be officially ordained into the ministry by the Chicago Presbytery. He was plain and simple with the ordination board, telling them that if Augustine didn't play in the National League, he would not know anything about him. Sunday would go on to preach against the sins of his day. Many thousands would "hit the sawdust trail" and be saved. Sunday would develop a preaching style that was distinct to say the least! Breaking booze bottles and throwing chairs was not unusual during one of his sermons. God would use this unique, anointed preacher to see a million souls saved.

Don't let what you are keep you from being who God wants you to be. Surrender your life to God. He has used a stuttering Moses, an impulsive Peter, a doubting Thomas, a gifted Paul, and He will have no difficulty using you!

April 16, 1896

The Joy of Soulwinning

"He that goeth forth and weepeth, bearing precious seed, shall doubtless come again with rejoicing, bringing his sheaves with him."—**Psalm 126:6**

Happiness alludes most people in this life. Even God's people struggle to maintain their joy. The trials of life wear away at us and the burdens steal our strength and happiness. In those seasons, there is a sure way to renew our joy.

Lee Scarborough was attending Yale University and felt that the Lord wanted him to preach God's Word. He would later describe his experience: "In Old Farnum Hall at Yale University, in my room, on my bed, with a broken heart I yielded. I thank God that since that time I have been trying to do His will." God took that broken heart and molded a servant. His preaching would have a profound influence on the ministry of evangelists John R. Rice and Hyman Appelman. He would later preach: "Oh, the joys and rich spiritual experiences of those who win souls. As I look back across the fifty-five years of my little life, I remember a happy home, though it was in a log house, on the frontiers of Texas, the joy of a gloriously good father and mother, and remember the joys of my own happy home through now twenty-five years with my blessed companion and our six children... As I look back over the years of study and recount the intellectual joy and comradeship of my friend and remember the social joys of my heart when I have been permitted by this same Saviour to bring to Him scarlet women, infidels, atheists, gamblers, murderers, whoremongers, moralists, and all sorts, thousands and thousands of them. There is no joy like the joy of soulwinning."

When is the last time you shared the good news of the Gospel? Have you given anyone a Gospel tract recently? Have you shared your testimony with someone in your family, at your workplace, or in your neighborhood? God promises that if we go with His message of salvation and a broken heart for the lost, we will have fruit. And the joy that accompanies that fruit is unparalleled by any earthly happiness we could hope to attain.

1 Samuel 30–31 // Luke 13:23–35

April 1944

The Greatest War

"I looked on my right hand, and beheld, but there was no man that would know me: refuge failed me; no man cared for my soul."—**Psalm 142:4**

When we hear of wars or even the rumors of war, we are troubled and often overwhelmed with the loss of life and devastation it brings. We are willing to put all of our resources and effort into finding the cause and terminating the conflict. Often, however, we are occupied with the strife between nations and peoples while at the same time overlooking an even greater war—the war for the soul.

John R. Rice got off the train in Buffalo, New York, in April of 1944 to conduct citywide evangelistic meetings. America was in the middle of the largest war in world history, but John R. Rice knew what America needed. More important than the battle for world domination, was whether people would spend eternity in Heaven or Hell. As World War II tore apart Europe, Rice knew that America needed the Gospel and the power of God to defeat the ultimate enemy. At the end of the evangelistic crusade, 997 people made a public profession of salvation. Just over a year later, America would win the war in Europe, and many of her soldiers would return home to hear the Gospel themselves.

The greatest war may be raging in the cubicle next to you at work in the soul of your co-worker. It may be in one of your children or grandchildren who are wrestling with salvation. Our cities are being ravished by sin and are headed to eternal destruction. Failure to engage in this conflict is as horrible as turning a deaf ear to the cries of those whose lives are threatened by chemical or nuclear war.

Will you enlist today to fight for the souls of men? Will you lift your eyes above the earthly battlefields and see the unseen war that rages in the hearts of men and women all around us?

April 19, 1908

Multitudes and Individuals Need Christ

"Then Philip went down to the city of Samaria, and preached Christ unto them.... And the eunuch answered Philip, and said, I pray thee, of whom speaketh the prophet this? of himself, or some other man? Then Philip opened his mouth, and began at the same scripture, and preached unto him Jesus."—**Acts 8:5,34–35**

J. Wilbur Chapman and Charles Alexander prayed before their last meeting in Philadelphia on the evening of April 19, 1908. This was their first campaign together with Chapman preaching and Alexander leading the singing. After the meeting, they received the results: a total of 1,470,000 attended and approximately 8,000 were saved. But Chapman and Alexander's focus was not on the crowd as much as the individual person. One night during the revival, Alexander asked if anyone would stand and sing "He Will Hold Me Fast," to which an African-American man stood and sang the song beautifully. Alexander asked, "Are you a Christian?" To which the man replied, "Yes, sir!" Alexander exclaimed, "We hardly need to ask that, do we? Everybody could tell by his face that he was singing from his heart." The man shouted out, "And my name's Alexander too!" Charles was so thrilled to meet the man, he asked him to come up to the platform and sing an "Alexander duet," after which the man prayed for the meeting.

When the campaign was over, Chapman and Alexander heard the conclusion of the story. A woman was walking by the hall that night ready to take her life. She decided to come into the building to "have one more bit of fun before taking the fatal step," not knowing a service was being conducted. But when she heard the hymn, "He Will Hold Me Fast," saw the men singing together, and heard them pray, "she resolved to give her heart to God, and with His help to face the struggle of life with new courage." Such was the impact of the Chapman-Alexander meetings on the multitudes and on the individual.

Jesus preached to the multitudes by the Sea of Galilee but also to the woman at the well, Nicodemus, and the thief on the cross. The soul of one and the souls of a city are both important to God and should be to us.

April 19, 1854

Are You Thirsty?

"For I will pour water upon him that is thirsty, and floods upon the dry ground...."
—Isaiah 44:3

God said through the prophet Jeremiah, "And ye shall seek me, and find me when ye shall search for me with all your heart" (Jeremiah 29:13). God never hides from the thirsty soul. He is not far from any one of us if we are looking for Him.

The young Dwight Lyman Moody could not imagine the amount of books that would be at his fingertips if he joined the Young Men's Christian Association. He wrote to his brother about his desire to join the YMCA to have access to the seemingly unlimited amount of books. He wrote, "Then I shall have a place to go to when I want, and I can have all the books I want to read and only have to pay a dollar a year." Moody would spend hours pouring over the books in the YMCA library. There is no doubt what he read softened his heart and prepared him for a soulwinning visit from a faithful Sunday school teacher named Edward Kimball almost a year later.

Are you willing to search the Scriptures? "My son, if thou wilt receive my words, and hide my commandments with thee; So that thou incline thine ear unto wisdom, and apply thine heart to understanding; Yea, if thou criest after knowledge, and liftest up thy voice for understanding; If thou seekest her as silver, and searchest for her as for hid treasures; Then shalt thou understand the fear of the LORD, and find the knowledge of God" (Proverbs 2:1–5).

The Bible contains all things that pertain to life and godliness. What a resource of knowledge, wisdom, and understanding at our fingertips! Will you "give attendance to reading, to exhortation, to doctrine" (1 Timothy 4:13)? God loves to reveal Himself to us every day through the pages of His Word.

April 20, 1718

God Never Leaves Us or Forsakes Us

"When thou passest through the waters, I will be with thee; and through the rivers, they shall not overflow thee: when thou walkest through the fire, thou shalt not be burned; neither shall the flame kindle upon thee."—**Isaiah 43:2**

David Brainerd, the sacrificial missionary to the American Indians, was born April 20, 1718 in Haddam, Connecticut, to Hezekiah and Dorothy Brainerd. David grew up with nine siblings and at a young age lost his father. Five years later his mother also died and David was left orphaned at the age of fourteen. He no doubt wrestled with what his future would hold. He would later attend Yale, but was kicked out for criticizing a professor.

David would soon develop a great burden for the mysterious American Indian and would be used of God to inspire millions of future missionaries. One incident sealed in his heart a burden for the Native Americans. F.W. Boreham described the moment when the Indians were watching Brainerd, ready to kill him: "But when the braves drew closer to Brainerd's tent, they saw the paleface on his knees. And as he prayed, suddenly a rattlesnake slipped to his side, lifted up its ugly head to strike. Flicked its forked tongue almost in his face, and then without any apparent reason, glided swiftly away into the brushwood. 'The Great Spirit is with the paleface!' the Indians said; and thus they accorded him a prophet's welcome."

What do you face today that causes you to worry or fear? Have friends or family forsaken you? Have your resources run out? Are you unsure what the future holds? "Be careful for nothing; but in every thing by prayer and supplication with thanksgiving let your requests be made known unto God. And the peace of God, which passeth all understanding, shall keep your hearts and minds through Christ Jesus" (Philippians 4:6–7). David Brainerd only lived to the age of twenty-nine, but God was with him every step of the way, and his short life still impacts ours today!

April 21, 1855

A Radical Change

"...one thing I know, that, whereas I was blind, now I see."—**John 9:25b**

Mr. Edward Kimball, a faithful Sunday school teacher, was burdened for the young boys in his class. He determined that he would visit each of them and ask them if they were saved. On April 21, 1855, Kimball made his way to the address of a shoe cobbler shop where one of his pupils worked. Mr. Kimball knocked on the door where a young Dwight Moody was finishing his work for the day. Through the conversation, Mr. Kimball told him, "I want to tell you how much Christ loves you." That day was a turning point for Dwight. His life would never be the same after he accepted Christ as his Saviour. Moody later said, "I was in a new world. The birds sang sweeter, the sun shone brighter. I'd never known such peace." He would devote the rest of his life to sharing that peace with the world. It is estimated that over 100 million people sat in one of Moody's services and heard him preach that same Gospel message of peace.

Salvation is a radical change that takes place the moment a person places their faith in Jesus Christ as Saviour. At that moment everything changes—your heart, your life, your eternity! "Therefore if any man be in Christ, he is a new creature: old things are passed away; behold, all things are become new" (2 Corinthians 5:17). Have you been born again? Have you experienced salvation? Have you passed from death unto life? Do you know that your sins are forgiven and you have eternal life? "And this is the record, that God hath given to us eternal life, and this life is in his Son. He that hath the Son hath life; and he that hath not the Son of God hath not life. These things have I written unto you that believe on the name of the Son of God; that ye may know that ye have eternal life, and that ye may believe on the name of the Son of God" (1 John 5:11–13).

If you never have, God would love to hear you confess that you are a sinner and ask the Lord Jesus Christ to be your Saviour. When you do, God promises, "For whosoever shall call upon the name of the Lord shall be saved" (Romans 10:13). Everything will change when you do!

April 20, 1909

God Blesses Faith

"And Jesus said unto them, Because of your unbelief: for verily I say unto you, If ye have faith as a grain of mustard seed, ye shall say unto this mountain, Remove hence to yonder place; and it shall remove; and nothing shall be impossible unto you."—**Matthew 17:20**

Noon was coming soon, the time of the first prayer meeting in Melbourne, Australia. J. Wilbur Chapman and Charles Alexander had crossed the Pacific Ocean in hope of sharing the Gospel with thousands more around the world. God had blessed their revival work in America, but now God had led them to take a tour around the world with the Gospel message. They prayed, sacrificed, and stepped out by faith. As the hall opened for the first time, Chapman and Alexander had no idea what the response would be to their arrival. God honored their faith as four thousand businessmen came into the hall for that first noon prayer meeting. And that was just the beginning of what God was about to do. During the last service in Melbourne, Chapman and Alexander would see two thousand conversions. At each stop as they circled the globe, Chapman and Alexander would see thousands upon thousands come to Christ as Saviour.

"...Nevertheless when the Son of man cometh, shall he find faith on the earth" (Luke 18:8)? These were the words of Jesus Himself. He wondered if any would walk by faith. If Jesus returned to earth today, would He find you living by faith or walking by sight? No doubt, revival often tarries and evangelistic fires burn low because God's people are not exercising faith in a God who can do beyond what we can ask or think.

We might say, "But I just don't see anything in this world today that would make me think God can bring about those kinds of results in our day." But remember: "Faith is the substance of things hoped for, the evidence of things not seen" (Hebrews 11:1). We may not *see* it, but faith never relies on what it can see. Faith focuses on the One who can do far more than we can see.

April 21, 1826

Holy Spirit Power

"Then he answered and spake unto me, saying, This is the word of the LORD unto Zerubbabel, saying, Not by might, nor by power, but by my spirit, saith the LORD of hosts."—**Zechariah 4:6**

How tempting it is in the Lord's work to rely upon our own power rather than God's. We are satisfied with what we have the ability to do rather than experiencing the mighty hand of God. When we are trusting ourselves we are actually inviting the resistance of God! "Thus saith the LORD; Cursed be the man that trusteth in man, and maketh flesh his arm, and whose heart departeth from the LORD" (Jeremiah 17:5). Not a whole lot can happen when we are under God's curse rather than His blessing!

Revival comes when we come to the end of ourselves, stop trusting ourselves, and begin again to seek the Lord and rely upon His power to change hearts and lives. As long as we are satisfied with the results that we can manufacture and manipulate, God will stand by and watch us fail. When we recognize our deficiency and beg God to step in and take over, revival will occur.

Charles Finney preached fearlessly in Rome, New York. As Finney conducted the services, a press reporter watched the entire service with curiosity and wonderment. He could not believe what he was seeing. No doubt the Spirit of God worked in his life as well. He would later write in his newspaper: "Mr. Finney came to help the pastor...After he came, the Spirit of God was shed down with such power that nothing seemed able to resist it...The revival is remarkable for its solemnity and deep heart-searching."

Nothing could resist it! Man can resist man, but no man can win against the power of God. In whatever we attempt to do today for the Lord, let's be certain that we step aside and allow His power to work. He may choose to use us, but as the psalmist states, "God hath spoken once; twice have I heard this; that power belongeth unto God" (Psalm 62:11).

April 21, 1783

God Uses the Foolish to Confound the Wise

"But God hath chosen the foolish things of the world to confound the wise; and God hath chosen the weak things of the world to confound the things which are mighty."—**1 Corinthians 1:27**

Had we lived in some of the different time periods of Bible history, we more than likely would not have chosen the same individuals that God did to accomplish His work. Would we have chosen Moses? A shepherd boy named David? Would Jonah have been our choice to preach to Nineveh? Would we have placed fishermen or a tax collector in our inner circle of leadership? God often defies human logic and reasoning so "that no flesh should glory in his presence" (1 Corinthians 1:29).

Many great evangelists had been born in Europe, Asia, and Africa throughout church history, but God was beginning to shift the focus of history to a distant land filled with mysterious sights and plentiful resources. A New World was on the horizon, and God would use that world to usher in a country founded on His principles, and in turn produce some of the greatest revivals the world would ever see. On the first page of chapter one of God's work in America was the birth of Asahel Nettleton. Nettleton may not be a household name to most, but it is said that he was the first native-born American Evangelist. Born in late April of 1783 in Connecticut, Nettleton had a tender heart for the things of God as a young boy. God would use Nettleton as a mighty preacher during the Second Great Awakening.

Are you resisting God's plan for your life because you feel less qualified or prepared than someone else? Are you sitting on the sidelines because of a supposed weakness or deficiency? No one is inadequate in the hand of God. It is through those weaknesses that God shows His strength. Your deficiency may be the thing that God will use to demonstrate His miraculous revival working power. Yield to Him today. Watch him take your "five loaves and two small fishes" and feed the multitudes with plenty left over!

April 25, 1887

Whatever It Takes

"And when they could not come nigh unto him for the press, they uncovered the roof where he was: and when they had broken it up, they let down the bed wherein the sick of the palsy lay."—**Mark 2:4**

Getting this sick man in Mark 2 to Jesus was a difficult task. The men in the story who are unknown to us by name, knew that this poor man had but one hope—Jesus! But he was bedridden, and Jesus was busy with the crowds that thronged Him. So they decided to pick up his bed and carry Him to the Lord. But alas, this too was impossible because the house where Jesus preached was packed to capacity. Not to be denied, these men climbed up on the roof and with passion mixed with ingenuity, cut a hole in the tiles and let down the bed upon which the sick man lay—right in the lap of the One who could do something about the problem.

Charles Fuller of the Old-Fashioned Revival Hour and Fuller Theological Seminary was born in Los Angeles on April 25, in 1887. He would use the relatively new invention of radio to reach millions with the Old-Fashioned Revival Hour program with the American Broadcasting Company. Broadcasting from a Hollywood sound stage and later an auditorium in Long Beach, Charles Fuller would not only influence the Los Angeles area for Christ in his generation, but also the entire country.

Have we exercised any creativity in getting the Gospel to lost people today? Some will come to preaching services if we ask them. Some might need a ride to church. Others might come if we fed them a meal first or after the service. Still others might read a book that explains the plan of salvation, or watch a video, or listen to a live-streamed service. Our neighbors might listen to us if we shoveled their snow or raked their leaves. A complete stranger might take that tract we offer if we bought them a cup of coffee first. Don't stop giving the Gospel just because one particular method didn't work. Let's do whatever it takes!

April 1902

Music Can Open Hearts to the Gospel

"Speaking to yourselves in psalms and hymns and spiritual songs, singing and making melody in your heart to the Lord;"—**Ephesians 5:19**

God was using both R.A. Torrey and Charles Alexander in evangelistic work. In April of 1902, the two men met in Melbourne, Australia, and began praying about combining their efforts together in order to reach more souls for Christ. Torrey was a powerful preacher and many were being converted in his crusades. Alexander had an amazing ability to prepare the hearts of the listener to Torrey's message through music.

Torrey described Charles Alexander's ministry: "'He used his gifts in such a way that he could set all sorts of people singing the praises of Jesus—peers and paupers, members of Parliament and members of baseball teams. University students and prisoners in the penitentiaries, grey-haired doctors of divinity and golden-haired children, Jews and Gentiles, Protestants and Roman Catholics, Buddhists and Mahommedans.' 'What feature of the musical side of the revival gives you the keenest delight?' he was once asked. Much as he loved music in itself, and the joy of producing it, his reply was, 'I should soon tire of this side of the work if it were not for the soul-saving part of it.'"

Music prepares the heart for revival and when revival comes, people love to sing. These two ministries always work hand in hand when God is orchestrating revival. Music is not the "exciting" part and the preaching "boring" or vice versa. As Alexander knew, when God is at work in revival, there is a power in the music that leads people to Christ just as the preached Word does. "Let the word of Christ dwell in you richly in all wisdom; teaching and admonishing one another in psalms and hymns and spiritual songs, singing with grace in your hearts to the Lord" (Colossians 3:16). How our congregational singing might change if we knew God could use our voices in music to draw the hearts of those around us to the Saviour.

April 27, 1913

Not for Sale

"But Peter said unto him, Thy money perish with thee, because thou hast thought that the gift of God may be purchased with money."—**Acts 8:20**

The power of God cannot be bought or sold. In the book of Acts, Simon thought that he could purchase power that would enable him to do the same miracles the apostles were doing. While most things in life work that way, Heaven operates completely different. God's anointing rests on those who are humbly surrendered in complete obedience to Him, not because they have large bank accounts.

Evangelist Billy Sunday saw amazing results in his revival crusades and wonderful things were sometimes written about him. The following appeared in the South Bend Tribune on April 27, 1913: "If the Creator had seen fit to make fifty Billy Sundays simultaneously instead of but one, I am firmly of the opinion that the army of Christianity would shortly become the most formidable organization the world has ever known. That number of evangelists of the Billy Sunday type with his organization behind them could revolutionize the world big as it is. The baseball evangelist is undoubtedly the most remarkable preacher of his age and the whole truth in regard to the effective work he is doing never has, and probably never will be known."

Several attempts were made by people in the entertainment business, like P.T. Barnum, to buy the services of Billy Sunday. He was once offered a million dollars by a Hollywood film company to make a movie about his life and preaching style. Sunday said, "I wouldn't sell the Gospel for all the money in the world!"

Would you like to have the power of God? You don't need a seven figure bank account. "If ye then, being evil, know how to give good gifts unto your children: how much more shall your heavenly Father give the Holy Spirit to them that ask him?" (Luke 11:13).

 1 Kings 1–2 // Luke 19:28–48

April 28, 1911

Will Somebody Pray?

"And he saw that there was no man, and wondered that there was no intercessor."
—Isaiah 59:16a

J. Wilbur Chapman's crusade in Shrewberry, England, was about to conclude. Chapman's mind reminisced to the early days of the campaign. The attendance was small and barren. But one night, John Hyde, the missionary who had been called, "Praying Hyde," "The Man Who Never Sleeps," and "the Apostle of Prayer," attended Chapman's meeting. Hyde's biographer Basil Miller would say about him: "Walking on such anointed ground...for thirty days and nights, or ten days on end, or remain on his knees for thirty-six hours without moving...when he returned to the field preaching from such seasons...he was thus possessed of a spiritual power which opened the dark hearts of India to his message."

Hyde came to the fifty-two-year-old Chapman's room that night and asked to pray with him for the meetings. As Chapman listened to Hyde's prayers, his heart burned within him. He jumped up from his knees and shouted, "Now I finally know what prayer is!" The meetings would bear much fruit as the result of the missionary's prayers. The forty-six-year old missionary would enter Heaven the next year with much fruit to his account because he knew the secret to it all—prayer!

Do we believe that God answers prayer? Do we believe the promises of God's Word regarding prayer? "And this is the confidence that we have in him, that, if we ask any thing according to his will, he heareth us: And if we know that he hear us, whatsoever we ask, we know that we have the petitions that we desired of him" (1 John 5:14–15).

So why don't we pray? Does revival tarry today because we do not? James 4:2 tells us, "...ye have not, because ye ask not." Hyde was identified as "Praying" Hyde. Would anyone place that verb in front of our names?

April 28, 1906

Fast Food Revivals

"These all continued with one accord in prayer and supplication, with the women, and Mary the mother of Jesus, and with his brethren."—**Acts 1:14**

Are we willing to stop the busyness of our lives long enough to have revival? Biblically and historically, revivals have come when God's people allow God to prepare their hearts for His supernatural outpouring of blessing. The early church in Jerusalem gathered in prayer and fasting for the promise of God's Holy Spirit power. Their normal schedule was interrupted; plans were put on hold; nothing was more important than for God to work.

Due to our fast-paced lives today we want to compress and compact revival into a three or four day set of services. We place revival on "our" calendar and, in a sense, demand God does something in those days. When the meetings end, we are glad the sacrifice of time and effort has ended and we can get back to normal. How foolish it would be for a soon-to-be mother to say, "I'm going to give four weeks of my life for this pregnancy—nothing more!" What if a parent said, "I'll devote one year to training my child—that's it." How about the owner of a business who only gives three hours a week to his responsibilities?

Revivals in the past were not one day or one week wonders. On this day in 1906, a Billy Sunday meeting commenced that went for five weeks with the tabernacle filled to its six-thousand seat capacity each night. A choir of five hundred voices faithfully practiced and sang for thirty-five consecutive nights! Our response to that is often, "things have changed—our schedules don't allow that anymore." Indeed, things have changed. True revival like those in the early 1900s is unheard of.

Revival doesn't come through a fast-food window or out of a microwave oven. Take time for God and His revival work in your heart today.

Spring 1892

God or Money

"No man can serve two masters: for either he will hate the one, and love the other; or else he will hold to the one, and despise the other. Ye cannot serve God and mammon."—**Matthew 6:24**

Billy Sunday hung up the phone. He had a huge decision to make. He had given the National League his resignation back in March, but in response they had just offered him a new five thousand dollar contract to play baseball in front of thousands of people. Earlier he had told the Lord that if he had a chance to get out of his baseball contract, he would do so and serve the Lord. The YMCA in Chicago was offering him eighty-three dollars a month to be the Assistant Secretary. A glamorous opportunity versus a lowly assistant position; a chance to be paid a tremendous salary verses a paycheck that would barely make ends meet; fame and fortune verses Christ and His reproach. God had answered his prayer. But the lure of another contract and the fame that would come with it was difficult to refuse.

Sunday would confess later, "I didn't eat for two days and I couldn't sleep. I saw $5,000 everywhere I looked." But his loving wife Nell would give him direction: "There is nothing to consider; you promised God to quit." The next day, Billy Sunday turned his back on the baseball path and entered the path of God's will. The world can be thankful that Sunday chose the latter of the two choices. He spent three years as "Assistant Secretary" at the YMCA, caring for the poor and preaching to the lowly. These years would become the formative years of Sunday's life. Little did he understand the ultimate plan God had for his life, but he knew that God would bless his obedience.

Who will we serve today? The temporal things look really important in the temporal, but in the eternal, the temporal will mean absolutely nothing. The choice isn't that difficult when you consider the promise that comes with it: "But seek ye first the kingdom of God, and his righteousness; and all these things shall be added unto you" (Matthew 6:33).

MAY

May 1, 1893

What Does It Take to Stop You?

"Whatsoever thy hand findeth to do, do it with thy might; for there is no work, nor device, nor knowledge, nor wisdom, in the grave, whither thou goest."
—**Ecclesiastes 9:10**

On May 1, 1893, Dwight Lyman Moody was preparing to leave London for the final time. Before his departure, he called upon a celebrated physician to give him a checkup before the voyage to America. Upon examination, the doctor informed Moody that his heart was weakening. He suggested that he slow down, travel less, and not preach so often. As Moody went home that night, he thought that he would take the physician's advice.

Half way across the Atlantic Ocean on the steamer Spree, it began to sink. Moody thought for sure that his work was finished and that not only would he slow down, he was quite sure he would never preach again! Moody later recalled: "On that dark night, the first night of the accident, I made a vow that if God would spare my life and bring me back to America, I would come to Chicago, and at the World's Fair preach the Gospel with all the power that He would give me." God spared his life that night and despite the warnings from his doctor, he determined to organize a great revival when the World's Fair came to his home town of Chicago. During that six-month revival campaign in 1893, Moody prayed that God would use him in ways that He had never before. The fifty-three-year-old Moody still longed for God to use him. Many would consider the World's Fair Campaign of 1893 the greatest of Moody's lifetime.

While we must be good stewards of all that God gives us, including our health, may we never lose our burden to serve the Lord with all that we have. "Whosoever will come after me, let him deny himself, and take up his cross, and follow me. For whosoever will save his life shall lose it; but whosoever shall lose his life for my sake and the gospel's, the same shall save it" (Mark 8:34b–35).

1 Kings 10–11 // Luke 21:20–38

May 2, 1992

A Big Day

"Then they that gladly received his word were baptized: and the same day there were added unto them about three thousand souls. And they continued stedfastly in the apostles' doctrine and fellowship, and in breaking of bread, and in prayers."
—Acts 2:41–42

Can big days of evangelism take place today like they did on days like Pentecost in the Bible? Before we say no, have we ever prayed for a day like that? Has our church ever worked to get as many people under the sound of the Gospel as possible? If three thousand people wanted to get saved, would there be enough personal workers to show them how? Would we be prepared to baptize them?

On May 2, 1992, Dr. Curtis Hutson was asked to preach for an evangelistic day at the First Baptist Church of Hammond, Indiana. The church labored for weeks in advance to get as many as possible in the Chicagoland area under the sound of the Gospel that day. In the morning service where Dr. Hutson preached, 1,035 people came forward. The baptism service took place afterward, and people were still being baptized when Hutson had to leave to go to his next meeting. Services were held all across Chicago and northern Indiana with 36,902 total people attending. Throughout the services, 4,720 people were shown the plan of salvation at the altar and trusted Christ.

We do not serve a small God. He is "...not willing that any should perish, but that all should come to repentance" (2 Peter 3:9). He desires for all men be saved and come to the knowledge of the truth. Even if your church is not at this moment preparing for a big Sunday, who could you invite to hear the Gospel this Sunday? Have you prayed for souls to be saved through the ministry of your local church? When is the last time you knocked on someone's door and invited them to church or at least read a Gospel tract? What God did in the first century, He can do in the twenty-first century.

May 3, 1850

Walking with God Requires the First Step

"Therefore we are buried with him by baptism into death: that like as Christ was raised up from the dead by the glory of the Father, even so we also should walk in newness of life."—**Romans 6:4**

The waters of baptism do not save us from our sin. "…the blood of Jesus Christ his Son cleanseth us from all sin" (1 John 1:7). Baptism is a picture of the Gospel that saves us—the death, burial, and resurrection of Jesus Christ. It is the first step that God commands us to take after we are saved. "Repent, and be baptized every one of you…" (Acts 2:38b). "Everyone of you" doesn't leave "anyone of us" out! This simple step of obedience opens the door of God's blessing and further leading in our lives. It is hard to steer a parked car, but once it gets moving, it is much easier to turn that car in the direction it needs to go. When we make the "move" to be baptized, God begins to steer our lives in an amazing way.

A sixteen-year-old was baptized in 1850 in the River Lark at Isleham, England. No one gave a second thought to the boy getting baptized, but God had a tremendous future in store for this surrendered teenager. This teenage boy would later be known as the "Prince of Preachers." Charles Haddon Spurgeon would quickly become a Sunday school teacher and would preach his first sermon in the coming winter and go on to pastor the largest Baptist church in England with over 5,500 members. He would later preach of the ordinance of baptism, "The baptism of believers, we believe to be a reasonable, scriptural, and profitable service, calculated to strengthen and perpetuate every right feeling and conduct."

Have you taken this important step? You can't walk with God until you do. It may seem a little scary and friends and family may not understand, but the blessing of God is promised to those who follow the Lord in obedience. When God begins to bless and use you like he did Spurgeon, you will rejoice in every step the Lord asks you to take. Don't delay—"obedience is the very best way to show that you believe!"

May 4, 1856

Don't Underestimate God

"And the publican, standing afar off, would not lift up so much as his eyes unto heaven, but smote upon his breast, saying, God be merciful to me a sinner."
—Luke 18:13

There are some who believe they are too great of a sinner for God to save them. Others who are saved believe that they do not possess what it takes to be used by God. We look at ourselves and wonder why the God of Heaven would be interested in us. "In this was manifested the love of God toward us, because that God sent his only begotten Son into the world, that we might live through him. Herein is love, not that we loved God, but that he loved us, and sent his Son to be the propitiation for our sins" (1 John 4:9–10).

When D. L. Moody joined the church in May of 1856, his Sunday School teacher, Edward Kimball, had this to say about this young convert: "I can truly say, and in saying it I magnify the infinite grace of God as bestowed upon him, that I have seen few persons whose minds were spiritually darker than was his when he came into my Sunday School class; and I think that the committee of the Mount Vernon Church seldom met an applicant for membership more unlikely ever to become a Christian of clear and decided views of Gospel truth, still less to fill any extended sphere of public usefulness."

When Moody was saved and later joined the church, no one could envision what God could see. "Now unto him that is able to do exceeding abundantly above all that we ask or think, according to the power that worketh in us, Unto him be glory in the church by Christ Jesus throughout all ages, world without end. Amen" (Ephesians 3:20–21). Everyone around him doubted his "public usefulness," but God would use Moody to shake two continents with the Gospel of Christ. Don't underestimate what God wants to do with your life. He will save "whosoever" (Romans 10:13), and He will use all who surrender to Him (Romans 12:1–2).

1 Kings 16–18 // Luke 22:47–71

May 5, 1917

From the Gridiron to the Gospel

"But by the grace of God I am what I am: and his grace which was bestowed upon me was not in vain; but I laboured more abundantly than they all: yet not I, but the grace of God which was with me"—**1 Corinthians 15:10**

Joe Boyd was born May 5, 1917, in Jacksonville, Texas. Playing tackle for Texas A&M University, he was chosen by the Sporting News, Collier's Weekly magazine, the New York Sun, Boy's Life magazine, and the Collegiate Writers as a first-team player on the 1939 College Football All-America Team. The Aggies would win the National Championship that year, and Joe would be drafted by the Washington Redskins of the National Football League. Because the salary of a professional football player wasn't much in those days ($8,000 per year), he took a job instead at Todd Shipyards in Houston, Texas, in the accounting department.

Although Dr. Boyd was saved as a boy, he had not surrendered his life to Christ until one day a hurricane shook the city of Houston. A short time later, while listening to Evangelist B. B. Crimm preach on soulwinning, Boyd gave his life completely to Christ. The next day God allowed him to win a cleaning lady to Christ in the office building where he worked. He would hit the Gospel trail from there winning thousands to Christ personally and in his revival campaigns until God took him home on June 1, 2009. Along with other books he had written, his most popular was a book of sermons titled *From the Gridiron to the Gospel.* He loved sharing his testimony of what Christ had done for him.

You may never wear a football championship ring like Joe Boyd, but your testimony is powerful. The grace of God that changed your life can change someone else's. When we truly understand what Christ has done for us, it is not difficult to set aside our aspirations and dreams to labor in the harvest fields reaching others with that same grace.

May 6, 1832

The Greatest Desire

"Brethren, my heart's desire and prayer to God for Israel is, that they might be saved."—**Romans 10:1**

Most people today seem to have a "bucket list" of things they want to do or accomplish before their life is over. Meeting a famous person, visiting a far off place, doing some crazy feat, or obtaining some valuable possession would only scratch the surface of people's desires. The Apostle Paul had a great desire that mirrored that of His Saviour—for people to be saved. Second Peter 3:9 explains, "The Lord is not slack concerning his promise, as some men count slackness; but is longsuffering to us-ward, not willing that any should perish, but that all should come to repentance."

Charles Finney's heart was burdened for the city of New York. He had travelled up and down the state of New York to preach and longed to start a great work in the largest city in America. On this day in 1832, Finney started the work God had laid on his heart. He called it the Chatham Street Chapel. In the first seventy days, between 1,500 and 2,500 people attended the chapel, and a lighthouse in New York City had begun.

Did you know that God grants the desires of our hearts when they are born of Him and not ourselves? "Delight thyself also in the LORD; and he shall give thee the desires of thine heart" (Psalm 37:4). Are you delighting in the Lord today? That's the key. God doesn't give us everything and anything we want, but when our hearts are in tune with His, the desires that He puts there are on His bucket list as well as our own. "And this is the confidence that we have in him, that, if we ask any thing according to his will, he heareth us: And if we know that he hear us, whatsoever we ask, we know that we have the petitions that we desired of him" (1 John 5:14–15).

Align your heart with your Saviour today and then dream big! Make it your desire to win friends and family members to Christ or see some new ministry started in your church. "I am the LORD thy God, which brought thee out of the land of Egypt: open thy mouth wide, and I will fill it" (Psalm 81:10).

May 7, 1893

Here Am I, Send Me

"Also I heard the voice of the Lord, saying, Whom shall I send, and who will go for us? Then said I, Here am I; send me."—**Isaiah 6:8**

Sitting on the Mount of Olives in the Holy Land, D. L. Moody thought on the city over which Jesus had wept. The Lord's compassion for the city of Jerusalem was undeniable. "And when he was come near, he beheld the city, and wept over it" (Luke 19:41). The thought of Christ's compassion for the city of Jerusalem brought tears to Moody's eyes. He thought of the vast city of Chicago where he was privileged to pastor. "He saw the gilded gambling halls and the dingy bar rooms, the parlors of shame and the miserable dives, the sacrilegious concert rooms and the vulgar variety shows, alike desecrating the day of rest. He saw, as few men see it, the chasm which divided the classes, and he knew that even with a church on every block in Chicago there would still be a vast unchurched population, a city in a city going down to death.... The closed church doors and the open saloons, the darkened house of God and the brilliantly lighted devil's den burdened his soul."

For the thirteen months following his trip to Israel, he worked with one great object in view. Moody's "opportunity of the century," the World's Columbian Exposition officially began on May 7, 1893. Moody had been holding services and preparing for the start of the Fair for a week. He held 125 Sunday services throughout this campaign, many in different languages, with thousands saved. By the end of the campaign, there were exactly 1,933,210 people who had heard the Gospel of Jesus Christ. Moody would not squander this "opportunity of the century" to share the Gospel with people from all across the world.

Has God placed an opportunity before you? Has He given you a burden for your co-workers, the neighbors on your street, or a town without a church? Have you placed that burden before the Lord, and said like Isaiah of old, "Here am I; send me?" Don't miss your opportunity to be used by God!

May 4, 1890

Rejoice When God Uses Others

"And grieve not the holy Spirit of God, whereby ye are sealed unto the day of redemption. Let all bitterness, and wrath, and anger, and clamour, and evil speaking, be put away from you, with all malice: And be ye kind one to another, tenderhearted, forgiving one another, even as God for Christ's sake hath forgiven you."—**Ephesians 4:30–32**

After not letting Charles Finney speak at his church, the pastor of First Church in Rochester, J. H. McIlvaine, wrote a letter of deep regret. He was disappointed that he had been caught up in the discord and gossip of jealous preachers against Finney. The letter written in 1890, read as follows: "In answer to your note of March 29th inquiring for particulars of Mr. Finney's labors in Rochester while I was there, I am happy to say that I regard them as connected with the greatest work of grace I have ever seen in any of the churches. I was not in sympathy with it at the time, and would not admit Mr. Finney into the pulpit of the First Church, of which I was then pastor; but I have long been convinced that I was totally wrong, and have since taken occasion to say so to the church itself. During the revival Rochester was rocked to its foundations. Great numbers of hopeful converts were added to all the churches during his labors. You are at liberty to make what use of these statements you please."

Are you jealous that God is using someone else in ways He hasn't used you? Do you find yourself becoming critical of that person and seeking ways to discredit them? Have you spoken to others in a gossiping manner about them? These actions grieve the Holy Spirit and bring revival to a halt. In 1 Corinthians 12, Paul explains that God gifts and uses people differently. He closes the chapter by telling us the best gift is love and then exhorts us to practice it: "Charity suffereth long, and is kind; charity envieth not; charity vaunteth not itself, is not puffed up. Doth not behave itself unseemly, seeketh not her own, is not easily provoked, thinketh no evil; Rejoiceth not in iniquity, but rejoiceth in the truth; Beareth all things, believeth all things, hopeth all things, endureth all things" (1 Corinthians 13:4–7).

May 10, 1885

Man's Resistance Turns into God's Redemption

"And he fell to the earth, and heard a voice saying unto him, Saul, Saul, why persecutest thou me? And he said, Who art thou, Lord? And the Lord said, I am Jesus whom thou persecutest: it is hard for thee to kick against the pricks."
—Acts 9:4–5

Saul of Tarsus was persecuting those who were following Jesus Christ. Throwing many into prison, harassing others, and killing some, Saul was determined to wipe out Christianity. But shortly after the stoning of Stephen in Acts 7, God made a personal visit to Saul. That day, Saul, a murderer, was gloriously saved! His life changed and by chapter 17 in Acts, he and a few others had "turned the world upside down" for Christ.

A tough riverboat captain named Thomas Green Ryman came to hear Evangelist Sam Jones preach on May 10, 1885. He came for one reason—to call out and heckle the preacher. But as he listened to the preaching, the Holy Spirit began to work in his heart. Sam Jones preached the Gospel fearlessly, and during the invitation, Thomas Ryman came forward and was saved. After the service, the harsh, sturdy captain approached Jones. He explained what God had done in his heart during the service and told Jones that he wanted to build a tabernacle to hold revivals in Nashville, Tennessee. God had opened the door for many souls to hear the Gospel as a result of the rough riverboat captain's salvation.

Don't give up on those who seem to be impossible to reach. No one is too hard for the Lord to save. God can tender their hearts through your prayers and the circumstances that only He can bring into their lives. Keep speaking the truth in love to them and have faith to believe that God can miraculously save them just like He did Saul of Tarsus and a riverboat captain named Thomas Ryman.

May 10, 1894

Encourage Your Pastor

"And his armour-bearer said unto him, Do all that is in thine heart: turn thee; behold, I am with thee according to thy heart."—**1 Samuel 14:7**

T. Dewitt Talmage's church, the Brooklyn Tabernacle, took a chance to encourage their discouraged pastor, even though he had resigned. They decorated the church, invited officials, and celebrated his twenty-five years of faithfulness. Talmage stood and addressed the great crowd: "Dear Mr. Mayor and friends before me, and friends behind me, and friends all around me, and friends hovering over me, and the friends in this room and the adjoining rooms, and the friends indoors and out of doors—forever photographed upon my mind and heart is this scene of May 10, 1894. The lights, the flags, the decorations, the flowers, the music, the illumined faces will remain with me while earthly life lasts and be a cause of thanksgiving after I have passed into the great beyond. Tonight I think that the heavens above us are full of pure white blessings. My twenty-five years in Brooklyn have been happy years. I could not tell the story of disasters without telling the story of heroes and heroines, and around me in all these years have stood with men and women of whom the world was not worthy. These twenty-five years have been to me years of great happiness."

Did you know that your pastor has tough days too? He is human and subject to loneliness, discouragement, and heartache. Jonathan in 1 Samuel 14 is the only one in the army of Israel willing to fight the Philistines. His father, King Saul had given up. Many of the men were hiding in the caves out of fear. Jonathan experiences one of the most spectacular victories recorded in the Bible that day, and there was one—his armour bearer—who encouraged him to do all that was in his heart for God.

Will you be one who encourages your pastor today to stay in the battle? Will you support him with your prayers, kindness, time, and energy? Perhaps a note, email, or text from you would be the very thing he needs to stay in the battle for the Lord. Only eternity will reveal the spiritual battles won because you took time to encourage your spiritual leader.

May 11, 1826

Not Everyone Loves Revival

"Yea, and all that will live godly in Christ Jesus shall suffer persecution."
—2 Timothy 3:12

There are many promises in the Bible, most of which encourage and thrill us. The promise of salvation to all who will call upon the Lord; the promise that God's Word will endure forever; the promise that Jesus Christ is coming again; the promise of God's protective care at all times in our lives, are just a few of the wonderful truths that "are in him, yea and amen!"

Occasionally, however, we read a promise in the Bible that causes us to take a step back. The promise of persecution to those who live godly is one. We are assured that God will bless those who trust Him and serve Him by faith, but He makes sure that we also understand there will be those who oppose us.

Daniel Nash, one of the great prayer warriors of American history, writes a letter describing the opposition he and Evangelist Charles Finney were facing: "The work of God moves forward in power, in some places against dreadful opposition. Mr. Finney and I have been hanged and burned in effigy. We have frequently been disturbed in our religious meetings. Sometimes the opposition make a noise in the house of God; sometimes they gather round the house and stone it, and discharge guns. There is almost as much writing, intrigue, and lying, and reporting of lies, as there would be if we were on the eve of a presidential election. Oh, what a world! How much it hates the truth! But I think the work will go on."

Jesus reminded us of an important truth: "If the world hate you, ye know that it hated me before it hated you. If ye were of the world, the world would love his own: but because ye are not of the world, but I have chosen you out of the world, therefore the world hateth you" (John 15:18–19). Remember, they didn't hate Jesus because He was wrong—they hated Him because He was right. Stay on His side!

May 13, 1867

Now Is a Good Time for Revival

"Redeeming the time, because the days are evil."—**Ephesians 5:16**

Emma Moody, married just five years, was suffering terribly from asthma and doctors suggested that she spend four months away from Chicago to recover. D. L. Moody took this opportunity to travel to England with his wife for the first time and set up a meeting with two men whom he had never met but greatly admired—Charles Spurgeon and George Müller. While in London, Moody began noon-day prayer meetings as well, which was his practice everywhere he travelled. Even during a time of rest and recovery for his wife, Moody would never let an opportunity go to waste to plant or water the seeds of revival. No wonder men like these saw great revivals in their day.

The devil doesn't care what we do as long as we don't do it today. Satan is the master-mind behind procrastination. If we are spending time in God's Word each day and listening to good Bible preaching every week, we are well aware of things we could be doing for the cause of revival. Too often, we are a hearer of those things, but not a doer. "But be ye doers of the word, and not hearers only, deceiving your own selves" (James 1:22). A sure deception it is to think that God will send revival while we live in disobedience to His truth. A sure way to begin revival is to begin doing what we already know. "Therefore to him that knoweth to do good, and doeth it not, to him it is sin" (James 4:17).

In what area should you be redeeming your time today? What on your busy to-do list will have any significance in eternity? Perhaps the first thing we should do is rearrange the things we need to do in a way that will please the Lord and make a difference for revival and evangelism. Today is a great day for revival!

May 13, 1894

Trials in God's Work Are Not Unusual

"Beloved, think it not strange concerning the fiery trial which is to try you, as though some strange thing happened unto you: But rejoice, inasmuch as ye are partakers of Christ's sufferings; that, when his glory shall be revealed, ye may be glad also with exceeding joy."—**1 Peter 4:12–13**

May 13, 1894, was a day of great celebration as T. Dewitt Talmage's church concluded their "Silver Jubilee." Over six thousand people packed the auditorium to give glory to God for the great things He had done and to thank their pastor. Talmage preached with great eloquence, but during the handshaking time after the service, something caught Mrs. Talmage's eye. She noticed fire spurting out of the top of the organ while it was being played. They quickly ushered everyone outside to safety, but within a very short time, the church building was completely destroyed by fire. This wasn't the first time a trial had come. This was the third such fire to destroy the building in the church's brief twenty-five year history.

Trials are never pleasant on the surface, and we immediately ask God *why* when they come. God doesn't always offer an explanation, but He does command us to rejoice in the midst of them. Just as fire purifies gold or silver, so the fiery trials in our lives purify us and make us more valuable in God's service. Few have experienced trials like those of Job in the Old Testament. But in hindsight, he could look back and say, "But he knoweth the way that I take: when he hath tried me, I shall come forth as gold" (Job 23:10).

You may be facing difficult adversity in your life today, but don't quit. In Job 13:15, the tried and battered Job said, "Though he slay me, yet will I trust in him: but I will maintain mine own ways before him." Keep doing what you know is right. Maintain those things in your life that God has commanded you. This isn't the time to quit attending church or stop reading your Bible. In hard times we need those things more than ever! One day God's glory will be revealed, and you will be able to rejoice with exceeding joy.

May 1874

A Song from Above

"Yet the Lord *will command his lovingkindness in the daytime, and in the night his song shall be with me, and my prayer unto the God of my life."*
—Psalm 42:8

In route between Glasgow and Edinburgh, Ira Sankey read a little piece of poetry in the corner of a newspaper column that touched his heart. Later at the end of a service that night, D. L. Moody called on him to sing a hymn. Pricked in his heart, he grabbed the small piece of newspaper and sat down at the organ. "As calmly as if he had sung it a thousand times," he pressed an A flat chord and started to sing the poem to his own improvised melody. The song would be known as "The Ninety and Nine." After Sankey performed the song, Moody with tears in his eyes asked him, "Where did you find that hymn?"

> There were ninety and nine that safely lay, In the shelter of the fold;
> But one was out on the hills away, Far off from the gates of gold.
> Away on the mountains wild and bare; Away from the tender Shepherd's care.
>
> "Lord, Thou hast here Thy ninety and nine; Are they not enough for Thee?"
> But the Shepherd made answer: "This of Mine Has wandered away from Me.
> And although the road be rough and steep, I go to the desert to find My sheep."
>
> But none of the ransomed ever knew, How deep were the waters crossed;
> Nor how dark was the night the Lord passed through, Ere He found His sheep that was lost.
>
> And all through the mountains, thunder-riv'n, And up from the rocky steep,
> There arose a glad cry to the gate of heav'n, "Rejoice! I have found My sheep!"
> And the angels echoed around the throne, "Rejoice, for the Lord brings back His own!"

God made sure those words were found that day so that another lost and wandering sheep could hear it and be brought into the fold.

May 16, 1870

I Once Was Lost—But Now Am Found

"To open their eyes, and to turn them from darkness to light, and from the power of Satan unto God, that they may receive forgiveness of sins, and inheritance among them which are sanctified by faith that is in me."—**Acts 26:18**

Melvin Trotter was born in Orangeville, Illinois, on May 16, 1870, to a bartender who "drank as much as he served." Unfortunately, Mel would follow in his father's footsteps and ruin his life and family through this horrible addiction. Trotter's thirst was so great that even at the funeral of his little baby girl, he reached inside the casket, untied her shoes, and later that day sold them for another drink. With his life in shambles and no relief from his bondage, he planned to commit suicide. But on his way to the place he had chosen to take his life, he passed by the Pacific Garden Mission in Chicago. By the grace of God, he stumbled inside and heard the preacher tell of God's love for sinners. Falling under conviction, Mel Trotter was saved.

God didn't just save him from sin and Hell, but quenched his thirst for liquor. Mel soon returned to his home town of Grand Rapids, Michigan, and opened a rescue mission to reach people as he had once been. During his life time, Mel Trotter assisted in starting sixty-six rescue missions across the United States. "Moreover the law entered, that the offence might abound. But where sin abounded, grace did much more abound" (Romans 5:20).

Be sure to thank God for your salvation today. Maybe you were not in the bondage that Mel Trotter was when God found you, but it took Jesus dying on the cross for every one of us to be saved. We were born separated from God because of our sin, "But God commendeth his love toward us, in that, while we were yet sinners, Christ died for us" (Romans 5:8). In His wrath, God could have destroyed us, but in His mercy, He chose to redeem us. "For ye know the grace of our Lord Jesus Christ, that, though he was rich, yet for your sakes he became poor, that ye through his poverty might be rich" (2 Corinthians 8:9). Hallelujah!

May 16, 1844

I'll Go Where You Want Me to Go

"Now the Lord had said unto Abram, Get thee out of thy country, and from thy kindred, and from thy father's house, unto a land that I will shew thee."
—Genesis 12:1

It is no doubt a good thing that we cannot see into the future as God does. We often wish that we knew what was ahead in our lives, but God has designed our lives to be of faith rather than sight. Abram did not know where God was leading, but he was willing to follow His orders in simple obedience. Those steps of obedience turned into magnificent blessing.

The pioneers who lived by faith are not limited to the pages of Scripture. Asahel Nettleton died of tuberculosis on May 16, 1844. Dr. Fred Barlow in his book *Profiles of Evangelism* says of this great man of God, "[He] is practically an unknown name in America today. But he was the first of that illustrious crop of soul-winning worthies called evangelists who blazed trails with the pioneer settlers across trackless wilderness, who journeyed into the isolated and wayside communities, who shook cities and helped preserve the spiritual and moral life and soul of our nation." These early evangelists did not know where their next meal was coming from or the next attack. By faith they were willing to leave comfortable lifestyles and pulpits and take the Gospel into uncharted territory.

Is God leading you in some ways that humanly don't make sense? Is He asking you to follow Him in paths that are uncomfortable and perhaps even frightening? Whether it's witnessing to your boss at work, learning to tithe, or answering the call to full time ministry, God will often see if we are willing to simply trust Him. Early America was saturated with the Gospel by those who were willing to go wherever God said to go. Will you follow Him in that next step of obedience in your life?

May 1948

Asking for a Hard Thing

"And it came to pass, when they were gone over, that Elijah said unto Elisha, Ask what I shall do for thee, before I be taken away from thee. And Elisha said, I pray thee, let a double portion of thy spirit be upon me. And he said, Thou hast asked a hard thing: nevertheless, if thou see me when I am taken from thee, it shall be so unto thee...."—**2 Kings 2:9–10**

Does your prayer list have anything on it that only God can do? Are you praying for miracles? For impossible things? Did you know that God specializes in answering those kinds of prayers? "And Jesus looking upon them saith, "With men it is impossible, but not with God: for with God all things are possible" (Mark 10:27). Elisha had asked a "hard thing"—a double portion of the power that Elijah had seen in his life. It is interesting that Elisha did exactly twice as many miracles as Elijah. The last one occurred after he was dead! A man was raised back to life as his corpse came into contact with the bones of Elisha. Now that's a hard thing!

It had been thirty years since an evangelist had preached in evangelistic meetings in Chicago. Known as "the town that Billy Sunday couldn't shut down," John R. Rice, Bob Jones Sr., and Paul Rood decided to join together to reach the city of Chicago in their generation. They organized and launched a revival crusade in May of 1948—the first since the Billy Sunday meetings in 1918. God blessed those efforts with 2,800 people trusting Christ as Saviour.

When someone says, "it can't be done" they are distrusting our omnipotent God! Don't put limitations on God. "Call unto me, and I will answer thee, and shew thee great and mighty things, which thou knowest not" (Jeremiah 33:3). God invites you to come "boldly" into His presence with your requests. Give Him a hard project! Pray an impossible prayer. Ask for a hard thing!

May 22, 1894

How Long Does Revival Take?

"For in six days the Lord made heaven and earth, the sea, and all that in them is, and rested the seventh day...."—**Exodus 20:11**

Reaching the world for Christ seems impossible. Billions of people have never heard the Gospel. Churches are needed in so many places. We need pastors, missionaries, evangelists, educators, and Christian servants in every walk of life. When we look at the task, it seems too big to accomplish in a lifetime. Life is too short—there just isn't time! But if God could create everything in the universe in six twenty-four hour days, God surely is able to take our limited time and resources and make them count in a big way.

Evangelist Gypsy Smith travelled to Australia anticipating what God would do. In May of 1894, he began a six-week revival crusade in Adelaide, Australia. From that meeting he moved on to Melbourne and then Sydney. Upon reaching Sydney, he received a cable that his wife Annie was very sick. He bought a return ticket and boarded a boat aborting his revival efforts after just three months in the country. In those three short months, however, God had used his preaching mightily and thousands had come to Christ. In fact, two thousand people would come to his send-off, looking forward to his return.

It only took one sermon for the entire city of Nineveh to repent and turn to God. It only took one sermon on the day of Pentecost for three thousand to be saved, baptized, and added to the church. The Apostle Paul was just one man, but through his life and ministry, the world was turned upside down for Christ. God isn't always looking for a multitude. "And I sought for a man among them, that should make up the hedge, and stand in the gap before me for the land, that I should not destroy it: but I found none" (Ezekiel 22:30). Will He find *you* faithful today? You may be the *one* through which many can be *won*.

May 22, 1883

Running in God's Race

"Wherefore seeing we also are compassed about with so great a cloud of witnesses, let us lay aside every weight, and the sin which doth so easily beset us, and let us run with patience the race that is set before us."—**Hebrews 12:1**

Billy Sunday's dream had come true. The twenty-one year old who had given his life to the sport of baseball debuted in the Major Leagues for the Chicago White Sox on May 19, 1883. After beating the fastest runner on the team in a foot race, Billy was signed to a major league contract. He was a fast runner, running one hundred yards in ten seconds, yet in his first game, he struck out each time he came to the plate. But Sunday would rise to be a baseball star in Chicago, running all four bases in fourteen seconds and becoming the first to use a bunt to get to first base (not surprising due to his poor batting skills). Known for his exciting style, he was fast becoming a star, and large contracts were on the horizon.

But fame and fortune could not buy him happiness. God stopped him dead in his tracks one night as he heard the Gospel at the Pacific Garden Mission. Billy Sunday gave up baseball a short time later and began a race far more significant.

What is your dream? To what do you aspire in this life? Does it have any eternal value? Someone has said, "If you want your life to count, live it for something that outlasts it." The only thing that will outlast this life is the souls of men. The fame or money that Sunday could have obtained in Major League Baseball would not go with him into eternity, but the one million people who were saved under his preaching are in Heaven forever!

"And they that be wise shall shine as the brightness of the firmament; and they that turn many to righteousness as the stars for ever and ever" (Daniel 12:3). "Only one life; twill soon be past, and only what's done for Christ will last." Make sure your running the right race today—the one that has an eternal reward.

May 20, 1925

The Impact of Revival

"Howbeit Jesus suffered him not, but saith unto him, Go home to thy friends, and tell them how great things the Lord hath done for thee, and hath had compassion on thee. And he departed, and began to publish in Decapolis how great things Jesus had done for him: and all men did marvel."—**Mark 5:19–20**

Mark 5 records the amazing conversion of a man who was possessed with a legion of devils. He lived in a cemetery and wore no clothes. When they tried to bind him with fetters or chains, the satanic power within him gave him the power to break the fetters and chains asunder. Someone described this man as "a nude dude in a crude mood!" But Jesus casts out the legion of devils and changes his life so that the people saw him, "...sitting, and clothed, and in his right mind" (verse 15). At that point however, the people of the region told Jesus He was no longer welcome in their parts.

This former demoniac saw that Jesus was leaving and wanted to go with Him, but the Lord sent him back to his people to tell them the good news of salvation. Amazingly when Jesus returned to the country of the Gadarenes some time later, "...the people gladly received him: for they were all waiting for him" (Luke 8:40).

The *Burlington Daily Times* published a letter from the mayor of their city describing Evangelist Mordecai Ham's campaign in 1925: "...I must say I have never seen the city of Burlington so thoroughly stirred as it has been by this campaign. Every department of our municipal government has felt the wonderful effects of this meeting..." Revival has to start with each of us individually. When it does, it will spread to those around us. As the apostles pointed out, "For we cannot but speak the things which we have seen and heard" (Acts 4:20). The world may not believe the message but they cannot deny the changes in our lives. Let revival spread through your life to those around you today.

May 21, 1921

The Quick and Powerful Scripture

"For the word of God is quick, and powerful, and sharper than any two-edged sword, piercing even to the dividing asunder of soul and spirit, and of the joints and marrow, and is a discerner of the thoughts and intents of the heart."
—Hebrews 4:12

In his own words, Evangelist Bob Jones Sr.'s "best crusade" began in Montgomery, Alabama, in 1921. Jones loved every minute of meeting the people, praising the Lord in the meeting, and preaching the Gospel to anyone in the town who would hear. Newspaper headlines the next day reported, "More Than Five Thousand Held Spellbound by Eloquence of Splendid Evangelist: Hundreds Turned Away at Each Sunday Service; Sermons Not Sensational." Bob Jones Sr. would turn the town upside down with the fiery preaching of God's Word.

Did you know that God will use His Word even when it isn't preached with fire or eloquence? God has chosen to use preaching without a doubt, but He blesses the preaching of "the Word." It is not the sermon outline, or the great illustration, or the personality of the preacher that God promises to bless. He promises to bless and use His Word. "For as the rain cometh down, and the snow from heaven, and returneth not thither, but watereth the earth, and maketh it bring forth and bud, that it may give seed to the sower, and bread to the eater: So shall my word be that goeth forth out of my mouth: it shall not return unto me void, but it shall accomplish that which I please, and it shall prosper in the thing whereto I sent it" (Isaiah 55:10–11).

You may not stand behind a pulpit today before a large congregation of hearers, but will you give someone God's Word? Just as a congregation needs a word from the Lord, that person next to you at work, on the bus, or in a classroom, needs that same word. "Go, stand and speak…to the people all the words of this life" (Acts 5:20).

May 22, 1888

Glory!

"According to my earnest expectation and my hope, that in nothing I shall be ashamed, but that with all boldness, as always, so now also Christ shall be magnified in my body, whether it be by life, or by death."—**Philippians 1:20**

After the doctor examined him, Billy Bray said, "Well, Doctor, how is it?" "You are going to die," the doctor solemnly replied. Billy instantly shouted, "Glory to God. Glory to God. I shall soon be in Heaven!" Then he added in a low tone, and in his own peculiar way, "When I get up there, shall I give them your compliments, Doctor, and tell them you are coming too?"

On his deathbed on May 22, 1888, William Trewartha Bray, known as Billy Bray to his fellow Englishmen, would utter his last word—"Glory." Someone once said of him, "He was blessing and praising the Lord all the day, so that Heaven was not to him very different than Earth." In 1984, the church that he had founded, named "Three Eyes Chapel," was dedicated in his honor.

What will be on your lips when you die? Will you die rejoicing that you are about to enter Heaven, or will you die bitter and angry that God is removing you from this Earth?

It's fair to propose that we will die exactly in the same manner as we have lived. If your life is full of bitterness, anger, worry, and fear—that is exactly the way you will die. But if your life is filled with peace, joy, contentment, obedience to God—you will die with "Glory" on your lips. When we love and walk with Christ on Earth, our hearts are the same as the apostle Paul's, "We are confident, I say, and willing rather to be absent from the body, and to be present with the Lord" (2 Corinthians 5:8).

Maybe instead of worrying about how we're going to live today, we should practice how we are going to die! Let Christ be magnified today whether in life or in death.

May 23, 1498

Living and Dying for Christ

"For to me to live is Christ, and to die is gain."—**Philippians 1:21**

Girolamo Savonarola considered his fate on the morning of May 23, 1498. He had been a Catholic friar, but was disturbed by the heresies that he saw promoted around him. He had preached fervently against the Pope and preached repentance to the city of Florence. Revival had begun to take hold on Florence, and the masses were beginning to turn away from the Pope and the false teachings of Catholicism. After attempts to bribe him failed, the Pope had him arrested, tried, and convicted of "reforming the government and cleansing the temple."

As Savonarola and two other men were led to the executioner in Florence, Italy, a peace came over his heart. Girolamo had no regrets. The bishop who was overseeing his execution declared, "I separate you from the church militant, and the church triumphant." Savonarola replied, "Not from the church triumphant! That is beyond thy power." His hands were tied behind his back, and he was hung as a heretic. His body would be burned later to deny him the honor of being buried by his followers. Savonarola's faithful testimony would greatly impact those who watched him die, and his testimony would inspire others who later led the Reformation in Europe.

Martyrdom seems like a difficult thing to face, but in reality "to be absent from the body [is] to be present with the Lord" (2 Corinthians 5:8). Dying for Christ in that sense is a promotion or gain, as Paul called it. The tough part is *living* for Christ. Every day we must die to self, to sin, and to the world in order to live for Jesus Christ. That isn't always easy but it is the only way for us to experience personal revival. We hope we would be willing to die for Christ if it came to that; but are we willing to *live* for Him today? God will give you the grace to do so, and when it comes time to die, even if as a martyr—His grace will be sufficient then too.

May 24, 1738

Salvation Settled

"He that hath the Son hath life; and he that hath not the Son of God hath not life. These things have I written unto you that believe on the name of the Son of God; that ye may know that ye have eternal life, and that ye may believe on the name of the Son of God."—**1 John 5:12–13**

John Wesley had struggled with his salvation. As he journeyed to America as a missionary, he was drawn to the singing of some Moravians who were on board. The joy that came from their hearts through their singing was something he longed for but did not have. After a frustrating and unfruitful mission endeavor in the New Land, he returned to England wrestling in his soul about eternal life.

On the evening of May 24, 1738, he decided to visit a Moravian meeting on Aldersgate Street in London. His heart was "strangely warmed" by what he saw and heard. The Word of God was piercing his heart and convicting him of his sin. He would later describe the significance of this visit in his journal: "In the evening, I went very unwillingly to a society in Aldersgate Street, where one was reading Luther's Preface to the Epistle to the Romans. About a quarter before nine, while he was describing the change which God works in the heart through faith in Christ, I did trust in Christ, Christ alone in salvation, and an assurance was given me that he had taken away my sins, even mine, and saved me from the law of sin and death." John Wesley's "Aldersgate Experience" would change his life and direction forever.

Is your salvation settled? Are you certain that you are a child of God? Do you have assurance that your sins are forgiven and that you have a home in Heaven? You can settle that right now. "For whosoever shall call upon the name of the Lord shall be saved" (Romans 10:13). Agree with God that you are a sinner and acknowledge that Jesus Christ is the only One who can save you. Ask Him to forgive you of your sin and give you eternal life. Then, "...though your sins be as scarlet, they shall be as white as snow; though they be red like crimson, they shall be as wool" (Isaiah 1:18).

May 25, 1925

The Bible Withstands Attack

"Thy word is true from the beginning: and every one of thy righteous judgments endureth for ever."—**Psalm 119:160**

It is not unusual for the Bible to come under attack. Man does not attack and reject the Bible because he thinks it is false. There is no such thing as an atheist. John 1:9 says of Jesus Christ, "That was the true Light, which lighteth every man that cometh into the world." C. S. Lewis states that there has never been a civilization anywhere whose laws did not mirror the Ten Commandments. No group of people, according to Lewis, has ever been discovered who allowed stealing, or taking another's wife, etc., even though those people had never seen a Bible. Why is that? Romans 2:14–15 sheds light on this fact: "For when the Gentiles, which have not the law, do by nature the things contained in the law, these, having not the law, are a law unto themselves: Which shew the work of the law written in their hearts, their conscience also bearing witness…."

An influential Congregationalist, Dr. Glaslow, criticized Billy Sunday in the magazine *The Congregationalist* in May of 1925. He criticized Sunday's dogmatic stand against evolution saying that it highly offended him. He wrote that Sunday's uncompromising stand on such things was sending people to Hell. He critiqued his doctrine calling it "medieval salvationism," that, "Salvation is a matter of contract; hell is a literal pit of fire and brimstone; the Bible is verbally infallible; every man who teaches Higher Criticism is a liar."

Peter warned in his second Epistle that there would be "…scoffers, walking after their own lusts" (2 Peter 3:3). Man doesn't scoff because he doesn't think there is a God or that the Bible is untrue. He scoffs because he is not ready to stop sinning! Many a man has vowed to destroy God's Word, but the Bible is still standing and always will. "Concerning thy testimonies, I have known of old that thou hast founded them for ever" (Psalm 119:152).

May 24, 1874

The Glory of God's Creation

"The heavens declare the glory of God; and the firmament sheweth his handywork. Day unto day uttereth speech, and night unto night sheweth knowledge. There is no speech nor language, where their voice is not heard."—**Psalm 19:1–3**

"Arthur's Seat" in Edinburgh, Scotland, was described by Robert Louis Stevenson as "a hill for magnitude, a mountain in virtue of its bold design." On May 24, 1874, D. L. Moody returned to Edinburgh, Scotland, to preach at this renowned mountain. The beauty of God's creation was magnified in an even greater way through the preached Word of God. God's general revelation in creation combined with the specific revelation of God's Word, spoke to twenty thousand people that day. Three thousand, five hundred people were saved there at Arthur's Seat and in the previous meetings in Glasgow under the direction of Moody.

The psalmist in chapter 19, after explaining God's glory in creation in the opening six verses, explains the glory and value of the Word of God in verses 7–11: "The law of the LORD is perfect, converting the soul: the testimony of the LORD is sure, making wise the simple. The statutes of the LORD are right, rejoicing the heart: the commandment of the LORD is pure, enlightening the eyes. The fear of the LORD is clean, enduring for ever: the judgments of the LORD are true and righteous altogether. More to be desired are they than gold, yea, than much fine gold: sweeter also than honey and the honeycomb. Moreover by them is thy servant warned: and in keeping of them there is great reward."

God is seen on every canvas of nature and on every page of Scripture. Both nature and the Bible reveal the glory and love of God. Enjoy God today! Whether you are out and about in nature or reading God's Word, you can bask in the power and presence of your God.

May 27, 1828

Don't Criticize Revival Efforts

"But if ye have bitter envying and strife in your hearts, glory not, and lie not against the truth. This wisdom descendeth not from above, but is earthly, sensual, devilish. For where envying and strife is, there is confusion and every evil work."
—James 3:14–16

Criticism of revival became rampant in the early 1800s. Much of this divisiveness centered around Charles Finney. Finney and a few other evangelists, knowing that jealousy and a critical spirit would hinder the Spirit of God, agreed to discontinue publishing any information about their revivals so as not to stir up further controversy. The signed document read as follows and was signed on May 27, 1828: "The subscribers having had opportunity for free conversation on certain subjects pertaining to revivals of religion, concerning which we have differed, are of the opinion that the general interests of religion would not be promoted by any further publications on those subjects, or personal discussions; and we do hereby engage to cease from all publications, correspondences, conversations, and conduct designed and calculated to keep those subjects before the public mind; and that, so far as our influence may avail, we will exert it to induce our friends on either side to do the same."

How sad it is when God's people cannot rejoice over the blessings of revival work. Are their some tares among the wheat in revival? Of course, but the Lord gave instruction to let both grow until the harvest (Matthew 13:24–30). Will some methods be used that some might question? No doubt. Some were preaching in Paul's day from improper motives, but Paul writes in Philippians 1:18, "What then? notwithstanding, every way, whether in pretense, or in truth, Christ is preached; and I therein do rejoice, yea, and will rejoice." Let's follow Scripture and the leading of the Holy Spirit as carefully as we know how, but let's also be careful how we criticize the work of others in revival.

May 28, 1841

God's Thoughts and Ways Are Never Evil

"For I know the thoughts that I think toward you, saith the Lord, thoughts of peace, and not of evil, to give you an expected end."—**Jeremiah 29:11**

God's ways are not always our ways and His thoughts are so much higher than our own. As a result, we can become disappointed and even disillusioned by God's ways. While we can only see our present situation, our God's ways are "providential." The word *providence* comes from two words: *before* and *video.* God sees before something happens and thus prepares our way accordingly. That plan is never evil, though it may seem so at the time.

D. L. Moody's father was a bricklayer like his forefathers providing for his family in Northfield, Massachusetts. On this day in 1841, Dwight along with his family received the terrible news of his father's death. Dwight was only four years old at the time. His mother Betsey would now be responsible to raise the nine children of the Moody family alone with no provision left from her husband. She no doubt developed a deep bitterness against God, as she would never encourage Dwight to read the Bible or pray. He would only receive a fifth grade education, leaving school to provide for his mother and younger siblings. Yet God had an amazing plan for Dwight Moody that he could never have imagined at the time of his father's death.

Are you questioning something that God has allowed in your life? Are you becoming bitter or angry at God or people because of it? Joseph did not understand why he was mistreated, lied about, and thrown in prison. Daniel could not have understood being carried away as a slave to Babylon. The disciples did not understand the crucifixion of Jesus Christ. In time, however, all of these situations were necessary to bring about an "expected end" that God had planned from the beginning. Hang in there—God has not forsaken you!

May 29, 1921

A Six Week Revival

"A faithful man shall abound with blessings...."—**Proverbs 28:20a**

In a small rural town in Wisconsin, a six-week revival was scheduled in the spring of 1930. The Evangelist, Dennis Shannon, would preach each night, including Saturday nights. Most of the people in the area were farmers and with cows to milk, crops to tend to, and the distance to the church, it would not be the practice of most to go every night to the meeting.

David and Lily, however, were committed Christians. Every day they planned their schedule and worked diligently so as to be in the revival each night with their three small children. It was seven miles to the church and their old Model A Ford didn't travel all that fast, but each night for six weeks they were faithful. One night, their middle child, Marvin, at the age of nine, trusted Christ as Saviour! These were depression years in America, and while times were tough, the faithfulness of Marvin's Dad and Mom left a deep impression on him. He was forced to quit school after the eighth grade and by fifteen was farming his own land trying desperately to make a living. As tough as it was, he never missed a church service for anything and led his wife and three children to love God and serve Him faithfully.

Born on this day in 1921, Marvin was the best Christian I ever knew. He was my Dad! The blessings of his faithfulness continue to affect my life and my two siblings to this day. You may not feel like being faithful today, but think of the blessings that you and those coming after you will miss if you quit today. I'm grateful for a faithful pastor who decided to have a revival and for an evangelist who would come and preach for six weeks and for my grandfather who didn't miss a night and for a dad who got saved and was faithful until God took him home. Well done, thou good and faithful servants!

May 30, 1792

A Vision for the Lost

"Where there is no vision, the people perish: but he that keepeth the law, happy is he."—**Proverbs 29:18**

When William Carey got saved, he soon developed a burden for those who were lost in foreign lands. At that time, missionaries to a foreign field were unknown. As a teacher in a school, Carey had read of the voyages of Captain Cook and wondered about those in far off places who had never heard the Gospel. As a shoe cobbler, he would balance books on the wheel and study the Bible and foreign languages. He soon mastered seven languages including Hebrew and Greek. The Particular Baptists at the time were Calvinistic in their theology and did not buy into Carey's vision for foreign missions. At one meeting where he made his appeal, Dr. John Ryland stood up and declared, "Sit down young man! When God is ready to save the heathen, He will do it without your help or mine!"

Carey was persistent, however, and on May 30, 1792, at age thirty-one, he stood in the pulpit of Friar Lane Baptist Chapel in Nottingham, England, and preached a sermon that would spark the modern missionary movement. Carey preached two points: "Expect great things from God. Attempt great things for God." Later in the year, he would publish *An Enquiry into the Obligation of Christians to Use Means for the Conversion of the Heathen and Begin a Missionary Society.* He would leave his home country in April of 1793 to reach the unsaved in India. One historian described him in this way: "When he died at seventy-three, he had seen the Scriptures translated and printed into forty languages, he had been a college professor, and had founded a college at Serampore. He had seen India open its doors to missionaries, and he had seen many converts for Christ." Today we refer to Carey as the "Father of Modern Missions."

Don't let others quench your zeal to serve God. God blesses persistence. "Therefore, my beloved brethren, be ye stedfast, unmoveable, always abounding in the work of the Lord, forasmuch as ye know that your labour is not in vain in the Lord" (1 Corinthians 15:58).

May 28, 1942

Take the Gospel to All

"And he said unto them, Go ye into all the world, and preach the gospel to every creature."—**Mark 16:15**

God is interested in all the world. He is not willing that any should perish, but that all should come to repentance. (See 2 Peter 3:9.) "For this is good and acceptable in the sight of God our Saviour; Who will have all men to be saved, and come unto the knowledge of the truth" (1 Timothy 2:3–4). We can easily get tunnel vision when it comes to the lost. We are naturally concerned about our loved ones and friends, but what about those beyond our doors or city? Are we willing to step out of our comfort zone to reach them? Are we willing to "go" with the Gospel?

Charles Fuller's "Old-Fashioned Revival Hour" was gaining popularity in Los Angeles. Fuller was busy with his ministry in southern California and could have easily become content with the results he was seeing there. But as World War II was now raging across an ocean, Fuller was burdened to expand the influence of his Gospel outreach. Financially, the war years made it tough to think about doing any more, but Fuller lived with a passion to see people saved and young people called to the ministry.

Fuller wrote his friends, J. Elwin Wright and P. J. Zondervan, and the three of them planned an Old Fashioned Revival Hour service in late May of 1942, in Grand Rapids, Michigan. The "Old Fashioned Revival Choir" would sing and Rudy Atwood the beloved pianist would be at the piano. God blessed this service as these men stepped out on faith to take the Gospel wherever God would allow them.

But what about us? Will we leave our comfort zones to get the Gospel to all the world? Will we sacrifice to make it possible? God commands us and promises His blessing!

JUNE

June 1, 2009

What Is Your Passion?

"The fruit of the righteous is a tree of life; and he that winneth souls is wise."
—Proverbs 11:30

Once Joe Boyd surrendered his life to Christ, there was no stopping him. Opponents of Texas A&M had felt the blows of this All-American football player as the Aggies won the National Championship in 1939. But from that point on, it was the devil who felt the blows of this powerful preacher of the Gospel. "Brother Joe" had a way of getting an audience to laugh or enjoy a football story, only to quickly turn the tables and strike a blow to the heart. For over sixty years he traveled tirelessly preaching God's Word.

When Joe Boyd was found dead on June 1, 2009, the little kitchen table in his humble apartment told the story of his passion for preaching and soulwinning. Open on that table was his Bible, a commentary, a Spanish dictionary, and a yellow writing tablet with a sermon half-written in Spanish. Boyd first started learning Spanish after his eightieth birthday and loved to preach the Gospel to Spanish-speaking people. He hadn't preached for a couple of years prior to his death due to health reasons, but his heart still beat for revival and the preaching of God's Word. Whenever God would give him another opportunity to do so, he was determined to be prepared.

What is your passion? What are you living for today? As much as Joe Boyd loved football, he rarely watched a game once he started preaching. His desire was simply to win souls and train others to do the same. Even in his later years, when one met the tall, muscular Joe Boyd, they could tell he had played some "ball." But God didn't build him for football—God built Joe Boyd to preach the Gospel!

June 2, 1906

We Preach Not Ourselves

"For we preach not ourselves, but Christ Jesus the Lord; and ourselves your servants for Jesus' sake."—**2 Corinthians 4:5**

In a time when there wasn't much entertainment for people to consume, Billy Sunday was becoming a phenomenon that was sweeping the nation. People wanted to see this animated preacher as sometimes he would even stand on top of the pulpit to make his point. But while the former Major League baseball player was a huge draw, he viewed it only as a way for people to hear the truth, lift up righteousness, and point people to a Saviour.

Crowds were large everywhere he went, and newspapers carried the details of his preaching and recorded the statistics. One such account published on June 2, 1906 said, "Closing on June 2 with 1,365 converts. Rev. Sunday received $3,064.38 as a voluntary offering. Rev. Sunday wears no glasses, delivered his farewell on Monday night to a large audience in spite of a heavy rain storm. A powerful sermon with seventy-three conversions at the altar." Billy Sunday was forty-four years old and going strong for the cause of Jesus Christ.

The attention, large crowds, and mammoth love offerings would ruin most preachers. The largest love offering ever recorded for an evangelist was given to Sunday in his New York campaign and totaled nearly $125,000. Sunday took that offering and gave most to the Red Cross to help with their work during the War and the rest he gave to the Pacific Garden Mission in Chicago where he was saved. When he died, Sunday's assets totaled less than fifty thousand dollars. No doubt God blessed him because his life was not about himself but about his Saviour.

What is your life about? Is it evident to those who know you that your purpose is to live for Christ and to share Him with others? God blesses this kind of focus.

June 1, 1876

God Honors Sacrifice

"And there came a certain poor widow, and she threw in two mites, which make a farthing. And he called unto him his disciples, and saith unto them, Verily I say unto you, That this poor widow hath cast more in, than all they which have cast into the treasury."—**Mark 12:42–43**

The church in Chicago where D. L. Moody pastored had been meeting in the basement of an unfinished church building for two years. Everyone had given all they could in time, energy, and resources to see the building completed, but it was taking much longer than expected. Thousands of children contributed five cents each for a brick in the new building. Moody encouraged the people weekly, to stay faithful, continue to sacrifice, and never give up. He knew that if they would be faithful, God would see the project to completion and bless it mightily.

The day to open the building finally came on June 1, 1876, and God indeed did honor the faith of those people. Thousands would now flock to hear God's Word each week in downtown Chicago. The souls saved week after week were more than enough reward for the sacrificial giving of adults and children alike.

Does it seem like a goal or dream you've had when the work of God is being delayed? Are you becoming weary in well-doing? The Bible teaches in Galatians 6:9 that "…we shall reap if we faint not."

What if the people in Chicago had quit while meeting in the basement? What if they had decided the sacrifice wasn't worth it? Many of those little children who sacrificed a nickel to build the building lived to see thousands walk the aisles trusting Christ. "I waited patiently for the Lord; and he inclined unto me, and heard my cry" (Psalm 40:1). God hasn't forgotten you—stay faithful, and stay sacrificial.

June 4, 1768

Ready to Suffer

"Then Paul answered, What mean ye to weep and to break mine heart? for I am ready not to be bound only, but also to die at Jerusalem for the name of the Lord Jesus."—**Acts 21:13**

America was not always a free nation where free speech was enjoyed. In 1768, a group of Baptist evangelists were thrown in jail in the church-state of Virginia for preaching the Gospel without a license. Patrick Henry, who would become famous for his "Give me liberty or give me death" speech, rode fifty miles to defend the Baptist evangelists in court. Patrick stood in defiance against the judge and the court. William Smoot in *Reminiscences of Baptists Of Virginia* describes the scene and Henry's arguments: "'From that period when our fathers left the land of their nativity for settlement in these American wilds, for liberty, for civil and religious liberty, for liberty of conscience to worship their Creator according to their own conceptions of heaven's revealed will, from the moment that they placed their feet upon the American continent, and… sought an asylum from persecution and tyranny, from that moment despotism was crushed, the fetters of darkness were broken, and heaven decreed that man should be free, free to worship according to the Bible…

"'But may it please your Worships,' continued the speaker, 'permit me to ask once more, For what are these men about to be tried? This paper says, 'for preaching the Gospel of the Saviour to Adam's fallen race.' Then in tones of thunder he exclaimed; 'What law have they violated?'…and waved the indictment round his head. The court and audience were now wrought up to the most intense pitch of excitement. The face of the prosecuting attorney was pallid and ghastly, and he seemed unconscious that his whole frame was agitated with alarm; while the judge, in a tremulous voice, put an end to the scene, now becoming excessively painful, by the authoritative declaration: 'Sheriff, discharge those men.'"

Ask the Lord to give you boldness as you share the Gospel with freedom today. He will bless your courage!

June 914 B.C.

Turn Back to the Lord God

"And when Asa heard these words, and the prophecy of Oded the prophet, he took courage, and put away the abominable idols out of all the land of Judah and Benjamin, and out of the cities which he had taken from mount Ephraim, and renewed the altar of the LORD, that was before the porch of the LORD."
—2 Chronicles 15:8

After the preaching of Azariah, the son of Oded, King Asa decided to turn his heart and his nation back to God. Azaraiah preached, "…Hear ye me, Asa, and all Judah and Benjamin; The LORD is with you, while ye be with him; and if ye seek him, he will be found of you; but if ye forsake him, he will forsake you. Now for a long season Israel hath been without the true God, and without a teaching priest, and without law. But when they in their trouble did turn unto the LORD God of Israel, and sought him, he was found of them. And in those times there was no peace to him that went out, nor to him that came in, but great vexations were upon all the inhabitants of the countries. And nation was destroyed of nation, and city of city: for God did vex them with all adversity. Be ye strong therefore, and let not your hands be weak: for your work shall be rewarded" (2 Chronicles 15:2b–7).

King Asa gathered the nation together after hearing the preaching to lead them back to the Lord. The nation could see that the Lord was with Asa, and they sacrificed seven thousand oxen and seven thousand sheep. At the end of the ceremony, the entire nation entered into a covenant with the Lord that they would follow Him with all their hearts.

Are we willing to turn from our idols of self, pride, money, lust, and leisure today and covenant with God that we will serve Him? We can say that we will, but what will we sacrifice to show that commitment? These people in the Old Testament brought fourteen thousand animals to sacrifice as a sign of their true repentance and willingness to put the Lord in His rightful place. Show God how much you love Him today—use words only if necessary!

June AD 33

The Power of the Holy Spirit

"And, behold, I send the promise of my Father upon you: but tarry ye in the city of Jerusalem, until ye be endued with power from on high."—**Luke 24:49**

With Christ's orders in their minds, the early church gathered to wait and pray. Some no doubt were still dazed by the recent events of the death, burial, and resurrection of Jesus Christ. They wanted to tell others of this incredible story, but were told to wait for the power of the Holy Spirit. Suddenly, on the Day of Pentecost, everything changed! A powerful wind blew through the room and flames of fire descended from above. As the disciples emerged from the room, they found thousands of people celebrating the feast of Pentecost. As they began preaching and sharing the good news of the risen Lord, people were hearing the message in their own languages. Some accused these disciples of being drunk, but Peter stood up and set the record straight: "...Ye men of Judaea, and all ye that dwell at Jerusalem, be this known unto you, and hearken to my words: For these are not drunken, as ye suppose, seeing it is but the third hour of the day. But this is that which was spoken by the prophet Joel; And it shall come to pass in the last days, saith God, I will pour out of my Spirit upon all flesh: and your sons and your daughters shall prophesy, and your young men shall see visions, and your old men shall dream dreams: And on my servants and on my handmaidens I will pour out in those days of my Spirit; and they shall prophesy: And I will shew wonders in heaven above, and signs in the earth beneath; blood, and fire, and vapour of smoke: The sun shall be turned into darkness, and the moon into blood, before that great and notable day of the Lord come: And it shall come to pass, that whosoever shall call on the name of the Lord shall be saved" (Acts 2:14–21).

The Holy Spirit's power that had been promised by Christ Himself, had now come upon these disciples. The results were phenomenal and could have never been accomplished in man's power. Will you rely upon God's Holy Spirit and His power in your life today? Why would we settle for anything less?

June 7, 1913

The Old Rugged Cross

"For the preaching of the cross is to them that perish foolishness; but unto us which are saved it is the power of God."—**1 Corinthians 1:18**

The best way to pull away from discouragement, depression, criticism, and seeming failure is to reflect on the cross of Calvary. It is there where we get a glimpse of the One who loves us, not for what we do, but for who we are—sinners who are in desperate need of His mercy and grace.

After being criticized for his evangelistic work, George Bennard wrote the first verse to the beloved song, "The Old Rugged Cross." He first sang his song at an evangelistic meeting which he was conducting, but on this day in 1913, the entire hymn was sung for the first time by a small choir of five accompanied by guitar in Pokagon, Michigan. Let your mind and heart go back to that place called Golgotha as you read these words:

On a hill far away stood an old rugged cross,
The emblem of suffering and shame;
And I love that old cross where the Dearest and Best,
For a world of lost sinners was slain.

Oh, that old rugged cross, so despised by the world,
Has a wondrous attraction for me;
For the dear Lamb of God left His glory above,
To bear it to dark Calvary.

To the old rugged cross I will ever be true;
Its shame and reproach gladly bear;
Then He'll call me someday to my home far away,
Where His glory forever I'll share.

So I'll cherish the old rugged cross,
Till my trophies at last I lay down;
I will cling to the old rugged cross,
And exchange it someday for a crown.

June 8, 1878

Do You Long for Revival?

"Wilt thou not revive us again: that thy people may rejoice in thee?"
—Psalm 85:6

Evan Roberts was born in Loughor, Wales, to Henry and Hannah Roberts. At an early age, Evan would memorize Scripture at night and faithfully attend church. By the time he reached eleven years of age, he was working in the coal mines with his father.

David Matthews in his book *I Saw the Welsh Revival* states: "Following the calling of a coal miner, he was once in a minor colliery explosion when a page of his priceless Bible was scorched by the fiery elements. Stranger still to record, it was the words in 2 Chronicles 6 which lay open at the time of the disaster, where Solomon prayed for revival. When Mr. Roberts became world-known, a picture of this Bible went around the world. Was this young man always dreaming of revival? The incident cited seemed prophetic."

Matthews goes on to say: "Once, we are told, he heard a sermon on the words, 'But Thomas was not with them when Jesus came.' It is reported that those words made an ineffaceable impression on the mind of the youth. Perhaps we find in this incident the secret for his unflagging zeal for the services of the sanctuary. Never did he turn back." At age twenty-six, "Day and night without ceasing, he prayed, wept and sighed for a great spiritual awakening…." Roberts wrote, "for ten or eleven years I have prayed for revival. I could sit up all night to read or talk about revivals."

That hunger and thirst for revival turned into what history calls "The Great Welsh Revival." Evan Roberts was the primary preacher in the crusades that swept the country of Wales. Will you pray, weep, and sigh for a revival of that kind today? Matthew 5:6 promises, "Blessed are they which do hunger and thirst after righteousness: for they shall be filled."

June 7, 1873

In Sickness and in Health

"And I was with you in weakness, and in fear, and in much trembling. And my speech and my preaching was not with enticing words of man's wisdom, but in demonstration of the Spirit and of power: That your faith should not stand in the wisdom of men, but in the power of God."—**1 Corinthians 2:3–5**

With barely enough money for the tickets, Dwight Moody and his new music man, Ira Sankey, boarded the little boat *City of Paris* that would take them to England for the first time in early June of 1873. Sankey was originally a little skeptical of joining Moody on this trip, four thousand miles away from home. Moody did not do well on boats, and Sankey would later describe the seasickness that the evangelist endured: "He got sick when he bought the ticket." Moody would stay in his room the moment he boarded the ship to the moment the ship docked in England. But Moody's desire was to shake the country like John Wesley and George Whitefield had 125 years before, and Sankey wanted to be a part. As God promises, His strength was made perfect in their weakness (2 Corinthians 12:9) when the preaching of Moody, along with the singing of Sankey, shook England with the Gospel.

We live in a day when a little tiredness keeps us from our Bible reading and prayer. A sniffle or cough keeps us from God's house. The weather is usually too hot, too cold, too rainy, or too *something* for us to go out and tell anyone about the Lord. We are good at excuses. Although there are from time to time illnesses or uncontrollable obstacles to serving the Lord, let's not neglect our responsibilities and give ourselves a pass every time we aren't feeling 100 percent. When excuses pop into your mind, read 2 Corinthians 11:23–28. The Apostle Paul's testimony of endurance to serve the Lord will encourage and motivate you to do the same.

June 1910

Zealous Christians

"But it is good to be zealously affected always in a good thing, and not only when I am present with you."—**Galatians 4:18**

It is easy to get zealous about things that have only temporary value at best. Vacations, sports teams, hobbies, business ventures, and relationships are only a partial list of things to which people today easily give all of their attention and energy. Loss of sleep, sacrifice of money, and ridiculous hours only scratch the surface of the zeal we have for earthly things. We admire the zeal of those who build a great business or fanatically support their team or give millions of dollars to a cause. But where is the zeal of Christians for God's work? Where is our passion for revival and winning the lost?

Thomas E. Green described Billy Sunday's preaching in his article in June of 1910: "That's Billy Sunday, America's great evangelist." He wrote: "On the platform, he plays ball! Attitudes, methods, gestures—he crouches, rushes, whirls, bangs his message out, as if he were at the bat in the last inning, with two men out and the bases full. And he can go into any city in America and for six weeks, talk to six thousand people twice a day, and turn that community inside out."

People can deny what we believe, but they cannot deny how we behave. Has the Gospel changed your life? Does anyone want the life you live? How can we expect a lost world to be interested in a Christianity that no longer affects us?

Zeal can be contagious. God saved us to be a "...peculiar people, zealous of good works" (Titus 2:14b). Ask God to give you a zeal for the eternal today.

June 1935

Hope for Your Hometown

"But Jesus said unto them, A prophet is not without honour, but in his own country, and among his own kin, and in his own house."—**Mark 6:4**

Sometimes the most difficult people to reach are those who know us best. Perhaps it is because they have seen our inconsistencies of the past and think that whatever it is that we have now won't last. Often they are offended that we have rejected the way "they brought us up" and suspect that we are forsaking them or disrespecting them. Jesus Himself acknowledged that reaching one's own people is a difficult task.

Gypsy Smith grasped his Bible as he returned to his hometown to preach the Gospel. The Gypsies were known for their theft and deceit, and they reveled in their reputation. But God had transformed Gypsy Smith's life, and his greatest desire was to return and preach the Gospel to his own people.

Smith held a revival crusade in Epping Forest, six miles northeast of London, where he was born and grew up. To his surprise, ten thousand people came to hear his testimony of salvation, many of them accepting Christ as their Saviour at the conclusion of the service. A memorial stone stands in Epping Forest to this day, memorializing Gypsy Smith's life and testimony. After briefly describing his ministry, the bottom of the plaque reads with a quote from Numbers 23:23, "...What hath God wrought!"

Ask God to break through the resistance of your family, friends, or neighbors. You will have to live a consistent life, but God is more powerful than any human obstruction. It may take time, but God will use your faithful testimony as He used Gypsy Smith to reach those you care about the most for Christ.

Summer 1858

Occupy Until I Come

"How long wilt thou sleep, O sluggard? when wilt thou arise out of thy sleep? Yet a little sleep, a little slumber, a little folding of the hands to sleep: So shall thy poverty come as one that travelleth, and thy want as an armed man."
—Proverbs 6:9–11

In a biography about his father, William Moody described Dwight Moody's zeal for the Lord in the early years after he was saved: "Although Moody's Sunday mornings were occupied in securing young men to share his pews at Plymouth Church, his Sunday afternoons and evenings were free. His indomitable energy seemed to need no "day of rest," and a good night's sleep was always sufficient to recuperate the utmost drain upon his strength. Even in later days, he was wont to associate rest, not with inactivity, which he considered most wearisome, but with some change of occupation. 'How I do pity people who hang about these summer resorts doing nothing! My! It would send me crazy!' he would often exclaim. He soon solved the problem of occupying his leisure hours on Sunday afternoon by taking up Sunday school work."

Dwight Moody at age twenty-one formed a Sunday School class for children on the coast of Lake Michigan in the summer of 1858. These neglected children were looked down upon in society, but Dwight was determined to make a difference in their lives. With growing numbers of kids attending his class, the word began to spread across the city. Dwight Moody developed his first nickname through this time: "Crazy Moody." But as a result of Moody's faithfulness throughout the years, soon his title turned into "Brother Moody," then "Mr. Moody," and finally "D. L. Moody."

You may not possess the energy of a Moody, but are you wasting time that could be devoted to God's work? Out of 168 hours in a week do we need all 128 of those hours, after our obligations of work, for ourselves? Could time be devoted on your schedule this week for eternal things? The blessing of God on your life will be in direct proportion to your commitment to His church.

June 13, 1912

Honors from God

"How can ye believe, which receive honour one of another, and seek not the honour that cometh from God only?"—**John 5:44**

Billy Sunday received an honorary doctorate of divinity from Westminster College on June 13, 1912. But Billy did not have time for pomp and circumstance. Something was more important in his heart than his personal accolades—the Gospel. Dr. Robert McWatty Russell later declared, "Mr. Sunday was not able to be present, being engaged at evangelistic services at Beaver Falls, so the degree was conferred in absentia." Nothing would sidetrack "Dr. Sunday's" effort to see souls saved and lives changed with the power of the Gospel.

Do we live for the praise of men or the praise of God? Of course we are to give honor to those to whom honor is due. That is a Bible principle not to be neglected. But if we are living for the applause, approval, and accolades of men we will come up sadly short at the judgment of God.

John the Baptist preached fearlessly against the sins of King Herod. As a result, his execution was ordered by the king. "And immediately the king sent an executioner, and commanded his head to be brought: and he went and beheaded him in the prison" (Mark 6:27). "In the prison"! No one was there to applaud his faithful life, his testimony, or his martyrdom. Executed "in the prison" with no applause from the throngs or prayers by the saints. But in Luke 7:28, Jesus said of John, "...among those that are born of women there is not a greater prophet than John the Baptist...."

So which would you rather have? Thousands of people's praise at a commencement exercise or "Well done, thou good and faithful servant" at the Judgement Seat of Christ? Stay focused on the praise that comes from God!

June 14, 1910

A Line You Don't Want to Cross

"The LORD is merciful and gracious, slow to anger and plenteous in mercy. He will not always chide: neither will he keep his anger for ever."—**Psalm 103:8–9**

J. Harold Smith was born on this day in 1910. Smith would be a pioneer in using radio and television for the propagation of the Gospel. His "Radio Bible Hour" would begin in 1934 and continued broadcasting for over seventy-five years. He was also the first pastor to televise his church services in 1953. But perhaps his most famous accomplishment was a sermon entitled "God's Three Deadlines," in which he preached about the sins of blaspheming the Holy Spirit; of ignoring the day of grace, and the sin unto death. Even after Smith's death, many have come under deep conviction listening to this message on a recording.

We ought to thank the Lord each day that He is a merciful and gracious God. "It is of the LORD's mercies that we are not consumed, because his compassions fail not. They are new every morning: great is thy faithfulness" (Lamentations 3:22–23). But we dare not take advantage of God's grace. God told Noah that he would destroy the world with a flood of water. It would take Noah 120 years to build the ark and all the while he built it, he preached righteousness. But the people mocked Noah and resisted the message. One day the door to the ark was shut by God and the rain started to fall. The line had been crossed, and God's mercy and grace were not obligated to open that door.

This is why it is so important to obey God immediately when He speaks to us. Is the Lord convicting you of your need of salvation? Christian, is He asking you to take a step of obedience, repent of a sinful habit, or give your life to him in complete surrender? To delay is to presume upon God's grace and love. Don't cross that line!

June 1860

Is Your All on the Altar?

"I beseech you therefore, brethren, by the mercies of God, that ye present your bodies a living sacrifice, holy, acceptable unto God, which is your reasonable service."—**Romans 12:1**

D. L. Moody had heard a preacher say, "The world has yet to see what God can do with a man fully surrendered to Him." That night in his pew, Moody bowed his head and humbly prayed, "By God's grace, I will be that man!" Those words would echo in Moody's mind for years. He had been saved for five years now and had been contemplating a decision for some time. His burden for the souls of men was growing greater and greater, until he could not hold himself back anymore. His Sunday School for children had been growing, and God had been blessing his ministry. He officially decided to give his life to full-time Christian ministry by leaving his secular job in June 1860.

Does God want more of your life than you are currently giving Him? You might think that God could never use you, but Moody was never educated formally. He often spoke in double negatives and by some accounts "slaughtered the King's English." R.A. Torrey, a very intellectual man who was Moody's assistant for many years, marveled at how God used Moody despite his lack of education and training.

Upon his surrender, Moody gave himself tirelessly to the study of God's Word and the preaching of its truths. While he was not polished like some other preachers in his day, it was said that you felt like you were in a courtroom and on trial when he preached. He would not leave you alone until you confessed your guilt of sin and accepted the pardon provided by God's Son.

God can equip you for ministry after He calls you. "Faithful is he that calleth you, who also will do it" (1 Thessalonians 5:24). Perhaps the world is waiting today to see what God will do with another man or woman fully yielded to Him.

June 1870

There Is a Fountain Filled with Blood

"How much more shall the blood of Christ, who through the eternal Spirit offered himself without spot to God, purge your conscience from dead works to serve the living God?...And almost all things are by the law purged with blood; and without shedding of blood there is no remission."—**Hebrews 9:14, 22**

Dwight Moody met Ira Sankey, his future music man, for the first time in Indianapolis, Indiana. Moody's service was being led by a rather boring music director when Sankey came in. Sankey felt compelled to stand and sing the verse to the song with more passion. The first song Moody heard Ira Sankey sing was, "There Is a Fountain Filled with Blood." After finishing his song, the rest of the congregation had stopped singing to listen to Sankey sing. Moody approached Sankey and said, "You will have to come to Chicago and help me. I've been looking for you for eight years!" For the rest of their lives they would serve in evangelistic work together.

There is a fountain filled with blood, Drawn from Immanuel's veins,
And sinners plunged beneath that flood, Lose all their guilty stains:

The dying thief rejoiced to see, That fountain in His day;
And there may I, though vile as he, Wash all my sins away:

Dear dying Lamb, Thy precious blood, Shall never lose its power,
Till all the ransomed church of God, Be saved, to sin no more:

E'er since by faith I saw the stream, Thy flowing wounds supply,
Redeeming love has been my theme, And shall be till I die:

When this poor, lisping, stammering tongue, Lies silent in the grave,
Then in a nobler, sweeter song, I'll sing Thy power to save.

No doubt these two servants of Christ are singing that song today in a nobler and sweeter way than they ever dreamed of on earth. Sing this old hymn a time through and let it's words and melody draw you closer to the One who saved you.

June 17, 1859

Who Can You Encourage?

"And when Saul was come to Jerusalem, he assayed to join himself to the disciples: but they were afraid of him, and believed not that he was a disciple. But Barnabas took him, and brought him to the apostles, and declared unto them how he had seen the Lord in the way and that he had spoken to him, and how he had preached boldly at Damascus in the name of Jesus."—**Acts 9:26–27**

Evangelist J. Wilbur Chapman was born on June 17, 1859. As he grew, he attended a Quaker day school and Methodist Sunday school where he heard truths from God's Word. At seventeen years old, he was saved. In his own words, the preacher gave an invitation to the students to stand and trust Christ as their Saviour: "I think every boy in my class rose to his feet with the exception of myself. I found myself reasoning thus: Why should I rise, my mother was a saint; my father is one of the truest men I know; my home teaching has been all that a boy could have; I know about Christ and I think I realize his power to save. While I was thus reasoning, my Sunday school teacher (Mrs. C. C. Binkley, wife of Senator Binkley) with tears in her eyes, leaned around the back of the other boys and looking straight at me, said, 'Would it not be best for you to rise?' And when she saw that I hesitated, she put her hand under my elbow and lifted me up just a bit, and I stood upon my feet. I can never describe my emotions. It was a day when one of the most profound impressions of my life was made. Through these years I have never forgotten it, as it was my teacher who influenced me thus to take the stand—it was her personal touch that gave me courage to rise before the church and confess my Saviour."

Is there someone you could encourage today as Barnabas did for Saul of Tarsus or Mrs. Binkley did for J. Wilbur Chapman? It may be your words or gentle touch that would make a difference. J. Wilbur Chapman would become the link between the great evangelists D. L. Moody and Billy Sunday, continuing the traditions of evangelism and, most importantly, the passion for winning souls to Christ. That link would have been broken, however, had it not been for an encourager.

June 17, 1963

Who Has the Hearts of Your Children?

"Train up a child in the way he should go: and when he is old, he will not depart from it."—**Proverbs 22:6**

On June 17, 1963, the gavel fell in the verdict of Abington School District versus Schempp, declaring that prayer and Bible reading in American public schools was unconstitutional. The nation's reaction was split as the news media, national leaders, and average citizens all took sides on the issue. The ruling showed that the United States was drifting from its founding principles that were guided so carefully by Scripture and bathed in prayer. Satan was now given a foothold in public schools that is obvious to this day.

While we can blame the problems of our youth on others, we should be careful. Parents, what are you doing to diligently train your children in the ways of God? God places the responsibility of raising our children in God's Word squarely on Dad and Mom: "And these words, which I command thee this day, shall be in thine heart: And thou shalt teach them diligently unto thy children, and shalt talk of them when thou sittest in thine house, and when thou walkest by the way, and when thou liest down, and when thou risest up. And thou shalt bind them for a sign upon thine hand and they shall be as frontlets between thine eyes. And thou shalt write them upon the posts of thy house, and on thy gates" (Deuteronomy 6:6–9).

How much time do our children spend in front of a television, on the Internet, on social media, in front of a game console, or with their friends compared to the time they are influenced in some way by God's Word? Should we be surprised that they have little interest in God or spiritual things if we are not making an effort to whet their appetites? Do we wonder why they do not follow in our footsteps in their faith if we never spend time teaching them spiritual things? The public education system is not going to change any time soon. Our homes, however, could change the emphasis today. Spend some time today lovingly training your children in the way that they should go.

June 20, 1915

A Local Church Baptist

"That we should be to the praise of his glory, who first trusted in Christ."
—Ephesians 1:12

On June 20, 1915, Blaine Myron Cedarholm was born. His dad led singing in revival meetings often, and Cedarholm, hearing the Gospel early in life, was saved at the age of four. From that moment on, it seemed that he was destined to be a preacher of the Gospel. No doubt, he could have done other things. Blessed with tremendous size and physical strength, he won a letter in four sports at the University of Minnesota—football, swimming, boxing, and track. As a fullback for the Gophers, he won All-American honors his senior year.

Dr. Cedarholm was a "rapid-fire" preacher who could say more in an hour than most could say in a week of revival services. After receiving his theological training in Philadelphia, he pastored in that city for five years before traveling as an evangelist for the next twenty years. During that time on the road, he was instrumental in seeing nearly one thousand churches planted across the United States. As the Conservative Baptist Convention began to drift, Dr. Cedarholm took his stand and became an independent Baptist. His passion was now training the next generation of preachers which he did faithfully at Pillsbury Baptist Bible College in Owatonna, Minnesota, and at Maranatha Baptist Bible College in Watertown, Wisconsin.

He was known as a Baptist with a capital "B." He was unwavering in his stand for the principles that distinguished Baptist churches as New Testament churches. His life and legacy continue to influence his "preacher boys" to this day as his desire was to live for the praise of God's glory—nothing less.

Are you living to that end today? Are you standing for biblical truth? Are you faithful to a New Testament local church? Stand where God and the Bible stand. You will never go wrong, and you will live your life for the praise of His glory.

June 20, 1736

The Record Is on High

"But he that glorieth, let him glory in the Lord. For not he that commendeth himself is approved, but whom the Lord commendeth."—**2 Corinthians 10:17–18**

George Whitefield was twenty-two years old when he preached his ordination sermon on June 20, 1736, entitled "Let No Man Despise Thy Youth." Whitefield would become one of the most powerful evangelists in England and the American colonies. His booming voice could be clearly heard by twenty thousand people without a microphone. Despite his being cross-eyed, Whitefield would become almost a celebrity in his day, alongside the Wesley brothers and Jonathan Edwards. But Whitefield's focus was not on his fame or even his ministry. His continued focus was to be used of God to see revival in his generation. When his friends encouraged him to start a denomination for his followers, he refused. Very little is recorded in books about Whitefield's ministry and historians agree that the little preserved from his life and ministry was his own fault. He did not keep a diary or memoirs that could be produced and read later. In fact, he requested that his tombstone would bear the following words: "Here lies G. W. The record is on high." God used this humble servant to usher in the First Great Awakening in America through his preaching.

Do you have to get credit or be acknowledged by man for everything you do? Do you constantly speak of what you are doing for the Lord? Or are you okay with God keeping the record? His records are far more accurate than any ledger here on earth and His memory is unfailing. "For God is not unrighteous to forget your work and labour of love, which ye have shewed toward his name, in that ye have ministered to the saints, and do minister" (Hebrews 6:10). In fact, Jesus reminded us that the smallest of deeds will be remembered and rewarded. "And whosoever shall give to drink unto one of these little ones a cup of cold water only in the name of a disciple, verily I say unto you, he shall in no wise lose his reward" (Matthew 10:42). Just play the game and let God keep the score!

June 22, 1873

What Will It Take to Stop You?

"If thou faint in the day of adversity, thy strength is small."—**Proverbs 24:10**

D. L. Moody and Ira Sankey had arrived in England for the first time. God had used their ministry greatly in America, but they had never ministered in England where a different culture awaited them. Soon after they landed, they found out that the expense money for the trip had not been sent, and the two pastor friends who had originally invited them had both died. Sankey would later describe the situation: "It was anything but cheerful. Here we were in a strange country without an invitation, no committee, and mighty little cash." Moody, holding the letter, replied, "If the Lord opens a door, we'll go through. If not, we'll go back to America."

Moody was used to preaching to thousands in the States, but in Moody's first meeting in England, he would preach to only fifty people. Ira Sankey would describe in his autobiography that Moody did not show one sign of anxiety: "Less than fifty present! They took their seats as far away from the pulpit as possible! They wouldn't sing; they didn't take to the little organ, or the Yankee tunes."

But Moody was not a quitter. He was determined to preach the Gospel whether fifty or five thousand attended. And God blessed Moody's tenacity. Moody would continue his evangelistic campaign in England, and the British people would grow to love these American evangelists and respond to God's message.

Are you thinking about quitting because of some adversity in your life? Are you discouraged because the Christian life isn't what you expected? In your own strength you will wilt at every obstacle, so let God be your strength. He will see you through the difficult times. "God is our refuge and strength, a very present help in time of trouble" (Psalm 46:1).

June 22, 1750

Resolved to Be Faithful

"But Daniel purposed in his heart..."—**Daniel 1:8a**

Are we committed to serving Jesus Christ no matter what comes our way or have we given ourselves a way out of God's will should it become too difficult or trying? We have no idea what lies ahead of us in our journey as a child of God. There may be good times or bad times, easy roads or difficult paths. We may be called upon to serve in sickness or in health, in riches or poverty. Are we resolved regardless of the cost?

Nine years after Jonathan Edwards preached his groundbreaking message, "Sinners in the Hands of an Angry God," he was dismissed from his pulpit on June 22, 1750. He had poured his life and soul into his ministry, but his church became upset about his fearless preaching. Edwards was dismissed for preaching against ungodly books, the dance, and the unsaved taking communion. Despite his trials, his mind drifted back to his Resolutions as a young man. Resolution #1: "Resolved, that I will do whatsoever I think to be most to God's glory, and my own good, profit and pleasure, in the whole of my duration, without any consideration of the time, whether now, or never so many myriad's of ages hence. Resolved to do whatever I think to be my duty and most for the good and advantage of mankind in general. Resolved to do this, whatever difficulties I meet with, how many and how great soever."

God honors that kind of resolve. His church may have tired of his preaching with few coming to his defense. But the name Jonathan Edwards is forever linked with the First Great Awakening in America. His preaching continued to inspire and instruct others for years after the first great revival in the Colonies and especially sparked a fire in the hearts of young people to follow in his footsteps.

The response and results of our service is in God's hands—the resolve is in ours. Remain faithful, Christian.

June 23, 1909

The Simplicity of the Gospel

"For God so loved the world, that he gave his only begotten Son, that whosoever believeth in him should not perish, but have everlasting life."—**John 3:16**

Monroe Parker was born in Thomasville, Alabama, on this day in 1909, but he was raised in Texas where his father worked in a dry goods store. In his college years, Monroe was only known for his carousing, drinking, and partying, until one night at age nineteen, he heard Bob Jones Sr. preach a sermon entitled "The Perils of America." Parker's life changed that night. He would soon transfer to Bob Jones College and study to become a preacher.

Blessed with a quick wit and gifted mind, Monroe Parker became known as an eloquent speaker with the gift of an orator. He could paint a picture like no one else, and his illustrations of biblical truths touched the hearts of those who heard him. In one particular revival meeting, the pastor informed him that a number of preachers would be in the service that night. Upon hearing this, Parker wanted to preach something that would impress the preachers in the audience. That afternoon he prepared a masterpiece and looked forward to preaching it with his usual flair and style.

As he looked over the crowd during the singing, Parker noticed that the church folk had brought a large number of unsaved guests to the meeting. The Holy Spirit pricked the heart of the talented evangelist with the words of the last congregational hymn, "Christ receiveth sinful men." The words of the chorus struck a blow: "Make the message clear and plain, Christ receiveth sinful men." Just before stepping to the pulpit he tucked the notes to his masterpiece into his pocket and opened his Bible to John 3:16 and preached the simple message of salvation. Dozens were saved that night because of his obedience.

June 24, 1904

Life's Purpose

"For the Son of man is come to seek and to save that which was lost."
—Luke 19:10

On June 24, 1904, William Booth, founder of the Salvation Army, took a pen and some paper and wrote a simple poem describing his life purpose:

"Some men's ambition is art;
Some men's ambition is fame;
Some men's ambition is gold;
My ambition is the souls of men."

He had told his wife after a camp meeting in London many years before: "Oh, Kate, I have found my destiny. These are the people for whose salvation I have been longing all these years. As I passed the doors of the flaming sin-palaces tonight I seemed to hear a voice sounding in my ears, 'Where can you go to find such heathen as these, and where is there so great a need for your labours?' And there and then in my soul I offered up myself and you and the children to this great work. These people shall be our people, and they shall have our God for their God."

Eight short years after writing that simple poem, God would call William Booth home to Heaven. Booth, however, had raised up an army of workers who made the salvation of men their primary purpose.

What is your life purpose? Do you have one? The purpose of Jesus Christ in coming to this world to seek and save the lost (Luke 19:10) has been given to us: "To wit, that God was in Christ, reconciling the world unto himself, not imputing their trespasses unto them; and hath committed unto us the word of reconciliation…Now then we are ambassadors for Christ" (2 Corinthians 5:19–20). Will you serve in your position as an ambassador for Christ faithfully today?

June 25, 1868

The Encouragement of a Spouse

"Whoso findeth a wife findeth a good thing, and obtaineth favour of the LORD."
—Proverbs 18:22

Helen Thompson was born in Dundee, Illinois, to William and Ellen Thompson. She grew up in Chicago, where she taught Sunday school as a teenager and eventually went to Business College.

Soon after Billy Sunday was saved, he met Helen, often called "Nell" by her friends, at a church social, and they began courting. Billy Sunday would find a priceless treasure in his soon-to-be wife. God was bringing them together for a special time and a special reason. "Ma Sunday" as she was affectionately called by many, was her husband's biggest cheerleader and a faithful companion in the work of revivals.

Are you supportive of your spouse and his or her desire to serve the Lord? Are you walking in harmony on your journey of faith? So often a husband or wife is hindered by a spouse who doesn't have the same commitment to the things of God. The synergy of a husband and wife when centered in the will of God can produce so much more than the individuals could ever accomplish by themselves. The encouragement of a spouse can keep someone in the battle. "Two are better than one; because they have a good reward for their labour. For if they fall, the one will lift up his fellow: but woe to him that is alone when he falleth; for he hath not another to help him up" (Ecclesiastes 4:9–10).

Find a way to encourage your spouse today. If you are not yet married, ask God to help you lift up a friend and encourage them in their work for the Lord. Be a blessing to your pastor or someone on your church staff. We need each other! Determine to help someone on their journey today.

Job 3–4 // Acts 7:44–60

June 25, 1877

The Secret to Success

"Keep thy heart with all diligence; for out of it are the issues of life."
—Proverbs 4:23

"General" William Booth was always on the lookout for new evangelists to join the Salvation Army. Booth noticed the potential of the Smith family in the Salvation Army Christian Mission in London and invited Gypsy to be a "captain" in the ministry. Gypsy Smith would serve in the Salvation Army for six years, seeing 23,000 people saved through his ministry with General Booth. Later an old gypsy man would place his hand on Smith's head at the end of one of his evangelistic meetings. The old gypsy told him, "I'm feeling for the secret to your success." Gypsy Smith replied, "Well, my brother, you are too high. The secret of my success lies in my heart."

Is your heart tender toward God and ready to obey His commands? God mentions the "heart" over eight hundred times in the Bible. We tend to look on the outward appearance, but "the LORD looketh on the heart" (See 1 Samuel 16:7). Sadly there are many people today like those in Isaiah's day, who were described thus: "Wherefore the Lord said, Forasmuch as this people draw near me with their mouth, and with their lips do honour me, but have removed their heart far from me, and their fear toward me is taught by the precept of men" (Isaiah 29:13).

Revival is not a reformation of the outside but starts with an inner working of the Holy Spirit in our hearts. When the heart is revived, habits will be reformed. When the heart is pure, our practice will be honorable. Are you diligently guarding your heart from those influences that will keep you from revival? Are you cultivating a heart for God? A sensitive heart is the secret to success with and for God.

June 22, 1875

Let God Take Care of Your Enemies

"Recompense to no man evil for evil. Provide things honest in the sight of all men. Be not overcome of evil, but overcome evil with good."—**Romans 12:17, 21**

D. L. Moody was gaining prominence in 1875, and the news media was digging up dirt on the evangelist. The *New York Times* was, in Moody's son's words, "strong in its opposition to evangelists." They reported on Moody and Sankey that they were "credibly informed that messengers Moody and Sankey were sent to England by Mr. P.T. Barnum as a matter of speculation," referring to the Barnum and Bailey Circus. The *Saturday Review* reported on a different date that they were taken back when "so many persons go to hear the Americans. As for Moody, he is simply a ranter of the most vulgar type. His mission appears to degrade religion to the level of the 'penny gaff.'" The "penny gaff" was the lowest and cheapest form of entertainment in Moody's day, usually a short theatrical production in a back room or alley. The newspapers had degraded the preaching of the Gospel as a back-alley dance.

What do we do when people criticize, make unkind and false accusations, or ridicule our testimonies? Peter advises us to look to Jesus Christ as our model in 1 Peter 2:21–23: "For even hereunto were ye called: because Christ also suffered for us, leaving us an example, that ye should follow in his steps: Who did not sin, neither was guile found in his mouth: Who, when he was reviled, reviled not again: when he suffered, he threatened not; but committed himself to him that judgeth righteously."

Lost people will always act like lost people, but God's people should never respond like lost people. God will have the last word, and we can be sure that He will judge righteously. Like Moody and Sankey, overcome evil with good. They did not respond to the accusations, but rather went on preaching revivals and winning the lost to Christ. Is someone harassing you for your faith? Pray the prayer of Jesus, "Father, forgive them; for they know not what they do" (Luke 23:34a).

June 28, 1703

A Mother's Example

"Every wise woman buildeth her house: but the foolish plucketh it down with her hands."—**Proverbs 14:1**

John Wesley was born in Epworth, Lincolnshire, England, on this day in 1703. John Wesley was one of nineteen children and would owe much of his ministry to his godly mother's example and prayers. Susannah Wesley knew that if her children were to grow up and serve the Lord, they would need a godly home that would shape their lives from an early age.

Most women today struggle with raising two or three kids, much less nineteen! When did she possibly have time to pray for her children and how could she possibly keep her sanity well enough to be the example they needed? In the midst of nineteen children, Susannah Wesley knew that she needed quiet time with the Lord. The only way she could get it was to pull her apron up over her head, and, in those brief moments, she would block off all the distractions and talk to the Lord.

John and Charles Wesley would emerge from that home and become a powerful influence in the British Isles. They were so disciplined in their service for the Lord that they were soon labeled as "Methodists." John Wesley would be known for his preaching and writing while Charles would pen the words to some fifteen hundred hymns.

Susannah Wesley was a wise woman who did more than cook meals, wash clothes, and clean house. She molded children who would influence the world for revival!

In the frantic pace and busyness of our lives, can our children count on us to find time with God on their behalf? They must! Pull the apron over your head today, and ask God to use you to mold children who will influence others for revival.

June 28, 1914

A Man of God

"And he said unto him, Behold now, there is in this city a man of God...."
—1 Samuel 9:6a

There may never have lived a more unique individual than Lester Roloff. Born on June 28, 1914, Roloff was raised in Dawson, Texas. Following salvation at an early age, he sensed the call of God on his life and began preaching at the age of eighteen. He realized he needed some training and so went to Baylor University in Waco, Texas. He took his milk cow with him and sold her milk each day to pay his way through college.

Whether preaching in a church, flying his small airplane, raising money for his children's homes, or fighting legal battles in court against those who hated his ministry, both saved and lost people recognized quickly that this was a man of God. It seemed he was always in the middle of a big battle, but he had a big God and his faith in Him was unflappable. Often as he preached, he would just start singing, and no doubt his favorite song was "Living by Faith." The words would characterize his life.

I care not today what the morrow may bring,
If shadow or sunshine or rain,
The Lord I know ruleth o'er everything,
And all of my worry is vain.

I know that He safely will carry me through,
No matter what evils betide;
Why should I then care though the tempest may blow,
If Jesus walks close to my side?

Living by faith in Jesus above,
Trusting confiding in His great love;
From all harm safe in His sheltering arm,
I'm living by faith and feel no alarm.

June, 25 1907

Just Keep on Going

"So I spake unto the people in the morning: and at even my wife died; and I did in the morning as I was commanded."—**Ezekiel 24:18**

Life can sometimes wield unexpected blows. Trials and troubles can come out of nowhere and hardly give us time to think about what has happened. These knockout punches can leave many a strong person staggering and groping in despair and despondency.

Irene Chapman, the wife of J. Wilbur Chapman, had died twenty-one years before. Two years later after Irene's death, with a young daughter by his side from his first wife, he married Agnes Strain. Now, on June 25, 1907, God took his second wife home and Chapman was left alone once again.

Fortunately, Chapman had friends in the ministry like Billy Sunday and William Biederwolf who sent telegrams of encouragement and love. As Ezekiel of old, Chapman didn't stop to complain or stew in self pity, but continued to preach as God had commanded. The next year, he would begin his historic, worldwide campaigns with song leader Charles Alexander.

We cannot change the past, but we can change our reaction to the past. We can sulk in bitterness over our difficulties and losses, or we can claim the promise in Romans 8:28: "And we know that all things work together for good to them that love God, to them who are the called according to his purpose."

If life has taken an unexpected turn, keep going. God has promised: "I will never leave thee, nor forsake thee. So that we may boldly say, The Lord is my helper, and I will not fear what man shall do unto me" (Hebrews 13:5b–6). His plan is perfect, and if we trust Him completely, He will direct our paths for the future: "Trust in the LORD with all thine heart; and lean not unto thine own understanding. In all thy ways acknowledge him, and he shall direct thy paths" (Proverbs 3:5–6).

JULY

July 1, 1824

A Prayer Warrior

"O that one might plead for a man with God, as a man pleadeth for his neighbor!"—**Job 16:21**

St. Lawrence Presbytery met to ordain Charles Finney on July 1, 1824. Finney was called upon to preach an extemporaneous sermon. The council criticized his impromptu message because "he condescended to talk to the people in a colloquial manner...his exhortations were too vehement...[and] he spoke in too many strong terms of the hazard of life, and too severely blamed the people for their sin."

The pastor who ordained Finney would later regret his decision because of Finney's reputation as a fanatic. But this day would also mark Finney's first meeting with Daniel Nash, who would become his prayer warrior for revival. Finney would later describe the meeting: "At this meeting of the presbytery I first saw Rev. Daniel Nash, who is generally known as 'Father Nash.' He was a member of the presbytery. A large congregation was assembled to hear my examination. I got in a little late and saw a man standing in the pulpit speaking to the people, as I supposed. He looked at me, I observed, as I came in; and was looking at others as they passed up the aisles. As soon as I reached my seat and listened, I observed that he was praying. I was surprised to see him looking all over the house, as if he were talking to the people; while in fact he was praying to God."

Daniel Nash would go to a city two or three weeks before Finney would arrive, rent a room, and begin to fast and pray for the revival. Few knew him or of him, but Finney would later say that when Nash died, the power in his revival meetings began to wane.

No powerful revival will take place without the power of prayer! Will you plead with God for revival?

July 2, 1750

Compromise Kills Revival

"Your glorying is not good. Know ye not that a little leaven leaveneth the whole lump?"—**1 Corinthians 5:6**

It doesn't take but a pinch of yeast in the mixture of ingredients to cause a loaf of bread to rise as it is baked. The Apostle Paul teaches us that it doesn't take but a small compromise of truth, and the Spirit of God is quenched and the power of God stifled. Indeed, it is often "...the little foxes, that spoil the vines..." (Song of Solomon 2:15).

Shortly after the First Great Awakening, the Colonies passed what was called the Halfway Covenant. The Halfway Covenant allowed unsaved people to be baptized and join a church, primarily to bring in money to the state-church system. For someone to serve in government, they needed to be a church member, and thus the Halfway Covenant flooded churches with unsaved people wanting to be baptized. Many churches compromised and thus were filled with lost church members.

Jonathan Edwards took his stand against this covenant and was voted out of his church as a result by a 230 to 23 tally. As he left the church for the last time on July 2, 1750, this giant of the faith would be cast out of his own church, shamed and scorned by those around him because he would not compromise. At the time, Edwards may have wondered if he did the right thing. Few today, however, are aware of the Halfway Covenant, while most are well aware the role that the Great Awakening played in the formation of this country, with Jonathan Edwards leading the way.

Never sacrifice the future on the altar of the immediate. What is gained by compromise to truth will fizzle and fall, but the Word of God shall stand for ever. (See Psalm 119:89).

July 3, 1863

Keep Your Promises

"When thou vowest a vow unto God, defer not to pay it; for he hath no pleasure in fools: pay that which thou hast vowed. Better is it that thou shouldest not vow, than that thou shouldest vow and not pay."—**Ecclesiastes 5:4–5**

As a lady lay dying in the city of Chicago, she kindly asked her pastor if he would please find her wayward son and tell him about Christ. D. L. Moody made a promise before God that night that he would find her son and give him the Gospel. Moody learned that the boy worked as a bellboy in a downtown hotel. On the night before the Fourth of July in 1863, Moody made his way to the hotel. Upon locating the boy, he asked him where the quietest place was where they could talk. The young man took him up to the roof of the hotel overlooking downtown Chicago. Fireworks were exploding all around them as they stood on that rooftop. God quieted the young man's heart as this faithful soul winner shared the Gospel. In a few moments the boy was wonderfully converted to Christ. Moody described the scene: "Below was the tumult of the city. It was the night before the Fourth of July and they were firing off cannons and skyrockets. There on the roof, at midnight, this boy was praying!" No doubt the angels in Heaven were making some noise above them that rivaled the noise below! "Likewise, I say unto you, there is joy in the presence of the angels of God over one sinner that repenteth" (Luke 15:10).

Do you keep your promises? Have you told your pastor or a missionary that you would pray for them? Do you? Have you made a commitment at the altar after a sermon that you have not fulfilled? Have you made promises to your family that have been broken? Will you demonstrate your love to God and others by keeping your promises as God has kept His to you? "God is not a man, that he should lie; neither the son of man, that he should repent: hath he said, and shall he not do it? or hath he spoken, and shall he not make it good?" (Numbers 23:19). God doesn't send revival to liars—He sends revival to lovers! Those who love God keep their promises to Him.

July 4, 1820

Respect for the Reward

"By faith Moses, when he was come to years, refused to be called the son of Pharaoh's daughter...Esteeming the reproach of Christ greater riches than the treasures in Egypt: for he had respect unto the recompence of the reward."
—**Hebrews 11:24, 26**

Moses could have had fame, wealth, and power. He was in a perfect place and knew all the right people. His training had prepared him for a luxurious life in Egypt. Moses, however, knew that God's blessing now and in eternity was far more valuable than anything Egypt could offer. Turning his back on it all, he stepped out by faith and followed God.

Robert Sheffey, one of the key circuit-riding preachers of the nineteenth century, was born in Ivanhoe, Virginia, on July 4, 1820. When Robert was just two years old, his mother died and he was sent to live with his aunt. There he would enjoy the prominence of his family in the town and soon head off to Emory and Henry College. With wealth aplenty and esteemed training, his future was bright in whatever field he would choose. God would hijack his plans for earthly wealth and fame and call him to a work that would yield eternal rewards. Traveling by horseback, Sheffey would take the Gospel and stir the fires of revival in the small towns of the Appalachian Mountains.

God's rewards are of far more value than anything this world has to offer. We serve the Creator of the Universe. We don't have to worry if we will be taken care of. "Are not five sparrows sold for two farthings, and not one of them is forgotten before God? But even the very hairs of your head are all numbered. Fear not therefore: ye are of more value than many sparrows" (Luke 12:6–7). We simply need to follow God by faith, keeping our eyes on the eternal. In this, we have not only the example of Moses, but in a far greater way, the example of Christ: "Looking unto Jesus the author and finisher of our faith; who for the joy that was set before him endured the cross, despising the shame, and is set down at the right hand of the throne of God" (Hebrews 12:2).

Summer, 1953

Even the Deaf Shall Hear

"The blind receive their sight, and the lame walk, the lepers are cleansed, and the deaf hear, the dead are raised up, and the poor have the gospel preached to them."—**Matthew 11:5**

In 1939, Bill and Catherine Rice moved to Illinois to prepare for the field of evangelism. It was that same year that their little baby girl, Betty, became extremely ill with spinal meningitis. Though she survived, she lost her ability to hear because of a high fever.

As Dr. Rice traveled all across the country preaching revivals, he was burdened that his own daughter could not hear the plan of salvation. With pictures and a blackboard, Cathy communicated the Bible stories to her daughter which resulted in her salvation. In 1950, while preaching in Murfreesboro, Tennessee, God led them to buy some property west of the city, and the Bill Rice Ranch was born. In the summer of 1953, the first week of camp was held for deaf young people who could come free of charge to ride horses, go swimming, play games, but most importantly hear the Gospel preached through sign language.

What a great example of a tragedy turned to triumph by an Almighty God. Deaf and hearing people alike for decades now have rejoiced that the Rice's did not let unfortunate circumstances harden their hearts, but rather allowed those unfortunate events to lead them to reach multitudes who otherwise may never have "heard."

We tend to think of our trials as unfortunate events with little eternal value. That is not how God sees them. How might God want to use your trials for His glory?

July 6, 2000

Separated No More

"And God shall wipe away all tears from their eyes; and there shall be no more death, neither sorrow, nor crying, neither shall there be any more pain: for the former things are passed away."—**Revelation 21:4**

When Joe Boyd traveled as an evangelist, it was difficult to take his family with him to the revivals. For many years, Brother Joe would travel alone up and down the highways preaching revivals and evangelistic crusades while his wife Edith, whom he affectionately called "Dolly," stayed at home. Mrs. Boyd was active in her church, cared for her aged mother many of those years, and worked a part time job. Those reunions when Joe could get home were special for the Boyds. As departure day would come once again, they would say their goodbyes with hugs and kisses and then Brother Joe would always say, "Dolly, if one of us dies before the other, I will meet you just inside the Eastern Gate up yonder."

Mrs. Edith Boyd did die first, on this day in the year 2000. Dr. Boyd continued to preach for nearly another decade before God called him home as well. I'm sure they found each other just inside the Eastern Gate. Often when Brother Joe was alone, you could hear him humming or singing this old song:

I will meet you in the morning, just inside the Eastern Gate;
Then be ready, faithful pilgrim, Lest with you it be too late.
If you hasten off to glory, Linger near the Eastern Gate,

For I'm coming in the morning; so you'll not have long to wait.
Oh the joys of that glad meeting, with the saints who for us wait!
What a blessed, happy meeting just inside the Eastern Gate.

I will meet you, I will meet you, Just inside the Eastern Gate over there;
I will meet you I will meet you, I will meet you in the morning over there.

Thank God we don't sorrow as those who have no hope! There will be a reunion one day with those who have gone before us, never to be separated again.

July 7, 1887

Writing the History of the Future

"Now also when I am old and greyheaded, O God, forsake me not; until I have shewed thy strength unto this generation, and thy power to every one that is to come."—**Psalm 71:18**

The psalmist had one thing left on his "bucket list." He knew that his time on earth was running out, but he desired to pass on to the next generation the goodness and grace of God. While most have plenty to do without worrying about anyone else, it is essential and part of our obligation to train those coming behind us to serve the Lord.

When you read the biography of D. L. Moody, he was obviously a very busy man and gave his energy completely to reaching the lost for Christ. But Moody knew the heart of the psalmist as well. In July of 1887, he held his Student's Conference with 250 students attending representing eighty colleges in twenty-five states. Mornings were spent in sessions with Mr. Moody, and afternoons were spent in personal study or athletic competition. Moody's biographer would describe the atmosphere of the Student Conference: "a peculiar tenderness of feeling prevailed during the closing days of the meeting." God worked specifically in the heart of the young people in the area of missions with over 100 students announcing that God had called them to the mission field.

Moody would die before his sixty-third birthday, but the work of God would continue, in part, because of his willingness to invest in the next generation.

Who can you encourage that is coming after you? Scripture instructs us to pass the truths of God's Word on to others: "And the things that thou hast heard of me among many witnesses, the same commit thou to faithful men, who shall be able to teach others also" (2 Timothy 2:2). Time and training given to them allows you to "write the history of the future."

July 8, 1741

The Genesis of an Awakening

"To me belongeth vengeance, and recompence; their foot shall slide in due time: for the day of their calamity is at hand, and the things that shall come upon them make haste."—**Deuteronomy 32:35**

Pastor Jonathan Edwards was excited to hear the news of Evangelist George Whitefield's success in England and organized a trip for Whitefield to preach in Boston and at his church in Northampton. As Whitefield preached, the powerful evangelist reported and reminded them about the revivals that were sparking in the colonies and in England. During the entire sermon, Edwards was greatly moved for the need of revival in his own church.

Later on July 8, 1741, the frail, unimpressive pastor, after much fasting and prayer, would go to his pulpit in Enfield, Massachusetts, and preach the now famous message, "Sinners in the Hands of an Angry God." He would read his sermon that day, monotone and seemingly impassionate without animation or gesture. His text was Deuteronomy 32:35, and after reading it he began, "In this verse is threatened the vengeance of God on the wicked unbelieving Israelites, who were God's visible people, and who lived under the means of grace; but who, notwithstanding all God's wonderful works towards them, remained void of counsel, having no understanding in them." As he progressed in his message, the parishioners began to weep and grasp the pews in front of them, fearing God's judgement as Edwards continued reading his message.

Edwards closed his sermon with, "And let every one that is yet out of Christ, and hanging over the pit of hell, whether they be old men and women, or middle aged, or young people, or little children, now hearken to the loud calls of God's word and providence...Therefore, let every one that is out of Christ, now awake and fly from the wrath to come.'" The Great Awakening had begun!

July 9, 1838

Godliness with Contentment

"But godliness with contentment is great gain. For we brought nothing into this world, and it is certain we can carry nothing out. And having food and raiment let us be therewith content."—**1 Timothy 6:6–8**

Philip P. Bliss was born on this day in 1838 in a log cabin in Clearfield County, Pennsylvania. As an eleven-year old boy, he would hear the piano played for the first time, and he fell in love with the instrument. God placed the gift of music within him, and Bliss used it for the rest of his life for the glory of God.

Along with the musician Ira Sankey, Bliss traveled to many of D. L. Moody's meetings and wrote many of the songs that were used during the campaigns. He would be most known for composing the tune to the words written by H. G. Spafford after his four girls were lost at sea crossing the Atlantic Ocean: "It Is Well with My Soul."

Bliss' royalties for his songs in the year 1875 would amount to $60,000, a hefty amount for the mid-1800s. When Philip Bliss brought the entire amount as an offering, Evangelist Moody told him he should keep at least $5,000 for himself. Bliss replied, "Not a cent, it all belongs to God."

Everything we have is a gift from God. "A man can receive nothing, except it be given him from heaven" (John 3:27b). Our possessions and our priorities are linked together. "For where your treasure is, there will your heart be also" (Matthew 6:21).

Do you struggle giving your tithes and offerings to the Lord? God isn't asking us to give something that is impossible to do. He can put money in our pockets when we need it, but He is far more interested that we have Him in the first place of our heart.

July 10, 1934

Practice How You Preach

"Now therefore go, and I will be with thy mouth, and teach thee what thou shalt say."—**Exodus 4:12**

Moses was shocked that God wanted him to lead the nation of Israel out of Egypt into the Promised Land. He did not feel like he had the ability for such a task. He said, "...I am not eloquent...but I am slow of speech, and of a slow tongue" (Exodus 4:10). I wonder sometimes how many miracles have been missed because we as God's people are unwilling to place our dependence on God instead of ourselves. No one is worthy to serve the King of Kings and Lord of Lords. We are sinners saved by grace, and it is only by God's grace that we can serve Him.

The pastor and evangelist Curtis Hutson was born in Decatur, Georgia, on this day in 1934. He would later meet his future wife Barbara in high school and work at a textile mill after graduation. Hutson would travel to churches in the area around Atlanta while working as a mail carrier. He loved to hear preaching and longed to be used by God. With no formal training for ministry, Dr. Hutson would go in his garage and take a sermon that he had written and preach it. To simulate an audience, he would set some tin cans on the floor and preach to them. He was so burdened to say the right things, especially at the invitation after the message, that he tied strings to the cans and pulled them toward him as he exhorted his "audience" to come to Christ.

God used Dr. Hutson's faithful preparation and burden for the lost, allowing him to reach thousands of people for Christ and stir churches for revival. Can God use you? The only abilities God is looking for are availability, pliability, and dependability. Like Moses and Curtis Hutson, we are all candidates for God to use.

July, 1875

Never Give Up

"And there came thither certain Jews from Antioch and Iconium, who persuaded the people, and, having stoned Paul, drew him out of the city, supposing he had been dead. Howbeit, as the disciples stood round about him, he rose up, and came into the city: and the next day he departed with Barnabas to Derbe."
—Acts 14:19–20

The first trip by Moody and Sankey to England yielded few results, at least in comparison to their ministry in America. But these evangelists were determined that God wanted them to get the Gospel to these people. While many in England thought that revival was dead, they rose up and returned for a second visit.

God honored their tenacity as revival services were held throughout the city of London. The services were coming to a close after four and a half months of meeting. William Moody would record the statistics of his father's great London Crusade: "In Camberwell Hall, 60 meetings, attended by 480,000 people; in Victoria Hall, 45 meetings, attended by 400,000; in the Royal Haymarket Opera House, 60 meetings, attended by 330,000; in Bow Road Hall, 60 meetings, attended by 600,000; and in Agricultural Hall, 60 meetings, attended by 720,000; in all, 285 meetings, attended by 2,530,000 people. The mission cost £28,396 19s. 6d., nearly all of which was raised before the close of the meetings." What if they had quit after the first meeting? Over two and a half million people would have never heard the Word of God preached from these servants, and over 5,000 people would never have been saved!

Success is rarely calculated in days; it often takes decades of faithfulness to see the results of our labor. Don't give up! Your loved one can be saved. Your church can grow. Your city can be reached. Revival is never impossible! Most of us would have quit had we been stoned and left for dead like Paul, or felt like a failure in a revival campaign. But men like Paul and Moody were not to be stopped! Rise up, Christian, and go at it again.

July 12, 1875

The Tide of Materialism and Atheism

"So the people of Nineveh believed God, and proclaimed a fast, and put on sackcloth, from the greatest of them even to the least of them."—**Jonah 3:5**

Dr. Philip Schaff of New York described the farewell meeting of Moody in London, two years after his humble first service in Great Britain: "They have proved the elementary truths over the hearts of men more mightily than all the learned professors and eloquent pastors of England could do. As a Methodist revival, more than a hundred years ago, stopped the progress of deism, so these plain laymen from America turned the tide of modern materialism and athiesm. It is the grace of God behind these men which explains the extraordinary religious interest they have awakened all over Scotland and England. The farewell service given to the American evangelists on the 12th of July, in London, furnished abundant testimony to the fruits of their labors from the mouths of ministers and laymen of all denominations. It was a meeting which will not be forgotten."

Can the tide of materialism and atheism be stemmed in our day? It has happened before. Nineveh was not a city primed for a revival, but one sermon turned their hearts back to God. London had not received Moody on his first visit, but by the end of his second visit, the direction of the city had been altered.

Can God do these same things in the twenty-first century? Why not? He hasn't changed! "For I am the Lord, I change not..." (Malachi 3:6a). Men are still lost but the Gospel still has the power to save the lost. Yes, "...evil men and seducers shall wax worse and worse, deceiving, and being deceived. But continue thou in the things which thou hast learned and hast been assured of, knowing of whom thou hast learned them" (2 Timothy 3:13–14). We don't get a pass on our responsibilities to pray and work for revival just because our day seems to be evil. God does His best work at the worst of times!

July 10, 1873

Revival Drives Out Apathy

"So then because thou art lukewarm, and neither cold nor hot, I will spue thee out of my mouth."—**Revelation 3:16**

Nothing sickens the heart of God any more than Christian apathy. The lukewarmness of the Laodicean church is well documented in the third chapter of Revelation. The sad thing is, they were apathetic and thought they were awesome. "Because thou sayest, I am rich, and increased with goods, and have need of nothing; and knowest not that thou art wretched, and miserable, and poor, and blind, and naked" (Revelation 3:17). We are prone to become self-absorbed and self-sufficient thinking that we can get along without God in our lives, our homes, and our churches. This is why we need revival so desperately.

On July 10, 1873, *The Christian* magazine carried an article about the revival meetings conducted by Moody in the Northeast. "On Sunday morning, June 22nd, Mr. Moody preached in Salem Congregational Church to Christian workers; in the afternoon, in the Corn Exchange, to about a thousand persons, and in the evening in Wesley Chapel. Many were impressed. Every evening during the following week, Bible lectures were delivered in various chapels, each service resulting in the saving of souls, but especially in the quickening of believers. Formality and apathy are to a great extent dissipated, and Christians have been led to pray and work for the conversion of sinners."

Evangelism doesn't always produce revival, but revival always produces evangelism. Yes, God is not willing that one soul perish in Hell. But the world cannot be reached by apathetic and indifferent Christians. "Formality and apathy" must once again be "dissipated" and Christians led "to pray and work for the conversion of sinners."

July 10, 1743

Revival Is Never Easy

"For we wrestle not against flesh and blood, but against principalities, against powers, against the rulers of the darkness of this world, against spiritual wickedness in high places."—**Ephesians 6:12**

If you have read every devotional thus far in this book, you might come to the conclusion that revival was easy in the generations before us. We read of these mammoth crowds and large numbers being saved under Moody, Finney, Sunday, Rice, and Roloff, and perhaps assume that it was easy then.

On July 10, 1743, John Wesley wrote in his journal of a meeting that saw the resistance of Satan: "I preached at eight on Chowden Fell, on, 'Why will ye die, O house of Israel?' Ever since I came to Newcastle the first time, my spirit had been moved within me, at the crowds of poor wretches, who were every Sunday, in the afternoon sauntering to and fro on the Sandhill. I resolved, if possible, to find them a better employ; and as soon as the service at All Saints was over, walked straight from the church to the Sandhill, and gave out a verse of a psalm. In a few minutes, I had company enough; thousands upon thousands crowding together. But the prince of this world fought with all his might lest his kingdom should be overthrown. Indeed, the very mob of Newcastle, in the height of their rudeness, have commonly some humanity left. I scarce observed that they threw anything at all; neither did I receive the least personal hurt: but they continued thrusting one another to and fro, and making such a noise, that my voice could not be heard: so that, after spending near an hour in singing and prayer, I thought it best to adjourn to our own house."

We won't be able to pillow our head each night knowing that we were fruitful, but we can pillow our heads each night knowing that we were faithful. It was even said of Jesus in Matthew 13:58, "And he did not many mighty works there because of their unbelief." Revival has an enemy who never makes it easy.

July 11, 1922

Revival in Our Homes

"And, ye fathers, provoke not your children to wrath: but bring them up in the nurture and admonition of the Lord."—**Ephesians 6:4**

W.E. Biederwolf became the director of Winona Lake Christian Retreat in 1922. Winona Lake had been thrust into the national spotlight after Billy Sunday built his home there, and Christian retreats and conference centers sprang up all over the town. Biederwolf had travelled in evangelism as well, first as an apprentice to J. Wilbur Chapman and later on his own. Biederwolf had been used of God in a great way throughout the world and was excited about the prospect of serving in Winona Lake. He would labor there for forty years, twenty of those years as director. Burdened for the next generation to learn the doctrines of the Word of God, he would help begin the Winona Lake School of Theology. His burden for Christian homes and families would birth the Family Altar League, which by his death, would see over 250,000 families reading the Bible together and praying in a "family altar" time.

Are you leading your family in revival? Too often the revival spirit that is sought and prayed for in our churches is diminished the moment we walk through the front door of our homes. Husbands and wives feuding; children living in disobedience to their parents; ungodly influences of the media; and just plain busyness rob us of the revival we should be experiencing every day with our families. When the revivals of George Whitefield hit the city of Philadelphia, Benjamin Franklin stated, "One can hardly walk down any street in the evening without hearing songs and hymns coming from the inhabitants of every house."

Perhaps your nation or church is not ready for revival, but you could pray for one to begin in your home. Turn off the television, get off Facebook, power down your cell phone, get out God's Word, and spend some time there. Ask God to work in your life and in your family to bring about revival.

July 17, 1917

Don't Forget the Day You Were Saved

"Therefore we ought to give the most earnest heed to the things that we have heard, lest at any time we should let them slip. For if the word spoken by angels was stedfast, and every transgression and disobedience received a just recompence of reward; How shall we escape, if we neglect so great salvation...."
—**Hebrews 2:1–3a**

Charles Fuller, the creator of "The Old Fashioned Revival Hour" was saved July 17, 1917. Fuller became a student of R.A. Torrey and would influence Christianity in powerful ways through his radio broadcasts. Fuller never wanted to forget that special day in his life when he accepted Christ as his Saviour, so he began each radio program with the familiar song:

> We have heard the joyful sound: Jesus saves! Jesus saves!
> Spread the tidings all around: Jesus saves! Jesus saves!
> Bear the news to every land, Climb the steeps and cross the waves;
> Onward!—'tis our Lord's command; Jesus saves! Jesus saves!

When revival comes, our hearts and minds will be renewed as we remember what Jesus Christ did for us on an old rugged cross. Our salvation, no matter how long ago it occurred, must never grow old. Once neglected, we will lose our passion to share it with others.

Has the memory of your salvation slipped? Take a moment today to go back to the day you trusted Christ. Remember how sinful your life was made to appear to you by the conviction of the Holy Spirit and the wonderful joy that came when you asked Jesus Christ to save you. Let your heart be revived as you revel in the grace of God. "The works of the Lord are great, sought out of them that have pleasure in therein. His work is honourable and glorious: and his righteousness endueth for ever. He hath made his wonderful works to be remembered" (Psalm 111:2–4a).

July 17, 1994

Study to Show Thyself Approved unto God

"Till I come, give attendance to reading, to exhortation, to doctrine."
—1 Timothy 4:13

On this date in 1994, the "Monk" as he was often called, Dr. Monroe Parker entered Heaven. John R. Rimes remembered him as having "the best balance of knowledge and zeal." Upon his death, his Greek New Testament was "worn to a frazzle." Dr. Parker took the words of Paul to preachers seriously, "Study to shew thyself approved unto God, a workman that needeth not to be ashamed, rightly dividing the word of truth" (2 Timothy 2:15).

Not everyone has a responsibility to "rightly divide" God's Word as a preacher like Monroe Parker, but God does command us to study His Word. The truths of Scripture are not all found on the surface. We must dig and mine for them as we would silver or gold. "Yea, if thou criest after knowledge, and liftest up thy voice for understanding; If thou seekest her as silver, and searchest for her as for hid treasures; Then shalt thou understand the fear of the LORD, and find the knowledge of God" (Proverbs 2:3–5).

Some might think the Bible is way too complicated to understand and to get something from it for our lives each day. Here is a good prayer to pray before you begin to read: "Open thou mine eyes, that I may behold wondrous things out of thy law. I am a stranger in the earth: hide not thy commandments from me" (Psalm 119:18–19).

The truth is, finite man can never understand a Book written by an infinite God without His help. And did you know the Holy Spirit was given to us for that express purpose? "Howbeit when he, the Spirit of truth, is come, he will guide you into all truth" (John 16:13a). Ask the Holy Spirit to open your understanding to "all things that pertain unto life and godliness" (see 2 Peter 1:3). He is anxious to answer that prayer!

July 18, 1742

Peace and Assurance in Death

"Yea, though I walk through the valley of the shadow of death, I will fear no evil: for thou art with me; thy rod and thy staff they comfort me."—**Psalm 23:4**

John Wesley received word that his mother, Susannah Wesley, was on her deathbed. He wrote in his journal: "I left Bristol in the evening of Sunday, July 18, and on Tuesday came to London. I found my mother on the borders of eternity. But she had no doubt or fear; nor any desire but (as soon as God should call) 'to depart and be with Christ.' Wesley would credit his entire ministry to the faithfulness and influence of his godly mother.

Every person knows that they will one day die. No one has ever defeated the enemy of death unless God intervened in a miraculous way as He did with Enoch and Elijah. Barring the rapture, each of us will walk through this valley of the shadow of death.

Did you notice that God calls it the "shadow" of death? Shadows can be scary to a little child who first discovers them, but it doesn't take long to know that a shadow can do us no harm. The child of God likewise should not fear the "shadow" of death, for "We are confident, I say, and willing rather to be absent from the body, and to be present with the Lord" (2 Corinthians 5:8). The Apostle Paul determined to live for Christ, and if he died, it would be a promotion! "For to me to live is Christ, and to die is gain" (Philippians 1:21).

Often when someone dies, we say something like, "we lost a loved one today." But how can someone be "lost" when we know exactly where they are? When we come to Jesus Christ and accept Him as our Saviour, we never again have to worry about what happens when we die. "And I give unto them eternal life; and they shall never perish, neither shall any man pluck them out of my hand. My Father, which gave them me, is greater than all; and no man is able to pluck them out of my Father's hand. I and my Father are one" (John 10:28–30).

July 19, 1827

Greater Works of Revival Today

"Verily, verily, I say unto you, He that believeth on me, the works that I do shall he do also; and greater works than these shall he do; because I go unto my Father."
—John 14:12

The above verse is one of the most astounding in the Bible. Jesus is speaking and assures us that those who follow Him in obedience will see greater works for God than He did! How is that possible? While we may not have a complete answer to that question, we do know that He sent the Holy Spirit of God to live within us, and Paul reminded us in Ephesians 3:20, "Now unto him that is able to do exceeding abundantly above all that we ask or think, according to the power that worketh in us." We understand that it is not us—but God working in and through us who accomplishes these great works.

What we should note particularly, however, is that God is by no means finished with His work in this world. So many have a fatalistic attitude today that revival is impossible or that somehow we have passed by the opportunity for a mighty awakening. The old time evangelists saw amazing results in their meetings, but they too, were convinced that more of the same could be seen.

On July 19, 1827, a convention was held in New Lebanon, New York, to report on the meetings of Charles Finney. Documents from this meeting read in part, "That revivals of true religion are the work of God's Spirit, by which, in a comparatively short period of time, many persons are convinced of sin, and are brought to the exercise of repentance toward God, and faith in our Lord Jesus Christ; That the preservation and extension of true religion in our land have been much promoted by these revivals; That, according to the Bible and the indications of Providence, greater and more glorious revivals are to be expected than have yet existed." May we not be the generation that decides revival is impossible! That is contradictory to Scripture and history!

Psalms 23–25 // Acts 21:18–40

July 19, 1838

Preach the Blood

"...and the blood of Jesus Christ his Son cleanseth us from all sin."—**1 John 1:7b**

The powerful evangelist Christmas Evans had just finished his sermon in Swansea, Wales, and left his pulpit for the last time. He whispered, "This is my last sermon," and went to bed, never to return. Evans was known as the "Bunyan of Wales" because of his vivid imagination for teaching the truth of God's Word. Born with only one eye, he was somewhat hideous to behold, but his preaching swept the country of Wales. On his deathbed, before he passed, a group of preachers gathered to ask advice of the faithful preacher before he died. Evans replied, "Young men, preach the blood in the basin."

Some would criticize and reject the Bible because of its continuous emphasis on the blood. But the premise is made way back in Leviticus 17:11, "For the life of all flesh is in the blood: and I have given it to you upon the altar to make an atonement for your souls; for it is the blood that maketh an atonement for the soul." When the Old Testament believer would sin, they were required to bring a blood sacrifice to the temple in order that atonement or a covering could be made for their sin. This was to be an act of faith looking forward to the only true sacrifice for sins yet to come.

One day, Jesus Christ shed His blood on the cross as a final and complete atonement for sin. "By the which will we are sanctified through the offering of the body of Jesus Christ once for all. And every priest standeth daily ministering and offering oftentimes the same sacrifices, which can never take away sins: But this man, after he had offered one sacrifice for sins for ever, sat down on the right hand of God" (Hebrews 10:10–12). Without the message of the blood of Christ, we have no Gospel to preach!

> There is a fountain filled with blood drawn from Emmanuel's veins;
> And sinners plunged beneath that flood lose all their guilty stains.

July 1903

Rejoicing in Heaven

"Likewise, I say unto you, there is joy in the presence of the angels of God over one sinner that repenteth."—**Luke 15:10**

Do we rejoice when people walk the aisle to be saved in our churches or follow the Lord in believer's baptism, or have these events become laborious and disinteresting to us? Are we in a hurry for the service to end so that we can get on to our priorities? Do we complain about a long invitation or the care that is given to the new converts?

R.A. Torrey and Charles Alexander were amazed at what they had seen on their international tour. Hundreds of thousands of people attended their crusades, and thousands of souls were saved. As Torrey and Alexander's ship reached America again, the evangelists no doubt thanked the Lord for what they experienced in His ministry. After reaching Chicago, a crowd of ten thousand people tried to enter the auditorium of the Bible Institute to greet the evangelists and rejoice with them over the souls that were saved.

Maybe God isn't interested in sending revival because we aren't interested in receiving one! Perhaps the Lord has stopped sending visitors to our churches because we are no longer excited to have them. Could it be that no one has walked the aisle in a while because we didn't rejoice the last time someone did? The angels in Heaven rejoice over *one.* How many would it take for you to get excited?

If we are to experience revival, we must rejoice about the things in which God rejoices. Heaven is not impressed with our grand choirs and eloquent sermons. Our organization and administration does not impress the angels. Our new dress or fancy suit doesn't command the attention of those beyond the pearly gates. But the angels stop every time a sinner is saved and rejoice!

July 22, 1886

Wherever He Leads I'll Go

"I delight to do thy will, O my God: yea, thy law is within my heart."
—Psalm 40:8

Baylus Benjamin McKinney was born in Heflin, Louisiana, in 1886. He was known as a no-nonsense preacher who shot straight with anyone who was brave enough to listen. Joe Boyd heard him preach while he was running from God's will. Boyd was critical of his homely appearance and frail frame. During the message, McKinney looked right at Joe Boyd, pointed his finger and said, I've won 125,000 people to Christ since I got saved—how many have you won?" Dr. Boyd later said, "I was scared he was going to kill me, so I bowed my head and said, 'Lord if you will let me get out of this service alive, I'll try to win one.'" The next day Joe Boyd led his first soul to Christ.

B. B. McKinney grew up in Bistineau Baptist Church, which still holds an annual song service in his honor. He would become well-known for his evangelistic song writing. A humble and obedient man, the hymn that most characterized his life was, "Wherever He Leads I'll Go."

"Take up thy cross and follow Me," I heard my Master say;
"I gave My life to ransom thee, Surrender your all today."

He drew me closer to His side, I sought His will to know;
And in that will I now abide, Wherever He leads I'll go.

It may be through the shadows dim, Or o'er the stormy sea:
I take my cross and follow Him, Wherever He leadeth me.

My heart, my life, my all I bring, To Christ who loves me so;
He is my Master, Lord, and King, Wherever He leads I'll go.

Wherever He leads I'll go, Wherever He leads I'll go,
I'll follow my Christ who loves me so, Wherever He leads I'll go.

What might happen if you would "try to win one" person to Christ today?

July 23, 1742

It Will Be Worth It All

"Henceforth there is laid up for me a crown of righteousness, which the Lord, the righteous judge, shall give me at that day: and not to me only, but unto all them also that love his appearing."—**2 Timothy 4:8**

Susannah Wesley did not have an easy life. She was placed in jail twice because of a lack of money to pay bills. Twice her house burned down. In one of those fires, her son John Wesley had to be rescued from the second story window. She was not only the mother of nineteen children, but she was their school teacher as well. She taught them Latin and Greek as well as all of the classical studies. Susannah would read a sermon to her children every Sunday afternoon, and there was a point when over two hundred people would come to their house to hear her read. She wrote meditations and scriptural commentaries for use with her children on the Apostles Creed, The Lord's Prayer, and The Ten Commandments.

Susannah Wesley was buried in Bunhill Hills on July 23, 1742. This cemetery in London was for those who would not conform to the Anglican church. On her deathbed, she told those around her, "Children, as soon as I am released, sing a song of praise to God." Her son John wrote her epitaph:

"In sure and certain hope to rise
And claim her mansion in the skies.
A Christian here her flesh laid down,
Her cross exchanging for a crown."

Your cross in this life may be heavy as well, but one day you will exchange it for a crown! John and Charles Wesley, two of her sons, led the great Wesleyan revival in England at a time when the moral and spiritual conditions were at their worst. John would often say that he owed every victory in his ministry to his godly mother. Yes, it will be worth it all!

July 1739

Revival Fires

"...but his word was in mine heart as a burning fire shut up in my bones, and I was weary with forbearing, and I could not stay."—**Jeremiah 20:9b**

The spiritual fire that was lit in the heart of John Wesley by his mother Susannah raged within him from the moment he was sure of his salvation. He was not allowed to preach in the Anglican churches of his day, nor did he have the desire to do so. Those churches had long since abandoned the truths of God's Word and existed in compromise and demise. Wesley took to the countryside and preached to the common people. He often preached from Acts 16:31, a message entitled, "What must I do to be saved?" People by the hundreds would come from miles around to hear this young evangelist preach the Gospel.

D. L. Moody used to say, "Get on fire for God, and people will come and watch you burn!" Have you allowed the fire in your heart to burn low? Have you become complacent about soul winning? The summer months often get us out of our good disciplines and routines, but we must not neglect the harvest all around us.

Pastor Glen Teasdale, a man few have ever heard of, told some friends after his long life as a pastor was about to end. "I have been a pastor for over sixty years, but I do not recall a single week where I did not go out and knock on some doors and tell people about Christ. Even when we would go on vacation, I would slip away to a nearby town and spend an hour or two telling people about Jesus." The fire in his bones never went out!

Surely if we would ask the Lord to bring someone across our path today who needs the Gospel, He could do so. Wendall P. Loveless put his prayer in a little chorus: "Lead me to some soul today; O teach me, Lord, just what to say. Friends of mine are lost in sin, and cannot find their way; Few there are who seem to care, and few there are who pray. Melt my heart and fill my life; Give me one soul today."

July 1, 1800

Revive Thy Work

"O Lord, I have heard thy speech, and was afraid: O Lord, revive thy work in the midst of the years, in the midst of the years make known; in wrath remember mercy."—**Habakkuk 3:2**

The duration of the First Great Awakening was roughly five years. It was confined primarily to the Colonies where the vast majority of the population lived. By 1800, people were moving south and west claiming new land in search of their dreams. But unfortunately, they also moved away from the spiritual awakening their parents and grandparents had once experienced and enjoyed. Thoughts of God and religion were placed aside as new frontiers developed. Thomas Jefferson, a religiously controversial figure, was taking office as the President of the United States, and many were increasingly wary about the rise of humanistic thought in the nation. Churches were empty, and preachers were discouraged.

But God was ready to visit the nation again and once more awaken her to spiritual truth. The first Methodist camp meeting in America was held in Logan County, Kentucky, at the turn of the century. By 1801, a camp meeting in Cane Ridge, Kentucky, popularized the camp meeting as a way to counteract the increasingly secular culture. These camp meetings would soon spark the Second Great Awakening which would last over twenty-five years.

As we see the dangers of a secular culture today, we would agree with the psalmist who cried, "It is time for thee, Lord, to work: for they have made void thy law" (Psalm 119:126). Would you pray daily for revival? Would you ask others to pray with you? "Again I say unto you, That if two of you shall agree on earth as touching any thing that they shall ask, it shall be done for them of my Father which is in heaven" (Matthew 18:19).

July 26, 1827

Resistance from Within

"Beloved, follow not that which is evil, but that which is good. He that doeth good is of God: but he that doeth evil hath not seen God."—**3 John 11**

In this short epistle written by the Apostle John, he warned the church about a man named Diotrephes, who loved to have the preeminence and greatly withstood the ministry of the Apostle. John would deal with him upon his arrival. "Wherefore, if I come, I will remember his deeds which he doeth, prating against us with malicious words: and not content therewith, neither doth he himself receive the brethren, and forbiddeth them that would, and casteth them out of the church" (verse 10). How sad that sometimes resistance to the work of God comes from within. We expect the lost to oppose revival, but what a shame that some in the church do as well.

Charles Finney's ministry was not without controversy, and on July 26, 1827, a council meeting within his denomination was held to place restrictions and boundaries on the revivals held by Mr. Finney. While it is important that things be "...done decently and in order" (1 Corinthians 14:40) we must never let our personal jealousies and criticism quench the Holy Spirit's power. Many believe that the Second Great Awakening began to die because of those from within who became critical of the revivals.

In 3 John, the Apostle tells these believers to follow that which is good. We must keep our eyes on the Lord and our nose in the Book, as it were. Martha at the end of Luke 10 was intent on pleasing the Lord and doing her very best to serve Him. But her focus soon left the Lord and centered on her sister. She became critical and demanding. Her desire to please the Lord had been replaced by an envy of her sister (Luke 10:38–42). The Lord's rebuke of her is sufficient warning for each of us: "Martha, Martha, thou art careful and troubled about many things: But one thing is needful: and Mary hath chosen that good part, which shall not be taken away from her."

July 27, 1953

Closed to the Gospel?

"After they were come to Mysia, they assayed to go into Bithynia: but the Spirit suffered them not."—**Acts 16:7**

With Communism to the north, and freedom to the south, the armistice to end the Korean War was signed in the former Korean capital of Kaesong. The armistice ended the war that claimed over 545,000 lives and wounded over 2.5 million civilians. A demilitarized zone was established to separate North and South Korea. After the war, South Korea was open to missionaries and evangelists from America, and many went in to preach the Gospel and saw great spiritual fruit. Yet fifty years later, the North is still closed to the Gospel.

Churches in South Korea have funds stored up for the day when the dictatorship of North Korea is removed and the border opens. Korean pastors and evangelists stand ready to take the Gospel to their fellow men and women to the North who have never had a chance to hear the Gospel. How we need to pray for these "closed countries." There was a time when missionaries could not get into the former Soviet Union and yet today, while the situation is less than ideal, the Gospel is being preached. Missionaries are in Cuba, Laos, and Vietnam because God has cracked open the door at least for a time.

Why should we hear the Gospel twice when millions have never heard it once? May God use our generation to pray, store up funds, and train laborers to be ready to go to "Bithynia" when the Holy Spirit opens the door.

We must be careful in our thinking, however. Sometimes we assume that "open doors" mean that the going will be easy—that no sacrifice will be required. Yet, the Apostle Paul wrote, "For a great door and effectual is opened unto me, and there are many adversaries" (1 Corinthians 16:9). Any true work of God will encounter opposition, but God's grace is always greater.

July 28, 1757

By the Grace of God

"But by the grace of God I am what I am: and his grace which was bestowed upon me was not in vain; but I labored more abundantly than they all: yet not I, but the grace of God which was with me."—**1 Corinthians 15:10**

On July 28, 1757, John Wesley penned in his journal, "I do indeed live by preaching!" In one of his most popular messages "By Grace Are Ye Saved through Faith," Wesley preached: "All the blessings which God hath bestowed upon man are of his mere grace, bounty, or favor; his free, undeserved favor; favor altogether undeserved; man having no claim to the least of his mercies. It was free grace that 'formed man of the dust of the ground, and breathed into him a living soul,' and stamped on that soul the image of God, and 'put all things under his feet.' The same free grace continues to us, at this day, life, and breath, and all things. For there is nothing we are, or have, or do, which can deserve the least thing at God's hand. 'All our works, Thou, O God, hast wrought in us.' These, therefore, are so many more instances of free mercy: and whatever righteousness may be found in man, this is also the gift of God."

God's grace can be seen in our lives at every turn from the moment of our salvation until we stand before the Lord face to face. Both the victories and the defeats are part of His wonderful grace. We must not, however, "...frustrate the grace of God" (Galatians 2:21). Paul determined that God's grace would not be in vain. So many today take liberties in their grace to live as they please. But listen to the words of Paul on this matter in Titus 2:11–12, "For the grace of God that bringeth salvation hath appeared to all men, Teaching us that, denying ungodliness and worldly lusts, we should live soberly, righteously, and godly, in this present world."

Take a moment to thank the Lord for His grace in your life today and then make a commitment to live and labor in that grace in a way that pleases Him rather than yourself.

July 29, 1928

Salvation Is Not of Ourselves

"For by grace are ye saved through faith; and that not of yourselves: it is the gift of God: Not of works, lest any man should boast."—**Ephesians 2:8–9**

Monroe Parker had made a profession of salvation when he was eight years old but was continuing to live a sinful life. He would explain his testimony in later years, "I was a sinner, and I knew it." Parker eventually forsook his sinful lifestyle and became a Sunday school teacher in Birmingham, Alabama, but still was unsure of his salvation. Finally, on the morning of July 29, 1928, Evangelist Bob Schuler preached the Gospel and Monroe came under the Holy Spirit's conviction. He quickly accepted Jesus as His Saviour and shared his testimony with the church. Exactly a year later, on the same day in 1929, he was licensed to preach.

Every person knows that they are a sinner. The guilt of our conscience over wrong thoughts and deeds are constant reminders of our sinful nature. We are born in this dreadful condition. "Wherein in time past ye walked according to the course of this world, according to the prince of the power of the air, the spirit that now worketh in the children of disobedience: Among whom also we all had our conversation in times past in the lusts of our flesh, fulfilling the desires of the flesh and of the mind; and were by nature the children of wrath, even as others" (Ephesians 2:2–3).

Just like Monroe Parker, we can try to change our ways. We attempt to stop sinning and start doing something good. But salvation is "not of ourselves." Outside of Jesus Christ there is no work, reform, belief, or religion that can save us from sin. "Neither is there salvation in any other: for there is none other name under heaven given among men, whereby we must be saved" (Acts 4:12).

Has Jesus Christ saved you, or are you trying to save yourself?

July 30, 1845

We Preach Christ

"For the Jews require a sign, and the Greeks seek after wisdom: But we preach Christ crucified, unto the Jews a stumblingblock, and unto the Greeks foolishness;"—**1 Corinthians 1:22–23**

Evangelist Charles Finney would preach often at Oberlin College and spent time there training young preachers. In a periodical called *The Oberlin Evangelist,* published by the college, Finney wrote on July 30, 1845, "Alas, I cannot tell you how much my soul has been agonized to think that there could be a theological student here who could do this! Oh, let him only be full of Christ, and he will lecture on something very different from mesmerism and phrenology. Let all these young men be filled with Christ, and this institution can shake the world."

The New Testament preachers made Christ the emphasis of their sermons. John the Baptist—"The next day John seeth Jesus coming unto him, and saith, Behold the Lamb of God, which taketh away the sin of the world" (John 1:29). Peter—"Therefore let all the house of Israel know assuredly, that God hath made that same Jesus, whom ye have crucified, both Lord and Christ" (Acts 2:36). Philip—"Then Philip went down to the city of Samaria, and preached Christ unto them" (Acts 8:5). Paul—"And straightway he preached Christ in the synagogues, that he is the Son of God" (Acts 9:20). Apollos—"For he mightily convinced the Jews, and that publicly, shewing by the scriptures that Jesus was Christ" (Acts 18:28).

Let's tell someone about Christ today! All other subjects of conversation are of temporary value at best. Let's exalt the One whom God does. "Wherefore God also hath highly exalted him, and given him a name which is above every name: That at the name of Jesus every knee should bow, of things in heaven, and things in earth, and things under the earth; And that every tongue should confess that Jesus Christ is Lord, to the glory of God the Father" (Philippians 2:9–11).

July 31, 1932

God Works through Local Churches

"And I say also unto thee, That thou art Peter, and upon this rock I will build my church; and the gates of hell shall not prevail against it."—**Matthew 16:18**

Evangelist John R. Rice had begun open air revival meetings in Dallas, Texas. Many were saved in the services, and they needed a local church where they could be discipled and grow in their new-found faith. As a natural result of the evangelistic meetings in the city and his staunch belief in the importance of the local church, John R. Rice planted the Fundamental Baptist Church of Oak Cliff, Texas, for the converts to grow and fellowship in the Word of God. As the charter was signed on July 31, 1932, Rice along with those new Christians claimed the promise that God would build His church.

Are you being faithful in your local church? Sundays have become "fun days" for most in our culture today. Going to church is the last thing on their minds. Sleeping in, sports leagues for the youngsters, catching up on the work around the house, a trip to the lake or mountains, shopping, and more all seem to take precedence over the Lord's Day and His house. When the doors of our churches are open, we ought not to ask, "Are we going to church?" We ought to ask, "What time are we leaving?" "Not forsaking the assembling of ourselves together, as the manner of some is; but exhorting one another: and so much the more, as ye see the day approaching" (Hebrews 10:25).

If Jesus Christ loves the church and gave Himself for it (Ephesians 5:25), should it not have importance in our lives? Can we expect revival when we neglect the house of God? Can we expect our marriages to survive and our children to grow in spiritual matters, without the preaching and teaching of God's Word regularly? Can we expect our lost loved ones or neighbors to be saved, when we are negligent in such an important duty?

AUGUST

August 1, 1899

Longing and Looking for Revival

"For thus saith the high and lofty One that inhabiteth eternity, whose name is Holy; I dwell in the high and holy place, with him also that is of a contrite and humble spirit, to revive the spirit of the humble, and to revive the heart of the contrite ones."—**Isaiah 57:15**

One of Moody's last Northfield Conferences, called the General Conference of Christian Workers, began on August 1, 1899. Back in June, he had written a letter inviting preachers to the conference and explaining its purpose: "All of God's people who are interested in the study of His Word, in the development of their Christian lives, in a revival of the spiritual life of the church, in the conversions of sinners, and in the evangelization of the world, are cordially invited to be present…Many thoughtful men have come to feel strongly that the hope of the Church today is in deep and widespread revival. We are confronted with difficulties that can be met in no other way. The enemy has come in like a flood—it is time for those who believe in a supernatural religion to look to God to lift up a standard against him. Oh, for a revival of such power that the tide of unbelief and worthiness that is sweeping in upon us shall be beaten back; that every Christian shall be lifted to a higher level of life and power, and multitudes of perishing souls be converted to God! Why not? God's arm is not shortened, nor His ear heavy. I believe the sound of the going in the tops of the mulberry trees may already be heard."

I wonder what Moody would sense if he were alive today? I'm convinced he would be even more convinced that the only hope of our nation is revival! Not just a revival Sunday or week of meetings on the church calendar, but a mighty moving of God in our lives. It must start with brokenness and humility. It is the contrite and humble spirit that God visits in revival. "Though the LORD be high, yet hath he respect unto the lowly: but the proud he knoweth afar off" (Psalm 138:6). Revival is still a long way off if we are not willing to humble ourselves and repent of our sins.

August 1806

The Birthplace of Revival

"These all continued with one accord in prayer and supplication, with the women, and Mary the mother of Jesus, and with his brethren."—**Acts 1:14**

We love reading of the great results in Acts 2 on the day of Pentecost as three thousand people were saved, baptized, added to the church, and continued in discipleship and service. But it's important to recognize that the birthplace of this (or any other) revival was not in the public service with people, but in the private sanctuary with God. God powerfully used Peter's preaching on the day of Pentecost, but that sermon was preceded by days of prayer in the Upper Room, as we read in Acts 1. And so it has been for every revival of history. The birthplace is not in the pulpit, but in the prayer closet.

In August of 1806, five college men from Williams College held a prayer meeting in a grove of trees near the Hoosic River. As they prayed and discussed doctrine, a thunderstorm moved into the area, and the men had to take shelter from the rain inside a haystack. Samuel John Mills, James Richards, Francis L. Robbins, Harvey Loomis, and Byram Green prayed inside the haystack. After prayer, Samuel would look at his friends and utter the memorable words: "We can do it if we will."

Arthur Latham Perry later described the moments inside the haystack: "The brevity of the shower, the strangeness of the place of refuge, and the peculiarity of their topic of prayer and conference all took hold of their imaginations and their memories." Many historians point to this moment as the beginning of modern American missions. These men would soon form the American Board of Commissioners for Foreign Missions and would send missionaries to India, China, Hawaii, and Southeast Asia.

Your time in the closet of prayer today could change your life. The next prayer meeting at the church could change a nation or nations. Let's not overlook the birthplace of revival.

August 3, 1927

Satanic Opposition to Revival

"The thief cometh not, but for to steal, and to kill, and to destroy: I am come that they might have life, and that they might have it more abundantly."
—John 10:10

On this day in 1927, Mordecai Ham was crossing the street and was hit by a speeding car. He was immediately taken to the hospital where he lay bedridden for six months. The great preacher was frustrated that he could not be in his pulpit. A newspaper article in *The Oklahoman* would later quote Ham as he lay in bed recovering: "I have been lying here trying to figure out why I was hurt and who was to blame. You will remember that I had a great deal to say about the devil that was not complimentary to him. I also had announced a series of messages that I would preach on 'Satanic Cults' for this fall. I guess the devil tried to head me off. I want to serve notice on him now that unless he does a cleaner job of knocking me out I will have a great deal more to say about him just as soon as these doctors and my good wife will permit me to return to my pulpit." After the incident, his prayer meeting crowds grew to 2,200!

Satan is an unseen enemy, but he is no less real because he is invisible to us. His attacks on us, our churches, our pastors, and revival can be destructive and devastating. We cannot and must not attempt to fight him in our flesh. Second Corinthians 10:4 reminds us, "For the weapons of our warfare are not carnal, but mighty through God to the pulling down of strong holds." The devil is always upset when revival begins to crush the strongholds that Satan has spent centuries building. We are no match against him, but we have this promise in 1 John 4:4: "Ye are of God, little children, and have overcome them: because greater is he that is in you, than he that is in the world."

Anyone seeking revival is sure to face opposition from Satan, "But thanks be to God, which giveth us the victory through our Lord Jesus Christ" (1 Corinthians 15:57).

August 4, 1947

God's Word Always Works

"Now when they saw the boldness of Peter and John, and perceived that they were unlearned and ignorant men, they marveled; and they took knowledge of them, that they had been with Jesus."—**Acts 4:13**

Peter and John were rugged fishermen when Jesus called them to follow Him. They had no formal training in the synagogues or institutions of religious instruction in their day. But three years with Jesus changed their lives. They sat at the feet of the greatest Teacher who ever lived. The curriculum was without error and backed up with a perfect example of the truth taught. That kind of training caused the thinkers and scholars of their day to take notice.

Gypsy Smith died on the Queen Mary during his forty-fifth crossing of the Atlantic on August 4, 1947. His ashes would be spread in Epping Forest outside of London where he had been born eighty-seven years prior. A journalist once reported on his appearance as he preached: "A short, wiry, thick-set gentleman, with an elastic, springy step, dressed in common, everyday suiting, without style....a head well rounded and finely formed, a face of fair finish, and clear countenance, brown as the berries of the autumn bush, a heavy, dark mustache; dark eyes that glisten like diamonds, with the zeal of religious enthusiasm; a magnificent head of hair, black as a raven's wing, and strikingly suggestive of the nomadic race that gave him birth."

Smith once humbly described his life: "I didn't go through your colleges and seminaries. They wouldn't have me...but I have been to the feet of Jesus where the only true scholarship is learned." Will you spend time with Jesus today? Don't rush out into your day without a lesson at His feet. A reading of His Word and careful meditation on its truths, will equip you for the challenges you face in a far greater way than that business magazine, book on leadership, or blog on the Internet. "Come unto me, all ye that labour and are heavy laden...and learn of me" (Matthew 11:28–29).

August 1868

The Powerful Word of God

"The prophet that hath a dream, let him tell a dream; and he that hath my word, let him speak my word faithfully. What is the chaff to the wheat? saith the LORD. Is not my word like as a fire? saith the LORD; and like a hammer that breaketh the rock in pieces?"—**Jeremiah 23:28–29**

Henry Moorehouse visited Chicago again to hold revival campaigns in August of 1863. A young twenty-six-year-old Dwight Moody was eager to learn from the seasoned evangelist. He longed to preach with the kind of power and impact of a Henry Moorehouse. When Moorehouse visited his church previously, what he learned was perhaps at first unexpected. In his son's words, Moody learned that the preacher must "draw his sword full length, to fling the scabbard away, and enter the battle with a naked blade." In that revival Moorehouse preached on John 3:16 every single night! Moody would later say, "If a man gets up in that pulpit and gives out that text today, there is a smile all over the church." We have a tendency to discredit the power of Scripture when we think its truth is already familar to us—as if we no longer needed it.

Is there anything more powerful than the "naked blade" of the Sword of the Spirit? The machinery of methods and the manipulation of man will never change the heart. "For the word of God is quick, and powerful, and sharper than any two-edged sword, piercing even to the dividing asunder of soul and spirit, and of the joints and marrow, and is a discerner of the thoughts and intents of the heart" (Hebrews 4:12). And it always works! "Seek ye out of the book of the LORD, and read, no one of these shall fail…" (Isaiah 34:16). That's a promise from the One who wrote it and has commissioned the Holy Spirit to guide men and women into its truth!

We must know our weapon, use our weapon, and trust our weapon! No revival is possible with the Sword in the scabbard. Everything else, including heaven and earth, will pass away; "…but my words shall not pass away" (Mark 13:31).

August 1875

The Music of Revivals

"Speaking to yourselves in psalms and hymns and spiritual songs, singing and making melody in your heart to the Lord;"—**Ephesians 5:19**

Many of the hymns we sing and enjoy today were written during revivals. Many evangelists had musicians working with them in the campaigns, and it was natural for great songs to come to the minds of these gifted musicians as they heard Bible preaching night after night. Charles Wesley composed 1,500 hymns himself! During the Welsh Revival over 1,000 hymns were written. Proper preaching and proper music always go together because they come from the same source—the Word of God.

D. L. Moody returned to Chicago from traveling throughout England and America in August of 1875 and prayed about what the Lord would have his next project be. He felt like the Lord had laid on his heart to publish a hymnbook of the songs he collected from Ira Sankey and Philip Bliss. With the help of these men and others, Moody soon published his hymnal titled *Gospel Hymns and Sacred Songs.* Music was a key element in Moody's campaigns, and he was thankful to have a new resource for reaching souls with the Gospel and edifying the saints.

When a church is experiencing revival, the congregational singing becomes vibrant and worshipful once again. And why not—music is one of the best ways to express what God is doing in our heart. We even have an entire book of the Bible—Psalms—filled with the songs of God's people. Through its pages, we are often admonished, "O come, let us sing unto the LORD: let us make a joyful noise to the rock of our salvation" (Psalm 95:1).

We may not have a voice like Sankey or the gifts of Bliss to compose the notes, but even a "joyful noise" is pleasant to our God. Sing the Lord a song on your way to work today or maybe in a quiet place during lunch. As one little chorus puts it, "It's amazing what praising can do!"

August 1876

A Key Component

"Humble yourselves therefore under the mighty hand of God, that he may exalt you in due time."—**1 Peter 5:6**

It would be obvious to most Christians to include in the ingredients of prayer the importance of seeking God and confessing sin in the pursuit of genuine revival. But oddly, we often overlook the one God mentions first in 2 Chronicles 7:14 in His formula for an awakening: "If my people, which are called by my name, shall humble themselves...." Truthfully, we never advance much in prayer or seeking God or repentance until we humble ourselves. Humility is the component that enables the others. Without it, God stands afar off and revival is never experienced. In God's economy, the way up—is down. "Though the LORD be high, yet hath he respect unto the lowly: but the proud he knoweth afar off" (Psalm 138:6).

George C. Stebbins, who would become dear friends with Moody and Sankey and help edit the hymnal they would publish, described his first meeting with D. L. Moody at his home in Northfield in August of 1876 to help him with Sunday services: "This was the first time I had seen Mr. Moody since the night he left Chicago for his work in Great Britain, which was destined very soon to make him known throughout the Christian world. And yet, though he was then at the height of his fame, and conceded to be one of the great religious characters of his time, he was still the same unassuming and unaffected man that he was before his work had brought him into such prominence before the world." D. L. Moody's humility was a hallmark of his ministry, and one of the reasons God used him in such an amazing way.

The first step a child takes is the most difficult when learning to walk. It rarely turns out successful. The first step to revival is likewise not easy and we will fall more than once in trying to conquer our pride and self-sufficiency. Ask God to help you today—not to think less of yourself—but to not think of yourself at all.

August 8, 1738

The Presence of the Holy Spirit

"Now the Lord is that Spirit: and where the Spirit of the Lord is, there is liberty."—**2 Corinthians 3:17**

When John Wesley made his first trip to the New Land, he was miserable. Nothing went right. His sermons were dry, the people were unfriendly, and the results were scarce. He couldn't get back to England fast enough. As we saw in a previous devotion, Wesley found himself "strangely" at a service with Moravians on Aldersgate Street one night, and it was there that He trusted Christ as Saviour. I doubt that it was easy for a "missionary" to come to the realization of his lost condition and be saved, but the world is thankful that he did.

Less than four months after his conversion he returned to Georgia and was amazed at the spirit amongst the congregation that he and his brother Charles visited in the Colony of Georgia. He wrote in his journal on August 8, 1738, "What hath God wrought there in one-and-forty years?" His heart was touched by the power of real Christian ministry after he had found peace in his heart about his own eternity.

Without the Holy Spirit who enters our lives at salvation, spiritual activity and religious services will seem boring, dry, and useless. Why? Because you are still separated from God. When the Holy Spirit takes up residence in your life upon salvation, "…all things become new" (2 Corinthians 5:17).

Once we are saved, we cannot lose the presence of God for He has promised in Hebrews 13:5, "…I will never leave thee, nor forsake thee." But it is possible to quench the Holy Spirit by resisting His leading, living in sin, or neglecting our Christian duties. You can know when it's happening because you are no longer enjoying your time with God or other Christians. "Whosoever believeth that Jesus is the Christ is born of God: and every one that loveth him that begat loveth him also that is begotten of him" (1 John 5:1). How's your love for God? How's your love for other believers? Maybe it's time for revival!

August 1878

The Force of Words

"How forcible are right words!…"—**Job 6:25**

D. L. Moody invited Professor Henry Drummond to preach his sermon "The Greatest Thing in the World" at Northfield College in August of 1878. Professor Drummond had first preached this sermon three years prior alongside Moody in England. The crowd wanted Moody to preach in England, but he told them, "No, you've been hearing me for eight months, and I'm quite exhausted. Here's Drummond; he will give us a Bible reading." With that said, Drummond opened up his Bible and turned to 1 Corinthians 13. He gave a remarkable exhortation from the greatest chapter on biblical charity. The short sermon would eventually be published at Moody's "urgent plea," and literally multi-millions of copies were printed, read, and distributed.

The best place to find "right words" is in God's Word. What was supposed to just be a short, fill-in thought from Scripture, ended up affecting millions of people! We would be wise to forget what we want to say, and just say what God has already said. His words are so much more forcible than ours. We flounder and fail so many times in our witness and ministry because of what Jesus states in Matthew 22:29, "…Ye do err, not knowing the scriptures, nor the power of God." Paul adds in 1 Timothy 6:3–4, "If any man teach otherwise, and consent not to wholesome words, even the words of our Lord Jesus Christ, and to the doctrine which is according to godliness: He is proud, knowing nothing…."

Preacher, how much Bible is in your message for this Sunday? Sunday school teacher, count the verses in your lesson you plan to teach. Have you shared Scripture with a lost person lately or a wayward Christian? Does the music you listen to contain God's Word? Do the words of Scripture grace the walls in your home? How forcible are right words!

August 1–20, 1885–1899

No Sin to Confess?

"If we say that we have no sin, we deceive ourselves, and the truth is not in us. If we confess our sins, he is faithful and just to forgive us our sins, and to cleanse us from all unrighteousness. If we say that we have not sinned, we make him a liar, and his word is not in us."—**1 John 1:8–10**

After one of Moody's "August Conferences," a man approached him and boasted of his own holiness and piety. "Why, I have not sinned for years!" he bragged. "Haven't you?" replied Moody. "Well, before I shall accept your word for it I should like the testimony of your wife." Moody's son later described the man's response: "The perfectionist thereupon gave such an exhibition of temper as to warrant the spectators' sympathy for his wife and Moody's skepticism."

It seems that many have forgotten what sin is. We think it is only wrong if we get caught. Or we think that if everyone else does it, it is surely okay. First John 5:17 gives a simple, succinct definition: "All unrighteousness is sin…." The standard for righteousness is not your neighbor, your boss, or even your pastor. The only righteous one is God! So according to the Bible definition, anything "ungodlike" or "unrighteous" is sin. Have you ever filtered your thoughts, words, reactions, entertainment, friendships, and everything else in your life through Colossians 3:17? "And whatsoever ye do in word or deed, do all in the name of the Lord Jesus, giving thanks to God and the Father by him."

After you watch that movie or show, can you bow your head and thank God through Jesus name for it? How about your thoughts? Your relationships? Most of us know that we fall far short of the glory of God. That is why we need a Saviour to begin with. But many of us tolerate ongoing sin in our lives because we do not acknowledge it as such. No wonder revival tarries. We won't even acknowledge the sin that holds us back from God's Spirit working freely. "Your iniquities have turned away these things, and your sins have withholden good things from you" (Jeremiah 5:25).

August 1–20, 1885–1899

God's Supply

"I have been young, and now am old; yet have I not see the righteous forsaken, nor his seed begging bread."—**Psalm 37:25**

D. L. Moody's finances were getting low with his Bible institute and the coming summer conference. He needed ten thousand dollars to pay the bills. He described his situation: "I didn't see how I could do anything about raising the money, now, with this conference upon my hands, so I just committed the matter to the Lord." Soon, while graciously driving a lady to where she needed to go, she said, "Mr. Moody, I have decided to give you $10,000 to use for your school, just as you like." Moody rejoiced and commented, "It brings the Lord so near."

God never supplies all of our greed, but always all of our need! Philippians 4:19 promises, "But my God shall supply all your need according to his riches in glory by Christ Jesus." Why do we fret and worry when we have a God who supplies the need of the birds in the air and the lilies in the field? "Behold the fowls of the air: for they sow not, neither do they reap, nor gather into barns; yet your heavenly Father feedeth them. Are ye not much better than they? And why take ye thought for raiment? Consider the lilies of the field, how they grow; they toil not, neither do they spin: And yet I say unto you, That even Solomon in all his glory was not arrayed like one of these. Wherefore, if God so clothe the grass of the field, which to day is, and to morrow is cast into the oven, shall he not much more clothe you, O ye of little faith?" (Matthew 6:26, 28–30). How offensive it must be to God for us to suppose that He is unable to provide for us.

Commit your needs to the Lord today. Thank Him in advance for His promise to provide. Obey and serve Him with joy. Trust Him; and when He does come through for you in a miraculous way like He did for Mr. Moody—don't forget to rejoice and express your gratitude.

August 1891

God Uses the Unlikely

"But God hath chosen the foolish things of the world to confound the wise; and God hath chosen the weak things of the world to confound the things which are mighty; And base things of the world, and things which are despised, hath God chosen, yea, and things which are not, to bring to nought things that are: That no flesh should glory in his presence."—**1 Corinthians 1:27–29**

No one would have given a Gypsy boy much chance for success in life, much less in the ministry. From a poor home and a despised culture, God took Gypsy Smith and confounded the world. His first trip to America saw 1,500 people crowd into a building to hear him preach. During his second visit in 1891, a ten thousand seat auditorium was secured at a Methodist campground, and night after night each seat was filled. Gypsy Smith could never quite figure out why God would choose to use him, but the Bible makes it perfectly clear: "That no flesh should glory in his presence."

God doesn't share His glory. "I am the LORD: that is my name: and my glory will I not give to another, neither my praise to graven images" (Isaiah 42:8). Revival is often hindered because man wants too much of the glory. A powerful story is tucked away in Acts 12:21–23 that is well worth noting when we are tempted to take some of the glory for what God is doing. "And upon a set day Herod, arrayed in royal apparel, sat upon is throne, and made an oration unto them. And the people gave a shout, saying, It is the voice of a god, and not of a man. And immediately the angel of the Lord smote him, because he gave not God the glory: and he was eaten of worms, and gave up the ghost."

We can get too big for God to use us, but we can never get too small. Remember where and what you were when God saved you. Our only hope of accomplishing anything eternal is through Him. "I am the vine, ye are the branches: He that abideth in me, and I in him, the same bringeth forth much fruit: for without me ye can do nothing" (John 15:5).

August 13, 1908

The Memory of the Just

"The memory of the just is blessed: but the name of the wicked shall rot."
—Proverbs 10:7

The Scriptures teach, "A good name is rather to be chosen than great riches, and loving favour rather than silver and gold" (Proverbs 22:1). No one names their children after Ahab or Jezebel. Those names rot on the pages of history because of the wicked lives they lived. The memory of godly faithful Christians on the other hand are a blessing and of great encouragement. They leave behind them a legacy to follow as they followed the Lord.

The world lost a godly musician as Ira Sankey died in his sleep in his Brooklyn home on August 13, 1908. Glaucoma had blinded him the last five years of his life, giving him the same hardship as his friend Fanny Crosby. Sankey wrote over three hundred hymns and Gospel songs and was constantly at D. L. Moody's side until his death in 1899. The world will likely never again see an evangelistic team with the anointing of God as Moody and Sankey. One witness described the blessed ministry of these two men: "Every week the evening services are preceded by a service of song, conducted by Mr. Moody's co-laborer, Mr. Sankey, whose hymns, tunes, and voice (like those of Philip Phillips) have drawn and impressed many. Mr. Moody preaches the Gospel and Mr. Sankey sings it." The legacy of his music lives on each time we sing "Faith is the Victory," "Trusting Jesus," "Hiding in Thee," or "A Shelter in the Time of Storm."

You may not leave behind a hymn that will be sung for centuries after you pass, but what will you leave behind? A good name? A godly character? A faithful ministry? A sterling reputation? Will someone remember you for the encouragement you were to them? Will someone rejoice because it was you who led them to Christ? May we live today so that our memory is blessed!

August 14, 1875

Advance

"Brethren, I count not myself to have apprehended: but this one thing I do, forgetting those things which are behind, and reaching forth unto those thing which are before, I press toward the mark for the prize of the high calling of God in Christ Jesus."—**Philippians 3:13–14**

D. L. Moody's campaign in Europe was coming to a close. A year earlier just eight people had come to hear him. Now nearly six thousand filled the hall for a prayer meeting at 7:00 in the morning! Moody left them with the word he had repeated all through his meetings there—"Advance!" He then offered to shake hands with everyone there and departed the same day.

Often today, when a week of revival meetings ends, people are somewhat relieved as they can get back to their normal schedules and routines. But while the services may end, the revival should just begin. If revival truly came, it will in no way retreat, but advance!

One witness of Moody's campaign wrote: "A spirit of evangelism was awakened that has never died away. A large number of city missions and other active organizations were established…Bibles were reopened and Bible study received a wonderful impetus. Long-standing prejudices were swept away. New life was infused into all methods of Christian activity. An impetus was given to the cause of temperance such as had not been experienced in Great Britain before. No attempt was made to proselytize, but converts were passed over to existing churches for nurture and admonition in the things of the Lord."

Let's never be satisfied with simply a great service, or a big day, or a good week of revival meetings. May we pray for a fire to be lit in our hearts that can never be extinguished! Our love for Christ must never wax cold, and our service for Him must never diminish. As good soldiers of Jesus Christ, lets advance and continue to claim new territory for the honor and glory of our Saviour.

August 15, 1899

Investing in Lives

"And I will very gladly spend and be spent for you."—**2 Corinthians 12:15a**

Four months prior to his death, D. L. Moody was still going strong for the Lord. Six years earlier, the Young Women's Christian Association had started a conference for young women at Northfield, Massachusetts, but the accommodations in the little town were limited. Lodging places had been built for the men's conferences, but now this need arose. By faith, Moody built the Lowell Lodge so that young women could come and be challenged by the Word of God.

In his speech dedicating this Lodge, Moody said, "I am more than pleased with what has been accomplished here. We give the land very gladly because we believe it is going to open up a new plan, which I hope will be a great blessing not only to the town of Northfield, but to the country. If girls come here to Lowell and get stirred up by God's Spirit so that they go back and carry a blessing to others, we shall be a thousand times repaid for the little paltry that we give."

Sacrificial investment in the lives of others always pays! The little "paltry" that we give in time or resources may seem large now, but it will seem mighty small when someone in Heaven thanks us for the investment made in their life. A lost world thinks the child of God foolish to spend so much time in church, or out soulwinning, or giving tithes and offerings, or using talents for the work of God. But eternal dividends can never be tabulated on earth's calculators. Paul tells us to "...be rich in good works, ready to distribute, willing to communicate; Laying up in store for themselves a good foundation against the time to come" (1 Timothy 6:18b–19a). And Jesus instructed His disciples, "...lay up for yourselves treasures in heaven, where neither moth nor rust doth corrupt, and where thieves do not break through nor steal: For where your treasure is, there will your heart be also" (Matthew 6:20–21).

August 16, 1875

Finish the Race with Joy

"...so that I might finish my course with joy, and the ministry, which I have received of the Lord Jesus, to testify the gospel of the grace of God."
—Acts 20:24

Charles Finney who had traveled across the length and breadth of his country preaching the Gospel was now on his final lap. On this day in 1875, he would enter Heaven. Finney sensed the end was near and went outside and took a walk. As he did, he sang the hymn written by Charles Wesley, "Jesus, Lover of my Soul."

Jesus, lover of my soul, Let me to Thy bosom fly,
While the nearer waters roll, While the tempest still is high.
Hide me, O my Saviour, hide, Till the storm of life is past;
Safe into the haven guide; Oh, receive my soul at last.

Other refuge have I none, Hangs my helpless soul on Thee;
Leave, ah! leave me not alone, Still support and comfort me.
All my trust on Thee is stayed, All my help from Thee I bring;
Cover my defenseless head, With the shadow of Thy wing.

Thou, O Christ, art all I want, More than all in Thee I find;
Raise the fallen, cheer the faint, Heal the sick, and lead the blind.
Just and holy is Thy Name, Source of all true righteousness;
Thou art evermore the same, Thou art full of truth and grace.

Plenteous grace with Thee is found, Grace to cover all my sin;
Let the healing streams abound; Make and keep me pure within.
Thou of life the fountain art, Freely let me take of Thee;
Spring Thou up within my heart; Rise to all eternity.

Will your last lap of the race finish with a song of faith, trust, and joy? Most people die in the same way they lived! We may be closer to the end of the race than we realize. Enjoy His presence, His provision, His protection, and His power. Determine to finish your course with joy.

Psalms 94–96 // Romans 15:14–33

August 1905

Who's in the Limelight?

"But he turned, and said unto Peter, Get thee behind me, Satan: thou art an offence unto me: for thou savourest not the things that be of God, but those that be of men."—**Matthew 16:23**

The minute God begins to use us as Christians in some way, a strange thing happens—we start thinking it is us and not God who is accomplishing the work. Even the disciples, with Jesus right there with them, fell to this temptation. We naturally appreciate appreciation! Our flesh likes praise and is never satisfied with a little. Our appetite to be noticed or recognized is difficult to deny. We often make sure that everyone knows who thought of an idea or accomplished a task. But Proverbs 27:2 is pointed: "Let another man praise thee, and not thine own mouth; a stranger, and not thine own lips." The Apostle Paul reminds us when that urge to glory in ourselves comes, we must quickly reroute the praise: "But he that glorieth, let him glory in the Lord. For not he that commendeth himself is approved, but whom the Lord commendeth" (2 Corinthians 10:17–18).

By August 1905, Evan Roberts had seen over 100,000 souls come to Christ in the Welch Revival. He had been praying for the Lord to give him that many souls through his ministry, and the Lord had graciously answered. But Roberts was not the type of man to bring attention to himself. Roberts would often be seen on his knees for hours in the middle of the night, interceding for souls with tears running down his face.

Why did God bless the prayers of Evan Roberts? No doubt, his humble desire to lift up Christ was a major factor. When God gave Solomon His prescription for revival in 2 Chronicles 7:14, He included a significant order. "If my people, which are called by my name shall humble themselves" and then "pray, and seek my face, and turn from their wicked ways," then God will hear and heal our land. Our prayers can only be heard when our hearts are humbled.

Let's get back in the shadows and put Jesus in the limelight of glory. Only then will God hear our prayers and send revival.

August 18, 1688

The End of the Journey

"So Moses the servant of the LORD died there in the land of Moab, according to the word of the LORD."—**Deuteronomy 34:5**

No matter how faithful and diligent a Christian is in this life, there comes an end to the journey. God took Moses from a basket in the bulrushes to the brink of the Promised Land. The journey was not always easy, and he made his share of mistakes, but God records a powerful statement about him in Deuteronomy 34:10, "And there arose not a prophet since in Israel like unto Moses, whom the LORD knew face to face."

Thirteen days before he would enter the Celestial City, John Bunyan preached his final sermon at 7:00 AM in London, England. His text was John 1:33: "And I knew Him not: but He that sent me to baptize with water, the same said unto me, Upon Whom thou shalt see the Spirit descending, and remaining on Him, the same is He which baptizeth with the Holy Ghost." Most know the name John Bunyan for his masterpiece, *The Pilgrim's Progress.* He wrote that wonderful allegory while in the Bedford Jail in England because he would not take a license from the State to preach the Gospel. He could have been released at any time if he would conform to the law (which would have limited him from freely preaching salvation), but he spent thirteen years in a cell rather than compromise his convictions. One day, a new law was passed and Bunyan was released, and along with him, his literary classic that would affect millions for generations to come.

Will you be faithful to the end of the journey? When our health is good, the burdens are light, and God blesses our ministries, it is easy to be faithful. But what about when the tables turn? Can God count on us to be faithful in the valley as well as the mountaintop? Thirteen years in jail was a long time, especially when he could have walked out at any time if he would just recant his convictions. It has now been well over three hundred years since Bunyan preached his last sermon this day in 1688, yet lives are still being changed through what God did in those thirteen faithful years in prison.

August 19, 1561

No Fear of Man

"The Lord is on my side; I will not fear: what can man do unto me?"
—Psalm 118:6

Mary, Queen of Scots, arrived in Scotland to assume the throne on August 19, 1561. She had been given the throne when she was just six days old, but now after living in France for thirteen years, it was her time to rule the nation. Upon her arrival as a Catholic monarch, Scotland was torn between Protestantism and Catholicism. John Knox would preach against Mary, Queen of Scots, and soon he was arrested and brought before the queen herself. After he would not recant his position, he was charged with treason and thrown in prison. Knox was no stranger to prison, since his preaching against the Catholic Church had often resulted in imprisonment. Even though he was now in his fifties, Knox was not afraid to suffer for the faith of the Gospel. He would later be acquitted and continue to preach faithfully until his death in 1572. At his grave, the Earl of Morton would say of Knox: "Here lies one who never feared any flesh."

Our fear of God must always be greater than our intimidation by man. An unsaved spouse or family member can be unkind. A boss at work who has no time for Christianity is difficult to tolerate. Our neighbors get tired of our witness and may make it difficult for us. We live in a post-Christian culture and no doubt things will become much worse. But while 2 Timothy 3:13 promises, "But evil men and seducers shall wax worse and worse, deceiving, and being deceived, " the next verse exhorts us to continue despite the pressure of the world.

Safety and security is never to be found in conformity to the world's demands or caving under the pressure of their harassment. "The fear of man bringeth a snare: but whoso putteth his trust in the Lord shall be safe. Many seek the ruler's favour; but every man's judgment cometh from the Lord" (Proverbs 29:25–26). Will we fear God or will we fear flesh? Think of it this way before you decide: Will you one day give an account to God or man? An eternal perspective makes temporary decisions much easier.

August 20, 1895

Our Families Must Come First

"But if any provide not for his own, and specially for those of his own house, he hath denied the faith, and is worse than an infidel."—**1 Timothy 5:8**

The first institution God gave to man was the family. If revival is not happening in our homes, we can hardly expect our local churches, or our communities to experience one. Too often we put time and resources into everything but our families. Marriage may no longer be respected as sacred, and raising godly children may seem impossible, but God has not changed His plan when it comes to the home. The Lord uses love and submission between a husband and wife to picture the relationship between Christ and His people. (See Ephesians 5:22–31). The picture God intended is sadly and badly out of focus. Revival ought to recalibrate our priorities and that process should start with our marriages and our children.

D. L. Moody's first granddaughter, Irene Moody, was born on this day in 1895, just four years before his death. Moody loved this new addition to his family with a selfless love. His son wrote about his father: "As a grandfather, he seemed to experience a special joy, and entered into sweetest and happiest relations with the little ones that laid hold of his heart." That little girl would never remember hearing D. L. Moody preach, but she would remember the love and attention he gave her.

We cannot be right with God and wrong at home. That just isn't possible in God's economy. Are there things that need to be made right in your home? Ask the Lord to help you make those confessions, corrections, and changes. No doubt, if He is working on your heart, He is also working on the members of your family as well. A revival at home will lead to a revival at church. As a young boy, it was said of our Lord Jesus, "And Jesus increased in wisdom and stature, and in favour with God and man" (Luke 2:52). Perhaps we need to work on favor with both today as well.

August 1899

What Happens to Little Children When They Die?

"...I shall go to him, but he shall not return to me."—**2 Samuel 12:23**

Yesterday we noted the joy that D. L. Moody had for his granddaughter, Irene. That joy would soon turn to immense sadness as God would take this little girl home to Heaven at the age of four. Moody had lost his only grandson a few months before. F. B. Meyer spent time with Moody during his granddaughter's illness and recalled those difficult hours: "How his strong frame would shake with convulsive sobs as we prayed that her life might be spared! God, however, knew better, and took the little one home that she might be there in time to greet the strong, true nature that loved her so sincerely, when in turn His servant was called to enter his reward." Moody himself would pass away four months later.

It is in these times that we find comfort in the experience of David as recorded in 2 Samuel. David had committed his infamous sin of adultery with Bathsheba. Many months later after David had killed her husband to hide his sin from the public, the prophet Nathan came to the king to confront his sin. Part of the judgment pronounced was that the baby would die. David repented of his sin, prayed earnestly for the child, and fasted for seven days. But on that seventh day, the child died. No servant wanted to share the depressing news with the king, but when David heard them whispering behind him, he called, "Is the child dead?" They answered him, "He is dead." David suddenly rose up from the ground, cleaned himself up, and came to the tabernacle to worship. When asked why he had stopped praying and fasting, he replied, "...While the child was yet alive, I fasted and wept: for I said, Who can tell whether God will be gracious to me, that the child may live? But now he is dead, wherefore should I fast? can I bring him back again? I shall go to him, but he shall not return to me" (2 Samuel 12:22–23). In that last statement, we can find comfort. When a baby who has not yet reached an age when they can understand how to be saved dies, God promises that we will see them again. The heartbreak is real when we consider that they will never come back to us. But we will go to them just as Moody was reunited with his four-year-old granddaughter.

August 22, 1743

Using Time Wisely

"Walk in wisdom toward them that are without, redeeming the time. Let your speech be alway with grace, seasoned with salt, that ye may know how ye ought to answer every man."—**Colossians 4:5–6**

While riding to his next meeting on this day in 1743, John Wesley had horse trouble: his mare had lost a shoe. While waiting for the eighteenth-century "flat tire" to be fixed at the local blacksmith's shop, he shared the Gospel with the workers who were assisting him. He wrote in his journal, "This gave me an opportunity to talk closely, for near half an hour, with both the smith and his servant. I mention these little circumstances to show how easy it is to redeem every fragment of time (if I may so speak), when we feel any love for those souls for which Christ died."

Time is a precious commodity that can never be refunded. We are all given the same twenty-four hours in a day, but sometimes we waste the opportunities that are given to us, especially when we are in the midst of a trial. The Apostle Paul challenged the believers in the church at Colossae to be "redeeming the time." Often this phrase becomes trite in our churches, and even used as an excuse to burn out. We may even feel guilty because we are not as busy or productive as someone else.

So how is it that we can biblically and effectively "redeem our time?" Paul instructs us in his words that surround this common phrase. Our walk should be in wisdom. Our speech should be with grace. And our answer should always be ready.

How's your walk today? Paul is not speaking of your physical steps, but your testimony, your lifestyle. Does it honor God and point others to Christ? Are your actions demonstrating wisdom each day? How is your speech? Are your words "seasoned with salt," giving grace to those around you? How is your answer? Are you ready to answer every man who asks about the hope that is in you? Only as we keep these three areas in constant check can we truly "redeem the time."

August 29, 1920

The Infallible, Inerrant, and Inspired Word of God

"For verily I say unto you, Till heaven and earth pass, one jot or one tittle shall in no wise pass from the law, till all be fulfilled."—**Matthew 5:18**

At the Winona Lake Bible Conference, Bob Jones Sr. and William Jennings Bryan spoke in a special rally. During the meeting, Bryan leaned over to Jones and said, "If schools and colleges do not quit teaching evolution as a fact, we are going to become a nation of atheists." A few years later, Bryan would prosecute an evolutionist in the Scopes Trial and would lose against lawyer Clarence Darrow. Many Christians would point to a specific moment that lost the case for Bryan and for Christians across the land. Clarence Darrow was cross-examining Bryan about creationism and asked specifically about the literal six days of creation. Bryan would reply that he did not believe that the days in Genesis were literal twenty-four-hour days, and with that statement Darrow found the opportunity he was looking for. He criticized Bryan for not believing the Bible was fully and completely true. In Darrow's mind, if they were not literal twenty-four-hour days as the Bible says, but instead representative of eras, what else in the Bible is not to be taken at face value? At that moment, the case was lost for Bryan, and many would point to the Scopes trial as the beginning of the decline of religion in America. Bryan's prophecy during the Winona Lake rally would come true as a result of his own doctrinal error.

We believe the "verbal, plenary, inerrant" inspiration of the Bible. *Verbal*, meaning every word is inspired—in Jesus' own words, every "jot" and every "tittle," referring to the smallest of the Hebrew lettering and accent. *Plenary,* meaning every word is equally inspired—there is not one word that is more important or more inspired than another. And *inerrant,* meaning that there is not one error in the sacred text of the Word of God. We believe that we have the complete, inspired Word of God today. Be very careful of those who begin to explain away the words in the Bible. Thank the Lord today for the truth that you hold in your hand. Determine today to live it, defend it, and use it to reach others.

August 1894

Serve the Lord in Your Youth

"Let no man despise thy youth; but be thou an example of the believers, in word, in conversation, in charity, in spirit, in faith, in purity."—**1 Timothy 4:12**

No matter how young we are, we can serve the Lord. There is no age requirement to be used by God. In fact, Paul told Timothy to be an example to every believer around him as to what a Christian should be. In his speech, his lifestyle, his love, his spirit, his faith, and his purity, Paul instructed Timothy to model the Christian life for the believers in his church.

Bob Jones Sr. would be saved at the age of eleven in 1894. Even before his salvation, Jones would call all the kids in the neighborhood together in the woods and preach to them—when he was just seven years old. He preached his first message after his salvation when he was thirteen years old, and he would hold his first revival meeting at fifteen, under a wood arbor he built himself. At the age of sixteen, he had pastored some small Alabama country churches. Bob Jones Sr. no doubt understood and lived out the verse, "let no man despise thy youth."

Many young adults today by age twenty-five have still not determined God's direction in their lives as they float from college to college, job to job, and relationship to relationship. God never intended our early years of life to be wasted. "Remember now thy Creator in the days of thy youth, while the evil days come not, nor the years draw nigh, when thou shalt say, I have no pleasure in them" (Ecclesiastes 12:1). Good habits must be established early in life if they are to be maintained in later life.

You may not know the full scope of what direction God has for your life. But do not put off until later what you know God would have you do for Him today—regardless of your age.

August 25, 1912

Less than the Least

"Whereof I was made a minister, according to the gift of the grace of God given unto me by the effectual working of his power. Unto me, who am less than the least of all saints, is this grace given, that I should preach among the Gentiles the unsearchable riches of Christ;"—**Ephesians 3:7–8**

Bill Rice was born in Dundee, Texas, on August 25, 1912. His father would raise eight children, including evangelists John R. Rice and Joe B. Rice. He would be saved at an early age and would be called to preach at the age of nineteen. He would later reminisce: "When I was nineteen years old, I surrendered to preach. There was no question in my mind but that God had called me to preach. The Lord, however, had forgotten to call anyone to listen to me preach." The book *Profiles of Evangelism* retells the story of his first preaching invitation: "Bill received his first invitation to preach in a church. The kids were dismissed after lunch to go and play, the women cleaned up the tables and the pastor mentioned to the men, 'Of course, some of you men may want to smoke for a while instead of coming in the church and hear Brother Bill Rice.' But Rice relates, 'Oddly enough, I was honored more than I knew how to say. For the first time in my life, I had been invited to preach in a real church with electric lights and everything just like uptown! What's more, the pastor had called me 'Brother Rice.' That in Texas means *preacher*!"

The highest calling of God is to be a preacher of the Gospel. It is "According to the gift of the grace of God" and "by the effectual working of his power…" To preach the Word of God is a great privilege, but an attitude of humility must follow—"unto me, who am less than the least of all saints." We are not the least, but "less than the least" of all saints. For only when we have a right view of ourselves can we experience the powerful grace that is given to God's servants, the grace to preach the Gospel. Whether you have never preached your first sermon or have been preaching for decades, never lose sight of the humility and grace of our Saviour. Only then can we be fully used of God to proclaim "the unsearchable riches of Christ."

August 26, 1748

Always under Attack

"...Most gladly therefore will I rather glory in my infirmities, that the power of Christ may rest upon me."—**2 Corinthians 12:9**

John Wesley wrote a letter on August 26, 1748, to the authorities about the treatment he had received the previous day in their town: "Yesterday, between twelve and one o'clock, while I was speaking to some quiet people, without any noise or tumult, a drunken rabble came, with clubs and staves, in a tumultuous and riotous manner, the captain of whom...said he was a deputy-constable, and that he was to bring me to you. I went with him; but had scarce gone ten yards, when a man of his company struck me with his fist in the face with all his might; quickly after, another threw his stick at my head: I then made a little stand; but one of your champions, cursing and swearing in the most shocking manner, and flourishing his club over his head, cried out, 'Bring him away!' As we tried to leave, the mob followed hurling oaths, curses, and stones, one of which knocked me to the ground."

There are always three enemies lurking around us ready to attack: the world, the flesh, and the devil. The world has always resisted truth and if they hated Jesus Christ, you can be sure they will hate you. (See John 15:18–19). The flesh is our own internal desire to live contrary to God. Our flesh is still sinful and often presents quite an enemy to righteousness (See Romans 7:14–21). The devil may be an "unseen enemy" but he is no less real and powerful. He never rests or takes a vacation. (See 1 Peter 5:8).

Our first thought when we come under attack should not necessarily be, "What am I doing wrong?" The attack has more likely come because you are doing right! If there is no resistance to your life as a Christian, you are probably going the wrong way. We dare not overlook our enemies, but with God in us, we should never be overpowered by them either.

August 27, 1874

The Blindness of Bitterness

"Let nothing be done through strife or vainglory; but in lowliness of mind let each esteem other better than themselves."—**Philippians 2:3**

Bitterness seems like a personal right sometimes, doesn't it? We've been wronged or offended in some way, and we assume that we are justified in our anger, resentment, and attitude. Until *they* apologize we have every right to treat them the way we do.

On August 27, 1874, D. L. Moody was preaching in the town of Inverness, Scotland. A man in the city was vocal against the revival and Mr. Moody. He vowed that he would never go and hear the American evangelist preach. On this night, however, as he walked, he passed by a large auditorium where a large group had gathered. From the outside the preacher sounded interesting, so the man stepped in to listen. The Holy Spirit began to work on his heart, and that night he accepted Christ as Saviour. After trusting Christ, he asked those around him the name of the preacher as he thought he might like to meet him. How surprised he was to learn that the very man he said he would never hear—the man he disliked—was the one God used to reach him with the Gospel.

Has bitterness blinded you from some of God's blessings? Jesus sets an example for us in our hearts toward others. Knowing who we were—sinners, lost and undone, alienated from and enemies of God—He still came to us, and He gave His life for us. "For ye know the grace of our Lord Jesus Christ, that, though he was rich, yet for your sakes he became poor, that ye through his poverty might be rich" (2 Corinthians 8:9).

To Christians often suffering for their faith at the hands of ungodly people, Paul wrote, "Dearly beloved, avenge not yourselves, but rather give place unto wrath: for it is written, Vengeance is mine; I will repay, saith the Lord. Therefore if thine enemy hunger, feed him; if he thirst, give him drink: for in so doing thou shalt heap coals of fire on his head. Be not overcome of evil, but overcome evil with good" (Romans 12:19–21).

August 28, 1840

Use Your Talents for the Lord

"Then wrought Bezaleel and Aholiab, and every wise hearted man, in whom the LORD *put wisdom and understanding to know how to work all manner of work for the service of the sanctuary, according to all that the* LORD *had commanded."*
—Exodus 36:1

According to 1 Corinthians 12, God has given each of us gifts to be used for Him in the work of the Lord. These are not identical: "Now there are diversities of gifts, but the same spirit....For as the body is one, and hath many members, and all members of that one body, being many, are one body: so also is Christ." We should never boast of our talents nor should we diminish the talents of others even when they are different than our own.

Most of the time when we think of revival, we think of a preacher. Charles Finney, John R. Rice, or Billy Sunday might come to mind. But others with very different gifts were also greatly used by God in those times when God moved in a unique way. Ira D. Sankey was born in Edinburgh, Pennsylvania, to David and Mary Sankey on this day in 1840. At age sixteen he was saved at an evangelistic meeting. After fighting as a soldier during the Civil War, he worked for the Internal Revenue Service and spent time volunteering at the YMCA. One day Sankey was asked by D. L. Moody to leave his successful career and become his music pastor in Chicago. Later he would travel the world with Moody in revival meetings. Dr. Fred Barlow would write that Ira Sankey was "the evangelist of music" and that in large measure the revivals, though largely a result of great Gospel preaching, also came about in great measure by great Gospel singing.

How have you given your talents to the Lord? In the book of Exodus, God tells us of two men whom He appointed to use their talents in the service of the Lord, Bezaleel and Aholiab. These men were "wise-hearted," and God had given them specific abilities for them to use to build the tabernacle where God would be worshipped. Whether we have the abilities of a Bezaleel, a Aholiab, a Sankey, or a Moody, may we all be found faithful today using our talents to do God's work.

August 29, 1792

Our Will or God's Will?

"I delight to do thy will, O my God: yea, thy law is within my heart."
—Psalm 40:8

Charles Finney was born in Warren, Connecticut, on this day in 1792. His family would soon move to upstate New York as farmers, and Charles would never have the opportunity to go to college. The Finneys attended a Baptist church in Henderson, New York, but Charles was more interested in studying law as an intern, hoping to make it big as a lawyer one day. Charles had no interest in the things of God and would be bored when he heard of God's love. Upon finishing his law degree and while waiting in an attorney's office for a job interview with a large firm, Finney was stunned by the Holy Spirit's voice in his heart? "Are you going to serve yourself for the rest of your life, or will you serve Me?" Finney jumped from his seat, cancelled the interview, and began preaching.

Does the will of God sound boring to you? Are you more interested in what you can accomplish in this world than in what you can do for the next world? Satan is good at convincing us that if we serve the Lord we will be miserable. We will be poor, unhappy, and unfulfilled without any real joy or contentment. Satan tells us that it is in his way of the world that we will be happy, have friends, become famous, and have material possessions. The devil thus convinces us that we have a choice to make between pleasure and misery. If we want to be miserable—serve God, but if we want to have pleasure—follow him. But that is not the choice at all!

The choice is between pleasure and pleasure! We simply must decide how long we want the pleasure to last. Hebrews 11:25 tells us that there is "pleasure in sin for a season." There *is* pleasure in living in our flesh and enjoying the things that life has to offer, but unfortunately it is only for a season. But Psalm 16:11 tells us, "...at thy right hand there are pleasures for evermore."

Charles Finney continues in eternity to clip the coupons of following the will of God. Will we?

August 30, 1902

Pure Religion

"Pure religion and undefiled before God and the Father is this, To visit the fatherless and widows in their affliction, and to keep himself unspotted from the world."—**James 1:27**

What does it mean to you to be religious? Going to church? Singing in the choir? Teaching a class? Giving money to your church? Being moral and upright? Knowing the Bible? God's definition in James 1:27 is different, isn't it? Keeping ourselves from the pollution of this world is hard enough, but on the positive side of the equation, how many fatherless children have you helped? How many widows have you cared for?

Robert Sheffey died in White Gate, Virginia, on August 30, 1902. Sheffy suffered from rheumatism in his last years and had to be cared for by others. This great circuit-riding preacher had seen amazing answers to prayer and miraculous conversions everywhere he went throughout the Appalachian Mountains. His gravestone, however, would say nothing about his preaching, praying, or revival work. The epitaph simply reads: "The poor were sorry when he died."

Toward the end of His ministry, Jesus told of the saved standing before their Saviour in Heaven. Christ, the King, announces, "Come, ye blessed of my Father, inherit the kingdom prepared for you from the foundation of the world" (Matthew 25:34). He describes how these faithful servants had given him food when He was hungry; they had given him drink when He was thirsty; they had given him clothes when he was naked; when he was sick, they had visited Him; and when He was in prison, they came to Him. The people are confused at the comment of their Saviour? "When did we ever do those things to You, Jesus?" they asked. And the King answered, "...Verily I say unto you, Inasmuch as ye have done it unto one of the least of these my brethren, ye have done it unto me" (Matthew 25:40).

What could we do for someone less fortunate than ourselves today? Would Jesus do it? Would He want us to do it for Him? Man's religious definition doesn't require it—but God's does!

August 31, 1688

Reconciling Our Differences

"Moreover if thy brother shall trespass against thee, go and tell him his fault between thee and him alone: if he shall hear thee, thou hast gained thy brother."—**Matthew 18:15**

John Bunyan was riding horseback to London to meet his friend John Strudwick. He had heard, however, of a father and son in Berkshire who had been quarreling with one another and decided to take a detour to see if he could reconcile them. Afterward, while traveling on from Berkshire, he encountered a snowstorm and due to the plunging temperatures, became very ill. A few months later, on August 31, 1688, he passed away. John Bunyan, the great preacher and writer, would risk and give his life to try to reconcile a father and son whom he had never even met.

Conflict and bitterness come so quickly into our lives. Sometimes animosity festers in someone's heart without the other person even knowing about it. So Jesus, in Matthew 18:15–17, gives us a pattern to follow when conflict comes into the church. Whether someone has been guilty of an unknown mistake or an intentional hurt, Jesus tells us how to take care of the conflict. The first step He gives is to go to the individual and seek to make it right. Often, this opening of communication results in an admission of guilt, a desire for forgiveness, and a friend is restored. If the person is unwilling to communicate and sets the problem aside, Jesus commands us to bring another person with us to discuss the issue, perhaps a pastor or a deacon. If there is still no repentance, then the issue must be brought before the church.

Why does Jesus take disagreement between His children so seriously? A few verses later, He explains that the secret to power in the church is in its unity: "Again I say unto you, That if two of you shall agree on earth as touching any thing that they shall ask, it shall be done for them of my Father which is in heaven. For where two or three are gathered together in my name, there am I in the midst of them" (Matthew 18:19–20).

Do you need to call someone today or make a visit?

SEPTEMBER

September 1, 1785

Never Be Ashamed of the Gospel

"For I am not ashamed of the gospel of Christ: for it is the power of God unto salvation to every one that believeth; to the Jew first, and also to the Greek."
—**Romans 1:16**

We tend to pre-judge people based on their education, employment, or material wealth. We tend to be intimidated by those who are "higher" than us in some realm of life. We may be less likely to share the Gospel with our boss than a coworker. We may avoid some wealthy areas of our community, thinking they would not be interested in the Gospel and would certainly think less of us if we tried.

Peter Cartwright was born on September 1, 1785, near the James River in Virginia. His family was poor and in time would move to Kentucky, where he would live a rebellious life against God. At age sixteen, he would be saved after hearing the Gospel in an evangelistic meeting, and thus began the ministry of this rugged itinerant. He would travel for the next fifty-three years in eleven circuits, preaching over fourteen thousand sermons, and seeing ten thousand people saved and added to the church. His testimony lives on as a man whose very presence would cause the unsaved to accept Christ as their Saviour. On one instance when Cartwright was preaching on "What doth it profit a man if he should gain the whole world and lose his own soul," the crowd began to murmur, "General Jackson has come in!" Cartwright continued to boldly proclaim the Gospel, and even announced, "Who is General Jackson?" After the service, Andrew Jackson told Cartwright how impressed he was with his boldness: "If I had a few thousand such independent, fearless officers as you are, and a well-drilled army, I could take old England."

We dare not do selective evangelism. God's heart is that all would be saved and come to the knowledge of the truth (1 Timothy 2:3–4). We look on the outward appearance and naturally make judgments. But every man is the same on the inside—he is lost and needs a Saviour. Whoever God brings across our paths today, let's not be ashamed of the Gospel!

September 1, 1904

Death Has Lost Its Sting

"O death, where is thy sting? O grave, where is thy victory?"
—1 Corinthians 15:55

John R. Rice, who was often called the "Will Rogers of the Pulpit," lost his mother at age six, and he would remember her death for the rest of his life. In his fundamental periodical, the *Sword of the Lord*, Rice recalled that sober moment: "I remember the November day when we laid her body away....The rain beat down upon us and a friendly neighbor held an umbrella over our heads. O death! death! DEATH!" Being only six years old at the time, Rice struggled with the lonely realities of death. But six years later, on September 1, 1904, John R. Rice would experience victory over the sting of death as he asked Christ to be his Saviour.

Of course we mourn when a loved one or close friend dies. We miss them and long to be with them. We take great comfort and hope as believers in the words of Paul in 1 Thessalonians 4:13–18, "But I would not have you to be ignorant brethren, concerning them which are asleep, that ye sorrow not, even as others which have no hope. For if we believe that Jesus died and rose again, even so them also which sleep in Jesus will God bring with him. For this we say unto you by the word of the Lord, that we which are alive and remain unto the coming of the Lord shall not prevent them which are asleep. For the Lord himself shall descend from heaven with a shout, with the voice of the archangel, and with the trump of God: and the dead in Christ shall rise first: Then we which are alive and remain shall be caught up together with them in the clouds, to meet the Lord in the air: and so shall we ever be with the Lord. Wherefore comfort one another with these words."

This is why we must lead our loved ones and friends to Christ. Then, as children of God we can say with Paul, "O death, where is thy sting? O grave, where is thy victory? The sting of death is sin; and the strength of sin is the law. But thanks be to God, which giveth us the victory through our Lord Jesus Christ" (1 Corinthians 15:55–57).

September 1, 1934

Dr. Law and Dr. Grace

"Moreover the law entered, that the offence might abound. But where sin abounded, grace did much more abound: That as sin hath reigned unto death, even so might grace reign through righteousness unto eternal life by Jesus Christ our Lord."—**Romans 5:20–21**

Lester Roloff was ordained at the age of twenty-one in early September of 1934. One of the great sermons Dr. Roloff would preach was entitled "Dr. Law and Dr. Grace." In his message, he would describe a "patient" who was ill. He described Dr. Law and Dr. Grace as two doctors who are always correct in their diagnosis and never charge a fee. The patient enters the office of Dr. Law and says, "My hands are the problem. They want to fight." "No, the problem is in your heart," Dr. Law replies. "But Doctor, my eyes want to look at sinful things." "No, your problem is a heart problem." But my tongue wants to curse and my feet want to go to sinful places." "Your problem is still in your heart," replies Dr. Law.

The patient is upset and wants a second opinion. Dr. Law tells him that if he cannot admit his heart problem, other doctors cannot help him. The patient checks in with Dr. Vain Religion, who prescribes doing good things to make him feel better. The patient likes this advice, but after doing his best, nothing changes. Soon, the patient walks through the door of Dr. Law again. He admits that his heart is the problem, and Dr. Law prescribes a new heart. He informs the patient that he cannot do the surgery—there is only one who can—and leads him next door to the office of Dr. Grace.

Dr. Grace is warm and friendly and tells him that he can perform the surgery without help and without charge. "The consultation is free," Dr. Grace explains, "but the operation is actually very expensive. Thankfully, someone has already paid the price." By faith, the patient submits to Dr. Grace's knife. His old sinful heart is taken out, replaced with a heart that pumps new life throughout his body. On his way out of the office, the patient meets the Friend with nail-pierced hands Who paid for his operation and decides to live the rest of his life in devotion to Him.

September 4, 1932

Loving and Following God's Word

"And take not the word of truth utterly out of my mouth; for I have hoped in thy judgments. So shall I keep thy law continually for ever and ever."
—**Psalm 119:43–44**

As J. Harold Smith sat on his sister's front porch and listened to the Gospel, the Holy Spirit began tugging at his heart. Responding to the Holy Spirit's leading, he bowed his head and accepted Jesus Christ as his personal Saviour on this day in 1932. Smith would soon surrender to preach, and his ministry would touch the entire world through his radio preaching. "Radio Bible Hour," the program he founded, later described his ministry: "He accepted the Bible as he found it, preached it as the truth, and lived by its principles." Following Smith's death in 2001, Adrian Rodgers would say this about J. Harold Smith: "He had one of the boldest preaching styles married to and joined with the sweetest spirit of any evangelist that I know. He was fearless in his denunciation of sin, but faithful in his proclamation of Jesus."

Throughout the longest chapter in the Bible, Psalm 119, the psalmist describes his love and devotion for the Word of God. He praises the Lord for the precious gift of His Word and promises to follow its truths all of his life. He begs God to not let him forget these precepts as he gets older, for it is his source of daily hope and strength.

Do you love the Word of God? People search their whole lives for happiness when it is right at their fingertips every day. "Happy is the man that findeth wisdom, and the man that getteth understanding. For the merchandise of it is better than the merchandise of silver, and the gain thereof than fine gold. She is more precious than rubies: and all the things thou canst desire are not to be compared unto her. Length of days is in her right hand; and in her left hand riches and honour. Her ways are the ways of pleasantness, and all her paths are peace. She is a tree of life to them that lay hold upon her: and happy is every one that retaineth her" (Proverbs 3:13–18).

September 5, 1888

Two Are Better than One

"But from the beginning of the creation God made them male and female. For this cause shall a man leave his father and mother, and cleave to his wife; And they twain shall be one flesh: so then they are no more twain, but one flesh. What therefore God hath joined together, let not man put asunder."—**Mark 10:6–9**

Billy Sunday was married to the love of his life, Helen "Nell" Sunday, on September 5, 1888. They had met at a church social shortly after Billy was saved, and now they were united together in the service of their Lord. Throughout the years, Helen would lovingly be nicknamed "Ma" Sunday, and she would be the greatest help to Billy Sunday's campaigns in administration and support. In September 1913, the couple celebrated their silver wedding anniversary, and the press reported that, "The evangelist is just as devoted to his wife today as he was a quarter of a century ago when he was courting 'Ma,' then Nell, in Chicago while he played on the old Chicago White Sox baseball team."

The Pharisees and the Sadducees were trying to trip up Jesus in His teachings to embarrass Him in front of the people who admired Him. One of their clever questions was about divorce. "Is it lawful for a man to put away his wife?" they asked. Jesus replied, "What did Moses command you?" Knowing the Law and thinking they had Jesus trapped, they answered, "Moses suffered to write a bill of divorcement, and to put her away." But Jesus explained to them that only because of the hardness of the peoples' hearts was that law made, and he continued to teach on the sanctity of marriage. Ever since God created Adam and Eve, God has given us a plan for marriage: one man and one woman leaving father and mother and becoming one. There is great companionship and momentum, as a man and woman serve the Lord together in marriage. Complementing each other's strengths and weaknesses, a married couple create a synergy that is powerful in God's work. Perhaps that is why Satan strives constantly to get inside the home and break up what God has put together. Don't look for a way out; ask God to strengthen your marriage today!

September 7, 1769

Faithfulness Will Produce Fruitfulness

"That the trial of your faith, being much more precious than of gold that perisheth, though it be tried with fire, might be found unto praise and honour and glory at the appearing of Jesus Christ:"—**1 Peter 1:7**

On this day in 1769, Shubal Sterns was lost in an early and unexpected fall snow, uncertain if he could survive the blizzard. Looking behind and before him, Sterns was confused at even which direction to go in the freezing temperatures. Sterns began to reflect on his ministry for Christ, and prayed that the Lord would deliver him from the blizzard. After his prayer, he was encouraged in his heart to keep pressing on. He felt as if God had reassured him that the work he was doing would last for many generations to come. The Holy Spirit was whispering in his heart not to give up. Sterns heard God correctly in the blizzard. The results of his ministry are still felt in the "Bible Belt" of America today.

The trials of our lives can wear us down spiritually and sap us of the energy we desire in order to do our best for the Lord. We wonder what God has in mind as these difficulties curtail our usefulness and effectiveness. But it is during these times that people watch our testimonies more closely. Without the trial, we could preach or teach better, parent better, witness better, and generally serve better, but our faithfulness through the difficulty speaks in ways that our best sermons cannot. God never wastes a trial and we must be sure that we don't either.

Paul thought that his "thorn in the flesh" was limiting his effectiveness and asked the Lord to remove it on three occasions. But God knew that his effectiveness would be enhanced by the thorn, as He would grant the additional grace needed. Thus Paul declared, "Most gladly therefore will I rather glory in my infirmities, that the power of Christ may rest upon me" (2 Corinthians 12:9b). God doesn't mind if we ask Him to remove a trial, but if He doesn't, don't let your faithfulness stop there. Your faithfulness through the trial will multiply rather than diminish your fruitfulness.

September 7, 1952

The Powerful Influence of Music

"It came even to pass, as the trumpeters and singers were as one, to make one sound to be heard in praising and thanking the LORD; and when they lifted up their voice with the trumpets and cymbals and instruments of musick, and praised the LORD, saying, For he is good; for his mercy endureth for ever: that then the house was filled with a cloud, even the house of the LORD; So that the priests could not stand to minister by reason of the cloud: for the glory of the LORD had filled the house of God."—**2 Chronicles 5:13–14**

After a terrible car accident, B. B. McKinney died in Bryson City, North Carolina, at the age of sixty-six. He was on his way to preach in a revival meeting when God called him home. While McKinney was a powerful and compassionate preacher, he was also an engaging song leader and was known to say as he led, "Let's mean these words as we sing!" A plaque still hangs in Bistineau Baptist Church, his home church, commemorating his ministry. The plaque reads: "Baylus Benjamin McKinney...Composed over 500 hymns and Gospel songs...His life goal was to lead people to Christ through music."

As King Solomon finished his project of building the Temple for the Lord, he and the people organized a dedication ceremony. As the Ark of the Covenant was brought into the Temple, the choirs and orchestras began to glorify God in music. What an indescribable sound that must have been! Combined with their humble prayer and obedience, the music brought the presence of God to the Temple, so much that the priests could not even stand inside. The holiness of the Lord was lifted up through music, and the presence of the Lord followed.

Next time you go to church, would you decide that you are going to enhance the power of the preaching by preparing your heart through prayerful and humble obedience to sing in the congregational music? Music is not first and foremost for our enjoyment or entertainment. Nor is it our chance to exhibit our abilities or creativity. Music is designed to draw us closer to God and the preaching of His Word.

September 1907

God Blesses Those Who Serve

"And there was great joy in that city."—**Acts 8:8**

Stephen has just been stoned to death at the hands of Saul of Tarsus. There is great persecution against the church according to Acts 8:1. These early Christians are being harassed, jailed, and in many cases put to death. As the persecution intensifies, the people of God are scattered, but they take the Gospel with them wherever they go. Philip, one of the early leaders in the church at Jerusalem, is found preaching in Samaria and a great revival breaks out. Despite these difficult and dangerous times, there was "great joy in that city."

Something very similar took place in the town of Fairfield in September of 1907 during one of Billy Sunday's revivals. Theodore Thomas Frankenburg would later describe Billy Sunday's service in his book, *The Spectacular Career of Rev. Billy Sunday: Famous Baseball Evangelist:* "I have seen many a university football victory celebration; I have seen several riots of joy after a Yale-Harvard boat race; I was in the headquarters of District Attorney Jerome of New York when the word came on election night that he had beaten independently the candidates of all the regular parties. But I have never seen any crowd more beside itself than was the congregation of the tabernacle when the meeting was over…There were a hundred dangerous rushes to the platform…And when it was announced that altogether Sunday had won 1,118 Fairfield souls from the Devil for Christ, it seemed as though the roof was tugging at the rafters."

Do revivals, prayer meetings, preaching services, and souls being saved get you excited? Do they bring joy to your heart? Or do you just endure them and hope they don't go over their allotted time? Nehemiah declared "…the joy of the LORD is your strength" (Nehemiah 8:10). Ask the Lord to rekindle your joy for the things that bring Him joy. Would to God, that all of our church services would have so much joy of the Lord, "the roof would tug at the rafters!"

September 11, 1940

God's Yoke Is Easy and His Burden Light

"Come unto me, all ye that labour and are heavy laden, and I will give you rest. Take my yoke upon you, and learn of me; for I am meek and lowly in heart: and ye shall find rest unto your souls. For my yoke is easy, and my burden is light."
—**Matthew 11:28–30**

Mel Trotter had a heart attack in Kannapolis, North Carolina, and met the Lord who had so graciously saved him from a wasted life of sin. The *Grand Rapids Herald* printed his obituary: "Melvin E. Trotter, a soul-winner who fought the world, the flesh, and the devil up and down the United States and the foreign lands for decades, founder of the City Rescue Mission here and its successful superintendent for more than forty years died Wednesday morning, September 11, 1940, at his summer home at Macatawa Park." Trotter had a burden to reach those on the streets of our cities and helped start sixty-five rescue missions across the United States. He had assisted R. A. Torrey with his revivals, preached for Billy Sunday, and ministered to the soldiers during World War I. Trotter's legacy of serving the downtrodden of the world continues to this day through Mel Trotter Ministries in Grand Rapids, Michigan.

Satan likes to convince us that a life of sin is the fast track to fun, fulfillment, and happiness. God says just the opposite: "…the way of transgressors is hard" (Proverbs 13:15). "There is a way that seemeth right unto a man, but the end thereof are the ways of death" (Proverbs 14:12). Jesus promises that His yoke is easy and His burden is light. Satan's way is a slavery to sin, regret, and ultimately destruction. God's way is full of rest and joy. Jesus calls today to all those who are tired of the devil's lies and the disillusionment that sin has produced. He calls you to take up His yoke, learn of Him, and follow Him. To be sure, the Christian life is not always without challenges, but we have a Saviour who is on the other side of the yoke, carrying us and supporting us every step of the way. Satan will bind you to a yoke of bondage—Christ will get in a yoke of service with you, and with Him, that yoke becomes easy and your burdens become light.

September 10, 1830

The Word of God Prevailed

"...And fear fell on them all, and the name of the Lord Jesus was magnified. And many that believed came, and confessed, and shewed their deeds...So mightily grew the word of God and prevailed."—**Acts 19:17–18, 20**

One of the greatest revivals in New Testament history fell on the city of Ephesus during the ministry of the Apostle Paul. Paul had come to the affluent city, known for its wicked displays in worshipping the goddess Diana. Paul preached the Word of God faithfully, and as Paul's name drew many jealous people, a group of Jews tried to cast out a demon in Jesus' and Paul's name. The demon's infamous words to the Jews were, "Jesus I know, and Paul I know; but who are ye?" This incident stirred up the city and many went to Paul to hear of Jesus Christ. The Holy Spirit began to move and many were converted to Christ. These newly-saved people took their books of witchcraft and demonism to burn as a public testimony of turning to the Lord. The people confessed their sin to God and publicly stood for the Lord.

On September 10, 1830, Charles Finney began his meetings in Rochester, New York. It was recorded that over 100,000 people were saved by the meetings end in 1831. Paul Reno in his book *Daniel Nash: Prevailing Prince of Prayer* described how the meetings caused a great change in the city: "The whole character of the city was changed....And the city has been famous ever since for its high moral tone, its strong churches, its evangelical and earnest ministry, and its frequent and powerful revivals of religion....Even the courts and prisons bore witness to its blessed effect. There was a wonderful falling off in crime. The courts had little to do, and the jail was nearly empty for years afterwards." All classes of society were equally influenced. "The only theatre in the city was converted into a livery stable, the only circus into a soap and candle factory," the "grog shops were closed, and a new impulse was given to every philanthropic enterprise."

May we long and pray for these kinds of revivals today!

September 11, 1916

Satan Is Always Angry during Revival

"And the same time there arose no small stir about that way…And when they heard these sayings, they were full of wrath, and cried out, saying, Great is Diana of the Ephesians. And the whole city was filled with confusion…"
—Acts 19:23, 28–29

Yesterday we saw in our devotional that God's Word changed a whole community. Not only did destinies change from Hell to Heaven, but behaviors changed as well. We may ask God to give us those kinds of awakenings today that will alter the direction of our cities or nation. But be assured that the devil will get his licks in when it happens, as the verses above indicate in the city of Ephesus.

Mordecai Ham was conducting a campaign in Fort Worth, Texas. Opposition to the meeting began to grow as Ham fearlessly preached the Word of God to the city. One night, as Ham was walking through the Westbrook Hotel lobby, leaving for the service, he was maliciously assaulted, being struck on the back of head. He was left with gashes on the side of his face. Despite the hostility towards the evangelist, including angry protesters attempting to break up the service, over twelve thousand people attended the meetings and many were saved.

When revival comes, persecution follows. All through the Old and New Testaments and church history, the result of revival has always been persecution. When the Old Testament prophets and New Testament apostles preached for repentance, they were thrown in jail and beaten. After fire came down from Heaven for Elijah, Queen Jezebel sought to kill him. John the Baptist called out the sin of his day and lost his head. After Peter saw three thousand souls saved at Pentecost, the Sanhedrin arrested the apostles and beat them. Stephen preached and was martyred.

Whenever revival comes, persecution follows close after. The devil will fight tooth and nail to keep revival from spreading, but often the winds of persecution only spread the flames of revival further around the world.

September 12, 1927

God Can Do Anything

"Is any thing too hard for the LORD?"—**Genesis 18:14**

As they drove through Florida, Bob Jones Sr. was discussing with his wife, Mary, the threat of secularism and humanism on the youth of America. As they stopped for sandwiches, Jones announced to his wife that he was going to start a school to counteract the compromise exhibited in the denominational colleges. His wife turned to him and said, "Are you crazy, Robert?" About two years later, Bob Jones College was founded in St. Andrew's Bay, Florida, with eighty-eight students.

God often gives his children a distinct vision in their hearts for what He wants them to do. Others may think that God's will is crazy or silly, but God always gets the last laugh.

As three angels visited Abraham in the wilderness, Abraham's wife Sarah stayed inside the tent. God clearly told Abraham, "I will certainly return unto thee according to the time of life; and, lo, Sarah thy wife shall have a son." Sarah overheard what was said and laughed inside her heart. "After I am waxed old shall I have pleasure, my lord being old also?" she thought. But immediately, the Lord asked, "Wherefore did Sarah laugh, saying, Shall I of a surety bear a child, which am old?" And he pierced Sarah's heart with soul-searching question: "Is any thing too hard for the Lord?" He continued, "At the time appointed I will return unto thee, according to the time of life, and Sarah shall have a son." Sarah was incredibly embarrassed and denied laughing, but God knew her heart. "Nay; but thou didst laugh," was His reply. God would keep His Word, as He always does, and Sarah soon had a son, whom they named Isaac, which actually means "laughter."

Has God laid something on your heart that may cause others to laugh? Be sure that your goal is not self-centered or for your glory, for then God promises it shall certainly fail. But if your goal or desire is from God, remember God's promise to Abraham and move forward. Nothing is too hard for the Lord!

September 1911

Discipleship through the Local Church

"And they continued stedfastly in the apostles' doctrine, and fellowship, and in breaking of bread, and in prayers."—**Acts 2:42**

After the great revival at Pentecost, a natural result of the preaching of God's Word was that souls were saved and the church grew. God was adding to the church daily as they were in a continuous state of revival. At the end of Acts 2, we get a glimpse of these new believers as they continued steadfastly in learning the Word of God, fellowshipping with one another, participating in the Lord's Table, and in prayer meetings. The most amazing fact about Pentecost was not that three thousand people were saved, but that all three thousand continued in the program of the local church!

Billy Sunday was greatly concerned with converts—reaching souls with the Gospel was his highest priority in life. But he was also concerned with connecting them with a local church. Without a local church, a new believer would have no place to grow and learn. James S. Webb described the Billy Sunday campaign in Springfield, Ohio, in September of 1911: "The good work he did here still continues and the majority of our church members...are Billy Sunday converts."

When we have the privilege of seeing someone saved, we must be diligent to get them into our local churches so that they can grow and mature for Christ. The Bible describes them as "newborn babes" (1 Peter 2:2). When a mother gives birth to a child, her responsibility doesn't end—it just begins! She is now passionate to make sure that little child has everything needed to be healthy and strong.

Let's not be guilty of leaving our babies on the doorsteps for the world, the false cults, or unbiblical churches to devour. Like our own children, let's do our best in our churches to bring our new converts up in the nurture and admonition of the Lord!

September 1833

God Uses People to Spread the Gospel

"How then shall they call on him in whom they have not believed? and how shall they believe in him of whom they have not heard? and how shall they hear without a preacher? And how shall they preach, except they be sent? as it is written, How beautiful are the feet of them that preach the gospel of peace, and bring glad tidings of good things!"—**Romans 10:14–15**

The Particular Baptists in England were called so because they believed that Christ died for a "particular" group of people but not for all. This "Calvinism" has taken on many different forms throughout the centuries and unfortunately is very much alive today. In the early years of our nation, many believed that the salvation of sinners was accomplished independently of all human agency. The strength of the church, therefore, was to "sit still!" This group wasn't interested in evangelists or revivals, to say the least, as that would have called for an interference with the operation of divine sovereignty.

Thank God there were men like Jacob Knapp in September of 1833 who would launch out as evangelists despite this growing trend of apathy and indifference. Knapp was unwilling to be satisfied with the status quo even under a so-called spiritual label like Calvinism. He would join the ranks of the godly wanderers who preached the Gospel to anyone who would listen at any time and in any place.

God chose human instruments to "pen His Word" and today He uses human instruments to "pass His Word." What an honor it would have been to be a human writer of the Bible. Yet our privilege is similarly awesome! To give to others the message of God is a responsibility that we must not ignore. The eternity of people is dependent on whether or not we steward this privilege. Every saved person is "called to preach" the Gospel. We are all called to be missionaries and evangelists! What a joy is ours to spread the Gospel! Will you today?

September 1886

Are You Listening?

"He that hath an ear, let him hear what the Spirit saith unto the churches."
—Revelation 2:29

Evangelist Sam Jones was estimated to have preached one thousand sermons to approximately three million people from August 1855–September 1886. Jones would be known for his many quips throughout his powerful sermons. One such powerful quote was, "The roar of commerce, the click of the telegraph and the whistle of the engine have well-nigh drowned out the voice of God." If Sam Jones were alive today, he might say, "the app on our smart phone, the news of the television, and the chaos on Wall Street…." Or he might say, "the busyness of our schedules, the demands for our time, and the call to leisure…."

What has drowned out the voice of God in your life? As Jesus gave his messages to the seven churches in the book of Revelation, He reminded them of a simple truth that would ring clear for all who would read later: "He that hath an ear, let him hear what the Spirit saith unto the churches." When is the last time you listened to God's voice? Can you remember the last time you even heard His voice? Does God still call today? Oh yes He does, but sadly many of His people have their spiritual phones on "silent." They can look at God's message later and respond when it is convenient. Be careful! "To day if ye will hear his voice, Harden not your heart, as in the provocation, and as in the day of temptation in the wilderness: When your fathers tempted me, proved me, and saw my work. Forty years long was I grieved with this generation, and said, It is a people that do err in their heart, and they have not known my ways: Unto whom I sware in my wrath that they should not enter into my rest" (Psalm 95:7b–11).

Will you miss the victory and blessing in your life because you have turned a deaf ear to God's voice? Let Him speak through His Word to you today; listen; and then obey. If you are struggling to understand God's message, ask the Holy Spirit to be your "hearing aid." He specializes in guiding us into the truth (John 16:13)!

September 1901

God Exalts the Humble

"Humble yourselves therefore under the mighty hand of God, that he may exalt you in due time."—**1 Peter 5:6**

Mordecai Ham had taken his calling to preach seriously. He had studied twenty-seven books to prepare for the ministry to which God had called him. In September of 1901, he visited the District Association of Bethlehem with his father. His grandfather had pastored there for over forty years, and he was looking forward to hearing his grandfather preach that morning. Much to his surprise, during the service his grandfather singled him out among the crowd and asked him to preach an impromptu message. Ham was shocked, but out of respect for his grandfather, he preached a message from Matthew chapter eleven. Following the service, he was invited to preach that same night in the First Baptist Church of Scottsville, and then asked to preach at the Mt. Gilead Baptist Church in Kentucky. The evangelism ministry of Mordecai Ham had begun quickly!

What was the message that Ham preached that morning from Matthew 11 that would propel him into ministry? It was Christ's commendation of the ministry of John the Baptist. He reminded his audience that it was John's humility that God blessed. John was not jealous when his crowds left him and followed Christ. His response was "He must increase, but I must decrease" (John 3:30).

The "impromptu" message of Mordecai Ham's heart that morning was on humility, and it was that very humility that caused his ministry to be exalted! It is indeed the branch that bows the lowest that is always covered with the most fruit. Humility is a do-it-yourself project. God instructs us, "Humble *yourselves....*" Of course, God can humble us if we prefer, but it is much more advantageous to do it ourselves. And when we do, God will lift us up to do His work.

September 1903

Pray Through

"For I know that this shall turn to my salvation through your prayer, and the supply of the Spirit of Jesus Christ,"—**Philippians 1:19**

In September of 1903, R. A. Torrey and Charles Alexander were holding a revival campaign in Liverpool, England. The crowds became so large that they were forced to hold two meetings each night, one for the men and the other for the women. They saw God save five thousand people during that four week meeting.

Charles Alexander would later share one of his experiences in Liverpool that inspired him to write the song "Pray Through": "I was standing at a bank counter in Liverpool, waiting for a clerk to come. I picked up a pen and began to print on a blotter, in large letters, two words which had gripped me like a vice: PRAY THROUGH. I kept talking to a friend, and printing, until I had the big blotter filled from top to bottom with a column. I transacted my business and went away. The next day my friend came to see me and said he had a striking story to tell me. A man had gone into the bank soon after we had left. He had grown discouraged with business troubles. He started to transact some business with that same clerk over that blotter, when his eye caught the long column of PRAY THROUGH. He asked who wrote those words, and when he was told, exclaimed, 'That is the very message I needed. I will pray through. I have tried to worry through in my own strength, and have merely mentioned my troubles to God; now I am going to pray the situation through until I get an answer.'"

The Apostle Paul wrote to the church of Philippi thanking them for "praying him through." He would experience the great supply of the Lord through the prayers of those who loved him. Do you need to "pray through" something? Do you need to "pray someone else through" a trial or difficulty? Don't stop until you get an answer!

September 18, 1856

God Is in the Changing Business

"For our conversation is in heaven; from whence also we look for the Saviour, the Lord Jesus Christ: Who shall change our vile body, that it may be fashioned like unto his glorious body, according to the working whereby he is able even to subdue all things unto himself."—**Philippians 3:20–21**

A year after he was saved, D. L. Moody packed his bags and moved to Chicago, quite the change for the young New Englander. The bustling metropolis would ignore the young man as he entered the city limits, but the day would come when the city would be impacted mightily under his preaching. Moody quickly found a job in a shoe store and became involved in his local church. He joined a mission band, visited and distributed tracts wherever he could, and nearly doubled the Sunday school that he taught. As the Sunday school overflowed with kids, people began to notice this humble young preacher.

God brings about change in our lives in order to use us. We don't always like the "upsetting of the apple cart" that comes with change. Growth is often awkward and growing pains are not unusual in the physical realm. Spiritually, we don't always enjoy what God is doing and fail to see the big picture that necessitates the changes God is bringing our way. Getting us out of our comfort zones can give us a fresh perspective of our lives and the God we serve.

Someday, there will be a great change for all of us—a change that we can all look forward to. Paul tells the Philippian believers that Jesus will one day change our sinful bodies into glorified bodies through His great power. We will no longer have bodies that suffer from disease, stress, ailments, exhaustion, or fatigue. That will be a change we can all live with! Forever! Don't fret or worry, complain or gripe, or resist or rebel when God does a "change order" in your life. God has never made a mistake, and He's not going to make His first on you!

September 1904

God Calls Participants, Not Spectators

"And Elijah came unto all the people, and said, How long halt ye between two opinions? if the Lord be God, follow him: but if Baal, then follow him. And the people answered him not a word."—**1 Kings 18:21**

R. A. Torrey and Charles Alexander held meetings at Bolton, Wales, in September of 1904. In this meeting, they saw 3,600 people trust Christ as Saviour. Mrs. Alexander told of what took place during the invitation after the preaching one night: "Mr. George Davis stood upon the platform, eagerly looking out over the crowd, on the watch for striking incidents about which he could write. Alexander was leading the choir in songs of invitation…His quick eye caught sight of Mr. Davis, and at the first chance between the hymns he was down beside him. Several people below the platform had come forward to take their stand for Christ, amongst them some boys. All the personal workers seemed busy, and no one was at hand to talk and pray with these waiting seekers for Christ. Alexander made a call for more workers at the front, and then said to Mr. Davis, 'What are you doing here, Davis, while people are down there waiting to be led to Christ?' 'I'm watching for incidents for my articles,' was the reply. 'Get off the platform and lead some of those people to Christ,' said Alexander, 'and you'll have some first-hand incidents to tell.' A firm, though gentle, push accompanied the words, and almost before he knew it, Davis had descended the steps, and with Bible in hand stood ready for business and approaching a group of boys made the way clear to them. As one boy after another said he would take Christ as his Saviour, the heart of Mr. Davis thrilled with the joy of soul winning in a way never experienced before. From that day onward he grew and developed in the exercise of soul winning, a characteristic of his life ever since."

Are you merely watching the miracles of salvation that are taking place at your church? Don't stand on the sidelines. Be a part of what God is doing in the lives of others. It's wonderful to write about revival and soul winning but much more exciting to personally be right in the middle of it.

September 20, 1921

Are You Forgetting Something?

"Till I come, give attendance to reading, to exhortation, to doctrine. Neglect not the gift that is in thee, which was given thee by prophecy, with the laying on of the hands of the presbytery."—**1 Timothy 4:13–14**

John R. Rice had just graduated from Baylor University a year prior and was now getting ordained for the ministry. Ordination is a special moment in a preacher's life as the leaders, often from the past generation and those he respects, surround him, place their hands on him, and pray for God to use him. Rice would begin the ministry as an assistant pastor in Plainview, Texas, and the following year, he would begin as a senior pastor in Shamrock, Texas. God would use John R. Rice powerfully to preach as an evangelist, as editor of the *Sword of the Lord*, and as an author of numbers of books that are considered classics today.

The Apostle Paul knew his life would end soon. Awaiting his execution, Paul wrote to Timothy, his son in the faith, to encourage and challenge him one last time. Paul's only crime was being a Christian and sharing the Gospel in the Roman Empire. Paul called Timothy to remember his upbringing, doctrine, and the special moment in his life when the pastors had placed their hands on him to send him into the ministry. Lois and Eunice, his godly and faithful grandmother and mother, had brought him up in the nurture of God's Word. Paul had invested in Timothy as a mentor. But now it was up to him to continue in the training he had been given. Paul encouraged Timothy to give time to reading and study so he could preach God's truth clearly and correctly. Paul did not want Timothy to forget the moment he was set apart to preach the Gospel. Timothy was not to neglect the precious gift he had been given, the privilege to preach the Word of God.

Are you neglecting the gifts God has given you? Or are you seeking to enhance those gifts and be used in a greater way? One day, we will give an account of our stewardship of those gifts. "...For unto whomsoever much is given, of him shall be much required..." (Luke 12:48).

September 1907

God Uses the Unconventional

"And he said unto them, What manner of man was he which came up to meet you, and told you these words? And they answered him, He was an hairy man, and girt with a girdle of leather about his loins. And he said, It is Elijah the Tishbite."—**2 Kings 1:7–8**

The *American Magazine* published a seventeen-page article in September of 1907 criticizing Billy Sunday's hellfire and brimstone preaching: "He began by slapping every church tradition of procedure in the face. In the course of his first sermon becoming over-warm, he ripped off his coat and then his waistcoat and then his tie and collar. And even then his gestures, more vehement even than his words, caused the drops of sweat to fly from his brow and ears as he beat the pulpit and tossed his head until he was hoarse in execration of the devil and the hardness of the human heart."

The *Magazine* would quote the Reverend Pearse Pinch, pastor of the Fairfield Congregational Church: "He has outraged every ideal I have had regarding my sacred profession. But...my congregation will be increased by hundreds. I didn't do it! God did it through Billy Sunday! It is for me to humble myself and thank God for his help. He is doing God's work. That I do know!"

Sometimes we can be so cautious of "false fire" that we have no fire at all. When a person physically needs to be revived at the scene of a car accident, the paramedics don't worry about how fast they move, or how loud they bark orders, or if sweat is dripping from their faces. They have a life to save!

The revival of men and the salvation of souls is far more urgent. Maybe you wouldn't preach like a particular evangelist or get as excited about soul winning as someone else in the church—that's okay. At least attempt to please God in your way, and by all means don't criticize those who are trying to honor God and preach truth in revival work.

September 25, 1822

God Always Has a Perfect Plan

"But he knoweth the way that I take: when he hath tried me, I shall come forth as gold."—**Job 23:10**

Daniel Nash was heartbroken. The church he had poured his life into asked him to leave. He had finished building the church sanctuary, started a Sunday school, and continued a powerful mission work in the South. But the members wanted a younger pastor, and at age forty-six, Nash was too old for their liking. The members he loved decided to take a vote in a secret meeting to dismiss him as the pastor. Nash was heartbroken and could not understand what God was doing. But God never closes a door without opening another. Soon Nash would meet a new friend, Evangelist Charles Finney. He would begin travelling with Finney and become his constant prayer warrior. Finney left revival work after Daniel Nash died. He said, "the power is gone."

The furnace of affliction can be hot and uncomfortable. It is never the place we desire to be. God never unveils His entire plan for us to see because He wants us to trust Him rather than ourselves. Nash would soon realize that God was not finished with him at forty-six; rather He was about to commence on his life work that would bring incredible fruit.

God's words in Hebrews 12:2–3 are comforting and helpful when we are in those valleys of uncertainty: "Looking unto Jesus the author and finisher of our faith; who for the joy that was set before him endured the cross, despising the shame, and is set down at the right hand of the throne of God. For consider him that endured such contradiction of sinners against himself, lest ye be wearied and faint in your minds." If we look around us, we will be confused by our circumstances; if we look below us, we will see the one who seeks to destroy us; but if we look up to Jesus, we will see the One who loves us and will never forsake us!

September 23, 1857

Two or Three Can Make a Difference

"Again I say unto you, That if two of you shall agree on earth as touching any thing that they shall ask, it shall be done for them of my Father which is in heaven. For where two or three are gathered together in my name, there am I in the midst of them."—**Matthew 18:19–20**

Jeremiah Lanphier had a burden for revival in New York City. The stock market was collapsing, and economic disaster seemed inevitable. Religion seemed unimportant as revival meetings that had so characterized the region during the First and Second Great Awakenings ceased. Lanphier asked a business friend of his to join him for prayer in the Dutch Reformed Church on this day in 1857. From noon until 1:00 PM those two godly men prayed for revival. By the end of the week, twenty men gathered for prayer. Within three months more than fifty thousand men gathered in churches, fire stations, and schools to pray for revival. Two years later over one million people had come to Christ through the "Prayer Meeting Revival" of 1857–58.

Do you know someone who is of a like mind who you could pray with on a regular basis for revival? When R. A. Torrey arrived in Australia for his first revival there, he met two single ladies who had prayed every day for fifteen years that God would bring him to their country. No wonder God moved in such a spectacular way in those meetings! Don't worry about those who don't pray—find someone who does and join your hearts together. God promises His presence at prayer meetings of two or three. If we can get God at our prayer meetings—watch out! "And this is the confidence that we have in him, that, if we ask any thing according to his will, he heareth us: And if we know that he hear us, whatsoever we ask, we know that we have the petitions that we desired of him" (1 John 5:14–15). Praying for revival would hardly seem out of the will of God! There were two Great Awakenings. Could there be two Prayer Meeting Revivals?

September 29, 1867

Bringing People to Jesus

"One of the two which heard John speak, and followed him, was Andrew, Simon Peter's brother. He first findeth his own brother Simon, and saith unto him, We have found the Messias, which is, being interpreted, the Christ. And he brought him to Jesus..."—**John 1:40–42a**

The first church that W. E. Biederwolf would pastor was the Broadway Presbyterian Church of Logansport, Indiana, near his hometown of Monticello. Born on September 29, 1867, Biederwolf would later serve in the Spanish American War as a chaplain, giving the Gospel to every soldier he met. After his time in the war, Biederwolf entered evangelism, where he would serve thirty-five years travelling the country. He would then become the director of the Winona Lake Bible Conference grounds where Billy Sunday lived and often preached, and he would travel around the world to preach the Gospel to all who would hear. He was known for preaching on the fundamental doctrines of the Bible and wrote books on "The Diety of Christ," "The Resurrection," "The Second Coming," and "The Incarnation of Christ."

With such a resumé, we might assume that Biederwolf was raised in church by godly parents. But in reality, when he was a teenager, some of his friends invited him to a Sunday night church meeting. Those friends walked nearly twenty miles out of their way that evening to take a friend to church, and that night William Biederwolf was saved. Have you ever gone out of your way to bring someone to church to hear about Christ? Are you willing to use your car to go to an area of your town and tell people about the Lord?

Would Peter ever have been saved if Andrew did not care enough to bring him to Jesus? What if those teenagers in the late 1800s were too occupied with their own selfish interests to care about the lost soul of a friend? No doubt, they were exhausted by day's end, yet the seed planted that night would bring fruit one hundred fold.

September 25, 1872

None of These Things Move Me

"But none of these things move me, neither count I my life dear unto myself, so that I might finish my course with joy, and the ministry, which I have received of the Lord Jesus, to testify the gospel of the grace of God."—**Acts 20:24**

Peter Cartwright died in Pleasant Plains, Illinois, on September 25, 1872. He had described his life of evangelism in the rugged frontier vividly in his autobiography: "People, unacquainted with frontier life, and especially frontier life fifty or sixty years ago, can form but a very imperfect idea of the sufferings and hardships underwent at that day, when Methodist preachers went from fort to fort, from camp to camp, from cabin to cabin, with or without road, or path. We walked on dirt floors for carpets, sat on stools or benches for chairs, ate on puncheon tables (large casks), had forked sticks and pocket or butcher knives and forks, slept on bear, deer, or buffalo skins before a fire, or sometimes on the ground in the open air, had our saddles or saddlebags for pillows, and one new suit of clothes of homespun was ample clothing for one year for an early preacher in the West. We crossed creeks and large rivers without bridges or ferry boats, often swam them on horseback, or crossed on trees that had fallen over the streams, often waded waste deep; and if by chance we got a dugout, or a canoe, to cross in ourselves, and swim our horses by, it was quite a treat."

Many times we are stopped in our tracks by the most insignificant of trials. Cartwright would not let a lack of roads or bridges keep him from preaching the Word of God, and God blessed his tenacity.

Today we stop and cower at the least bit of rejection or testing. Oftentimes we wait for the perfect scenario to witness or serve. We will either be tenacious to serve because of our love for Christ, or just as tenaciously run from our opportunities for such by our love for self.

September 26, 1889

Training Laborers for the Harvest

"Then saith he unto his disciples, The harvest truly is plenteous, but the labourers are few; Pray ye therefore the Lord of the harvest, that he will send forth labourers into his harvest."—**Matthew 9:37–38**

In 1886, D. L. Moody addressed his church with a burden that God had laid on his heart: "I tell you what I want, and what I have on my heart. I believe we have got to have gap-men to stand between the laity and the ministers; men who are trained to do city mission work. Take men that have the gifts and train them for the work of reaching the people." As a result, R. A. Torrey helped to found the Chicago Evangelistic Society with his mentor D. L Moody on September 26, 1889. The Chicago Evangelistic Society would later be renamed after D. L. Moody's death as the Moody Bible Institute. R. A. Torrey would serve as superintendent for many years and later would assume the pastorate of the Chicago Avenue Church, renamed the Moody Church. The Moody Bible Institute became the premier Bible college of the early 1900s for students who desired to change the world for Christ. R. A. Torrey would lead the institution in fundamental doctrine and passionate evangelism.

According to Baptist records, in 1901 there were 54,000 men and women in Baptist colleges, seminaries, and academies preparing their lives to serve the Lord in the ministry. The population of the world at that time was 1.7 billion. Today, the population has reached 7.5 billion. Does God know math? It seems that if God needed 54,000 to reach 1.7 billion, He would need roughly 245,000 to reach the world now with the same number of workers. So where are they? Training places are struggling to keep their doors open for lack of students. The need is not lessening with each passing hour, month, and year. God is still calling. Will you answer? "Also I heard the voice of the Lord, saying, Whom shall I send, and who will go for us? Then said I, Here am I; send me" (Isaiah 6:8).

September 27, 1940

The Cattle on a Thousand Hills

"For every beast of the forest is mine, and the cattle upon a thousand hills...If I were hungry, I would not tell thee: for the world is mine, and the fullness thereof."
—**Psalm 50:10, 12**

John Sephus Mack, a Christian business man who financed Bob Jones Sr.'s great crusades, died on this day in 1940. He first met Bob Jones at a crusade in his hometown of McKeesport, Pennslyvania, when he sat on the platform because there were no seats left in the auditorium. Jones turned to him and said, "Help me get ahold of this crowd." As a result, they knelt down and prayed together in the service. Being a devout Presbyterian, Mack had never publically sought God in prayer like he did that night. After the service, John Mack told Evangelist Jones that he wanted to finance any needs that he might have. He soon financed much of Bob Jones's college and his future crusades.

Why do we doubt God's provision? Is God not big enough, or smart enough, or caring enough to provide for us? When God asks us to sacrificially give for His work, why do we start working the figures instead of working our faith? Elijah in 1 Kings 17 had declared that it would not rain for three and a half years because of the wickedness of the nation and its leadership. God took care of Elijah for a time at the brook Cherith. When the waters there dried up, He sent him down to a widow's house who was preparing to fix her last meal and die in poverty. But when she trusted God by faith, an amazing miracle took place! "For thus saith the LORD God of Israel, The barrel of meal shall not waste, neither shall the cruse of oil fail, until the day that the LORD sendeth rain upon the earth. And she went and did according to the saying of Elijah: and she, and he, and her house, did eat many days. And the barrel of meal wasted not, neither did the cruse of oil fail, according to the word of the LORD, which he spake by Elijah" (1 Kings 17:14–16).

Ready for a miracle? "Give, and it shall be given unto you..." (Luke 6:38).

September 28, 1934

The Sword of the Spirit

"When I blow with a trumpet, I and all that are with me, then blow ye the trumpets also on every side of all the camp, and say, The sword of the LORD, and of Gideon."—**Judges 7:18**

John R. Rice had a burning desire to get fundamental sermons into the hands of Christians in Dallas, Texas. Started as a four-page paper published by the Fundamentalist Baptist Church, Rice published the first edition of the *Sword of the Lord* on September 28, 1934. John R. Rice had begun a periodical that would influence Christianity for generations to come. The Sword's purpose statement to this day is: "An Independent Christian Publication, Standing for the Verbal Inspiration of the Bible, the Deity of Christ, His Blood Atonement, Salvation by Faith, New Testament Soul Winning and the Premillennial Return of Christ; Opposing Modernism (Liberalism), Worldliness and Formalism."

This generation still needs the trumpet of the Gospel to be blown and the sword of the Spirit to be held high. As many push to compromise God's Word, we should hold to the doctrines of God courageously. As Gideon and his three hundred men were surrounded by thousands of Midianites, he was well aware that only through the power of God would they see a victory. Gideon gave the signal by shouting, "The sword of the Lord and of Gideon!" And the three hundred men ran down the mountain, crashing their pitchers and sounding their trumpets. The Midianites thought they were outnumbered by their enemies in the night and quickly retreated. Today, we are still outnumbered by the world, the flesh, and the devil, but God is not influenced by the numbers or the odds stacked against Him. All He needs is a few of His servants to get thoroughly right with Him and courageously follow wherever He leads. The devil is getting his forces ready for the battle of all time. The world is using every bit of its resources to silence the cause of Christ. And the flesh is being fed and bombarded with the lusts from within. Will you claim the promise of victory through the Sword of the Spirit? Get more familiar with your weapon today, and use it!

September 29, 1951

God Commendeth His Love Toward Us

"But God commendeth his love toward us, in that, while we were yet sinners, Christ died for us."—**Romans 5:8**

Evan Roberts died in Cardiff, Wales, on this day in 1951. By this time, an obscure figure, forty-seven years after the Welsh Revival which he had led and was so mightily used. Roberts had suffered a collapse from his demanding schedule in 1906 and lived in depression for many years after. Away from the public spotlight, Roberts devoted his life to supporting others in prayer. His obituary read, "He was a man who had experienced strange things. In his youth, he had seemed to hold the nation in the palms of his hands. He endured strains and underwent great changes of opinion and outlook, but his religious convictions remained firm to the end." His words of revival still ring out after his death: "I would have burst if I had not prayed. What boiled me was that verse, 'God commending His love.' I fell on my knees with my arms over the seat in front of me, and the tears and perspiration flowed freely. I thought blood was gushing forth. For about two minutes it was fearful. I cried, 'Bend me! Bend me! Bend us!...What bent me was God commending His love (Romans 5:8), and I not seeing anything in it to commend. After I was bent, a wave of peace came over me, and the audience sang, 'I hear thy welcome voice.' And as they sang I thought of the bending at the Judgment Day, and I was filled with compassion for those who would be bent on that day, and I wept. Henceforth the salvation of souls became the burden of my heart...."

Has the truth of God's amazing love and grace faded from your mind? Have you lost sight of what He did for you that day on Golgotha? The picture of the Son of God pouring out His blood for us should never diminish in our minds. The only reason we even have the potential to love Him in some meager way is because He first loved us. Our love for Christ will keep us in love with the ministry. When we allow that love to wax cold, everything He asks us to do will become a burden. Come back to your first love today.

September 30, 1770

A Cross for a Crown

"For to me to live is Christ, and to die is gain."—**Philippians 1:21**

George Whitefield's body was slowing down, but his spirit was still energized by the thought of revival. He would be quoted as saying, "I would rather wear out than rust out." Whitefield passed away from his poor health the morning after preaching his last sermon. His desire was to be buried beneath his pulpit in the Old South Presbyterian Church in Newbury Port, Massachusetts. George Whitefield's legacy would continue as a powerful evangelist. Dr. James Hamilton described his ministry: "When it is realized that his voice could be heard by twenty thousand, and that ringing all over England, as well as America, he would often preach thrice on a working day, in that he has received in one week as many as a thousand letters from persons awakened by his sermons, if no estimate can be formed of the results of his ministry, some idea may be suggested of its vast extent and singular effectiveness." Dr. Fred Barlow would memorialize his death: "On September 30, 1770, just shy of his fifty-sixth birthday, George Whitefield, who preached for thirty-four years, crossed the Atlantic thirteen times, preached more than eighteen thousand sermons, influenced one of the greatest revivals, died at Newberry Port, Massachusetts, and is found 'suddenly exchanging his life of unparalleled labors for his eternal rest.'"

Whitefield worked tirelessly for the cause of Christ, and over two hundred fifty years after his death, we can still be thankful for his impact on the world. We do not advocate burning out or neglecting our Lord's clear commands, but most of us do not come near either one! Revival will not come to lukewarm churches or Christians. It will come to churches and Christians who are passionately in love with their Saviour and making Him preeminent in their lives. There will be no revival meetings or evangelistic efforts in Heaven. "I must work the works of him that sent me, while it is day: the night cometh, when no man can work" (John 9:4). Today we must labor—rest will come sure and soon!

OCTOBER

October 5, 1913

God Is Never Far from Those Who Seek Him

"And hath made of one blood all nations of men for to dwell on all the face of the earth, and hath determined the times before appointed, and the bounds of their habitation; That they should seek the Lord, if haply they might feel after him, and find him, though he be not far from every one of us."—**Acts 17:26–27**

God is not an abstract being or a figment of our imaginations. He is very much alive and attentive to each and every person on planet Earth. At times, He may seem far away, but the Bible teaches that He will hear even the faint whisper of those who seek Him. On Mars Hill, the Apostle Paul noticed an altar with the inscription, "To the unknown God." He may have been unknown to them, but God knew exactly who they were and was waiting for them to call upon Him.

J. Wilbur Chapman and his wife Mabel had sailed to England on the *Lusitania* the previous month, and now on October 5, 1913, it was time for the Chapman crusade to open at Andrew's Hall in Glasgow, Scotland. These meetings would continue for eleven weeks and by the final week, Chapman asked three other churches if they would open their doors to house the crowds that were coming. Thousands were turned away from the final service in Andrew's Hall because there just wasn't room for them. Chapman would see over twelve thousand people trust Christ during those eleven weeks of revival.

Many today are still searching for the "unknown God." They look for Him in pleasure, careers, relationships, status, and more only to come up empty and unfulfilled. Like Paul in Acts 17, we must be willing to go out of our way to stop at the Mars Hill of our day. It is important that we give them God's Word, for "...faith cometh by hearing, and hearing by the word of God" (Romans 10:17). Let's carry Gospel tracts with us, and let's be looking for opportunities today to talk about Jesus Christ. Christ commanded us to make known "the unknown God!"

October 2, 1858

Unlocking the Prayer Closet

"Be careful for nothing; but in every thing by prayer and supplication with thanksgiving let your requests be made known unto God. And the peace of God, which passeth all understanding, shall keep your hearts and minds through Christ Jesus."—**Philippians 4:6–7**

The first prayer meeting at noon in 1857 in the Dutch Reformed Church was just two men praying for revival. But soon thousands of people in New York City had responded to God's call to pray. Describing the great Prayer Meeting Revival on October 2, 1858, the "*Daily Tribune*" of New York City reported, "Soon the striking of the five bells at 12 o'clock will generally be known as the Hour of Prayer." By mid-March, the three-thousand seat Burton's Theatre was filled for the prayer meetings.

Anxiety, stress, and fear grip us today as we endeavor to juggle and meet the demands of our lives. With the economy hitting rock bottom in the middle 1800s, what did Jeremiah Lanphier decide to do? Work harder? Work smarter? Cut this—add that? Lanphier had listened to his pastor faithfully preach about the revivals of the Bible and in American history. He took them to heart and decided that the only thing that could bring peace to his heart and the nation's heart was prayer!

When is your hour of prayer? When is your time to get alone with your Creator and spend time with Him? The Christian life cannot be won without intimate moments with God. We cannot expect to have victory in our personal lives or in our ministries without those times in the closet. We should pray with thanksgiving in our hearts to the Lord, *praising* His goodness towards us. We should take our *requests* to Him, *asking* him to answer according to His will. And we should *yield* to His calling on our lives, begging Him to use us in His service. After we spend time in prayer with our Heavenly Father, we are filled with a unique peace that passes all human understanding. Is your life in disarray or confusion? It's time to unlock the prayer closet. Peace awaits!

October 3, 1994

I'm on the Winning Side

"For whatsoever is born of God overcometh the world: and this is the victory that overcometh the world, even our faith."—**1 John 5:4**

At the Southwide Baptist Fellowship meeting at Northside Baptist Church in Charlotte, North Carolina, a frail man stood in front of his preacher friends to challenge them in the faith. Curtis Hutson's body was riddled with cancer, yet his desire was to encourage the next generations of preachers to stand on the Word of God. He preached a classic sermon entitled, "Things That Are Different Are Not the Same" from 2 Timothy 2:2—"And the things that thou hast heard of me among many witnesses, the same commit thou to faithful men, who shall be able to teach others also." He concluded his message from 2 Timothy 4:6–7, "For I am now ready to be offered, and the time of my departure is at hand. I have fought a good fight, I have finished my course, I have kept the faith." Tears flowed as many could sense this would be the last sermon of the great evangelist and soul winner. But Hutson lifted his weak voice and began to sing, "I'm on the winning side!"

Once I drifted out in sin, had no hope nor joy within,
And my soul was burdened down with pride.
Then my Saviour came along and He showed me I was wrong,
Now I know I'm on the winning side.

From the straight and narrow way I was drifting ev'ry day;
Out upon the waters deep and wide.
But it all is over now, glory light is on my brow,
And my soul is on the winning side.

Well, I am on the winning side, yes, I am on the winining side,
Out in sin no more will I abide;
I've enlisted in the fight for the cause of truth and right,
Praise the Lord, I'm on the winning side!

Every child of God is on the winning side! May we live as victors today so that one day we can sing victoriously even in death!

October 4, 1880

Are You Closer to God Today Than You Were Yesterday?

"And my people are bent to backsliding from me: though they called them to the most High, none at all would exalt him."—**Hosea 11:7**

Homer Rodeheaver was born in Cinco Hollow, Ohio, on this day in 1880. His family would soon move to Tennessee, where he would work at the lumberyard with his father. Homer developed an early love for music and would learn to play the cornet and later the trombone, for which he would become famous. Rodeheaver would travel in evangelism with W. E. Biederwolf and later Billy Sunday as their music man, using God's gift of music to reach the masses with the Gospel. "Rody," as he was lovingly called, had a love for humor, often describing his beloved trombone as a "Methodist trombone" that sometimes "backslides."

In all seriousness, we should be in the practice of examining our lives every day to prevent backsliding. The prophet Hosea preached fervently against the backsliding of his nation. Though they would call the Lord their God, they would not act like one of his followers. They were actively forsaking their God and as a result judgment was coming. Hosea's message from the Lord was the last call for repentance that God would send before the Assyrian Empire conquered the people. But most did not understand the importance of Hosea's preaching. They did not see any problem with how they were living and no strange prophet was going to prove to them otherwise. Whether in the old days of Israel or in our modern day, backsliding happens slowly over time. No Christian plans to backslide, but over a long period of time, backsliding happens in our lives if we do not stay on guard and attentive to God's Word.

Someone has rightly said, "If you were ever closer to the Lord than you are now, you have backslidden." Are you willing to admit that spiritually you are not where you should be or once were? That's an important first step. The next step is to "Draw nigh to God, and he will draw nigh to you…" (James 4:8).

October 5, 1703

A Valley of Dry Bones

"So I prophesied as I was commanded: and as I prophesied, there was a noise, and behold a shaking, and the bones came together, bone to his bone."
—Ezekiel 37:7

The Old Testament prophet Ezekiel told of a vision he had received from the Lord. He was taken to a valley full of dry bones, no doubt the remains of a vicious battle. The Lord told Ezekiel to preach to the dry bones and to call for the Spirit of God to breathe upon them. As a result of Ezekiel's obedience, they were miraculously revived. The key elements of Ezekiel's dream were the Word of God and the Spirit of God. With those two supernatural forces, Ezekiel was able to watch the dry bones all around him be revived as a great army for the Lord. Though the specific application of this passage is about the nation of Israel, there is tremendous application to the child of God and revival. Are we relying on the Word of God and the Spirit of God? Are we living in obedience to these two voices?

Jonathan Edwards was born on this day in Windsor, Connecticut, in 1703. Jonathan would go to college at age thirteen, a prodigy in religious education. Edwards' great accomplishment, however, was not in his great knowledge, but his great willingness to be used of God. Edwards would become one of the key influencers of the Great Awakening of America. Realizing that most in his church were unsaved, Edwards preached God's truth week after week, year after year with great prayer and personal courage. During the beginning sparks of the Great Awakening, Edwards would write of his church that "300 of the 670 communicants were savingly brought home to Christ." He wrote, "the town seemed to be full of the presence of God. The noise amongst the dry bones waxed louder and louder. The revival struck the hearts first of the young people and then of their elders all over the town…The tavern was soon empty. People had done with their quarrels, backbiting, and intermeddling with other men's matters." Lord, shake our dry bones today through your Word and your Spirit in another Great Awakening!

October 6, 1536

The Bible Stands

"Wherein I suffer trouble, as an evildoer, even unto bonds; but the word of God is not bound."—**2 Timothy 2:9**

William Tyndale had been arrested and sentenced to death for translating the Word of God into English and distributing the Bible to the common people, which he knew was the key to their salvation and turning of the nation back to God. After betrayal by a close friend, Tyndale was imprisoned in Brussels and sentenced to be strangled and burnt at the stake in Vilvoorde, Belgium. Tyndale was led to the stake, hands tied behind his back, in what appeared to be a defeating moment. But before he was strangled to death, Tyndale shouted before the onlookers, "Lord! Open the King of England's eyes!" God would answer the prayer of this martyr that day. In the next four years, four successive translations of the Bible were written in English, based on the work of Tyndale, and in 1611, the King of England himself would publish the King James Version of the Bible.

Throughout history, many evil men have tried to remove the Word of God from the face of this earth. The Roman Catholic Church during the Middle Ages kept the people in the dark for hundreds of years, forbidding the Bible to be translated or read in the common language. Later in history, wicked men like Voltaire, Adolf Hitler, Karl Marx, and Joseph Stalin had made the purpose of their lives to remove the Bible from the world. In the United States, the atheist Madalyn Murray O'Hair founded "American Atheists" and served as president from 1963 to 1986. Her activism caused the Supreme Court to remove prayer and Bible reading from our public schools. But the Word of God lives on.

Never in the course of history has a book been so hated, and yet survive. How could a book be supernaturally protected through the ages? The Apostle Paul's words to Timothy shed great light: "The word of God is not bound." Yes, many who have proclaimed the Word of God have been bound, beaten, tortured, and killed, but the Bible cannot be restricted, silenced, or destroyed. Let it live in and through your life today!

October 7, 1747

Remember Now Thy Creator

"Remember now thy Creator in the days of thy youth, while the evil days come not, nor the years draw nigh, when thou shalt say, I have no pleasure in them."
—**Ecclesiastes 12:1**

Joseph Bellamy preached in Stratfield, Connecticut, on October 7, 1747. His text was Ecclesiastes 12:1 and he powerfully and bluntly called to his audience: "I see you and know the way you take. I pity you, I call to you, I warn you. I command you! Remember the Creator, be mindful of God now, without any further delay—in the days of thy youth." Bellamy who was mentored by men like Jonathan Edwards knew well what an Awakening looked like.

Bellamy was challenging his listeners that day to heed the words of King Solomon. Solomon had literally all that the world had to offer. Throughout the book of Ecclesiastes, he describes his life passions. He turned to pleasure, productivity, possessions, and prudence for happiness. But at the end of his life, he declares that all is vanity. The emptiness of this world discouraged him. Maybe not to the same extent, but all of us can testify to the emptiness of the world's offers. In our youth, we turn to pleasure for satisfaction. Soon, we realize that we need some sort of income, so we plan a career and turn to productivity. Once we have earned enough money to be comfortable, we are tempted with possessions. And towards the end of our lives, we turn to prudence for fulfillment. But without God, all is vanity. Solomon concludes his book by pleading that we do not do as he did, but do as God says! "Remember now thy Creator in the days of thy youth…." He continues: "Let us hear the conclusion of the whole matter: Fear God, and keep his commandments: for this is the whole duty of man. For God shall bring every work into judgment, with every secret thing, whether it be good, or whether it be evil" (Ecclesiastes 12:1, 13–14).

Will you heed the warning of the wisest, richest, and most powerful human being who ever lived? Remember God today—or regret it tomorrow!

October 8, 1871

Fire!

"But the heavens and the earth, which are now, by the same word are kept in store, reserved unto fire against the day of judgment and perdition of ungodly men."
—2 Peter 3:7

The dark Sunday night sky was interrupted by a spark at the O'Leary farm on October 8, 1871, as D. L. Moody finished his evening message. The fire became untamable after the city watchman had reported the wrong area to the firefighters. He soon realized his mistake but was too embarrassed to correct the firemen. Many historians believe that if the watchman would have corrected his mistake as soon as he realized it, the city would have been saved from the Great Chicago Fire. Because most of the city was built of wood, the disaster would consume more than two thousand acres of the city and devastate a third of the population. The fire eventually destroyed Moody's church and home as well as the homes of many of his members. Moody, in his own words, saved "nothing but his reputation and his Bible" that horrible night.

But God warns us of another fire coming in the future. This fire will destroy the entire earth in judgment against "the perdition of ungodly men." The Word of God that created this world, will someday cause it to be destroyed. God will take his hands off the very atoms that hold our world together, and the entire earth with its corruption and sin will explode in fire. The Apostle Peter reminds us of this day so that we will view everything around us in that perspective. We are but pilgrims on this earth. In the words of the old song, "This world is not my home. I'm just a-passing through. My treasures are laid up somewhere beyond the blue. The angels beckon me from Heaven's open door, and I can't feel at home in this world anymore."

How "at home" are you in this world? Everything in this world will someday be consumed. How will you live with that "Great Fire" in mind today?

October 9, 1871

Another Fire

"And of some have compassion, making a difference: And others save with fear, pulling them out of the fire; hating even the garment spotted by the flesh."
—Jude 22–23

When the Great Chicago Fire erupted, Ira Sankey escaped the city in a row boat. Along with many others out on Lake Michigan, he watched as flames engulfed the vast city. In His mercy, God sent rain on the evening of October 9 that would assist in the putting out of this horrible fire. Over three hundred people lost their lives, and one third of the population were left homeless. For months preachers like Sankey and Moody would spend hours upon hours trying to help people recover and assist in any way that they could. Their great desire though it all, however, was to rescue men's souls from an awful fire still coming.

If we really believed in an eternal place called Hell, we would do everything within our power to tell others of the only way of escape. We would not worry what people think about us or how many would laugh. We would not think about our awkwardness or timidity. Nothing would keep us from getting the message to as many as possible in as many places as possible.

Many today do not like to talk about Hell. It's too negative and causes fear. But Jesus spoke much more about Hell than He did Heaven. There are 239 warnings in the New Testament alone about this horrible place. We simply must not ignore this subject. "The wicked shall be turned into hell, and all the nations that forget God" (Psalm 9:17).

The way of escape is not through religion, good deeds, or sterling character. "Neither is there salvation in any other: for there is none other name under heaven given among men, whereby we must be saved" (Acts 4:12). Show someone the escape route today. Don't wait until it is everlastingly too late!

October 10, 1958

The Old Rugged Cross

"But God forbid that I should glory, save in the cross of our Lord Jesus Christ, by whom the world is crucified unto me, and I unto the world."—**Galatians 6:14**

The Apostle Paul gloried in the cross of Christ and refused to glory in anything else. He gladly took up his own cross spiritually, following in Christ's footsteps, and gloried in the trials of his life that were a result of his faith. He was crucified unto the world with no desire to return. The lust of the flesh, the lust of the eyes, and the pride of life—all that is in the world—was dead to him.

George Bennard, the evangelist known for writing "The Old Rugged Cross," died in Reed City, Michigan, on this day in 1958. Bennard preached to thousands throughout his ministry with the Salvation Army. Undoubtedly his greatest contributions to all Christians was his beloved hymn, "The Old Rugged Cross." The town of Reed City, Michigan, constructed a cross in front of Bennard's house to memorialize his contribution to Christian hymnology, and a museum remains in the town of his life and ministry. He is today buried in Inglewood, California. Bennard went to his grave living the words of the fourth stanza, and they ought to motivate us today as well.

> To the old rugged cross I will ever be true;
> Its shame and reproach gladly bear;
> Then He'll call me someday to my home far away,
> Where His glory forever I'll share.
> So I'll cherish the old rugged cross,
> Till my trophies at last I lay down;
> I will cling to the old rugged cross,
> And exchange it someday for a crown.

Will you cherish the opportunity you have today to take up your cross and follow Jesus Christ? Yes, it may bring some shame and reproach your way. But one day, you will exchange that cross for a crown.

October 10, 1821

Faithful in Proclaiming the Gospel

"And daily in the temple, and in every house, they ceased not to teach and preach Jesus Christ."—**Acts 5:42**

While hoping to make a fortune as a lawyer, Charles Finney heard the Gospel, and his life pursuits were changed dramatically. Immediately after his salvation on October 10, 1821, Finney could not keep the message of the Gospel to himself. "Finney went up and down the village street, like a merchant, like a salesman searching for customers, conversing with any with whom he might meet...Pious frauds, young Unitarian smart-alecs, booze-makers, the unsaved, scoffers—it made no difference who they were. 'A few words spoken to an individual would stick in their heart like an arrow.'" Finney would later speak of the day he was saved and first began to witness to others about the saving power of Christ: "I believe the Spirit of God made a lasting impression upon every one of them. I cannot remember one whom I spoke with who was not converted." The first day he accepted the Gospel was the first day he proclaimed it.

Are we able to go days without sharing the Gospel with someone? The apostles in the Book of Acts were so passionate about the Gospel that at the end of chapter five they "ceased not to teach and preach Jesus Christ." But at the beginning of chapter five, they were arrested, beaten, and jailed because of their witness. We have more freedom but less witness! Have we gotten lax because of our liberties? How sad it would be not to realize how valuable our freedoms are until they are taken away.

We may not be as fruitful as Finney on the first day of his salvation, but we can be just as faithful. When we are faithful, God will make us fruitful. What a privilege to be "labourers together with God" (1 Corinthians 3:9) in the grand task of reaching souls for Jesus Christ. When we plant the seed of the Gospel with our words and water it daily with our testimonies, God brings the increase.

October 12, 1906

Insignificant Becomes Significant

"But ye shall receive power, after that the Holy Ghost is come upon you: and ye shall be witnesses unto me both in Jerusalem, and in all Judaea, and in Samaria, and unto the uttermost part of the earth."—**Acts 1:8**

The 100th Anniversary celebration of the Haystack Prayer Meeting concluded after four days on October 12, 1906 in Williamstown, Massachusetts. No one would have guessed that a prayer meeting in the middle of a haystack in the middle of nowhere in the middle of a thunderstorm would spark the modern American missionary movement. Dr. Edward Warren Capen published an article commemorating the anniversary: "One hundred years ago there might have been seen on a late July or early August afternoon in Sloane's meadow near the Hoosac River in Williamstown, Mass., two piles of hay. The adjoining maple grove still stands, but the haystacks perished long ago. Nevertheless, the site of the northern one is marked by a monument surmounted by a globe and inscribed with these words, above and below a haystack carved out of the marble:"

The Field is the World
The Birthplace of American Foreign Missions
1806
SAMUEL J. MILLS
JAMES RICHARDS
FRANCIS L. ROBBINS
HARVEY LOOMIS
BYRAM GREEN

Names that have long since vanished in American history, but not from the pages of God's records. These men would turn the world upside down and their example would inspire many others to follow them to the uttermost part of the world.

October 13, 1920

For the Glory of God

"Unto him be glory in the church by Christ Jesus throughout all ages, world without end. Amen."—**Ephesians 3:21**

The great music evangelist Charles Alexander died in his sleep from a heart attack on this day in 1920 after a period of failing health. Dr. T. B. Davis described his powerful ministry: "The Apostle Paul toured much of the world in his day, but it was only a portion of our planet. Whitefield and the two Wesleys, and Moody and Sankey visited America and England in their wonderful missions for the salvation of the lost; but it remained for Dr. Reuben A. Torrey and Mr. Charles M. Alexander to completely circle the globe, and then for Mr. Alexander to make a second trip, revisiting old scenes, leading thousands in Gospel song, and preaching Christ to individuals on land and sea."

Alexander's tombstone bears his most beloved hymn:

When by the gift of his infinite grace,
I am accorded in Heaven a place,
Just to be there and to look on his face,
Will through the ages be glory for me.

Looking back one day from Heaven, we will regret ever living a single moment of our lives for anything but the glory of God? Jesus said in John 8:29 "...for I do always those things that please him." Could we say that? One of the greatest statements made about our Lord is the tribute given him by the Apostle Paul in Romans 15:3a "For even Christ pleased not himself." So much of our time is consumed with selfish interests and fleshly desires. Get in the habit of asking the Lord from time to time throughout your day, "Lord is this pleasing to you?" That little question will keep you spot on to the purpose God gave us in 1 Corinthians 10:31, "Whether therefore ye eat, or drink, or whatsoever ye do, do all to the glory of God."

October 14, 1857

Rich toward God

"But God said unto him, Thou fool, this night thy soul shall be required of thee: then whose shall those things be, which thou hast provided? So is he that layeth up treasure for himself, and is not rich toward God."—**Luke 12:20–21**

The national financial market collapsed in 1857, greatly affecting the pastors and evangelists of that day. One author described it as "a yawning earthquake, it shook down the palaces of the rich, no less than the humble dwelling of the poor, and swallowed up their substance. Men went to bed dreaming all night of their vast hoarded treasures, and woke up in the morning hopeless bankrupts." Because of the crash, the people of New York City were suddenly open to the Gospel, and revival would break out all across the city in less than a year.

Jesus tells us of a similar situation in the form of a parable. A man had worked his entire life to fill his barns and become wealthy. In his pride, he thought to himself, "...What shall I do, because I have no room where to bestow my fruits? And he said, this will I do: I will pull down my barns, and build greater: and there will I bestow all my fruits and my goods. And I will say to my soul, Soul, thou hast much goods laid up for many years take thine ease, eat, drink, and be merry" (Luke 12:17–19). Sounds like the thinking of most people today! The dreams of making it big so that I can live in ease and comfort.

God, however, has a completely different perspective. "But God said unto him, Thou fool, this night thy soul shall be required of thee: then whose shall those things be, which thou hast provided?" (verse 20). He closed that parable with some valuable advice for all who would read it: "So is he that layeth up treasure for himself, and is not rich toward God" (verse 21). It's strong language, but God calls us "fools" if all we have is material stuff and have neglected God. When your soul is required, will you be rich toward God?

October 15, 1906

Make Me Like You, Dear Lord

"Thou shalt not follow a multitude to do evil; neither shalt thou speak in a cause to decline after many to wrest judgment."—**Exodus 23:2**

Sam Jones boarded a train to head for home on October 15, 1906, after preaching a revival in Oklahoma City. Little did he know that the train would take him to the gates of Heaven. Over thirty thousand people would come to view his body and pay their condolences to the great evangelist. Dr. Will Houghton would later portray the "uniqueness" of his ministry:

"Jones was conducting a citywide revival campaign where great crowds were attending and many unsaved were turning to Christ. But the cooperating pastors felt Jones was preaching too many negative sermons against sin—too little on love. And they felt he should be more dignified, use more tact, etc. So the pastors agreed to meet secretly one afternoon to pray for their evangelist. Quite by chance Jones came in about the middle of the prayer meeting...and was overjoyed to find the ministers conducting a prayer meeting. It did not take him long, however, to discover he was the object of their prayers. 'Oh Lord, help Brother Jones to use more tact,' prayed one pastor. 'Help him to be more dignified in the pulpit,' prayed another. 'Change his mannerism,' besought another. 'Give him more respect for the clergy,' called out another....

"It was not until the last one prayed that they knew of Jones' presence. That was when he began to pray—'Lord, I hope you won't listen to a one of these preachers. They don't preach against sin, they don't visit door to door, they don't weep over sinners and they don't win souls. And they want You to change me until I'm most like them! Oh Lord, help these preachers to sense enough to realize that if You were to answer their prayers I would be just as worthless and no account as they are! Please God, don't make me like any of these fellers.' A group of very sheepish and subdued preachers listened as the evangelist went on to pray for a sweeping revival there—a prayer that God answered!"

October 16, 1874

Do You See the Multitudes?

"But when he saw the multitudes, he was moved with compassion on them, because they fainted, and were scattered abroad, as sheep having no shepherd. Then saith he unto his disciples, The harvest truly is plenteous, but the labourers are few; Pray ye therefore the Lord of the harvest, that he will send forth labourers into his harvest."—**Matthew 9:36–38**

God had been blessing the ministry of D. L Moody in Great Britain. The attendance on this second trip had been a far cry from his first when only eight people came to the initial service. Moody and Sankey traveled to Belfast, Ireland, and to his amazement, the services at the Botanic Gardens were so packed that they could only admit those with tickets. Moody was very clear, however, that tickets would only be administered to those who specifically wanted to be saved. Everyone else was turned away. As a result, the Botanic Gardens of Belfast was filled with the lost ready and eager to hear the Gospel.

Throngs of people came to hear Jesus Christ during his ministry a few thousand years ago. They saw His miracles, heard His words, and wanted more of His message. As the people flooded to meet Him, Jesus cast His eyes upon the masses of people. They were as sheep that did not have a shepherd. They were scattered abroad, confused, and distraught. Jesus' heart filled with compassion and love as He gazed upon them. He turned to His disciples, who, like us, needed to have their vision of this world altered. He wanted to teach them a simple lesson, "The harvest truly is plenteous, but the labourers are few; Pray ye therefore the Lord of the harvest, that he will send forth labourers into his harvest."

When you look at people around you, is that what you see—a sea of lost souls who need a Saviour? Have you discerned that there are not enough laborers to reach these masses of people? Are you willing to pray for laborers? Are you willing to give financially to those who want to train and go to the multitudes? Are you willing to be the answer to the prayer and become a laborer yourself?

October 16, 1777

Lift Up the Truth

"Blessed is the nation whose God is the Lord; and the people whom he hath chosen for his own inheritance."—**Psalm 33:12**

Lorenzo Dow, whose biography would become a best-selling book in America, preached an unusual revival meeting in October of 1777. During his sermon, the audience became extremely offended and began to leave the tabernacle. Dow ran to the back of the building and held the doors shut, keeping anyone from leaving, a practice probably not recommended! He then stood in that same spot and continued to preach the Gospel. Two thirds of the audience had accepted Christ by the end of the message. Lorenzo Dow would shake the young nation for Christ. His impact was so widespread and had such a lasting effect that in 1860, the most popular name given to baby boys that year was "Lorenzo" after the famed evangelist.

Revisionist historians today would have us believe that America does not have its roots in Christianity and the revivals we read about were short-lived and had little lasting impact. A mere walk through our nation's capital would prove otherwise. Monuments and engravings all through our nation testify to the rich biblical history of our nation. In our historic documents and speeches, we see clearly the roots that our nation has in the Bible.

But what will we do with this rich Christian heritage? How can we pass it on to our children and grandchildren? How can we counteract the deletion of God from our history? Jesus declares in Matthew 5:13, Ye are the salt of the earth..." Salt was used in Jesus day as a preservative for food prior to the technology of refrigeration. We are tasked by God Himself to be the preservative of truth. Of course, it must be preached in our pulpits, and propagated through our witness, but an ounce of example is worth a pound of sermons! In a day when "...truth is fallen in the street..." (Isaiah 59:14), may we lift that truth up in the way we think, live, and speak!

October 16, 1910

A Pure Church for a Pure Christ

"For I am jealous over you with godly jealousy: for I have espoused you to one husband, that I may present you as a chaste virgin to Christ."
—**2 Corinthians 11:2**

J. Wilbur Chapman began his Chicago revival campaign on this day in 1910. Just as God moved this city under the preaching of D. L. Moody and R. A. Torrey, He would do the same under the powerful preaching of Chapman. His biography by Ford Ottman would describe the meetings: "The opening service was held on Sunday afternoon, with a sermon based on the Song of Solomon 6:10, 'Who is she that looketh forth as the morning, fair as the moon, clear as the sun, and terrible as an army with banners?' Each day thereafter until the end of the campaign, with one or two exceptions, he held noon-day meetings in the Opera House, and conducted an evening service in the White City. On the thirty-first of October, the evening meetings were transferred to the Wilson Tabernacle and continued there until Sunday the sixth of November when they were transferred to the Austin Tabernacle where the great series of meetings was brought to a close on Sunday evening, November twenty-seventh. During all this period he preached from two to four sermons each day."

Whether we would agree or disagree with Chapman's hermeneutics, he preached from the Song of Solomon in that opening service on the church of God adorned for her husband Christ. The Apostle Paul rebuked the Corinthians for their lack of purity as a Bride for Jesus Christ. They had let sin creep into the church, and they did not have the courage to deal with it. Paul explained to them that Christ is jealous of His Church. He gave His life to redeem the church, and we should desire to be that pure bride when we stand before Him one day.

The challenge is great as we live in a polluted culture. The dirt and grime of sin attaches easily to us. Chapman may have taken some liberties with his text in Song of Solomon, but it's hard to get Paul's words wrong in 1 Timothy 5:22, "...keep thyself pure."

October 1905

Do Right 'Till the Stars Fall

"Therefore to him that knoweth to do good, and doeth it not, to him it is sin."
—James 4:17

Bob Jones Sr. married the love of his life, Bernice, in October of 1905. His beloved wife would die of tuberculosis after ten months of marriage, an indescribably difficult loss for the young evangelist. Throughout his life, "Dr. Bob" was known for his short quips, many of which were about perseverance, no doubt learned through his wife's Homegoing as well as other obstacles he faced throughout his life. Even today, he is remembered by some of these sayings: "The test of your character is what it takes to stop you." "The greatest ability is dependability." "Finish the job."

His most remembered saying is probably, "Do right 'till the stars fall." And sometimes he would add, "And if the sky does start falling, keep doing right while it does!" It is easy today to be distracted from the right things in our busy schedules. The fact that most others aren't doing right doesn't help either. But God says that if we know something is right and we don't do it, we have sinned. All of us are well aware of the sins of *commission*—lying, stealing, murder, envy, covetousness, etc. But we have a tendency to overlook the sins of *omission*.

Most of us who have children have quoted Numbers 32:23 a time or two to them. "...Be sure your sin will find you out." Perhaps we ask our children if they did something wrong, and they deny it. (Children are professional liars!) We can't prove they did, so we say, "Well, if you did it...be sure your sin will find you out." While there is nothing wrong with the application, and it is true that sin is always found out, the context of Numbers 32 deals with a sin of omission. Moses had given the people a number of commands and perhaps wondered if they would obey them. So he added in verse 23, "But if ye will not do so, behold ye have sinned against the Lord: and be sure your sin will find you out." What do you know to be right to do? Do it! Do it 'till the stars fall!

October 1, 1876

Pride Always Ends Revival

"Likewise, ye younger, submit yourselves unto the elder. Yea, all of you be subject one to another, and be clothed with humility: for God resisteth the proud, and giveth grace to the humble. Humble yourselves therefore under the mighty hand of God, that he may exalt you in due time:"—**1 Peter 5:5–6**

D. L. Moody had a great burden to reach his hometown with the Gospel. God had placed him in this thriving metropolis for a reason, and Moody was passionate to reach the individual soul and the masses in Chicago. His crusade began in October of 1876 in a 10,000-seat auditorium and lasted for sixteen weeks. The revival crusade produced anywhere between 2,500 and 10,000 converts. Before we are critical of the wide range of statistics, we must remember that Moody had a policy to never keep specific records of his decisions. Thus, many of his numbers may vary in his ministry. No matter what the numbers were, however, God was using this humble former shoe cobbler for His glory.

There is nothing wrong or sinful about keeping numbers of attendance or salvations, but we must be careful not to boast or take personal pride in numbers. God does not bless a boastful heart, and He resists the proud. The moment we are proud and brag about our accomplishments, the blessing of God is quickly taken away. "Pride goeth before destruction, and an haughty spirit before a fall" (Proverbs 16:18). None of us would pray for God's resistance on our lives or ministry. How foolish it would be for a preacher to pray, "God resist me as I preach this sermon today," or for a soul winner to pray before knocking on a door, "Lord, resist me as I witness to this soul today."

The truth is, however, that no matter how much we pray for God's power and blessing, if we are walking in pride, we are an abomination to the Lord (Proverbs 16:5). As God blesses you today, be sure to humbly thank Him and give Him all the glory.

October 5, 1833

Praying for Revival

"Ye also helping together by prayer for us, that for the gift bestowed upon us by the means of many persons thanks may be given by many on our behalf."
—**2 Corinthians 1:11**

Do your prayers influence others? The Apostle Paul was grateful for the faithful prayers of the believers in the church at Corinth. Because of their simple prayers, the Apostle Paul was able to minister to others and have a faithful testimony to the world. Paul knew that his fruit in ministry was largely due to the prayers of God's people on his behalf.

Charles Finney preached his installation service after he accepted the pastorate in a church in New York City in early October of 1833. Daniel Nash had died only a few years before, and now the great evangelist would settle down at the Chatham Street Chapel. It is interesting to note that Finney gave up evangelism only a couple months after his greatest prayer warrior had passed away. Finney would continue to preach for revival in his church and would train the next generation of preachers in his Oberlin College, but Daniel Nash's prayers would be greatly missed for the rest of his ministry.

Would your prayers be missed? What would change in your pastor's ministry if you stopped praying? Would your church and its members suffer if you didn't pray? The truth is, we may never know those answers, because we've never *started* praying!

What if Christians started to pray as we ought? Would there be a revival? Would missionaries be more effective? Would lost loved ones, neighbors, friends, and co-workers come to Christ if we prayed for them? Would relationships be restored, finances provided, and health come back to those who are ill? Prayer is a powerful tool in the hands of a humble child of God. "Let us therefore come boldly unto the throne of grace, that we may obtain mercy, and find grace to help in time of need" (Hebrews 4:16).

October 4, 1890

Choosing Christ over the World

"By faith Moses, when he was come to years, refused to be called the son of Pharaoh's daughter; Choosing rather to suffer affliction with the people of God, than to enjoy the pleasures of sin for a season; Esteeming the reproach of Christ greater riches than the treasures in Egypt: for he had respect unto the recompence of the reward."—**Hebrews 11:24–26**

Moses, through a series of circumstances uniquely designed by God, ended up in Pharaoh's house under the influence of the powerful leaders in Egypt. He was educated and equipped to go to the top and thus enjoy the finest that the world had to offer. But if he remained there, he would miss the will of God The choice to follow God would not always be easy as it would involve leading people who often didn't want to be led and would gripe and complain constantly. But the eternal rewards of that choice would far outweigh anything Egypt had to offer.

Billy Sunday's last Major League Baseball appearance was with the Philadelphia Phillies on October 4, 1890. Before the next season, he would turn down his contract to serve the Lord full time. God had extended a higher call and he accepted. So much more important than swinging a bat or throwing a ball around a field, no matter what it paid, were the souls of men and glorifying His Saviour. In a day when the sport of baseball was beginning to boom, Sunday decided that he would spend his life living for eternity instead of this present world.

The choices Satan throws our way may be much more subtle than those of Moses or Billy Sunday. We may not be choosing today between the world's riches and God's will or between a professional sports career and preaching the Gospel. The devil might, however, tempt us to overindulge on a hobby instead of spending time with our families. He might interest us in a lavish vacation instead of giving more money to missions. He could lure us away from a good church because of a slight job promotion. Be careful! Every decision leads to a direction, and every direction has a destination. A slight deviation today can have a devastating impact on the future.

October 23, 1740

Tomorrow May Be Too Late

"Boast not thyself of to morrow; for thou knowest not what a day may bring forth."—**Proverbs 27:1**

Nathan Cole, a farmer from Wethersfield, Connecticut, vividly described the Great Awakening and George Whitefield's preaching: "[One morning] all on a sudden, about 8 or 9 o'clock there came a messenger and said Mr. Whitefield preached at Hartford and Weathersfield yesterday and is to preach at Middletown this morning (October 23, 1740) at ten of the clock. I was in my field at work. I dropped my tool that I had in my hand and ran home and bade my wife to get ready quickly. I then ran to the pasture for my horse with all my might fearing that I should be too late to hear him. We had but an hour, but rode as fast as we could the twelve miles to the meeting house. When we came within about half a mile of the road on which the meeting house stood, I saw before me a cloud or fog rising....[which] turned out to be a cloud of dust from the horses racing as it were....every horse seemed to go with all his might to carry his rider to hear news from heaven for the saving of souls. It made me tremble to see the sight. When we got to the old meeting house there was a great multitude; it was said to be three or four thousand assembled together....I saw no man at work in his field, but all seemed to be gone. When I saw Mr. Whitefield come upon the scaffold he looked almost angelical, a young, slim, slender youth before the people with a bold undaunted countenance, and it sobered my mind, and put me into a trembling fear before he began to preach; for he looked as if he was clothed with authority from the Great God, and a sweet solemnity sat upon his brow. And my hearing him preach gave me a heart wound; by God's blessing my old foundation was broken up, and I saw that my righteousness would not save me..."

Oh that we would see an awakening of hearts again in this country for a Word from God! When work, recreation, leisure, and self-interest would be dropped like the tool in the hand of Nathan Cole, an urgency for our soul's need would be sensed and then acted upon.

October 24, 1867

God Hears Our Praise

"Ye that fear the LORD, praise him; all ye the seed of Jacob, glorify him; and fear him, all ye the seed of Israel. For he hath not despised nor abhorred the affliction of the afflicted; neither hath he hid his face from him; but when he cried unto him, he heard."—**Psalm 22:23–24**

Charles Alexander was born in East Tennessee on this day in 1867. He would grow up listening to his mother read the sermons of D. L. Moody each night around the fireplace, and at the age of thirteen, he trusted Christ as Saviour at a revival meeting. He would later hold thousands of revival meetings in his ministry as the music man for two great evangelists, R. A. Torrey and J. Wilbur Chapman. He would travel the world with each of them, becoming one of the only evangelists of his time who circled the globe twice with the Gospel. Charles Alexander's passion was singing and writing music that exalted Christ. His wife would later describe his singing: "No one who ever heard Charles Alexander sing needed to be told that he, like the birds, sang because there was within him a holy impulse which he could not resist. It was not his profession to sing; it was his life."

Alexander was once asked, "What feature of the musical side of the revival gives you the keenest delight?" As much as he loved music in itself and the joy of producing it, he replied, "I should soon tire of this side of the work if it were not for the soul-saving part of it." Alexander's life purpose was to glorify God through the gift of music by bringing souls to the Lord.

God hears our conversations, He hears our prayers, and He hears when we sing. The psalmist exclaims, "Nevertheless, he regarded their affliction, when he heard their cry:" (Psalm 106:44). When the sinner cries to God, He hears. When the afflicted cry to God, He hears. When those who fear God's name call to Him, He hears. What greater reason is there to praise the Lord? Let Him hear from you today! Of course, He can read your mind—but He loves to hear you sing! The music you sing to Him may be just the thing that draws someone else to the Saviour!

October 445 BC

Trendy or Traditional

"And Ezra the priest brought the law before the congregation both of men and women, and all that could hear with understanding, upon the first day of the seventh month."—**Nehemiah 8:2**

Christians and churches get swept into all kinds of trendy ideas and methods today. Not all new ideas are bad for sure, but when they replace Scriptural tradition, that trend can be tragic. For example, church services have gone through quite an overhaul in recent years. Technology is a big part of that, but trends that replace preaching time with entertainment and fellowship is dangerous. Even preaching in many churches has changed from the traditional sermon from the Bible to a talk about life with almost no reference to Scripture. Some argue, "That is what people want." No doubt! But what does God want, and what did He establish as a tradition when people gather for worship?

The Temple had been rebuilt in this month in 445 BC after much encouragement from the prophets Haggai and Zechariah, and the walls had been reconstructed under the leadership of Nehemiah. Now, to rededicate the holy city to the Lord, Nehemiah organized a great dedication ceremony for the people of Jerusalem. Ezra the scribe would read the Word of God (The Old Testament Law from start to finish) while the people stood and listened. This took the entire morning according to Nehemiah 8:3 and the people were "...attentive unto the book of the law."

The reading was not dry or uninteresting. In verse 8 it says, "So they read in the book of the law of God distinctly, and gave the sense, and caused them to understand the reading." All of this was done from "upon a pulpit of wood, which they had made for the purpose" (verse 4). When they finished, the people responded, "And all the people answered, Amen, Amen, with lifting up their hands: and they bowed their heads, and worshipped the Lord with their faces upon the ground..." (verse 6). They responded in agreement and bowed humbly in worship and decision. Revival depends on that kind of biblical tradition!

October 26, 1928

Do You Have Answers?

"But sanctify the Lord God in your hearts: and be ready always to give an answer to every man that asketh you a reason of the hope that is in you with meekness and fear: Having a good conscience; that, whereas they speak evil of you, as of evildoers, they may be ashamed that falsely accuse your good conversation in Christ."—**1 Peter 3:15–16**

If someone today asks you to prove to them that there is a literal Heaven or a literal Hell, could you do it? Which is right: evolution or creation? Can you prove your answer to be true? How do we know that the Bible is accurate? Was Jesus God? Why does God allow wars to take place or children to die of starvation? What is the purpose of earthquakes or fires or tornados? Does prayer really work? Do all religious beliefs lead to Heaven? God instructs us to be prepared to answer these kinds of questions. Sadly, many Christians do not spend enough time in God's Word to discover those answers to give to those who need them.

Evangelist R. A. Torrey died in Asheville, North Carolina, at the age of seventy-two on this day in 1928. He had circled the globe preaching the Gospel. He led the Moody Church and Moody Bible Institute for decades and had used the mind God gave him to put many things in print defending the Bible against its critics and providing answers to those seeking them. "*The Fundamentals*," included ninety classic essays defending the fundamental doctrines of the faith. Robert Harkness, Torrey's pianist for many years, wrote that "he was skilled in the art of meeting the difficulties of the unbeliever. He was powerful in answering the hackneyed arguments of the infidel."

Torrey had followed 1 Peter 3:15 and lived his life to respond to the attacks against God and the Bible in his day. Today, the truth of God's Word is under attack as never before. Are you prepared to defend that truth? "Study to shew thyself approved unto God, a workman that needeth not to be ashamed, rightly dividing the word of truth" (2 Timothy 2:15).

October 27, 1935

How Will You Die?

"And brought them out, and said, Sirs, what must I do to be saved? And they said, Believe on the Lord Jesus Christ, and thou shalt be saved, and thy house."
—Acts 16:30–31

Paul and Silas were arrested for casting a demon out of a girl at Philippi. This miracle upset those who were making a profit off of this girl, and Paul and Silas were beaten and thrown into prison. These faithful preachers could have become bitter or angry at God. They could have decided it wasn't worth serving the Lord any longer. But instead, with their backs bleeding and their feet in stocks, they took a deep breath and sang praises to the God whom they loved. The prison echoed with the hymns from their lips. For all they knew this could be their last night on earth, but they were determined to make even their last breath count for Jesus Christ.

Billy Sunday wasn't feeling well. Earlier in the year, he had suffered a heart attack, and doctors tried to persuade him to slow down. Despite the warnings, Sunday wanted to keep his commitment to preach at the First Methodist Church in Mishawaka, Indiana, on October 27, 1935. He knew he was rounding the final turn and headed for the home stretch of life. As it turned out, this night would indeed be his last time to preach. I suppose Sunday could have preached on some deep theological passage to show off his understanding and knowledge of Scripture. He could have dazzled the audience with stories from his celebrated baseball career, his miraculous conversion to Christ, or his amazing evangelistic crusades. Instead, when this seventy-three-year-old evangelist took the pulpit for what would be the last time, the title of his message was: "What Must I Do to Be Saved?" At the invitation, forty-four precious souls found Christ as Saviour! Ten days later, the former Major League baseball player would slide safely into "home plate," his race here on earth completed.

Billy Sunday died the same way he had lived—telling people about Christ. How do you want to die? It's best we start "living" that way today!

October 27, 1771

How Will You Invest Your Life?

"Lay not up for yourselves treasures upon earth, where moth and rust doth corrupt, and where thieves break through and steal: But lay up for yourselves treasures in heaven, where neither moth nor rust doth corrupt, and where thieves do not break through nor steal: For where your treasure is, there will your heart be also."
—**Matthew 6:19–21**

Francis Asbury was appointed as John Wesley's general assistant in America and arrived in the colonies ready to begin his ministry in the New World. As he sailed across the Atlantic, he wrote in his journal: "I will set down a few things that lie on my mind. Whither am I going? To the new world. What to do? To gain honor? No, not if I know my own heart. To get money? No; I am going to live to God, and to bring others so to do." When Asbury set foot on Colonial soil, there were 80 Methodist preachers in the colonies, with roughly 14,000 people in their congregations. By the time Asbury died, there were about 200,000 members, 2,000 local pastors, and 500 itinerant preachers who called themselves Methodist. Historians have estimated that around five million people lived in America at this time, and the Methodists had reached at least two million of them.

Asbury's desire was simply "to live for God and to bring others so to do." He was not concerned with the accolades or wealth of this world; God's plan was his priority. He was laying up treasures in Heaven, where his investment would last for eternity. Life cries out to us to live for the temporary—a new car or house; a dream vacation; a fool proof investment for our retirement days. Are we laying up any treasure in Heaven? Someone has wisely said, "If you want your life to count, live it for something that outlasts it." What will outlast your time here on earth? The only things we can take with us when we leave this world are the souls of men. Does anything on your to-do list today have anything to do with that?

In the temporary, everything temporary looks really important. But in eternity, nothing in the temporary will be important at all. Let's invest in the eternal today!

October, 1874

Lift Up the Cross

"But God forbid that I should glory, save in the cross of our Lord Jesus Christ, by whom the world is crucified unto me, and I unto the world."—**Galatians 6:14**

Prayer meetings had been held for months in Dublin, Ireland, before the arrival of D. L. Moody and his evangelistic team. The crusade began in late October of 1874 at the Exhibition Palace, the largest meeting hall in the city. The London *Christian* reported: "The inhabitants of Dublin are becoming alive to the fact that we are now in the enjoyment of a great time of refreshing, and that our gracious God is working powerfully among us by the instrumentality of these, His honored servants. Such a sight has never been witnessed here as may now be seen every day—thousands flocking to the prayer meeting and to the Bible reading, and, most of all, to the evening services in the great Exhibition Palace. It fills the heart of a child of God with deepest emotion to stand upon the platform from which Mr. Moody preaches, and to cast one's eye over the vast concourse of people hanging on the speaker's lips as in burning words he discourses of life and death, and 'Jesus and His love.' One cannot but ask the question, 'What is the magic power which draws together these mighty multitudes and holds them spellbound?' Is it the worldly rank or wealth of learning or oratory of the preacher? No, for he is possessed of little of these. It is the simple lifting up of the cross of Christ—the holding forth the Lord Jesus before the eyes of the people."

The world, and even some churches have proven that you can draw a large crowd with various forms of entertainment. Many enjoy being amused or amazed, but few want to be spiritually awakened and altered. The average person will tolerate religion of some kind, but wants little to do with revival. Is anything powerful enough to cut through this coldness and deadness? Must we wait for a gifted speaker to arrive? Is there some new technology we lack? First Corinthians 1:18 informs us of the only power that can radically change lives: "For the preaching of the cross is to them that perish foolishness; but unto us which are saved it is the power of God."

October 30, 1883

Character Is What Stands Out to God

"But the LORD said unto Samuel, Look not on his countenance, or on the height of his stature; because I have refused him: for the LORD seeth not as man seeth; for man looketh on the outward appearance, but the LORD looketh on the heart."
—1 Samuel 16:7

Bob Jones Sr. was born October 30, 1883, in Dale County, Alabama, to William and Georgia Jones. Bob would help out on the farm at a young age, and often go door-to-door selling the goods from the Jones farm. Bob Jones would later recall, "We may have been a little undernourished, but we built some character." Bob Jones would exhibit a God-given ability to preach and communicate with people, but at the very beginning of Bob's life, he was first taught character. Jones knew that without character, he would be of no use to His Saviour. He would later teach his students: "Your character is what God knows you to be; your reputation is what men think you are; and the test of your character is what it takes to stop you."

The prophet Samuel was sent by God to the house of Jesse to anoint a new king over Israel. When Samuel arrived, it was obvious to him who that next king would be. Eliab was tall, handsome, and impressive to look upon. He had "leader" written all over the outside. God, however, looks past the outside and straight to the heart. God cannot use all of the personality and talent if He doesn't have control of a man's heart. What is on the inside of a man or woman is far more important to God than what is noticed on the outside. "I the Lord search the heart, I try the reins, even to give every man according to his ways, and according to the fruit of his doings" (Jeremiah 17:10).

When God looks in our hearts, what does He see? An oak tree can look healthy and stand tall in the forest, but if hollow on the inside, it will come crashing down in the next storm. We may pass the "eye test" of our friends and family members, but we must remember that God's eye looks past the outward and directly to the heart of a man. God can take one man with character and do the impossible!

October 31, 1875

Surprising the Skeptics

"But the natural man receiveth not the things of the Spirit of God: for they are foolishness unto him: neither can he know them, because they are spiritually discerned."—**1 Corinthians 2:14**

As Christians, we find it difficult to understand why people are not excited about spiritual things as we are. Often those we invite to church have no desire to come no matter how great we try to make it sound. Some would even call us crazy for spending our time and even our money on the things of God. The world, however, is blinded to spiritual truth.

Brooklyn, New York, became the site of D. L. Moody's first citywide evangelistic campaign in America. The meetings began on this date in 1875. William Moody, in his biography about his father, wrote of this first meeting: "From the first the work was attended with greatest encouragement. Large throngs attended the meetings and the music which had proved so great a factor in London was no less effective in Brooklyn. The *New York Herald* descried the opening scene as one 'never before witnessed in any city on this continent.' And editorial expressed surprise at 'the lack of novelty or genius,' and wonderment at the crowds. Nevertheless it continues to accord space to reports of the services. As the meetings proceed, the paper states, 'The more we see of Messengers Moody and Sankey, the more are we puzzled on account of their success.'"

The newspapers could not understand or reconcile the success of these preachers. They could not fathom how some twenty thousand people were turned away from the five thousand seat auditorium because there was simply no room for them. There was nothing profound about the man D. L. Moody or his song leader, Ira Sankey. There was nothing "genius" about their methods. Moody's success was based on a promise as old as time itself: the Word of God is powerful. From the first day of creation, God's Word spoke into existence the heavens and the earth, and to this day, the Word of God will bring amazing change everywhere it is proclaimed.

NOVEMBER

November 1, 1961

Christ Versus Antichrist

"And this is love, that we walk after his commandments. This is the commandment, That, as ye have heard from the beginning, ye should walk in it. For many deceivers are entered into the world, who confess not that Jesus Christ is come in the flesh. This is a deceiver and an antichrist."—**2 John 6–7**

The battles we face in the Christian life are varied and it seems there is no limit to the size and scope of the obstacles that a child of God will face. Financial pressure, physical illnesses, relational conflicts, and personal temptations are real and attack us regularly. While the battles are many, they are all part of a great war between Christ and the Antichrist.

Mordecai Ham died in Louisville, Kentucky, at the age of eighty-four on November 1, 1961. From 1901 to 1941, Ham conducted 289 revival meetings in twenty-two states, which produced 303,387 professions of faith. Over 7,000 people surrendered to full-time Christian service under his preaching. Edward E. Ham would summarize Mordecai Ham's ministry in his biography of his uncle: "God raised up Evangelist Ham to do more than hold meetings in the great cities of the South. He ordained him a prophet to do more than lead great campaigns against liquor during the pre-prohibition days. God raised him up to remind Christian America of the main spiritual issue that has been in existence since man's beginning on this earth: Christ versus the Antichrist."

In his second epistle, John warns his readers of "many deceivers" who had already come and denied the basic truths of Christianity. When people deny that Jesus Christ is the Son of God and deceive others about who Christ is, they are preparing the way for the Antichrist. These are false teachers, and God clearly commands us to stand against them. The spirit of an antichrist surrounds us today as we draw closer to the end of the age. The only thing that can cut through the powerful deception of Satan is the Word of God. "Is not my word like as fire? saith the Lord; and like a hammer that breaketh the rock in pieces" (Jeremiah 23:29). Speak the truth in love today and let God break with His hammer the spirit of antichrist.

November 2, 1828

The World Needs Jesus

"The same came therefore to Philip, which was of Bethsaida of Galilee, and desired him, saying, Sir, we would see Jesus."—**John 12:21**

The great preacher A. B. Earle responded to the Gospel and was saved at the age of eighteen on this day in 1828. He would later travel 325,000 miles, preach 19,780 sermons, and see 150,000 people saved. Earle was known for simply lifting up Christ. He always kept his eyes on his Saviour and kept the memory of the cross fresh in his mind.

A Christian newspaper in England would later describe his preaching ministry: "His preaching was not eloquent. His delivery was not beyond the average. His voice had no special power. His large angular frame and passionless mouth were decidedly against him. His sermons seemed sometimes as though composed thirty years ago, before we so often heard, as now, the clear and ringing utterances of free grace, and the name of Jesus in almost every sentence. He expressed his own emotions very simply, and did not often refer to them. His rhetoric was often at fault, and sometimes even his grammar. Truly the enticing words of man's wisdom were wanting in his case.

"The first time I heard him I came away in wonder as to wherein his unusual Gospel power lay; but as I listened to him again and again, I could not help realizing how the congregation, and my own soul with them, were held by the power of God. When he preached on the value of a human soul, I do not remember a single thought or illustration that was new to me; and yet I came away overwhelmed in this realization of the infinite preciousness of each child of Adam, and found myself as I awoke the next morning, weeping in sorrow and anxiety for lost sinners."

Will people see Jesus in our lives today? Will they hear us speak His name? When they do, will they know He is more than just a name to us? Let's make sure the world sees less of us and more of Jesus today!

November, 1893

God Takes Care of Every Need

"I have been young, and now am old; yet have I not seen the righteous forsaken, nor his seed begging bread."—**Psalm 37:25**

D. L. Moody concluded his once-in-a-lifetime opportunity at the Chicago World's Fair in early November of 1893. In an interview after the six-month campaign, Moody stated: "The principal result of our six months' work is that millions have heard the simple Gospel preached by some of the most gifted preachers in the world; thousands have been genuinely converted to Christ, and Christians all over this land have been brought to a deeper spiritual life and aroused to more active Christian effort for the salvation of others…I have learned to appreciate more than ever the power that there is in concentrated and united Christian action."

The reporter then asked him about the finances needed for such a venture. Moody reported that $60,000 had been raised to cover the cost of this great effort for revival and evangelism. When asked if he knew where those monies would come from before the meetings began, he replied: "I only knew the work ought to be done, and that we have a God who will always sustain us in doing what we ought to do." Moody claimed the truth that God always supplies where He leads, and He praised God for His wonderful provision.

Will you trust God for your needs today? God is more than able to pay for whatever He orders. He owns the cattle on a thousand hills (Psalm 50:10)—and He owns the hills as well! "The earth is the LORD's, and the fulness thereof; the world, and they that dwell therein" (Psalm 24:1).

Our needs are not bigger than God's resources. "But my God shall supply all your need according to his riches in glory by Christ Jesus" (Philippians 4:19). He doesn't promise to meet all your *greed* but definitely all your n*eed*. When we do God's will in God's way, we can trust Him to meet every need.

November 4, 1883

Revival Again and Again

"Wilt thou not revive us again: that thy people may rejoice in thee?"
—Psalm 85:6

Moody knew that the work of God was never over. Some had questioned the need for another revival crusade in London after the last one was so successful. But D. L. Moody knew that revival needs to happen again and again. Even the word *revival* itself with the prefix "re" speaks of the need for revival constantly in our lives. None of us in this life will reach a state of perfection and thus are constantly in need of an awakening from God.

After two new auditoriums were erected prior to his coming, Moody began his second London Crusade on November 4, 1883. In his opening remarks on the first evening, he said, "I have come to London with high hopes and great expectations. I have about one hundred times more faith than I had when I came here eight years ago. Some people have said that the former work in London hasn't lasted. I want to say that since then I have been preaching all through America—from Maine to the Pacific slope—and that wherever I have gone I have found the fruit of that London work; it is scattered all over the earth."

History proves that there was much work yet to be done in London during this second meeting. Over two million would hear the Gospel preached. Wilfred Grenfell, the future medical missionary to Newfoundland and Labrador, was saved. C. T. Studd's father would also be reached with the Gospel during these meetings, and C. T. would forsake his well-followed cricket career to become a great missionary to the people of China, India, and Africa. Thank God, Moody was not content with one moving of God in London! May we never be satisfied with what God has done in the past, but pray and work that God may "do it again" for His glory!

November 6, 1889

Biblical Repentance

"...Repent, and turn yourselves from all your transgressions; so iniquity shall not be your ruin."—**Ezekiel 18:30**

No lasting revival can take place unless there is legitimate repentance. For a true change to occur there must be a change of mind which leads to a change of direction. If you were driving east on a highway and decided you were going the wrong way and needed to be going west, you would make a decision to turn around which would require making a U-turn and heading the opposite direction. Too many people today want to add a "Jesus decision" of some kind in their lives but continue cruising through life in the same direction.

Dr. Edward Beecher wrote of Charles Finney in 1889: "I was pastor of Park Street Church when he [Finney] was first invited to preach in Boston, and I invited him to preach for me. He complied with my request, and preached to a crowded house the most impressive and powerful sermon I ever heard...No one can form any conception of the power of his appeal. It rings in my ears even to this day. As I was preaching myself, I did not hear him again. But I met good results in all who heard him, and have ever honored and loved him, as one truly commissioned by God." Finney's passionate plea for sinners to come to repentance rung clear through the nation. His burden for souls and his passion of revival was blessed by God in a unique way. He boldly preached to the saved and the unsaved to repent and turn to God.

Does God want you to turn from something today? "He that covereth his sins shall not prosper: but whoso confesseth and forsaketh them shall have mercy" (Proverbs 28:13). When God convicts of sin, we must deal with that sin scripturally. That requires confessing it but also forsaking it. Have you turned your back on sin? Have you turned away from the world and all it offers and set your eyes on following Christ. How can we expect revival if we are walking away from God? Turn around today in true repentance of sin.

November 6, 1904

Sparks of Revival

"The sacrifice of the wicked is an abomination to the LORD: but the prayer of the upright is his delight."—**Proverbs 15:8**

Beginning on October 31, nightly prayer meetings were held in the Moriah Chapel by Evan Roberts. Every night, the power and presence of God intensified on the congregation, and many people were saved. On November 6, Evan Roberts told the crowd at the meeting to pray the same prayer together: "O send the Holy Spirit now for Jesus Christ's sake." As that assembly prayed deep into the night, God began to work in an amazing way.

The beginning of the Welsh Revival is difficult to pinpoint, but this prayer meeting at the beginning of November is one of the many sparks that would contribute. Those meetings in the Moriah Chapel would later be described by one in attendance: "The revival meetings were extraordinary; some people would be crying for joy; others crying for sorrow over their sin. Several people would be praying at the same time; for their friends, parents or children. Some would be singing; others telling people about the joy they now experienced. The chapels were filled to capacity and there were crowds of people on the roads outside. Yet there was no disorder in the meetings. They lasted until two, three, or four o'clock in the morning.... The Revival spread like wildfire from place to place all over the country where people had been praying that such a thing would happen."

To see God work in amazing ways, the beginning is always bathed in prayer. But we must be sure that our prayers are not hindered by our sin. God delights in the prayer of His child who is right with Him. When our relationship with the Lord is not right, however, our prayer becomes an abomination. It does not matter what we do or how we pray, God will not bless a person who is living in sin against His commands. Only when we are completely right with God, will our prayers become a delight to our Heavenly Father. Is there anything in your life hindering your prayers today? Inspect before you intercede, and whatever God shows you, eliminate so that your prayers will be His delight.

November 7, 1935

Absent from the Body

"We are confident, I say, and willing rather to be absent from the body, and to be present with the Lord."—**2 Corinthians 5:8**

The last sermon Billy Sunday preached was entitled, "What Must I Do to Be Saved?" One week later, November 7, 1935, the *New York Times* announced his death with the heading: "Billy Sunday Dies; Evangelist Was 71; Former Ball Player Induced Thousands to 'Hit Sawdust Trail' to Conversion." Sunday had been in poor health since February of 1933 but had continued to preach. On November 6, 1935, in the home of his brother in law, he complained of chest pains. A doctor was called and an ice pack was placed on his chest. With the pain reduced he rested until supper that evening when he told his wife Nell, who sat by his bedside answering letters, that he felt dizzy. Billy Sunday rounded third base for the last time that night and arrived "safe" at home in the presence of the Lord.

The world lost a great preacher that day and many lost a dear friend. But in reality he was not lost, for the Bible assures the child of God that the moment we leave this world through death we are immediately in the presence of Jesus Christ in Heaven. Sunday had heard the roar of a crowd in a baseball stadium more than once and he had preached to huge crowds of people throughout his revival ministry, but the throng in Heaven of those who had gone before him was a sight never seen by Billy Sunday on this earth. But no doubt as the host of angels and saints rejoiced at his arrival, the old revival preacher could only focus on One. The One he had loved and served since the day of his conversion. The One he had faithfully preached to the world. The One who would greet him at home plate and say, "Well done, thou good and faithful servant."

Do you know the Lord Jesus Christ as your Saviour? If not, you can today. "But as many as received him, to them gave he power to become the sons of God, even to them that believe on his name" (John 1:12). If you are a child of God, are you living for Christ today? One day the game will end and the final score will be posted. What will be the result of your life?

Fall 1912

The Power of God

"Jesus answered and said unto them, Ye do err, not knowing the scriptures, nor the power of God."—**Matthew 22:29**

The Pharisees and the Sadducees wanted to trap Jesus with their sly questions to turn the people against Him. As the Sadducees asked Jesus about the resurrection of the dead, Jesus rebuked them for their lack of knowledge. They did not know the Scriptures and the truth that Jesus was teaching, but they had missed something else as well. They had no knowledge of the power of God

The *Evening Times* of McKeesport, Pennsylvania, published the following announcement after the conclusion of a Billy Sunday crusade in their town: "From this date forward the Evening Times will not accept the advertisement of any distillery, brewer, or wholesale or retail liquor dealer. This rule is made a part of the policy of the advertising department of this newspaper…It is the desire of the management of this newspaper that it shall be a force for the betterment of its city and district, and no effort will be spared to make and keep its columns so clean that it may read every day with entire safety and real benefit by persons of all ages and both sexes."

God's power can change a city. Satan tries to make himself look more powerful than God, but the biblical record and the historical record both prove otherwise. God's power is limitless and universal. It knows no boundaries and no barrier can restrict or restrain it.

Are you experiencing that power in your life today? As you read God's Word today ask the Holy Spirit to reveal those areas of your life that quench God's power. Confess those areas as sin and then as a clean vessel ask the Lord to fill you with His Holy Spirit's power. The power of God can still make a difference in a life, in a city, in our world!

November 20, 1881

Dwelling Together in Unity

"Behold, how good and how pleasant it is for brethren to dwell together in unity!"—**Psalm 133:1**

D. L. Moody and C. H. Spurgeon had their differences. One was of British descent and the other American. One was a pastor, and the other an evangelist. One was an eloquent speaker, and the other struggled to pronounce long words. But the two men became good friends and enjoyed serving the Lord together. They both held the same doctrine from God's Word, and they loved the Lord.

These two great preachers had met in 1867 as Moody visited London with his wife Emma to seek medical treatment for her. Spurgeon invited Moody to preach at his church, and Moody responded with the following letter: "Dear Mr. Spurgeon...I am thankful for your very kind note. It quite touched my heart. I have for years thought more of you than of any other man preaching the Gospel on this earth; and, to tell you the truth, I shrink from standing in your place. I do not know of a church in all the land that I shrink from as I do from yours;—not but what your people are in sympathy with the Gospel that I try to preach, but you can do it so much better than I can. I thank you for inviting me, and I will be with your good people November 20...Remember me to your good wife, and accept of my thanks for your letter of cheer. Yours truly, D. L. Moody."

God admonishes us to dwell in unity with godly friends who love the Lord. "Iron sharpeneth iron; so a man sharpeneth the countenance of his friend." (Proverbs 27:17) What friends has God placed in your life to challenge and sharpen you? "A man that hath friends must shew himself friendly: and there is a friend that sticketh closer than a brother." (Proverbs 18:24) Are there friends in your life whom you can encourage in spiritual things today?

November 10, 1822

Trials Can Make Us Bitter or Better

"Looking diligently lest any man fail of the grace of God; lest any root of bitterness springing up trouble you, and thereby many be defiled."—**Hebrews 12:15**

Daniel Nash was voted out of his church as pastor. He had nowhere to go and so continued ministering as best he knew how in the place where God had put him. The population of that little town was only two thousand, but during that interim period in his life, Daniel Nash was able to see two hundred of them accept Christ as Saviour. He longed, however, to be in the ministry once again and began to succumb to defeat and bitterness in the next two years. At an ordination service, God brought Charles Finney and Daniel Nash together, and that partnership of preaching and prayer would shake the United States. As Finney would conduct revival campaigns, Nash would lock himself in a room and pray for God's power to fall upon the city. Turning his back on the bitter disappointment of the past, Nash set his mind and heart on God's better plan for his life.

Oftentimes events happen in our lives that we do not understand. Hurtful and wrong decisions can leave their lasting scars upon us. But we must never become bitter against God's plan. The seeds of bitterness are always sown after a difficult season in life, but we must never let them take root. If the root of bitterness is hidden in our hearts, it will soon raise its ugly head and ruin our lives. Like any root it is best to deal with it earlier rather than later. Has a root of bitterness begun to grow in your life? Is it choking out the good seed of God's Word? Do you recognize that your growth spiritually is stunted as a result and the fruit of the Spirit is rarely evident?

God did not intend the trials of your life to ruin you, but rather revive you. He designed them to bring you closer to Him rather than drive you away. Give the hurt in your life to the Lord. Ask Him to remove the bitterness from your life and make you better. When you do, the joy and peace will flood your heart once again and God will use you as an instrument of revival.

November 12, 1906

True or False

"Now I beseech you, brethren, mark them which cause divisions and offences contrary to the doctrine which ye have learned; and avoid them. For they that are such serve not our Lord Jesus Christ, but their own belly; and by good words and fair speeches deceive the hearts of the simple."—**Romans 16:17–18**

After many difficult days, Evangelist Mordecai Ham started a revival crusade in Houston, Texas, in a downtown skating rink on November 12, 1906. His meetings started small, but eventually the power of God swept the city. Soon the crowds swelled to over four thousand, and five hundred trusted in Christ. After much success, a group of charismatics began to disrupt the meeting by speaking in "tongues," and the revival meeting ended. Think what could have happened had Satan not won a victory. In fact, Ham would return to Houston thirty years later and see over seven thousand come to Christ!

Satan has many means of distracting us from revival. He will try anything within his power to keep souls from being saved and lives from being revived. Sometimes he will use discord among the brethren, other times confusion about doctrine. He does not really care what method, as long as it is successful in carrying out his wicked agenda. God commands us to worship him "decently and in order" (1 Corinthians 14:40), and He desires for us to stand for the truth of His Word. Be careful of the false doctrines of men that are propagated by those who use "good words and fair speeches." These false teachers teach a Gospel that does not include the doctrine of sin and lifts up a person's mystical experiences instead of the Word of God. They will always lead you down the path of confusion and deception. God commands us to mark them and avoid them.

The key is to saturate yourself in God's Word. "Order my steps in thy word: and let not any iniquity have dominion over me" (Psalm 119:133). "Seek ye out of the book of the Lord, and read: no one of these shall fail" (Isaiah 34:16a). "Heaven and earth shall pass away: but my words shall not pass away" (Mark 13:31).

November 12, 1873

Drawing Near to God

"Let us draw near with a true heart in full assurance of faith, having our hearts sprinkled from an evil conscience, and our bodies washed with pure water."
—**Hebrews 10:22**

The British people did not know quite what to think about D. L. Moody—this American evangelist from "across the pond." William Moody described the skepticism of the English people to his father's evangelistic campaign in Great Britain: "When an all-day meeting was announced to be held at Newcastle on November 12th, many anticipated failure, but those who had felt the reviving power and the love of God and had made this meeting a matter of earnest prayer knew that it could not fail. Not only did the people from Newcastle attend in large numbers, but visitors from Sunderland, Shields, Jarrow, and neighboring towns came in by train and filled the church and galleries. Business, home cares and work, pleasure and idleness had been left behind by the hundreds of earnest Christians who came to worship God and to hear His Word."

A six-hour meeting staggers the mind of most modern Christians. We think if we give God an hour on Sunday it is plenty and then the preacher better not go past noon! For those who truly want revival, however, we must draw nigh to God before we can expect Him to draw nigh to us. James 4:8 admonishes and promises, "Draw nigh to God, and he will draw nigh to you...." Too often, even in church, our minds are on something other than God and His Word. We are cumbered and burdened with the cares of this world, and the seed of God's Word falls on hard ground and is easily plucked away by Satan.

What will you do to prepare the soil of your heart before you attend a service at your church this week? As we enter the house of God may we take a moment to quiet our hearts before God so that He can speak and be heard. And let's not be in a hurry to leave but rather ponder that which we have heard and determine to respond in obedience throughout the days ahead.

November 12, 1873

Our Father's Business

"I must work the works of him that sent me, while it is day; the night cometh, when no man can work."—**John 9:4**

Henry Moorehouse stood and addressed the crowd in Newcastle, England, with his reasons why God used D. L. Moody:

1. He believes firmly that the Gospel saves sinners when they believe, and he rests on the simple story of a crucified and risen Saviour.
2. He expects, when he goes to preach, that souls will be saved, and the result is that God honors his faith.
3. He preaches as if there never was to be another meeting, and as if sinners might never hear the Gospel sound again: these appeals to decide now are most impressive.
4. He gets Christians to work in the after-meetings. He urges them to ask those who are sitting near them if they are saved.

D. L. Moody would seek and seize every opportunity to share the love of Christ with everyone around him. He knew that his opportunity would soon be over, and he wanted to give the Gospel to the whole world.

God blesses the simple, unselfish, sacrificial faith of his servants, whether they lived two hundred years ago or today. Are you living with an urgency to get the Gospel to your friends, family, co-workers, and neighbors? Do we expect God to bless our efforts? Do we pray and live in faith believing that we serve a God who "…is able to do exceeding abundantly above all that we ask or think" (Ephesians 3:20a)? Revival will not come to the fatalist! God is looking for men and women of faith who simply believe His Word and act upon it. In our busyness, let's not forget our Father's business!

November 14, 1909

Go Ye into All the World

"All the ends of the world shall remember and turn unto the LORD: and all the kindreds of the nations shall worship before thee."—**Psalm 22:27**

J. Wilbur Chapman looked behind him as he and his team boarded the *Empress of China* for home. He and Charles Alexander could have never imagined the great success they would see in Australia and Asia. Many of their new friends in Japan had come to the dock to see them off and bid them farewell. Chapman's biographer Ford Ottman tells us what Chapman's mind was focused on during his trip home: "The long Pacific voyage had given Dr. Chapman the rest he so greatly needed. His mind, however, had been busy with a prospective program for the coming year. His plan well defined, strength and courage renewed, he started eastward, eager to tell what God had wrought in Australia and the Orient."

As long as there are lost souls in the world, we must never be satisfied with what God has done in the past. Like Chapman, our minds must constantly look forward to the work yet to be done. Whether it is through prayer, giving, or going ourselves, we cannot rest until all have heard. Apathy and indifference will quickly take over the life of anyone who is distracted from "the fields that are white already to harvest." We must not succumb to the thought that "...There are yet four months, and then cometh harvest..." as the disciples in John 4:35. The devil will go to all lengths to draw our attention away from the task God has commissioned us with: "Go ye therefore, and teach all nations, baptizing them in the name of the Father, and of the Son, and of the Holy Ghost: Teaching them to observe all things whatsoever I have commanded you" (Matthew 28:19–20a).

No doubt your to-do list is filled with many things today that are necessary and needed. As you look at your list, however, is there anything there that has to do with eternity? Will we commit any time today to reaching someone with the Gospel? As C. T. Studd reminds us, "Only one life and it will soon be past; only what's done for Christ will last."

Lamentations 3–5 // Hebrews 10:19–39

November 22, 1755

The Local New Testament Church

"So that ye were ensamples to all that believe in Macedonia and Achaia. For from you sounded out the word of the Lord not only in Macedonia and Achaia, but also in every place your faith to God-ward is spread abroad; so that we need not to speak any thing."—**1 Thessalonians 1:7–8**

Shubal Stearns had moved to the South to plant a church in Liberty, North Carolina. His church charter was signed by sixteen people and the Sandy Creek Baptist Church had begun. No one knew the significance of this one country church being planted. Stearns' church would grow to influence churches all across the region. Sandy Creek Baptist Church would grow to over six hundred people and begin planting many other Baptist churches in the South. In the first seventeen years of the Sandy Creek Baptist Association, forty-two churches would be planted by Shubal Stearns. As Whitefield and Edwards preached in the North during the Great Awakening, Stearns was busy planting churches in the South.

The Apostle Paul commended the church of Thessalonica for being examples to the churches in the nearby areas. Their faith had been "spread abroad" among the region and had encouraged hundreds of people in the Roman Empire.

The impact of one church cannot be described this side of Heaven. God's plan is that churches start other churches, multiplying around the world. Church planters and missionaries are needed and must be supported so that God's plan can come to fruition. Satan is good at luring the church into a status quo of stagnation and satisfaction. We must fight the tendency of luke-warmness and indifference. We must be fully engaged in the soul winning and missionary outreach of our local churches. We must encourage the young people of our congregations to give their lives to ministry. And we must be faithful ourselves to proclaim the Gospel whether it is to those around the corner or around the world.

November 16, 1899

Excuses

"Then said he unto him, A certain man made a great supper, and bade many: And sent his servant at supper time to say to them that were bidden, Come; for all things are now ready."—**Luke 14:16–17**

The sixty-two-year-old Dwight Moody mounted the pulpit to preach his last sermon in Kansas City, Missouri. Entitled "The Great Supper," Moody preached on excuses from Luke 14:16–24. He preached: "Suppose we should write out tonight this excuse? How would it sound? 'To the King of Heaven: While sitting in Convention Hall, Kansas City, Missouri, November 16, 1899, I received a very pressing invitation from one of your servants to be present at the marriage supper of Your only-begotten Son. I pray Thee have me excused.' Would you sign that, young man? Would you, mother? Would you come up to the reporters' table, take a pen, and put your name down to such an excuse?...I doubt if there is one here who would sign it. Will you then pay no attention to God's invitation? I beg of you, do not make light of it. It is a loving God inviting you to a feast, and God is not to be mocked. Go play with forked lightning, go trifle with pestilence and disease, but trifle not with God. Just let me write out another answer: 'To the King of Heaven: While sitting in Convention Hall, Kansas City, Missouri, November 16, 1899, I received a pressing invitation from one of Your messengers to be present at the marriage supper of Your only-begotten Son. I hasten to reply. By the grace of God I will be present.'"

At the end of the service, Moody leaned on the organ and asked the pastors if he could have a last word with them. "Oh," he said, "I'm sick and tired of this essay preaching! I'm nauseated with this 'silver-tongued orator' preaching! I like to hear preachers, and not windmills." Moody became very ill later that night and telegrammed his family: "Doctor thinks I need rest. Am on my way home." Indeed! He was on "his way Home." Home at last with Christ after living a life without excuses. Will you execute God's will in your life today or will you find some way to excuse yourself? One day you will stand before God having done one or the other.

November 17, 1876

Every Soul Is Important to God

"And they sung a new song, saying, Thou art worthy to take the book, and to open the seals thereof: for thou wast slain, and hast redeemed us to God by thy blood out of every kindred, and tongue, and people, and nation;"—**Revelation 5:9**

At sixteen years of age, on November 17, 1876, Rodney "Gypsy" Smith was gloriously saved. His mother had passed away; his father had been witnessing to him; he had the opportunity to hear Ira Sankey sing; and he had visited John Bunyan's former home in Bedford—all events progressing to this special night. As he came forward during the invitation, someone whispered, "Oh, it's only a gypsy boy." Rodney would teach himself to read and write as a young boy, and immediately began preaching and singing to his friends. He would leave home a year later to begin travelling in the Salvation Army as an evangelist. He would later say, "Anyone can preach to a crowd, but it takes the grace of God to preach to one man."

The value of one soul is priceless. No matter what background or setting they are from, God cares for and loves every single person with an eternal love. He loved the world so much that He gave His Son as a sacrifice for our sins so that we could spend eternity in Heaven with Him. When the choir of the redeemed sing a new song in Heaven, every tribe, every tongue, every nation, every kindred will have a part. The Lamb of God was slain for all people from every part of the globe.

Who can you witness to today? It will take the grace of God, but God will always help those who endeavor to do His work. Jesus had one purpose in coming to this earth: "For the Son of man is come to seek and to save that which was lost" (Luke 19:10). He has given to each of His children that same purpose. Will you recruit someone for that grand choir in Heaven today? What a joy it will be to sing forever with those we have brought to the Saviour!

November 27, 1872

The Call to Preach

"But we preach Christ crucified, unto the Jews a stumblingblock, and unto the Greeks foolishness; But unto them which are called, both Jews and Greeks, Christ the power of God, and the wisdom of God."—**1 Corinthians 1:23–24**

Shortly after watching his father pass away, Sam Jones was saved after listening to his grandfather preach. Not long after he would preach his first sermon on Romans 1:16, he would be licensed to preach November 27, 1872. Dr. Fred Barlow would later depict Jones' wife Laura's reaction to his becoming a circuit riding preacher: "His wife stood by him, suffered through his drinking days, but she stubborned herself against his desire to preach, threatening to leave him if he pursued his plan to become an itinerant preacher. The night before the conference when he was licensed, she became violently ill, repented of her resistance, and at six o-clock the next morning awakened her mate to a hot Southern breakfast and saw him off on the train with her prayers." Jones was elated to be licensed as a circuit-riding preacher at age twenty-five. His salary would be $65 a year. Jones would later say, "I don't care what they pay or don't pay: I have a place to preach now, and I am so happy."

When God lays on the heart of a man to preach, a burning fire rages in his heart to proclaim the Word of God. Nothing else in life can distract him from the mission God has given him. No matter the payment or the responses, he will preach the Gospel fearlessly to anyone who will hear. To some, the Gospel is a stumbling block, something they struggle with and cannot understand. To others the Gospel is foolishness, something that they do not want to believe or give their lives to. But to the Christian, the preaching of the Gospel is the power and the wisdom of God. No calling can replace the call to preach God's Word. Has God called you? Have you ever asked Him? Is God calling someone in your family to preach? Are you resisting and trying to dissuade them? May God raise up preachers in our day as never before, and may we support them wholeheartedly when He does!

November 19, 1862

An Eternal Crown

"Know ye not that they which run in a race run all, but one receiveth the prize? So run, that ye may obtain. And every man that striveth for the mastery is temperate in all things. Now they do it to obtain a corruptible crown; but we an incorruptible."—**1 Corinthians 9:24–25**

William Ashley Sunday was born in Ames, Iowa, into poverty during the Civil War. His father would die a month later from pneumonia in a Union Army camp. Mrs. Sunday moved into her parents' home after the death of her husband, but the two boys became too difficult for her to handle. Billy's mother would send him and his brother to an orphanage when he was ten years old. Many around him would soon notice his athleticism, and he would work up the ranks of sports to play for the Chicago White Sox in Major League Baseball. God had designed Billy Sunday for something more than baseball, however. Soon Sunday would be saved at the Pacific Garden Mission and would preach to over 100 million people, seeing at least one million of them saved.

Billy Sunday's athleticism certainly made a way for him in this life, but his focus would soon change to the next life. The Apostle Paul described the sports of his day oftentimes in his letters. He frequently referred to the race of the Christian life, and in 1 Corinthians 9, he compares the athletes of his day to the Christians in the church at Corinth. The athletes of his day, just as the athletes of our time, worked extremely hard to be rewarded. But the crown of leaves which they received would shrivel and die a few days later. In contrast, the crown that Christ gives is incorruptible. Just as the athletes in professional sports work toward receiving a trophy and the Olympians strive to win a medal, we must run our spiritual races full of faith and self-discipline. All the trophies of this world will be thrown into a trash heap someday, but our crowns will be cast at our Saviour's feet. Will you run today so that you may obtain that crown? Or will you stand before the King one day without one crown to cast at His feet?

November 20, 1871

Pardoned

"...Unto him that loved us, and washed us from our sins in his own blood,"
—**Revelation 1:5b**

A biography of Charles Weigle written by the staff of Tennessee Temple University begins: "On the banks of the Wabash River stands the prosperous mid-western city of LaFayette, Indiana, county seat of Tippecanoe County, and hometown of Purdue University. When Purdue was a young, growing school just two years old, Charles Frederick Weigle was born, November 20, 1871, into the family of a God-fearing German baker and his devoted wife." Weigle would be saved at the age of twelve during revival services held at the Methodist Church of LaFayette. Weigle would later share his testimony of the night he was saved: "One night, as I sat on a rear seat, the Holy Spirit, the High Sheriff of Heaven, arrested me and led me to the front in sight of all the people present. I was convicted and condemned, and confessed my guilt to Almighty God. There seemed no hope for me. My sins towered up before me. Then Jesus came and quieted my fears. He paid the penalty for all my sins and guilt. He pleaded my case in the high court of Heaven and won my pardon. When this great truth dawned upon my mind, my heart was filled with gratitude and praise. There came a great love into my heart for my Saviour. That love has grown until He has the chief place in my life. Some day I expect to see Him face to face. That will be heaven for me." Charles Weigle would soon enter evangelism and be best known for writing the song, "No One Ever Cared for Me Like Jesus."

Jesus Christ does care about us, and He proved it by coming to this world and shedding His blood on a cross that we might have eternal life. "For ye know the grace of our Lord Jesus Christ, that though he was rich, yet for your sakes he became poor, that, ye through his poverty might be rich" (2 Corinthians 8:9). What more motivation would we need to serve Him today who has done for us what we could never have done for ourselves?

November 21, 1875

God's Work Done Properly

"Let all things be done decently and in order."—**1 Corinthians 14:40**

At the height of his evangelistic ministry, D. L. Moody began his crusades in Philadelphia on November 21, 1875. Twelve thousand people attended each evening. The ushers were well trained, capable of seating 1,000 people per minute, and vacating the premises of 12,000 in four minutes if needed. The doors were opened one and a half hours before the service began, and in 10 minutes the 12,000 seats were taken. The total attendance for the meetings was 1,050,000 with 4,000 saved. God was blessing the ministry of D. L. Moody with great power and unction.

God blesses when His house is organized and orderly. We should desire to do things with excellence in God's work. The Apostle Paul was in the middle of giving direction to the church at Corinth regarding their use of spiritual gifts in the church. The Corinthian church had misused and abused some of what God had given them, and Paul was correcting them quite strongly. He wrote to them regarding the use of tongues, the ordinance of the Lord's Supper, and the blatant sin and divisions that plagued their church. Paul summarizes most of his book in one verse for the Corinthians to read: "Let all things be done decently and in order." To serve God effectively, we must have order and organization. We must follow the guidelines of the Word of God and organize our ministry effectively. In this order and decency, there is room for the Holy Spirit to work and have freedom as well.

Our lives, our homes, and our churches must not be disorganized and haphazard. God has given us careful guidelines in His Word and when followed there is liberty for God to work. When we neglect those instructions, the devil will be sure to disrupt and cause division and defeat. "Order my steps in thy word: and let not any iniquity have dominion over me" (Psalm 119:133).

November 22, 1873

It Is Well

"Run now, I pray thee, to meet her, and say unto her, Is it well with thee? is it well with thy husband? is it well with the child? And she answered, It is well."
—2 Kings 4:26

Horatio Spafford, an active member of Moody's campaigns, received incredibly horrific news. He had already lost a son to scarlet fever two years earlier, but nothing could prepare him for the tragedy that occurred this day in 1873. Spafford had sent his wife Anna and four girls Annie, Maggie, Tanetta, and Bessie ahead to London on the S.S. *Ville du Havre,* intending, after caring for some last minute business, to join them in time to help with the Moody campaign there. It was on this fateful day in late November, however, that the steamship collided with another vessel and Spafford's four children were killed. Mrs. Spafford would telegram her husband two words as soon as she arrived in England: "Saved alone."

On the voyage to England to meet his wife, the captain told Spafford that they were sailing over the very spot where his children drowned. Overcome with grief, Horatio Spafford took a scrap piece of paper out of his pocket and wrote:

> When peace, like a river, attendeth my way,
> When sorrows like sea billows roll;
> Whatever my lot, Thou hast taught me to say,
> It is well, it is well with my soul.
>
> And Lord haste the day, when the faith shall be sight,
> The clouds be rolled back as a scroll;
> The trump shall resound, and the Lord shall descend,
> Even so, it is well with my soul."

By faith, both H. G. Spafford and the woman in our scripture above could believe in the midst of great tragedy—It is well! That can only be possible as our trust and faith are focused and fixed on our God.

November 23, 1939

The Tongue Is a Fire

"Even so the tongue is a little member, and boasteth great things. Behold, how great a matter a little fire kindleth! And the tongue is a fire, a world of iniquity: so is the tongue among our members, that it defileth the whole body, and setteth on fire the course of nature; and it is set on fire of hell."—**James 3:5–6**

John R. Rice's Fundamentalist Baptist Church was serving the Lord faithfully and fervently in Dallas, Texas. The church had been started as a result of Rice's evangelistic campaigns in Dallas. *The Sword of the Lord* periodical had been started out of the church, and the church was passionate about reaching the community for Christ. However, while a visiting missionary from South America was speaking during an evening service, a fire began to shoot out above the baptistery. The congregation rushed out of the building, covering their faces from the smoke. The church would lose their building completely that day and would have to start over and build again.

Churches today are often burnt to the ground without many people being alarmed or even noticing. The fire that consumes them melts marriages, scars friendships, and brings to ashes all that God is endeavoring to build. This fire is in our words.

The words that proceed out of our mouths can either build up or tear down. "Even so the tongue is a little member, and boasteth great things. Behold, how great a matter a little fire kindleth! And the tongue is a fire, a world of iniquity: so is the tongue among our members, that it defileth the whole body, and setteth on fire the course of nature; and it is set on fire of hell" (James 3:5–6). Do our words help the work of God or are they a hindrance? A wise prayer each morning is found in Psalm 19:14, "Let the words of my mouth, and the meditation of my heart, be acceptable in thy sight, O LORD, my strength, and my redeemer." If our words and thoughts please the Lord, we will have little trouble being a blessing to those around us.

November 24, 1876

A New Song

"O sing unto the LORD a new song; for he hath done marvellous things: his right hand, and his holy arm, hath gotten him the victory."—**Psalm 98:1**

Over a thousand preachers had gathered for D. L. Moody's ministers meeting in the Farwell Hall of Chicago. Philip Bliss, who had been working on a new song stood before the preachers that night and took a deep breath. This would be the first night that the hymn "It Is Well with My Soul" would be sung in public. Bliss had taken the words of Horatio Spafford, and given them a melody and on November 24, 1876, this new song was heard for the first time.

Tragedy would surround the song once again as Philip Bliss himself would only live one more month. William Moody remembered Philip Bliss in the biography of his father: "A musical genius of unusual promise, he had been willing to sacrifice his taste for higher lines of composition to write music that would prove effectual in carrying the Gospel message to the greatest numbers. As a hymn writer as well as a composer he was equally successful, as "Hallelujah, What a Saviour!" and "Wonderful Words of Life" testify. His personality was most lovable, and the strong attachment between him and Mr. Moody made the bereavement a deep one." Philip Bliss's new songs would become some of the most loved hymns of history.

God has given us a new song as well. Those who are in Christ become new creatures and the old passes away and all things become new (2 Corinthians 5:17). "All things" includes our music! Our new nature loses its appetite for the tunes that once dominated our flesh. A new song that is characterized by "psalms and hymns and spiritual songs" (Ephesians 5:19) now appeals to our new nature. Whether we are musical or not, there is a desire to praise the Lord.

Would people know that you are a Christian by the music you listen to and enjoy? The song we sing is a powerful testimony!

Ezekiel 22–23 // 1 Peter 1

November 25, 1860

Others Are Watching

"Having your conversation honest among the Gentiles: that, whereas they speak against you as evildoers, they may by your good works, which they shall behold, glorify God in the day of visitation."—**1 Peter 2:12**

Young and newly saved, Dwight Moody had preached and shared the Gospel anywhere he was able. Moody could not even read some of the words from the Bible out loud and would often skip words that he could not pronounce. But that would not stop him from sharing God's Word, especially to the children of Chicago. Moody would gather children together and teach them the Bible. After just one year, he was teaching 650 children every week! The word about "Crazy Moody's" Sunday school travelled quickly, and in 1860, President-elect Abraham Lincoln visited Moody's class. After this visit, Moody and Lincoln formed a partnership that resulted in the North Market Sunday School sending over fifty soldiers in response to the President's call for troops when the Civil War broke out a few months later.

We all have a testimony to those around us. We all have people watching us. In D. L. Moody's case, the soon-to-be President was watching, but in our case, it may be a young child who looks up to us for inspiration or a servant of Christ who looks to you for leadership or perhaps a lost person who desires to know more about Christ. Whatever the case, we all have people who are watching our testimonies. Peter encourages us in his epistle to have our conversation, our lifestyle, honest among those who are watching, particularly those who are lost. Many of them would want to find fault with Christ or find a reason to reject the Word of God. But from our example, they may see our good works and give the glory to God. Whoever is watching, be sure to lead them in the right direction. Satan would love to get a foothold in your life and as a result, see many reject the Gospel of Christ. Let's make sure whoever is watching us today receives the right picture of God!

November 20, 1771

Invest in Eternity by Investing in the Local Church

"...I will build my church; and the gates of hell shall not prevail against it."
—Matthew 16:18b

Shubal Stearns died in 1771, but Stearns' Sandy Creek Baptist Church would live on for generations to come. A monument still stands outside of the church reading: "It is a mother church, nay a grandmother, and great grandmother. All the Separate Baptists sprang hence, not only eastward towards the sea, but westward towards the great river Mississippi, but northward to Virginia and southward to South Carolina and Georgia. The Word went forth...and great was the company of them who published it, in so much that her converts were as drops of morning dew."

Institutions, corporations, and even governments in this world come and go. The world is changing faster than many of us can keep up. But there is one institution that will never close or fade away. The *ecclesia,* God's local church will always be in existence. From the day Christ called His disciples to Pentecost and beyond, God will always bless His church. Persecution only causes it to grow in intensity and numbers. Not even the gates of Hell itself can prevail against it.

So what are you investing your life in? Are you looking for a way to make your life matter in the grand scheme of eternity? Look no further than your local New Testament church. You have God's promise that your investment will pay off with eternal dividends.

Shubal Stearns could not have imagined the impact Sandy Creek Baptist Church would have, but God surely surpassed anything he could have prayed. Our churches today can impact this world today and for generations to come.

November 27, 1775

Will Someone Pray?

"And judgment is turned away backward, and justice standeth afar off: for truth is fallen in the street, and equity cannot enter...And he saw that there was no man, and wondered that there was no intercessor..."—**Isaiah 59:14, 16a**

J. Paul Reno gives us a glimpse into the life of Daniel Nash who was born this day in 1775: "He pastored a small church in the backwoods of New York for six years, and travelled with and prayed for a traveling evangelist for seven more years until his death. As far as we know, he never ministered outside the region of upstate New York during days when much of it was frontier. His tombstone is in a neglected cemetery along a dirt road behind a livestock auction barn. His church no longer exists, its meetinghouse location marked by a historic marker in a corn field; the building is gone, its timber used to house grain at a feed mill four miles down the road. No books tell his life story, no pictures or diaries can be found, his descendants (if any) cannot be located, and his messages are forgotten. He wrote no books, started no schools, led no movements, and generally kept out of sight."

Yet this man saw revival twice in his pastorate, and then was a key figure of prayer in the revivals of Charles Finney. He is known exclusively for his powerful ministry of prayer. All around us today the truth is being trampled. No longer is God revered and the Bible respected. God is not surprised by evil men and seducers waxing worse and worse, but He does wonder why there is no one to pray!

Prayer binds our nothingness to God's almightiness. Prayer doesn't need proof; it needs practice. Perhaps revival tarries in our generation because of our tardiness in prayer. John R. Rice stated that "all of our failures are prayer failures." We dare not plant churches, organize revivals, and plan evangelistic outreaches if we are not willing to pray. Was Daniel Nash one of a kind? He doesn't have to be. You and I have access to God's throne today. God is waiting to hear and answer our prayers.

November 27, 1994

Satan Opposes Prayer

"Praying always with all prayer and supplication in the Spirit, and watching thereunto with all perseverance and supplication for all saints."
—**Ephesians 6:18**

Leonard Ravenhill died in Lindale, Texas, on November 27, 1994 after a life of calling others to revival. His dear friend A. W. Tozer said of him, "To such men as this, the church owes a debt too heavy to pay. The curious thing is that she seldom tries to pay him while he lives. Rather, the next generation builds his sepulchre and writes his biography—as if instinctively and awkwardly to discharge an obligation the previous generation to a large extent ignored."

Leonard Ravenhill's classic book entitled *Why Revival Tarries* continues to challenge our generation toward revival. He wrote: "Poverty-stricken as the church is today in many things, she is most stricken here, in the place of prayer. We have many organizers, but few agonizers; many players and payers, but no pray-ers; many singers, no clingers; lots of pastors, few wrestlers; many fears, few tears; much fashion, little passion; many interferers, few intercessors; many writers, but few fighters. Failing here, we fail everywhere…

"The preaching ministry is open to a few; the ministry of prayer—the highest ministry of all human offices—is open to all. Spiritual adolescents say, 'I'll not go tonight, it's only a prayer meeting.' It may be that Satan has little cause to fear most preaching. Yet past experiences sting him to rally his infernal army to fight against God's people praying."

Does the devil fear your prayers? Is his work at risk because you are praying for revival? Satan doesn't fear a revival meeting where there is no prayer meeting. We have never had a greater need for revival, but God's invitation stands—"Let us therefore come boldly unto the throne of grace, that we may obtain mercy, and find grace to help in time of need" (Hebrews 4:16).

November 29, 1874

The Start of Revival

"But ye, beloved, building up yourselves on your most holy faith, praying in the Holy Ghost, Keep yourselves in the love of God, looking for the mercy of our Lord Jesus Christ unto eternal life."—**Jude 20–21**

Evangelist D. L. Moody's revival meetings began in Manchester, Ireland, in a hall that seated fifteen thousand people. The hall, however, for this crusade which commenced in late November of 1874, was not large enough for a single service. Pastor W. Rigby Murray wrote of Moody's meetings in Manchester: "Mr. Moody has demonstrated to us in a way at once startling and delightful that, after all, the grand levers for raising souls out of the fearful pit and the miry clay are just the doctrines which our so-called advanced thinkers are trying to persuade the Christian world to discard as antiquated and impotent. These are, the doctrine of the atoning death of Jesus Christ; the doctrine of a living, loving, personal Saviour, and the doctrine of the new birth by the Spirit and the Word of Almighty God...And then how shall I speak of the gladness which filled our hearts as we heard, almost from day to day, of conversions in our congregations, of parents rejoicing over sons and daughters brought to Jesus, of young men consecrating their manhood and strength to God, and of converts offering themselves for all departments of Christian service?...Give us a revived ministry and we shall soon see a revived church."

The great revivals of the past all follow the same formula: earnest prayer, powerful preaching of God's Word, and Christians placing themselves at God's disposal to serve in any way possible. Today we often speak about the need for revival yet neglect prayer, miss preaching services, and have excuses when it comes to getting involved in the work of God. No wonder Peter wrote in 1 Peter 4:17, "For the time is come that judgment must begin at the house of God...." Let God's work of revival begin in you today. The spark that ignites in your heart can produce a firestorm of revival that touches the world.

November 30, 1623

The Blood of Jesus Christ

"But if we walk in the light, as he is in the light, we have fellowship one with another, and the blood of Jesus Christ his Son cleanseth us from all sin."
—1 John 1:7

Very little is recorded about John Bunyan's early years, as even his exact birthdate is unknown. The earliest record of his life was his baptism. Following the traditions of the Anglican Church, Bunyan was baptized on this day in 1623 at the age of five. He had no idea how to be saved from his sin or what Christ had done for him. John would later hear a Puritan preacher speak against breaking the Sabbath, and he would never forget his words. The guilt in his heart for breaking God's law weighed upon him. Yet, from the guilt, he discerned to himself that he would enter God's judgment whether or not he continued in sin. He continued his life lost in his sin without hope.

After much conviction from the Holy Spirit about his wicked lifestyle, he tried to obey the law and read the Bible faithfully to earn his way to Heaven, but again no peace entered his heart. One day, as he walked through the town of Bedford, he overheard a group of ladies from a Non-Conformist church speaking about being "born again." He listened closely to the truth that they were speaking of, a truth that he had never heard before. But Bunyan would only repeat the motions of religion, trying to earn his way to God's favor.

One night, he opened Martin Luther's commentary on Galatians. As he read, he suddenly realized that Christ had made the sacrifice for his sins, and that he no longer needed to work for his salvation. Finally, Bunyan understood what Christ had done for him on the cross, as he read in 1 John 1:7, "...The blood of Jesus Christ His Son cleanseth us from all sin." He would later say: "I saw, moreover, that it was not good frame of heart that made my righteousness better, nor my bad frame that made my righteousness worse, for my righteousness was Jesus Christ Himself, 'the same yesterday, and today, and forever.'"

DECEMBER

December 606 BC

The Bible Stands

"Now the king sat in the winterhouse in the ninth month: and there was a fire on the hearth burning before him. And it came to pass, that when Jehudi had read three or four leaves, he cut it with the penknife, and cast it into the fire that was on the hearth, until all the roll was consumed in the fire that was on the hearth."—**Jeremiah 36:22–23**

God had commanded Jeremiah to record his message in a scroll and deliver it to the king of Jerusalem. His assistant, Barach, had helped him write down the message for the king, and the scroll was delivered to the scribe's chamber. Soon Jehudi, one of the kings' princes, was sent by the king to find the scroll and bring it to the palace. Jehudi read the Word of God before the king and the other princes of Jerusalem. As he listened to the Word from the Lord, the king became infuriated. Before Jehudi could finish reading the scroll, King Jehoiakim grabbed the scroll out of his hands, cut it with his penknife, and threw it into the fire. The enraged king watched the scroll burn in the furnace.

But God would command Jeremiah to write another scroll and to proclaim his message to the city: "...Thus saith the LORD; Thou hast burned this roll, saying, Why hast thou written therein, saying, The king of Babylon shall certainly come and destroy this land, and shall cause to cease from thence man and beast? Therefore thus saith the LORD of Jehoiakim king of Judah; He shall have none to sit upon the throne of David: and his dead body shall be cast out in the day to the heat, and in the night to the frost. And I will punish him and his seed and his servants for their iniquity; and I will bring upon them, and upon the inhabitants of Jerusalem, and upon the men of Judah, all the evil that I have pronounced against them; but they hearkened not" (Jeremiah 36:29–31).

Men throughout the ages have desired to destroy the Word of God. But God's Word will always stand. It is a supernatural, living Book that God protects and preserves for every generation. Read God's Word today, meditate on it, and share it with others.

December 2, 1934

God Is Our Refuge and Fortress

"He that dwelleth in the secret place of the most High shall abide under the shadow of the Almighty. I will say of the Lord, He is my refuge and my fortress: my God; in him will I trust."—**Psalm 91:1–2**

Monroe Parker had grown up as a Methodist, and his hero and mentor in the faith, Bob Jones Sr., was a Methodist as well. Yet after graduating from Bob Jones College and serving in the ministry for six years in Methodism, Parker began to sense that modernism was beginning to creep into the denomination, something his mentor Bob Jones fought tooth and nail. Parker, however, became "convinced of the Baptist distinctives" and was ordained as a Baptist preacher in 1934. Parker would continue to serve the Lord as a Baptist for the rest of his life. His favorite passage of Scripture was Psalm 91.

We can be thankful for our Baptist heritage, and we should never be ashamed of the stand that our forefathers have taken. Many Baptists of yesteryear have claimed the verses of Psalm 91 throughout persecution. When the authorities knocked down the door to arrest those who possessed a copy of the Word of God and when the martyrs were flung to their deaths for refusing to baptize their infants, God gave them divine hope.

The passage of Psalm 91 answers the age-old question: Where can we find God? The answer is simple: in the secret place, away from all the stress and discontentment of this world. God asks us to abide in Him, to live our lives in the peaceful shadow of the Almighty. God desires to be our fortress and refuge, but we must place our complete trust in Him. If we know God and His power, why would we not want to trust Him? When difficulties and trials come, God's Almighty shadow will drive them all away.

Are you content under the shadow of the Almighty today or do you need something else or something more. Isn't God and His Word enough? He has proven Himself trustworthy to those in ages past and will prove Himself to you if you will let Him.

December 3, 1966

No Better Friend

"And the scripture was fulfilled which saith, Abraham believed God, and it was imputed unto him for righteousness: and he was called the Friend of God."
—James 2:23

Charles Weigle died in Chattanooga, Tennessee, after spending the last fifteen years of his life on the campus of Tennessee Temple University. His biography would read, "He saw the beginning of revival spirit as it began to flame again out of the ashes of the old spiritual awakening."

Charles Weigle's greatest legacy would be the song "No One Ever Cared for Me Like Jesus." This song was born out of tragedy in Weigle's life. After returning from an evangelistic meeting, his wife announced, "I'm leaving, Charlie. I don't want to live the life you are living. I want to go the other way—to the bright lights." She would take their only daughter on the train to California that night. He found his wife eight months later in Los Angeles, and she boasted to him about her life of sin. A few years later, she lay on her deathbed, a result of her life of rebellion against God, and asked her daughter, "If you know where your father is, please ask him to pray for me, and see if God can forgive such a sinner as I." Still grieving five years later, Charles Weigle would sit down at his piano with no intention of writing a song. But God would lead his hands across the keys to write about his best Friend.

I would love to tell you what I think of Jesus,
Since I found in Him a friend so strong and true;
I would tell you how He changed my life completely,
He did something that no other friend could do.

No one ever cared for me like Jesus,
There's no other friend so kind as He;
No one else could take the sin and darkness from me,
O how much He cared for me.

Truly, Jesus is *the* "friend that sticketh closer than a brother (Proverbs 18:24). Spend time with Him today. He loves you and cares for you.

December 4, 1905

The Love of God

"In this was manifested the love of God toward us, because that God sent his only begotten Son into the world, that we might live through him. Herein is love, not that we loved God, but that he loved us, and sent his Son to be the propitiation for our sins."—**1 John 4:9–10**

Evangelist Mordecia Ham's wife Bessie died from cerebral palsy on December 4, 1905, after only five years of marriage, devastating the twenty-eight-year-old preacher. Ham would lose fifty pounds in the coming months, shaken from his loss. About a month later, Ham would take a trip to the Holy Land to grieve and give his burdens to the Lord. No doubt, as he stood at Mount Calvary and the Garden Tomb, Ham was greatly moved at the sacrifice Christ made for him. The trip would transform his life's perspective. Ham would return to the States and conduct his most successful evangelistic campaign to date in Houston, Texas.

The Apostle John points to one event in history as the definition of love. He declared, "Herein is love," as he pointed to the cross. God manifested Himself to mankind through His only begotten Son. The death of Christ opens the gates of Heaven and reveals God's love to us, so that we can live through Him.

Love is not defined by man's standard, but by God's unending love for us. We can be thankful that He sent His Son to die as a perfect sacrifice for our sins and that Christ demonstrated His love for us on that old rugged cross. Take this day to focus on the cross. Meditate on the suffering and pain that Christ endured for you to be reconciled with God.

Whatever you are facing today, God loves you with an everlasting love. As we focus on Christ's love on the cross, it will change our perspective on life and open doors to renewed service to Him. "For the love of Christ constraineth us; because we thus judge, that if one died for all, then were all dead: And that he died for all, that they which live should not henceforth live unto themselves, but unto him which died for them, and rose again" (2 Corinthians 5:14–15).

December 519 BC

Draw Nigh to God

"Therefore say thou unto them, Thus saith the Lord of hosts; Turn ye unto me, saith the Lord of hosts, and I will turn unto you, saith the Lord of hosts."
—Zechariah 1:3

The people of Jerusalem had become comfortable in their newly constructed homes, but they had left the rebuilding of the Temple of God for someone else to worry about. So God raised up the prophets Haggai and Zechariah to stir the people to finish the work they had started. Zechariah preached with thunder in his voice: "The Lord hath been sore displeased with your fathers. Therefore say thou unto them, Thus saith the Lord of hosts; Turn ye unto me, saith the Lord of hosts, and I will turn unto you, saith the Lord of hosts. Be ye not as your fathers, unto whom the former prophets have cried, saying, Thus saith the Lord of hosts; Turn ye now from your evil ways, and from your evil doings: but they did not hear, nor hearken unto me, saith the Lord. Your fathers, where are they? and the prophets, do they live for ever? But my words and my statutes, which I commanded my servants the prophets, did they not take hold of your fathers? and they returned and said, Like as the Lord of hosts thought to do unto us, according to our ways, and according to our doings, so hath he dealt with us" (Zechariah 1:2–6). The people of Jerusalem listened to the preaching of the prophets, and unlike their forefathers, rose up and finished the Temple.

Zechariah gives the people a simple truth in the beginning of his book, a truth that still applies to us today: If we will turn to God in obedience to His Word, He will respond by sending revival to our hearts. James 4:8a puts it this way, "Draw nigh to God, and he will draw nigh to you."

Revival doesn't have to be as complicated as we make it. When we turn to God we will automatically turn away from the things that keep us from revival. God hasn't changed. Just as He responded to Zechariah five hundred years before Christ, He will respond to you today.

December 6, 1839

We Need to Wake Up

"And that, knowing the time, that now it is high time to awake out of sleep: for now is our salvation nearer than when we believed. The night is far spent, the day is at hand: let us therefore cast off the works of darkness, and let us put on the armour of light."—**Romans 13:11–12**

After Charles Finney returned from his sabbatical in the Mediterranean, he published the first of his "Revivals of Religion" lectures in the *New York Evangelist* in 1839, beginning a series of twenty-two lectures. Finney wrote in his preface: "I found a particular inducement to this course, in the fact, that on my return from the Mediterranean, I learned, with pain, that the spirit of revival had greatly declined in the United States, and that a spirit of jangling and controversy alarmingly prevailed.

"The peculiar circumstances of the church, and the state of revivals, was such, as unavoidably to lead me to the discussion of some points that I would gladly have avoided, had the omission been consistent with my main design, to reach and arouse the church, when she was fast settling down upon her lees."

Over one hundred and fifty years later, the church has fallen asleep again. Finney's description of "jangling and controversy" describes our generation of Christians as well. Many of our churches have turned into social clubs and entertainment centers instead of what God has ordained us to be, a pillar and ground of the truth (1 Timothy 3:15). The night is almost over, and the time of Christ's return, "our salvation," is coming near. Yes, the world is dark with sin, but God has called us to be a light. He has called us to proclaim the Gospel before the Son of God returns to gather His children to Him. Sadly many Christians have dimmed the light and hid it under a bushel, cowering in fear and worry.

Listen to the Word of God being preached by the evangelists of old, "Awake! The kingdom of God is at hand!" Will we wake up in time for God to send another revival in our generation?

December 3, 1833

Rightly Dividing God's Word

"Study to shew thyself approved unto God, a workman that needeth not to be ashamed, rightly dividing the word of truth."—**2 Timothy 2:15**

Evangelist Charles Finney had a burden to train the next generation in the ways of the Lord. He began the Oberlin Collegiate Institute, which later was renamed the Oberlin College. Everything around the campus was fresh and new. The road leading to the college was newly finished, and the entire area was filled with tree stumps from the trees that had been cut down to construct the buildings. God was beginning a great work that would encourage the next generation to study and meditate on the Word of God. Starting with eleven families with a desire to study God's Word on December 3, 1833, Finney's college would grow to 101 students the following year.

God commands us to be students of His Word. The devil delights in seeing Christians who are ignorant of the Word of God because they are easily swayed with every wind of doctrine. Only the Scriptures can keep us firmly grounded in God's truth. The Apostle Paul commanded his son in the faith, Timothy, to be a devoted student of God's Word, and an unashamed workman as he spent time in the Bible daily. Paul, the tentmaker, also used a sewing term to describe how we should study God's Word. Just as a tentmaker would be sure to cut the fabric correctly to the right pattern, as a student of the Bible we should rightly divide the Word of truth, carefully and precisely following its perfect pattern for our lives.

God's Word is a special gift to us, and we should devote our lives unashamedly to it. Don't just read the Bible today—let it read you! As it does, let it become the pattern that guides every aspect of your life.

December 1872

Fiery Trials

"Beloved, think it not strange concerning the fiery trial which is to try you, as though some strange thing happened unto you: But rejoice, inasmuch as ye are partakers of Christ's sufferings; that, when his glory shall be revealed, ye may be glad also with exceeding joy."—**1 Peter 4:12–13**

Pastor T. Dewitt Talmage's fifteen thousand-seat auditorium in Brooklyn had no longer been able hold the crowds who came to hear his preaching. Every Sunday people would be turned away because there was no more room in the sanctuary. Talmage had raised funds to add more seating, but even the additions to the building could not hold the throngs of people who wanted to hear the Gospel. Still the building had been described as "one of the best buildings in the country for speaking and hearing, and was unsurpassed in its arrangements for seating a large congregation."

One night, however, a fire consumed the city and Talmage's church burned to the ground in the worst fire the city had ever seen. After the fire, Talmage led his church to build a larger auditorium, seating four thousand, completed in 1874. This auditorium would be consumed in another fire in 1889, and the church built a third auditorium, this time on a different street. In 1894, this third church building would burn down as well. Satan was testing this faithful preacher, but Talmage called them "blessings in disguise" as each time God would strengthen His people and enlarge their influence.

Fires in our lives come in different ways. The Apostle Peter wrote to suffering Christians, being persecuted for their faith. He encouraged them that their "fiery trial" was nothing to be surprised at and that their suffering would lead to great joy in the future. Through the fires of life, God melts away the impurities and leads us to a new beginning. Often the greatest joys and triumphs of our lives follow the most difficult trials. Do not let the fiery trials of this life keep you discouraged and defeated. The best victories in your life may be just around the corner.

December 9, 1863

Training Our Children

"Train up a child in the way he should go: and when he is old, he will not depart from it."—**Proverbs 22:6**

G. Campbell Morgan was born in Tetbury, England, on the farm of George and Elizabeth Morgan on December 9, 1863. His father was a Baptist preacher and would mentor him throughout his weakened childhood. When Morgan was ten years of age, his father would take him to hear D. L. Moody preach for the first time, and he was inspired to be a preacher. Three years would pass, and he would preach his first sermon. Two years more and he would be preaching in churches across the country. Morgan would grow to become one of the most influential preachers of his generation in England and America, crossing the Atlantic fifty-four times.

The influence we have as parents is so very important in our children's lives. It is never too early to begin teaching your children about Christ and bringing them up "in the nurture and admonition of the Lord" (Ephesians 6:4b). The Apostle Paul recognized the early training of young Timothy: "And that from a child thou hast known the holy scriptures, which are able to make thee wise unto salvation through faith which is in Christ Jesus" (2 Timothy 3:15). Vladimir Lenin, the Communist leader, once stated, "Give me a child for the first five years of his life, and he will be mine forever." Lenin understood something that many Christian parents fail to understand. What you place into a child's heart early will be there the rest of his life and will influence their decisions, direction, and destiny.

Take time today to invest in your children's lives. Be sure the next time you are at church that you take time for the children. Find a ministry where you can be involved in the training of the next generation for Christ. As Christians, we are never more than one generation away from extinction. It is our privilege and responsibility to pass the truth on to them and then have the joy to see them walking in that truth (3 John 4).

December 1900

Pick up the Mantle

"And he took the mantle of Elijah that fell from him, and smote the waters, and said, Where is the LORD God of Elijah? and when he also had smitten the waters, they parted hither and thither: and Elisha went over."—**2 Kings 2:14**

Three centuries of Christian ancestry, including Roger Williams, would culminate in the life of Evangelist Mordecai Ham. His father had pastored six Kentucky churches at one time, and his grandfather had served the Lord faithfully as a Baptist preacher in the backwoods of America. Growing up in a Christian home, Mordecai had once tried to baptize a cat. Obviously the animal did not want to be plunged into a horse trough, and when it resisted, Ham shouted, "Go on, get sprinkled and go to Hell!" But Mordecai had drifted from his Baptist faith, and at the age of twenty-two, he was summoned to his grandfather's deathbed. There he would watch his grandfather pass into eternity. Dr. Fred Barlow would later explain the importance of that day: "That moment the twenty-two-year-old Mordecai knew his grandfather's mantle had fallen upon him." After he married Bessie Simmons, Ham left his business as a traveling salesman and joined the ranks of travelling preachers in December 1900.

As the prophet Elisha stood gazing up into the sky, his mentor Elijah threw down his mantle. Elijah left this earth in a fiery chariot of flames, and all that was left was his mantle. Elijah's God needed to become Elisha's God. Elisha took the mantle with him, and with the crowds watching curiously, he called, "Where is the Lord God of Elijah?" He smote the Jordan River with the mantle, and immediately, the river parted for Elisha to walk on dry ground. Elisha would go on and do twice as many miracles as his mentor. Has someone invested in your life? Have they left you a Christian legacy to follow? Don't forsake that mantle. Pick it up and serve the Lord in your generation as they did in theirs. "Remember them which have the rule over you, who have spoken unto you the word of God: whose faith follow, considering the end of their conversation" (Hebrews 13:7).

December 11, 1895

The World Needs Preachers

"Preach the word; be instant in season, out of season; reprove, rebuke, exhort with all longsuffering and doctrine."—**2 Timothy 4:2**

John R. Rice was born in Cooke County, Texas, on December 11, 1895. The Rice brothers, John and his younger brother Bill, would grow up and together shake the nation with the Gospel. John would become one of the leading soul winners in the nation for over fifty years, in personal evangelism, holding revival crusades, conferences for evangelists, and writing inspiring articles and books. He would challenge the nation with his book *Prayer: Asking and Receiving* and his periodical *The Sword of the Lord.* John R. Rice would preach to America and remind Christians that "all of our failures are prayer failures." Rice challenged the preachers of his day to preach boldly and fearlessly: "Preach on booze. Preach on the scarlet sin, adultery.…Preach on the dance, tell people that it is rotten as sin.…Preach on the movies…made by vile, lewd people, holding up rotten moral standards, breaking down respect for marriage, pure love, hard work, God and the Bible.…Preach against lodges.…Preach against evolution and false cults. Preach on death, sin, Hell, judgment! Such preaching with boldness, with love, with tears, with Scripture, with faith, will bring great revivals, will save hardened sinners." After his death, the *Sword of the Lord* staff would count 22,923 letters that Rice had received from those across the world who thanked him for sharing the Gospel with them.

John R. Rice was a fearless preacher who confronted the sin of his day and led thousands to Christ. But John R. Rice and his brother Bill are no longer with us. Who will fearlessly and faithfully preach God's Word today? God does not call everyone to be a preacher, but everyone ought to be willing to be one should God call them. The Rice brothers would no doubt be shocked at the sins and the ungodliness that is tolerated today. God give us preachers who will once again stand for truth with the boldness of John R. Rice and tears in their eyes!

December 1901

Revival Is in the Air

"O Lord, I have heard thy speech, and was afraid: O Lord, revive thy work in the midst of the years, in the midst of the years make known; in wrath remember mercy."—**Habakkuk 3:2**

"Revival is in the air," wrote Evangelist R. A. Torrey before he launched his evangelistic tour, preaching through China, Japan, Australia, Tasmania, New Zealand, India, Germany, the United Kingdom, and the United States. In his book *How to Promote and Conduct a Successful Revival,* published in 1901 as a handbook for his revival campaigns, Torrey explains his reasoning for launching out into the field of evangelism: "Thoughtful ministers and Christians everywhere are talking about a revival, expecting a revival, and, best of all, praying for a revival. There seems to be little doubt that a revival of some kind is coming, but the important question is: What kind of a revival will it be? Will it be a true revival, sent of God because His people have met the conditions that make it possible for God to work with power, or will it be a spurious revival gotten up by the arts and devices of men? A business man who is in touch with religious movements in all parts of the country said to me recently, 'There is little doubt that a revival of some kind is coming, and the revival that is coming will be either the greatest blessing or the greatest curse that has ever visited the church of Christ.'" Torrey and his team had spent countless hours in prayer and fasting, and now they felt that the Lord was leading them into the paths of revival.

How is God leading you? Not everyone is called to the office of the evangelist, but every Christian ought to "...do the work of an evangelist..." (2 Timothy 4:5). God has placed you in a certain place at a precise time for a specific purpose: to share the Gospel. Will you pray for your workplace to see revival? Will you be an instrument in the hands of God where God has put you? Will you pray for your church, your family, your neighborhood to experience revival? Perhaps God is calling you to a life of revival work. What will you do to see revival today?

December 18, 1853

Serve the Lord Today

"Whatsoever thy hand findeth to do, do it with thy might; for there is no work, nor device, nor knowledge, nor wisdom, in the grave whither thou goest."
—Ecclesiastes 9:10

The soon-to-be "Prince of Preachers" was walking down the street with his friend to join a young preacher and encourage him in his services in Teversham, England. Upon arriving at the chapel, Charles realized that there was no one there to preach. Spurgeon later recounted, "I soon realized that there would be no sermon unless I gave them one...Praying for divine help, I resolved to make an attempt. My text should be, "Unto you therefore which believe he is precious," and I would trust the Lord to open my mouth in honor of his dear Son. It seemed a great risk and a serious trial, but, depending upon the power of the Holy Ghost, I would at least tell out the story of the cross, and not allow the people to go home without a word." He told how as he finished his short message in the small cottage, one woman critiqued his new pulpit ministry: "'Bless your dear heart, how old are you?'...'I am under sixty,' was the reply. 'Yes, and under sixteen,' was the old lady's rejoinder. 'Never mind my age, think of the Lord Jesus and his preciousness,' was all that I could say...."

Thus it was that Spurgeon preached his first sermon in the middle of December 1853. In the same year, he would be called to pastor a small Baptist church in Waterbeach, Cambridgeshire. Spurgeon would later challenge his students after sharing his story: "Many of our young folks want to do great things, and therefore do nothing at all; let none of our readers become the victims of such an unreasonable ambition. He who is willing to teach infants, or to give away tracts, and so to begin at the beginning, is far more likely to be useful than the youth who is full of affectations and sleeps in a white necktie, who is studying for the ministry, and is touching up certain superior manuscripts which he hopes ere long to read from the Pastor's pulpit." What would God have you start doing today? Don't delay! Tomorrow may never come.

December 22, 1862

One Died for All

"For the love of Christ constraineth us; because we thus judge, that if one died for all, then were all dead: And that he died for all, that they which live should not henceforth live unto themselves, but unto him which died for them, and rose again."—**2 Corinthians 5:14–15**

On December 22, 1862, Billy Sunday's father died of pneumonia one month after Billy was born. At an army camp in Patterson, Missouri, Sunday's father became a casualty of the Civil War. He would later write in his autobiography *The Sawdust Trail*, "I never saw my father. He walked from Ames, Iowa, to Des Moines, thirty miles, to enlist in the Civil War…." He would later try to locate his father's final resting place, but even through the War Department and private investigators, he was still unable to find the grave. He did discover however that the War Department had taken many of the soldier's bodies to a cemetery near St. Louis, named Jefferson Barracks. While preaching a revival meeting there, he took a day to visit the cemetery: "I stood with uncovered head amid the thousands of graves of known and unknown Union soldiers, and prayed for the living relatives of the heroes, thinking that perhaps dad sleeps there under the protecting folds of Old Glory."

Many soldiers throughout history have died for our current freedom. They gave their lives on the battlefield to fight tyranny and evil. We should forever honor those who have gone before us who shed their blood for our freedom. But there is One who shed His blood for the entire world. His blood delivers us from the tyranny of sin and gives us the freedom to live for Him. Because of Jesus' death, we are "constrained" by His love to serve Him. He died so that we would not live for ourselves, but would live for Him who died and rose again! He gave His life for you—what have you given Him? We should honor and love our Saviour for giving us eternal life, and as that love grows in our hearts, it should spring forth to everyone around us. Let your love and thanksgiving for your Saviour today be manifested to someone around you.

December 15, 1918

Finish Strong

"...so that I might finish my course with joy, and the ministry, which I have received of the Lord Jesus, to testify the gospel of the grace of God."
—Acts 20:24b

J. Wilbur Chapman had been in the hospital earlier in the year, and had written to a friend in England who was inviting him to preach: "I cannot tell you how sorry I am that our correspondence has been so interrupted. I have been seriously ill in the hospital for many weeks and have just returned home. I have known for a year that I would be obliged sooner or later to have this operation. Of course I am weakened very much but I shall be perfectly well in the future." But God would take this powerful preacher to Heaven by the end of the year.

Even ten days before his death, J. Wilbur Chapman was proving his love for others. One of his former church members had come to hear him preach during what would be one of his final messages on this earth: "Doctor Chapman, immediately after the service, came down to the pew where we were seated and stated that he had recognized us from the pulpit. He was as friendly and interested in us and in the news of his old parishioners as in the days years ago." Later, on December 15, 1918, Chapman preached his last message, "Christ, Our Only Hope."

Chapman was truly an evangelist anointed by God. Records show that he had preached fifty thousand sermons to some sixty million people.

Do you ever wonder what the record will show at the end of your life? Regardless of how you have started your race or have run in the past, determine today that you will finish strong. Jesus Christ from the cross cried, "It is finished!" I'm glad our Saviour did not quit before the finish line. He expects you and me to likewise be faithful unto death.

December 16, 1716

The Greatest Work Is to Serve

"Let this mind be in you, which was also in Christ Jesus: Who, being in the form of God, thought it not robbery to be equal with God: But made himself of no reputation, and took upon him the form of a servant, and was made in the likeness of men:"—**Philippians 2:5–7**

Thomas and Elizabeth Whitefield were keeping an inn on Southgate Street in Gloucester, England, when their fifth son, George, was born on this day in 1716. The Bell Inn still stands to this day as a monument to the famed evangelist's birthplace. With low business at the inn, his parents were unable to help George through college, so he became a "servitor," a servant-student who waited on the other students in the college. He paid for his tuition by doing much of their housework and cleaning. At college, he met two brothers, John and Charles Wesley, who would become some of his closest friends.

God would use the deprived baby in a crib that cold December day in an unbelievable way. Thousands would stare into his cross-eyed gaze and be convicted of their need for a Saviour. One historian would "sample" Whitefield's amazing results in preaching to his readers: "A scattered sampling of Whitefield's attendances: Mooreheads—1739—30,000 in attendance sometimes. Philadelphia—12,000; 22,000. Boston—'weather wet, but above 8,000 followed into the fields.' 'Saturday, about 15,000 people on the Common.' Farewell sermon 'to nearly 30,000 people, though the whole population of Boston at that time did not exceed 20,000.' The list is endless. The attendances are the more remarkable in the light of the fact that those were days of infidelity, profligacy, debauchery and formalism in England and America."

The world would mock or dismiss the life of a cross-eyed, servant boy born in a poor inn, but God would see his humility and lift him up as one of the most powerful preachers who ever lived. In a world where many fight for the top of the ladder, take ahold of the bottom rung. Someday God will turn that ladder upside down!

December 25, 1847

Learning How to Live and Die

"For we know that if our earthly house of this tabernacle were dissolved, we have a building of God, an house not made with hands, eternal in the heavens."
—2 Corinthians 5:1

Charles Finney's wife of twenty-three years had just passed away, leaving a massive hole in the heart of the evangelist. In his periodical *The Oberlin Evangelist,* he wrote a touching eulogy to his wife that was published on Christmas Day in 1847: "My dear wife used to look up to me as her spiritual guide and teacher under God, but in justice to her I would say that she taught me many more valuable lessons. She showed me in many things how to live, and now she has shown me how to die. Oh, I ask myself, Can I die like that? Certainly not without the abounding and sovereign grace of God." Lydia Finney had taught her husband that our lives here on earth should point to our lives in eternity.

The hymn writer wrote: "I will love Thee in life; I will love Thee in death." No doubt loving the Lord in life will lead us to love Him in death. When we realize that our earthly lives are a blink of the eye compared to our time in eternity, our live's pursuits and priorities quickly change.

Our days are merely an introduction to eternity. Yet many times, the thoughts and cares of this life distract us from the life to come. Such meaningless pursuits and temporal pleasures divert us from our main purpose in life. But when our eyes are on Christ, our perspectives change. Then, and only then, can we enjoy the blessings of God in both lives.

No one said it better than Paul under the inspiration of the Holy Spirit in Colossians 3:1–3, "If ye then be risen with Christ, seek those things which are above, where Christ sitteth on the right hand of God. Set your affection on things above, not on things on the earth. For ye are dead, and your life is hid with Christ in God."

December 18, 1707

The Music of Christmas

"And suddenly there was with the angel a multitude of the heavenly host praising God, and saying, Glory to God in the highest and on earth peace, good will toward men."—**Luke 2:13–14**

Charles Wesley was born in Epworth, Lincolnshire, England, on this day in 1707. He was the eighteenth child of nineteen. He would be taught how to read as soon as he was old enough to speak. As a child, he learned Greek and Latin and excelled at both. His mother, Susannah Wesley, would pray and have devotions with her children each night, leading them in the ways of the Lord. Charles would join his older brother John in college and graduate with a Master's Degree in classical languages and literature. Perhaps Charles' greatest contribution to Christianity were his hymns. "And Can It Be?" "Christ the Lord Is Risen Today," "O For a Thousand Tongues to Sing," and "Hark, the Herald Angels Sing" would be the most remembered of his six thousand hymns. At this Christmas season, meditate on the powerful doctrine in his beloved Christmas carol:

> Hark! The herald angels sing, "Glory to the newborn King;
> Peace on earth, and mercy mild, God and sinners reconciled!"
> Joyful, all ye nations rise, Join the triumph of the skies;
> With th'angelic host proclaim, "Christ is born in Bethlehem!"
> Hark! the herald angels sing, "Glory to the newborn King!"
>
> Christ, by highest Heav'n adored; Christ the everlasting Lord;
> Late in time, behold Him come, Offspring of a virgin's womb.
> Veiled in flesh the Godhead see; Hail th' incarnate Deity,
> Pleased as man with man to dwell, Jesus our Emmanuel.
> Hark! the herald angels sing, "Glory to the newborn King!"
>
> Hail the heav'nly Prince of Peace! Hail the Sun of Righteousness!
> Light and life to all He brings, Ris'n with healing in His wings.
> Mild He lays His glory by, Born that man no more may die;
> Born to raise the sons of earth, Born to give them second birth.
> Hark! the herald angels sing, "Glory to the newborn King!"

December 19, 1955

Expressing the Christmas Story

"And the shepherds returned, glorifying and praising God for all the things that they had heard and seen, as it was told unto them."—**Luke 2:20**

Homer Rodeheaver, Billy Sunday's right-hand man, took his last breath from heart failure at Winona Lake, Indiana. Rodeheaver was the driving force behind the music of the Billy Sunday evangelistic campaigns. With an outgoing and fun-loving personality, Rodeheaver loved to lead the music with his trombone during the revival services. Rodeheaver's obituary written the day after he died on December 19, 1955 read, "Dr. Rodeheaver's death culminates a most brilliant and colorful career as world evangelist, Gospel song writer and publisher, and philanthropist." Music, evangelism, and a life of service became the expression of what God had done in the life of Homer Rodeheaver.

After the shepherds heard the Good News that the Messiah was born in Bethlehem, they ran to see the manger where He laid. No doubt moved by the tender scene of the divine Baby wrapped in rags and laid in a horse's trough, the shepherds could not believe their eyes. Mary and Joseph were gazing upon the newborn, thanking God for the privilege of being used in His plan. The shepherds left the stable that night changed by what they had seen. As they returned to the fields, they sang and glorified God for the miracle He had done.

Singing praise and glorifying God is a natural manifestation of the inner working of the Holy Spirit in a revived life. One of the best indications of a thriving, revived church can be seen and heard in the song service. And one of the best indications of a thankful, revived individual is that there is a desire to sing and tell others about the grace of God.

The shepherds would glorify God, praise His name, and tell everyone around them about the Saviour Who was born in the manger. Will you glorify God today in your song? Will you tell others of the message of Christmas?

December 20, 1831

Can God Count on Us to Pray?

"And said unto them, Why sleep ye? rise and pray, lest ye enter into temptation."
—Luke 22:46

Daniel Nash, Charles Finney's prayer warrior, literally died on his knees on this day in 1831, a fitting end to his life-changing ministry. Charles Finney told of his death: "Said a good man to me, 'Oh, I am dying for the want of strength to pray! My body is crushed, the world is on me, and how can I forbear praying?' I have known that man to go to bed absolutely sick, for weakness and faintness, under the pressure. And I have known him to pray as if he would do violence to Heaven, and then have seen the blessing come as plainly in answer to his prayer as if it were revealed, so that no person could doubt it any more then if God had spoken from heaven. Shall I tell you how he died? He prayed more and more; he used to take the map of the world before him, and pray, and look over the different countries and pray for them, till he expired in his room, praying. Blessed man! He was the reproach of the ungodly, and of the carnal, unbelievingly professors; but he was the favorite of Heaven, and a prevailing prince of prayer."

What excuses are we offering for our lack of prayer? The testimony of a man who was cast out of his pastorate and travelled the rugged country with an itinerant evangelist certainly dwarfs our best excuses. The prayers of Daniel Nash changed the evangelistic ministry of Charles Finney and changed the eternity of thousands of souls. Our flesh is often weary, but we should not be as the disciples, who slept while Christ agonized and sweat as it were great drops of blood in the Garden of Gethsemane.

Will you make time for prayer today? It isn't always easy or convenient. Our schedule's demands rob us of that time in the throne room with God. Instead of making excuses, excuse yourself from less important things and meet with God in prayer. The lives you impact will one day thank you.

December 25, 1908

The Reason for the Season

"And the angel said unto them, Fear not: for, behold, I bring you good tidings of great joy, which shall be to all people. For unto you is born this day in the city of David a Saviour, which is Christ the Lord."—**Luke 2:10–11**

Billy Sunday was thrilled to travel to Spokane, Washington, for a revival campaign that would begin on Christmas night. With a population of 100,000 people, this would be the largest city Sunday had preached in to date. The newly-constructed Billy Sunday tabernacle was built to seat 10,000 people. Dr. Conrad Bluhm commented on the night: "His meetings were begun Christmas night. I had feared the opening night, it happening on Christmas...but, the citizens gave him a reception that swept the evangelist off his feet—the place was packed to the doors." The people of Spokane knew Who was to be the focus of the Christmas season, and 5,666 souls would be saved during Sunday's meetings in Spokane.

Amid the lights and the shopping and the stress of the season, never lose sight of the One whom we should be worshipping. The night Jesus was born, many people missed the celebration of the Messiah. Everyone in Bethlehem was concerned about the census, the Romans, and finding a place to stay for the night. The exception were some lowly shepherds. That night, they were privileged to see the most spectacular celebration in Heaven or on earth, as the angels rejoiced and proclaimed the news of the birth of the Messiah. The skies rang with music and lights, as a heavenly host praised this birth, "Glory to God in the highest, and on earth peace, good will toward men" (Luke 2:14).

Do not be the one who misses the reason for the season. Don't let the busyness and stress keep you from worshipping the Lord Jesus Christ during this month. "O come, let us worship and bow down: let us kneel before the Lord our maker" (Psalm 95:6). He alone is worthy of our worship!

December 22, 1899

No More Death

"And God shall wipe away all tears from their eyes; and there shall be no more death, neither sorrow, nor crying, neither shall there be any more pain: for the former things are passed away."—**Revelation 21:4**

"Some day you will read in the papers that D. L. Moody, of East Northfield, is dead. Don't you believe a word of it! At that moment I shall be more alive than I am now, I shall have gone up higher; that is all; out of this old clay tenement into a house that is immortal—a body that death cannot touch; that sin cannot taint; a body fashioned like His glorious body. I was born of the flesh in 1837. I was born of the Spirit in 1856. That which is born of the flesh may die, that which is of the Spirit will live forever."

D. L. Moody died at age sixty-two in his home days before the new century would turn. As he lay on his deathbed breathlessly, his last words as he approached eternity were, "I see earth receding; heaven is approaching. God is calling me. This is my triumph. This is my coronation day. It is glorious. God is calling and I must go. Mama, you have been a good wife… no pain…no valley…it's bliss."

R. A. Torrey, a close friend and the new leader of Moody's ministry, later said of his mentor: "The first thing that accounts for God's using D. L. Moody so mightily was that he was a fully surrendered man. Every ounce of that two-hundred-and-eighty-pound body of his belonged to God; everything he was and everything he had, belonged wholly to God." When life is focused as Moody's was on God, death has no sting! "O death, where is thy sting? O grave, where is thy victory? The sting of death is sin; and the strength of sin is the law. But thanks be to God who giveth us the victory through our Lord Jesus Christ" (1 Corinthians 15:55–57).

Do you fear death? If you have Christ as your Saviour, you need not fear. "Yea, though I walk through the valley of the shadow of death, I will fear no evil: for thou art with me" (Psalm 23:4).

December 23, 1744

A Fire Inside

"But his word was in mine heart as a burning fire shut up in my bones, and I was weary with forbearing, and I could not stay."—**Jeremiah 20:9b**

The Church of England did not approve of John Wesley's preaching and did not allow him to preach in any of their churches. But the Word of God was burning inside his bones, and he could not wait any longer. After being convinced by George Whitefield that preaching in the open air was appropriate, the polished preacher stood at Snow Fields in Epworth, England, on December 23, 1744. Slamming his Bible on his father's tombstone for a pulpit, he preached the Gospel to anyone who passed by and would listen. "I look on the world as my parish," Wesley would later declare. Little did Wesley know that revival would break out in England and God would use his powerful outdoor preaching to see thousands turn to Christ. He would preach eight straight days from his father's tombstone, and his last open-air service in the cemetery would last more than three hours as the commoners turned to the Gospel of Jesus Christ.

No matter where the Gospel is given, it will always exceed our expectations. As Christ stood in the synagogue to preach, he turned to the book of Isaiah and read the prophecy concerning Himself. Christ's purpose was to preach the Gospel to the poor and to heal the brokenhearted (Luke 4:18), and our purpose should be the same.

The power of God flows through the good news of the death, burial, and resurrection of Jesus Christ. Whether the Gospel is preached in Wesley's graveyard or the neighborhood where you live, it has the power to change lives. "For I am not ashamed of the gospel of Christ: for it is the power of God unto salvation to every one that believeth; to the Jew first, and also to the Greek" (Romans 1:16). Pause and reflect upon the day that God saved you and then let Him build a fire in you to tell someone else.

December 24, 1885

Touched with Our Infirmities

"For we have not an high priest which cannot be touched with the feeling of our infirmities; but was in all points tempted like as we are, yet without sin. Let us therefore come boldly unto the throne of grace, that we may obtain mercy, and find grace to help in time of need."—**Hebrews 4:15–16**

On this Christmas Eve in 1885, the New York Times published an article with the headline, "UNREGENERATE ST. LOUIS: Evangelist Sam Jones Fails to Redeem the Wicked City." The article on the front page opened: "Sam Jones and Sam Small, the evangelists, closed their campaign here this morning. It would be superfluous to speculate as to whether Jones' work here was a failure or not. He has admitted that it was repeatedly in the last ten days, and those who know the man know that he would not make such a confession unless he believed it." Even the prince of evangelists Sam Jones had failures and setbacks. This Christmas Eve was a day of discouragement for one of the great evangelists of yesteryear.

Every servant of God has moments in his or her life that could be described as a setback, a time when things did not go as planned. Everything in our plan is not in God's plan, but we are sure that He never makes a mistake.

This Christmas Eve, we can rest in the truth that though we may face discouragement, there is a Saviour who has been tempted just as we are, yet without sin. We can go to Him in all boldness and lay our burdens at His feet. Tomorrow we celebrate the day that our Saviour was born in a lowly manger, fully aware and willing to endure all of the hardships of this world. Now, He sits on His heavenly throne "that we may obtain mercy, and find grace to help in time of need." Our Lord invites you to cast "...all your care upon him; for he careth for you" (1 Peter 5:7).The world looked bleak on that Christmas Eve over two thousand years ago, but the next morning was the greatest day in the history of mankind!

December 25, 1766

Two Evangelists Are Born

"For unto us a child is born, unto us a son is given: and the government shall be upon his shoulder: and his name shall be called Wonderful, Counsellor, the mighty God, The everlasting Father, The Prince of Peace."—**Isaiah 9:6**

Christmas Day is a universal holiday celebrated among Christians in all parts of the world. The prophecies of a Messiah were fulfilled on this day though few knew it at the time. He had come for one reason: "For the Son of man is come to seek and to save that which was lost" (Luke 19:10). Evangelism was indeed the purpose of the Lord Jesus Christ as "The Lord is not slack concerning his promise, as some men count slackness; but is longsuffering to us-ward, not willing that any should perish, but that all should come to repentance" (2 Peter 3:9).

On a Christmas morning in 1766, another evangelist was born to Samuel and Joanna Evans. They would name him "Christmas!" Like Jesus, Christmas Evans was not born into a family of favor or wealth as his parents were poor shoemakers in Cardiganshire, Wales. However, that cold Welsh Christmas night would bring forth one of the most powerful and unique evangelists of his century. He would be described as a "gargantuan preacher: the tallest, stoutest, greatest man ever known…whose head is covered with thick, course, black hair. His gait unwieldy, his limbs unequal. He has but one eye—if it might be called an eye—more properly, a brilliant star over against a ghastly empty socket." The Baptist preacher would see revival in his pastorate and his evangelistic ministry for forty-eight years.

Christmas Evans would dedicate his life to worshipping Christ and proclaiming the Good News of salvation. We should be thankful that Christ came this Christmas season, but we should also share the message of Christmas with all those who have yet to hear about Him.

December 26, 1899

We Sorrow Not as Others

"But I would not have you to be ignorant, brethren, concerning them which are asleep, that ye sorrow not, even as others which have no hope. For if we believe that Jesus died and rose again, even so them also which sleep in Jesus will God bring with him."—**1 Thessalonians 4:13–14**

D. L. Moody's son William gave us a glimpse into the memorial service of the evangelist who was laid to rest on this day in 1899. "In seeming accord with Mr. Moody's feelings that 'everything before a true believer is glorious,' even Nature assumed no sign of mourning on the day that his earthly tabernacle was laid to rest on Round Top. December 26 was the date fixed for the funeral services, and, as someone expressed it, it was 'one of the Lord's own days.' The winter's first snow rested on the distant hills of southern Vermont and New Hampshire, while a clear sky and a frosty atmosphere combined to make it a day of unusual brightness. During the morning, friends arrived from all directions, representing every phase of society and every shade of theological belief." C. I. Scoffield and R. A. Torrey presided over the events that day, and no one was allowed to wear mourning clothing, due to Moody's request. Moody's daughter-in-law and her father wrote a song that was sung by the Northfield Quartet at the end of the service:

> Blessed hope, blessed hope, Blessed hope of the coming of the Lord!
> How the aching heart it cheers, How it glistens thro' our tears,
> Blessed hope of the coming of the Lord! A star in the sky, a beacon bright to guide us,
> An anchor sure to hold when storms betide us, A refuge for the soul,
> Where in quiet we may hide us, Is the hope of the coming of the Lord.

Sometimes at death, we say, "we've lost a loved one." In reality they are not lost, for we know exactly where they are. When a Christian dies, "We are confident, I say, and willing rather to be absent from the body, and to be present with the Lord" (2 Corinthians 5:8). What a blessed hope that is!

December 1734

The Surprising Work of God

"Being confident of this very thing, that he which hath begun a good work in you will perform it until the day of Jesus Christ:"—**Philippians 1:6**

"The Spirit of God began extraordinarily to set in and wonderfully to work among us," Jonathan Edwards wrote after he began his sermon series "Justification by Faith" in his Northampton church. Seven years before his famous sermon "Sinners in the Hands of an Angry God," Edwards began to preach and to pray for people in his church to be saved, and God was slowly beginning to work.

He would continue to write the following year in his *Faithful Narrative of the Surprising Work of God*: "This Work of God, as...the Number of true Saints multiplied, soon made a glorious Alteration in the Town; so that in the spring and summer following, Anno 1735, the Town seemed to be full of the Presence of God; it was never so full of Love, nor of Joy, and yet so full of distress, as it was then. There were remarkable Tokens of God's Presence in almost every House. It was a time of Joy in families on account of Salvation being brought unto them....More than 300 Souls were savingly brought home to Christ, in this Town, in the Space of half a Year....I hope that by far the greater Part of persons in this Town, above sixteen Years of age, are such as have the saving Knowledge of Jesus Christ."

God blesses the faithfulness of his servants. Often in our fast-paced, instant society, we expect God to begin working immediately, and we lose patience. But God delights in the patience of his children and blesses their persistent petitions. When Jesus' disciples asked Him to teach them to pray, he told them a parable to teach them the importance of praying with importunity. Jesus closed his story with this promise: "And I say unto you, Ask, and it shall be given you; seek, and ye shall find; knock, and it shall be opened unto you...If ye then, being evil, know how to give good gifts unto your children: how much more shall your heavenly Father give the Holy Spirit to them that ask him?" (Luke 11:9, 13). Be patient and persistent in your prayer life, and God will answer in surprising ways as well.

December 29, 1876

Tomorrow Is Not Guaranteed

"Go to now, ye that say, To day or to morrow we will go into such a city, and continue there a year, and buy and sell, and get gain: Whereas ye know not what shall be on the morrow. For what is your life? It is even a vapour, that appeareth for a little time, and then vanisheth away."—**James 4:13–14**

Philip Bliss, the composer of "Wonderful Words of Life," "Hallelujah, What a Saviour," and the music to Horatio Spafford's lyrics "It Is Well with My Soul," had been travelling with D. L. Moody as a songwriter and soulwinner. After visiting their family for Christmas, Philip Bliss and his wife Lucy boarded the train in the brisk morning temperatures. They were travelling to Chicago to meet up with Mr. Moody once again, but the familiar trip would end in disaster. That night in the freezing temperatures, the train derailed over a bridge in Ashtabula, Ohio, plunging over seventy feet into the canyon. Moody would soon receive the word that his two beloved fellow-servants were taken to Heaven. Moody's son would later write: "Mr. Moody never ceased to miss their aid in his work, and often spoke in warmest appreciation of their beautiful ministry."

We never know when our last day will be on this Earth. The Bliss family was looking forward to the day that they would see their Saviour, but they did not understand that it would be that cold December night of 1876. Likewise, we do not know the time or the hour that God will take us Home, whether through the Rapture or through death. We must live every day with the realization that this may be our last moment to make a difference in our world. If your family and friends, co-workers and acquaintances, remembered you from only your words and actions today, what would they remember? Would you have any regrets? What will your Saviour say when you meet Him face-to-face? Before the moment comes that we are ushered to Heaven, be sure that you are ready to meet your King. In the words of Philip Bliss:

"When He comes, our glorious King, All His ransomed home to bring,
Then anew His song we'll sing: Hallelujah! What a Saviour!"

Zechariah 5–8 // Revelation 19

December 29, 1745

The Power of Effectual Prayer

"Confess your faults one to another, and pray one for another, that ye may be healed. The effectual fervent prayer of a righteous man availeth much."
—James 5:16

In David Brainerd's journal on December 29, 1745, he wrote of a momentous breakthrough in his ministry with the American Indians: "After public worship was over, I went to my house, proposing to preach again after a short season of intermission. But they soon came in one after another; with tears in their eyes, to know, 'what they should do to be saved.' And the divine Spirit in such a manner set home upon their hearts what I spoke to them, that the house was soon filled with cries and groans. They all flocked together upon this occasion, and those whom I had reason to think in a Christ-less state, were almost universally seized with concern for their souls. It was an amazing season of power among them, and seemed as if God had 'bowed the heavens and come down…' and that God was about to convert the whole world."

God was blessing this ministry of evangelism tremendously, but Brainerd would die just two years later in Jonathan Edwards' home, at twenty-nine years of age, completely drained by his sacrificial ministry.

Perhaps the reason that God blessed Brainerd's ministry with such power was through his intercessory prayer. In his journal, published after his death, readers find repeated mentions of many hours spent in prayer. Prayer is our greatest weapon against the world, the flesh, and the devil, but so many times, we lose our desire or simply forget in our busy schedules. But God answers prayer and invites us to access His throne of grace. "Let us therefore come boldly unto the throne of grace, that we may obtain mercy, and find grace to help in time of need" (Hebrews 4:16). As we are now just hours away from a New Year, why not resolve to be more in prayer for the souls of men in this coming year?

December 30, 1946

All Things...for Good

"And we know that all things work together for good to them that love God, to them who are the called according to his purpose."—**Romans 8:28**

Monroe Parker and his wife Harriette loved serving the Lord together. They had met during a revival meeting where Billy Sunday had preached. Parker had arrived early and found a seat in the front near the organ. Shortly after, Harriette came up to play the organ, "Hello, Monk Parker. May I sit by you? I am going to play the organ." He was immediately smitten and made sure to sit in the same seat every night! This led to their dating and eventual marriage.

Parker describes a "lean" time in his evangelistic ministry. He had received a letter from a dear old missionary pastor at Bevier, Kentucky. It read, "You have been recommended to me as an evangelist. We can't offer you anything but a bed." He did not say whether that was in the house. "But," he said, "if you have the missionary spirit, come to us." After reading the letter, he handed it to Harriette. She read it and handed it back to him. Parker placed the letter under his pillow, and he and his wife fell asleep. When they awakened in the morning, Parker described the conversation thus: "Have you decided what we are going to do?" I said, "Yes," and she said, "I know what it is." I asked, "What?" She said, "We are going to Kentucky." I said, "You are mighty right we are. If I don't have a missionary spirit, I am not fit to preach."

For unknown reasons, however, God took away the love of his life. Monroe Parker's wife of twelve years died suddenly in a car crash on December 30, 1946. On the drive back from the funeral, Monroe's brother James turned the radio to a Cleveland station, where Monroe heard himself preaching from Romans 8:28. His own preaching ministered to him that day as he was again assured that all things work together for good.

That promise is just as certain for you as it was for Monroe Parker. Claim it today and live in the joy of God's goodness.

December 31, 1887

Count Your Blessings

"I had fainted, unless I had believed to see the goodness of the LORD in the land of the living."—**Psalm 27:13**

Billy Sunday told the story of the New Year's Eve night he proposed to his soon-to-be wife, Helen Thompson: "She had on an ox-blood cashmere dress, and a natural-colored lynx neckpiece thrown about her shoulders, which her parents had given her for Christmas, and which I had never seen before. Oh, boy! She was a knock-out! She looked like I imagine the Queen of Sheba did when she visited Solomon. She had ditched her beau, and I had given the gate to a girl I had out in Iowa. So I braced right up, just before midnight, and asked 'Nell, will you marry me?' She came back at me so quick it almost floored me: 'Yes, with all my heart.' I went home feeling as though I had wings on my feet. I didn't sleep that night. Visions of those black eyes stared at me from the darkness and turned night into day."

Helen's father would have objections to his daughter marrying a baseball player, but later that year, Sunday would receive a much anticipated telegraph from his "Nell": "Dad says it's all right." That afternoon, Sunday played one of his best games with "three hits and had five put-outs!"

As we close this year and open another, let us take a moment to consider the blessings that God has given to us. Through the good times and the bad, God has given us His presence, His provision, His protection, and most of all His promise of eternal life.

We so easily forget God's goodnesses in our lives and become discouraged or overwhelmed. And yet, Psalm 68:19 exclaims, "Blessed be the Lord, who daily loadeth us with benefits, even the God of our salvation. Selah."

As you look forward to a new year, take a few moments to reflect on this past year and thank God for what He has done for you. As the song says, "Count your blessings, name them one by one. Count your many blessings; see what God hath done."

BIBLIOGRAPHY & INDEXES

Bibliography

A & E Networks and the History Channel. *This Day in History.* San Diego, Tahabi Books, 2003.

Alexander, Helen. *Charles Alexander: A Romance of Song and Soul Winning.* Marshall Brothers, LTD. London, Edinburgh, New York. circa 1920.

The American Magazine, "The Rev. Billy Sunday and His Way on the Devil," Volume 64, September 1907.

Author Unknown. *The Life Story and Songs of Charles F. Weigle. Chattanooga, Tennessee:* Tennessee Temple Schools, 1963.

Banks, Louis Albert, Talmage, Frank De Witt, and Binkerd O.W. *T. DeWitt Talmage: His Life and Work* : Biographical Edition, Presbyterian Church, 1902.

Barlow, Dr. Fred. *Profiles in Evangelism.* Sword of the Lord Publishers, Murfreesboro, TN, 1976.

Brainerd, David. *Mr. Brainerd's Journal: In Two Parts.* Scotland: The Honourable Society for Propagating Christian Knowledge, 1749.

Brittain, Vera. *In the Steps of John Bunyan: An Excursion into Puritan England,* London: Rich and Cowan, 1950.

Budge, Tom. Memories of Carey. Central Baptist Church of Leicester.

Cairns, Earle E. *An Endless Line of Splendor: Revivals and Their Leaders from the Great Awakening to the Present.* Tyndale House Publishers, 1986.

Chapman, John Wilbur. *Papers of John Wilbur Chapman.* Philadelphia: Presbyterian Historical Society, 1880-1918.

Dorrien, Gary J. *The Remaking of Evangelistic Theology,* Westminster John Knox Press, 1998.

"Evangelistic Preaching," *The Sword of the Lord* (September 20, 1940).

Frankenburg, Theodore Thomas. *Billy Sunday, His Tabernacles and Sawdust trails: A Biographical Sketch of the Famous Evangelist.* Columbus, Ohio: The F.J. Heer Printing Company, 1917.

Frankenburg, Theodore Thomas. *The Spectacular Career of Rev. Billy Sunday: Famous Baseball Evangelist.* Columbus, Ohio: McClelland & Company, 1913.

"God's Wonderful Working: The First Great Awakening in New England & The Middle Colonies." Christian History: Issue 23, 1989.

Hopkins, Jerry. "No Guarantees: Mordecai F. Ham, Evangelism and Prohibition Meetings in Texas, 1903-1919." *East Texas Historical Journal:* Volume 44, Issue 2, Article 10.

Jones, Laura. *The Life and Sayings of Sam P. Jones: A Minister of the Gospel.* 2nd and rev. ed. Atlanta: Franklin-Turner Co., 1907.

Knapp, Christopher. *Miscellaneous Writings of Christopher Knapp*. New York: Irving Risch, 2015.

Lawson, James Gilchrist. *Deeper Experiences of Famous Christians*. Glad Tidings Publishing Company, 1911.

Matthews, David. *I Saw the Welsh Revival*. Asheville, NC: Revival Literature, 2004.

Minnex, Kathleen. Laughter in the Amen Corner: The Life of Evangelist Sam Jones. University of Georgia Press, 2010.

Moody, William R. *The Life of Dwight L. Moody*. New York: Fleming H. Revell Company, 1900.

Murray, Iain H. *Revival and Revivalism*. The Banner of Truth Trust, 1994.

New York Times Archives. query.nytimes.com.

The Oklahoman, 9/5/27.

Ottman, Ford C. *J. Wilbur Chapman: A Biography*. New York: Doubleday, Page and Company, 1920.

Perry, Arthur Latham. *Williamstown and Williams College: A History*. Published by the Author, 1899.

Peterson, Merrill D. and Vaughan Robert C., editors. *The Virginia Statute of Religious Freedom: It's Evolution and Consequences in American History*. Cambridge University Press, 1988.

Ravenhill, Leonard. *Why Revival Tarries*. Grand Rapids: Bethany House Publishers, 1959.

Reese, Ed. *The Life and Ministry of Reuben Torrey*. Knoxville, Tennessee: Reese Publications. (n.d. Web. 12 October 2017).

Reid, W. Stanford. *Trumpeter of God*, New York: Charles Scribner's Sons, 1974.

Reno, J. Paul. *Daniel Nash: Prevailing Prince of Prayer*. Asheville, NC: Revival Literature, 1989.

Rice, John R. *The Evangelist*. Murfreesboro, Tennessee: Sword of the Lord Foundation, 1968.

Rouse, Anderson R., "Making the South New, Keeping the South 'Southern': Bob Jones, Fundamentalism, and the New South" (2015). All Theses. Paper 2163.

Rusk, John. *The Authentic Life of T. DeWitt Talmage, The Greatly Beloved Divine*. L.G. Stahl, 1902.

The Scofield Study Bible, King James Version. C.I. Scofield, editor. New York: Oxford Press, 1917.

Spurgeon, Charles. *C.H. Spurgeon, An Evaluation: His Life, Sermons, and Ministry, An Appraisal*. Dallas, TX: The Electronic Bible Society, 1999.

Sunday, William A. *The Sawdust Trail: Billy Sunday in His Own Words.* Iowa City: Universtiy of Iowa Press, 2005.

Torrey, R.A. *How to Promote and Conduct a Successful Revival.* Chicago: Fleming H. Revell Company, 1901.

Turner, Daniel L. *Standing Without Apology: The History of Bob Jones University* Bob Jones University Press, 1997.

Walden, Viola, *John R. Rice: The Captain of Our Team.* Murfreesboro, TN: Sword of the Lord Publishers, 1990.

Wesley, John. The Journal of John Wesley. Chicago: Moody Press, 1951.

Whitefield, George. The Journals of George Whitefield. England: Quinta Press, 2009.

Wilhoit, Bert H. *Rody: Memories of Homer Rodeheaver*. Greenville, S.C.: Bob Jones University Press, 2000.

Wright, G. Frederick *Charles Grandison Finney*. University of Michigan Library, 1891.

Title Index

January

February

March

April

May

June

July

August

September

October

November

December

Scripture Index

Proverbs

Ecclesiastes

Song of Solomon

Isaiah

Jeremiah

Lamentations

Ezekiel

Daniel

Hosea

Amos

Jonah

Habakkuk

Zechariah

Malachi

Matthew

Mark

Luke

John

Acts

Romans

1 Corinthians

2 Corinthians

Galatians

Ephesians

Philippians

Colossians

1 Thessalonians

1 Timothy

2 Timothy

Titus

Hebrews

James

1 Peter

2 Peter

1 John

2 John

3 John

Jude

Revelation

About the Authors

DR. JOHN GOETSCH is the executive vice president of West Coast Baptist College in Lancaster, California. He has served the cause of revival in America and around the world since 1974 as a dynamic evangelist and preacher of the Word of God. He and his wife, Diane, have been married for forty-four years and have four adult children and eleven grandchildren.

NATHAN BIRT graduated from West Coast Baptist College in 2013 with a major in Evangelism and married his wife Alyssa the same year. The Birts make their home in Lancaster, California, where Nathan serves as the director of children's ministries at Lancaster Baptist Church.

OTHER DEVOTIONAL BOOKS WE THINK YOU WILL LOVE...

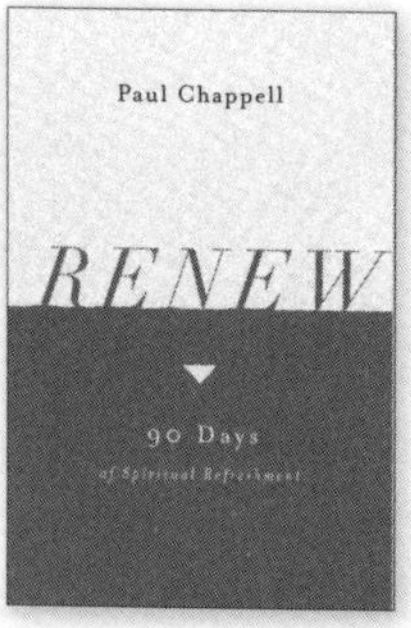

Renew By Paul Chappell

90 Days of Spiritual Refreshment

This ninety-day devotional guide will encourage you to seek God's face and renew your heart in His Word. Each devotion includes a Scripture passage and provides an encouraging or admonishing truth regarding your walk with the Lord.

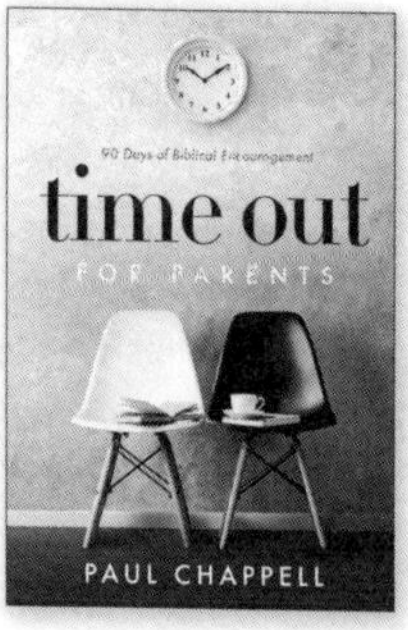

Time Out for Parents By Paul Chappell

90 Days of Biblical Encouragement

The ninety devotions in this book are written to encourage parents to seek God's wisdom as they raise their children for Him. At the close of each devotion is a single actionable thought given as "Today's Parenting Principle."

Disciple By Paul Chappell

Daily Truths from the Gospel of Luke for Followers of Jesus

Each daily reading in Disciple will take you on a journey through the Gospel of Luke and the chronological account of the life of Christ. As these brief devotions draw you closer to the Lord, you'll be challenged and encouraged to follow Jesus more closely and to walk with Him each day.

Striving Together Publications
New
Books
Church Leadership
Curriculum
Music
Print & Video
Spanish
Sale Items
CHURCH MEDIA
HIGH DEFINITION VIDEOS
PRESENTATION GRAPHICS
PROMOTIONAL ARTWORK
MOTION LOOPS
NEW ARRIVALS
PRINT MATERIALS